This book is dedicated
with respect and admiration to
all the members of the
Society of Saint Pius X.

Archbishop Marcel Lefebvre
Founder and Superior General of
The Society of Saint Pius X

APOLOGIA
PRO
MARCEL
LEFEBVRE

Part I
1905 - 1976

THE ANGELUS PRESS, INC.
2918 TRACY
KANSAS CITY, MO 64109

LIBRARY OF CONGRESS NO. 80 65104
ISBN NO. 0-935952-00-4

FIRST PRINTING—August, 1979
SECOND PRINTING—December, 1979
THIRD PRINTING—February, 1992

Printed in the United States of America

APOLOGIA
PRO
MARCEL LEFEBVRE

PART I ❧ 1905 - 1976

Michael Davies

THE ANGELUS PRESS
2918 Tracy Avenue
Kansas City, Missouri 64109

BOOKS BY MICHAEL DAVIES

Dossier on Catechetics

Cranmer's Godly Order

Pope John's Council

Pope Paul's New Mass (forthcoming)

Newman Against the Liberals
Twenty-five Classic Sermons by John Henry Newman
selected and edited by Michael Davies

The Order of Melchisedech
A Defense of the Catholic Priesthood

PAMPHLETS

Archbishop Lefebvre—The Truth

The Tridentine Mass

The New Mass

The Roman Rite Destroyed

Communion in the Hand

The True Voice of Tradition
The Story of Saint Athanasius

Communion Under Both Kinds (forthcoming)

A complete list available from The Angelus Press.

Contents

	Archbishop Lefebvre's Foreword	vii
	Author's Introduction	ix
	Illustrations	following page 102

I	Who Is Marcel Lefebvre?	1
II	A New Apostolate	11
III	Archbishop Lefebvre in His Own Words	25
IV	The Campaign Against Ecône	35
V	The Condemnation	57
VI	The *Credo* Pilgrimage	75
VII	The Rejection of the Appeals	103
VIII	The War of Attrition	133
IX	The Consistory Allocution	173
X	The War of Attrition Continues	193
XI	The Ordinations of 29 June 1976	201
XII	The Suspension	215
XIII	The Mass at Lille	253
XIV	The Audience with Pope Paul VI	273
XV	The October Condemnation	301
XVI	The End of a Momentous Year	345
	Chronological Index	355
	Appendices	363
	Index	451

**SÉMINAIRE INTERNATIONAL
SAINT PIE X**

Ecône CH 1908 RIDDES
Tél. 026/6 23 08 - 6 25 01 - 6 29 27

Mr Michael Davies est désormais connu
du monde catholique comme le meilleur
écrivain de langue anglaise, en ce qui concerne
les douloureux problèmes de l'Église catholique
depuis le Concile Vatican II

On ne peut que louer son érudition, son
objectivité, la prudence et la fermeté de ses
jugements guidés par son profond attachement
à l'Église catholique, dont il demeurera
pour la postérité l'un des meilleurs serviteurs.

En toute vérité, les pages qui suivent ne
font que confirmer cette appréciation. J'en
remercie vivement l'auteur.

Dieu fasse que ces ouvrages porteurs de vérité
et de lumière contribuent à la véritable réno-
vation de l'Église, au Règne de notre Seigneur,
au bienfait de la civilisation chrétienne et au
salut des âmes.

+ Marcel Lefebvre

Highclere, le 21 Juin 1989

Foreword by His Grace
Archbishop Marcel Lefebvre

Michael Davies is already recognized in the Catholic world as the most outstanding English-language writer concerned with the painful afflictions of the Catholic Church since the Second Vatican Council.

He merits praise for his erudition, his objectivity, and the wisdom and soundness of his judgments which are governed by his profound attachment to the Catholic Church among whose most faithful servants posterity will place him.

There can be no doubt that the pages which follow will confirm this tribute. I thank him profoundly.

God grant that his books, bearers of truth and light, will contribute to the true renewal of the Church, to the Kingship of Our Lord, to the benefit of Christian civilization and to the salvation of souls.

† Marcel Lefebvre
Highclere, 21 June 1979

Author's Introduction

I must begin my introduction with an explanation of the title of this book. Many of those who read it will know little or nothing about Archbishop Lefebvre when they begin. If they are Catholics they will have gathered from the official Catholic press that he is a French bishop who refuses to use the new rite of Mass and has a seminary in Switzerland where he trains priests in defiance of the Vatican. He will have been presented to them as an anachronism, a man completely out of step with the mainstream of contemporary Catholic thought, a man who is unable to adapt, to update himself. He is portrayed as little more than an historical curiosity, of no significance in the post-conciliar Church, a man whose views do not merit consideration. The Archbishop is often subjected to serious misrepresentation; he is alleged to have totally rejected the Second Vatican Council or to be linked with extreme right-wing political movements. A sad example of this form of misrepresentation is a pamphlet published by the Catholic Truth Society of England and Wales in 1976. It is entitled *Light on Archbishop Lefebvre* and the author is Monsignor George Leonard, at that time Chief Information Officer of the Catholic Information Office of England and Wales. I wrote to Mgr. Leonard pointing out that he had seriously misrepresented the Archbishop and suggested that he should either substantiate or withdraw his allegations. He answered in strident and emotive terms refusing to do either. I replied to Mgr. Leonard's attack on the Archbishop in a pamphlet entitled *Archbishop Lefebvre—The Truth*. This evoked such interest that several reprints were necessary to cope with the demand and it gained the Archbishop much new support. In this pamphlet I explained that the only way to refute the type of attack made by Mgr. Leonard was to present the entire truth—to write an *apologia*. The early Christian apologists wrote their "apologies" to gain a fair hearing for Christianity and dispel popular myths and slanders. It is in this sense that the word *"apologia"* is used in my title, i. e. as "a reasoned explanation" and not an "apology" in the sense of contemporary usage.

The classic *apologia* of. modern times is the *Apologia Pro Vita Sua* of Cardinal Newman. Newman had been seriously misrepresented by Charles Kingsley who refused to provide the unqualified public apology which was requested. Newman's reply proved to be one of the greatest autobiographies in the English language and almost certainly the greatest prose work outside the realm of fiction to appear in English during the nineteenth century—and ironically our thanks for it must be directed to an implacable opponent of Newman and Catholicism.

My own *Apologia Pro Marcel Lefebvre* may be devoid of literary merit but it is certainly not without historic interest and those who appreciate its publication must direct their thanks to Mgr. Leonard without whom it would never have been written.

Incidentally, my pamphlet replying to Mgr. Leonard proved so popular that the publisher followed it up with others and thus began the Augustine Pamphlet Series which now has sales running into tens of thousands and includes works by theologians of international repute.

Although this book certainly would not have been written had it not been for Mgr. Leonard it could not have been written had it not been for Jean Madiran, the Editor of *Itinéraires.* * *Itinéraires* is certainly the most valuable Catholic review appearing in the world today. It contains documentation that would not otherwise be published together with commentaries and articles by some of France's most outstanding Catholic intellectuals; men, alas, who have no counterpart in the English-speaking world. The debt my

*4, rue Garancière, 75006, Paris, France.

book owes to *Itinéraires* is incalculable. It provides the
source for most of the original documents included together with the articles by Jean Madiran and Louis Salleron
which I have had translated. Some of the material in my
commentaries on the documents also originates with *Itinéraires*. A detailed list of sources for all the material in the
Apologia will be provided in Volume II.

The scope of the *Apologia* is limited. It deals principally
with the relations between the Archbishop and the Vatican.
It does not deal with the activities of the Society of Saint
Pius X in any individual country. I am certainly not committed to the view that every action and every opinion of
the Archbishop, still less of every priest in the Society, is
necessarily wise and prudent. I mention this because the
reader who is not familiar with the "Ecône affair" may consider that my attitude to the Archbishop and the Society is
too uncritical and therefore unobjective. My book is objective but it is not impartial. It is objective because I have
presented all the relevant documents both for and against
Mgr. Lefebvre, something his opponents have never done. It
is partial because I believe the evidence proves him to be right
and I state this. However, the reader is quite at liberty to
ignore my commentary and use the documentation to reach
a different conclusion. Clearly, the value of the book derives
from the documentation and not the commentary.

I am convinced that the *Apologia* will be of enduring historical value because I am convinced that the Archbishop will
occupy a major position in the history of post-conciliar
Catholicism. The most evident trend in mainstream Christianity since the Second World War has been the tendency to replace the religion of God made Man with the religion of man
made God. Although Christians still profess theoretical concern for the life to come their efforts are increasingly taken
up with building a paradise on earth. The logical outcome of
this attitude will be the discarding of the supernatural element of Christianity as irrelevant. Since the Second Vatican
Council this movement has gained considerable momentum
within the Catholic Church, both officially and unofficially,

and, during the pontificate of Pope Paul VI, appeared to be sweeping all before it. No one was more aware of this than Pope Paul VI himself who made frequent pronouncements condemning this tendency and stressing the primacy of the spiritual. But in practice, Pope Paul VI did little or nothing to halt the erosion of the traditional faith. He reprimanded Modernists but permitted them to use official Church structures to destroy the faith, yet took the most drastic steps to stamp out the Society of St. Pius X. At the time this introduction is being written, June 1979, there are signs of hope that Pope John Paul II will be prepared not simply to speak but to act in defense of the faith. This is something we should pray for daily. It hardly needs stating that the criticism of the Holy See contained in this first volume of the *Apologia* applies only to the pontificate of Pope Paul VI. Not one word in the book should be construed as reflecting unfavorably upon the present Holy Father. It is my hope that in the second volume I will be able to give the details of an agreement between the Pope and the Archbishop. This is also something for which we should pray.

The reason I believe that Archbishop Lefebvre will occupy a major position in the history of the post-conciliar Church is that he had the courage and foresight to take practical steps to preserve the traditional faith. Unlike many conservative Catholics he saw that it was impossible to wage an effective battle for orthodoxy within the context of the official reforms as these reforms were themselves oriented towards the cult of man. The Archbishop appreciated that the liturgical reform in particular must inevitably compromise Catholic teaching on the priesthood and the Mass, the twin pillars upon which our faith is built.* The sixteenth-century Protestant Reformers had also realized that if they could undermine the priesthood there would be no Mass and the Church would be destroyed. The Archbishop founded the Society of St. Pius X with its seminary at Ecône not as an act of rebellion but to perpetuate the Catholic priesthood,

---

*Let anyone who doubts this compare the new and old rites of ordination. A detailed comparison has been made in my book *The Order of Melchisedech.*

and for no other purpose. Indeed, as my book will show, the Society at first enjoyed the approbation of the Holy See but the success of the seminary soon aroused the animosity of powerful Liberal forces within the Church, particularly in France. They saw it as a serious threat to their plans for replacing the traditional faith with a new ecumenical and humanistically oriented religion. This is the reason they brought such pressure to bear upon Pope Paul VI. There is no doubt that the demands for the destruction of Ecône emanated principally from the French Hierarchy which, through Cardinal Villot, the Secretary of State, was ideally placed to pressurize the Pope.

A number of those who have reviewed my previous books have been kind enough to say that they are very readable. Unfortunately, the format of *Apologia* is not conducive to easy reading. My principal objective has been to provide a comprehensive fund of source material which will be useful to those wishing to study the controversy between the Archbishop and the Vatican. After various experiments I concluded that the most satisfactory method was to observe strict chronological order as far as possible. This meant that I could not assemble the material in a manner that was always the most effective for maintaining interest. The fact that I had to quote so many documents in full also impedes the flow of the narrative. However, if the reader bears in mind the fact that the events described in the book represent not simply a confrontation of historic dimensions but a very moving human drama, then it should never appear too dull. Mgr. Lefebvre's inner conflict must have been more dramatic than his conflict with Pope Paul VI. No great novelist could have a more challenging theme than that of a man whose life had been dedicated to upholding the authority of the papacy faced with the alternative of disobeying the Pope or complying with an order to destroy an apostolate which he honestly believed was vital for the future of the Church. Let no one imagine that the decision the Archbishop took was taken lightly or was easy to make.

The reader will find frequent suggestions that he should

refer to an event in its correct chronological sequence and to facilitate this a chronological index has been provided on page 355. If this page is marked it will enable the reader to refer to any event mentioned in the book without difficulty.

As the reader will appreciate, I could never have written a book of this extent without considerable help—particularly as I was working on two other books simultaneously. Some of those who gave their help unstintingly have expressed a wish to remain anonymous, including the individual to whom I am most indebted for help with the translations. I must also thank Simone Macklow-Smith and my son Adrian for assistance in this respect. I must make special mention of Norah Haines without whose help the typescript would still be nowhere near completion. I am indebted to David Gardner and Mary Buckalew whose competent proof-reading will be evident to the discerning reader. Above all I must thank Carlita Brown who set the book up single-handed and had it ready for publication within three months. She would certainly wish me to mention all the members of the Angelus Press who have contributed to the publication of the *Apologia Pro Marcel Lefebvre*.

Despite all our efforts, a book of this size is certain to contain at least a few errors and I would appreciate it if they could be brought to my attention for correction in any future printing or for mention in Volume II. I can make no promise regarding the publication of the second volume of *Apologia* beyond an assurance that it will appear eventually. It will almost certainly be preceded by a book on the treatment of the question of religious liberty in the documents of Vatican II. The Archbishop's stand on the question of religious liberty is less familiar to English-speaking traditionalists than his stand on the Mass but it is no less important as it involves the very nature of the Church. He refused to sign *Dignitatis Humanae*, the Council's Declaration on Religious Liberty, because he considered it incompatible with previous authoritative and possibly infallible papal teaching. My book will provide all the necessary documentation to evaluate this very serious charge which is also examined briefly in Appendix IV to the present work.

Finally, I would like to assure the reader that although I have written much that is critical of the Holy See and Pope Paul VI in this book this does not imply any lack of loyalty to the Church and the Pope. When a subordinate is honestly convinced that his superior is pursuing a mistaken policy he shows true loyalty by speaking out. This is what prompted St. Paul to withstand St. Peter "to his face because he was to be blamed" (Galatians 2:11). The first duty of a Catholic is to uphold the faith and save his own soul. As I show in Appendices I and II, there is ample precedent in the history of the Church to show that conflict with the Holy See has sometimes been necessary to achieve these ends. Archbishop Lefebvre has stated on many occasions that all he is doing is to uphold the faith as he received it. Those who condemn him condemn the Faith of their Fathers.

Michael Davies

20 June 1979
St. Silverius, Pope and Martyr.

Si diligis me, Simon Petre.
pasce agnos meos,
Pasce oves meas.
Introit.

I

Who is Marcel Lefebvre?

MARCEL LEFEBVRE was born at Tourcoing in northern France on 29 November 1905. His parents were exemplary Catholics. His father owned a textile factory and was a daily communicant who would assist at Mass at a quarter past six each morning and recite his rosary before arriving at the factory to begin work ahead of his employees. Each evening he would be the last to leave. The welfare of his employees was always a primary consideration for him. The textile industry was to a very large extent dependent upon fluctuations of the market and in 1929, the year of Marcel's ordination, Monsieur Lefebvre was declared bankrupt and the family suffered financial ruin. But with characteristic resolution he set to work and succeeded in building up his business again.

From the age of eighteen he had been a *brancardier* at Lourdes, work to which he remained faithful throughout his life. He was also a tertiary of the Third Order of St. Francis. When the First World War broke out he joined a society dedicated to saving wounded soldiers and he made frequent trips

to Belgium, passing through the crossfire of the French and
German armies to bring back wounded soldiers to hospital
in Tourcoing. When Tourcoing came under German occupation he organized the escape of British prisoners. He later
escaped to Paris and worked for the French Intelligence Service under the name of Lefort for the rest of the war, frequently undertaking the most dangerous missions. All this
became known to the Germans who kept his name on record.
When Tourcoing was occupied during the Second World War
he was arrested and sent to prison at Sonnenburg where he
was confined in the most degrading conditions and treated
with extreme brutality His companions in prison have testified to his extraordinary courage, his complete resignation
to the decisions of divine Providence, and the inspiration he
imparted to them all in the midst of terrible suffering. His
greatest sorrow was that he had to die without seeing his
children again.

The mother of the Archbishop was born Gabrielle Watine.
All who knew her considered her to be a saint. The story of
her life was written by a French priest in 1948. Gabrielle
was celebrated not simply for sanctity but for strength of
character. During the absence of her husband in the First
World War she directed the factory, looked after her children, cared for the wounded, found time to visit the sick
and the poor, and organized resistance against the Germans.
She was arrested and subjected to an extremely harsh im-
prisonment, was distraught at the separation from her children, and became gravely ill. The German Commandant,
anxious and embarrassed, promised to release her if she
would write a note begging him to pardon her. She refused
to do so, being prepared to die rather than compromise on
a matter of principle. Fearing the consequences of her death,
the Commandant ordered her release and she returned to
her children broken in health but unbroken in spirit. When
she eventually died after long years of suffering all who knew

her testified that her death was the death of a saint, and there are numerous testimonies to favors obtained through her intercession.

Marcel was brought up in a family characterized by the highest standards of piety, discipline, and morality—and it was the example of the parents which above all formed the characters of the eight children. Five of them are now priests or religious and the entire family still remains closely united. As a child Marcel was always good humored and industrious with a particular love of manual work. While a seminary student he installed an electrical system in his parents' home with all the skill of a professional electrician.

After his vocation to the priesthood became apparent he studied in his own diocese and then in the French Seminary in Rome. He obtained doctorates in philosophy and theology. He was ordained priest on 21 September 1929.

His first appointment was to the working-class parish of Marais-de-Lomme, where he was extremely happy and well loved by the parishioners. The impact he made is well illustrated by an incident involving the death of a virulent anticlerical. This type of person is virtually unknown in English-speaking countries, where those who are not religious tend to be indifferent. In most Catholic countries there are people possessed by a fierce hatred for the Church and above all for the clergy, whom they associate with everything that is retrogressive and repressive in life. This particular individual remained inflexible until the end, but just before his death he said that he would see a priest—but it would have to be the young curate as he at least wasn't "one of them"!

In 1932 Father Lefebvre joined the Holy Ghost Fathers and was sent to Gabon as a missionary, where he remained throughout the war. This was, he testifies, one of the happiest periods of his life.

In 1946 he was recalled to France to become Superior of a seminary at Mortain, but he returned to Africa when he was appointed Vicar-Apostolic of Dakar on 12 June 1947. On 22 September 1948 he was appointed Apostolic Delegate (the Pope's personal representative) for the whole of French-speaking Africa—a mark of the great confidence placed in him by Pope Pius XII. He was appointed as the first Archbishop of Dakar on 14 September 1955.

Even Mgr. Lefebvre's most severe critics have been forced to testify to the efficacy of his apostolate in Africa. In 1976, a Swiss priest, Father Jean Anzevui, who had been welcomed as a guest at Ecône on a number of occasions, published a most distasteful attack upon the Archbishop, entitled *Le Drame d'Ecône*. Father Anzevui's assessment of Mgr. Lefebvre's apostolate is all the more remarkable from an avowed opponent. He states:

During his thirty year apostolate in Africa the role of Mgr. Lefebvre was of the very highest importance. His fellow missionaries still remember his extraordinary missionary zeal which was revealed in his exceptional abilities as an organizer and a man of action. He persuaded a number of congregations which had previously shown no interest in the missions to undertake work in Africa. He was responsible for the construction of large numbers of churches and the foundation of charitable works of every kind . . . . they are all agreed in recognizing his magnificent career, his courtesy, his affability, his natural and simple distinction, the dignity of his perfect life, his austerity, his piety and his absolute devotion to any task which he undertook.*

The Testimony of Father Cosmao

On 8 September 1977 Suisse Romande Television devoted a long programme to the Ecône seminary and Mgr. Lefebvre. During the programme there was a discussion between the commentator and Father Cosmao, a Dominican who had

*J. Anzevui, *Le Drame d'Ecône* (Sion, 1976), p. 16.

been Superior of the house of his order in Dakar for several years while Mgr. Lefebvre was Apostolic Delegate and Archbishop of Dakar. The testimony of Father Cosmao carries considerable weight and it is included here in full together with some comments by Louis Salleron. Text and commentary appeared in the *Courrier de Rome*, No. 175, p. 12.

Commentator: Was the prelate (Mgr. Lefebvre) an important person in the Church?

Fr. Cosmao: He had complete power in the Church in the whole of French Africa, from the Sahara to Madagascar. In the Africa which at that time was still French. And he was one of the most important personages in the Church at the end of Pius XII's pontificate.

Commentator: Did he do well, standing for the Church in Africa of that period?

Fr. Cosmao: He did indeed. Christians and priests thought of him as one of themselves. He really stood for that Church at the time. The fact is, it is the Church which has changed, not Mgr. Lefebvre. The Church has changed most profoundly and in particular because she has come to accept what has been happening in Europe since the end of the 18th century, in the train of the philosophy of illuminism and the French Revolution.

Commentator: What, in fact, has been happening?

Fr. Cosmao: Until then the Church made the kings, and by that made the organization of society sacrosanct. When that organization of society no longer corresponded to the actual relations between social groups, it was necessary, in order to transform that social organization, to take away its sacred character, and in so doing to tear the Church away from the position she held in European societies; and finally the Church, in the course of the decades, has come to understand that the criticism of her role under the *Ancien Régime* was justified, and that it was that very criticism which could renew her from top to bottom. I think that Vatican II, in

large part, is the conclusion of that process of growing awareness; and it is that conclusion and the whole process leading
to it which Mgr. Lefebvre cannot accept, because, to my
mind, he is really the representative of that Church which
was sure of its truth, its right, its power, and which thought
she alone had the power to say how society should be organized. And today Mgr. Lefebvre reproaches the Church not
with no longer speaking Latin and no longer offering Mass
in the rite of Saint Pius V but, as others put it, surrendering
to the World on the pretext of a desire to enter it, and sub-
jecting herself to the new world. That is the reproach which
issued logically from the Church of yesterday. It is he who is
faithful, in a certain way; but his fidelity is to a Church
whose attitude in history, as we have come to understand,
some more quickly than others, is in contradiction with the
demands of the Gospel.

Professor Salleron comments:

"For Fr. Cosmao's candor there can be nothing but praise.
In his opinion, it is not Mgr. Lefebvre who has changed but
the Church. In a certain way it is Mgr. Lefebvre who is
faithful. The fact is that Mgr. Lefebvre's reproach to the
Church of today concerns not Latin and liturgy primarily
but her alliance with the World etc....

Nostalgia? Vague remorse? Provocation? Indifference? It
is hard to discover Fr. Cosmao's secret feelings. But he bears
witness to a *fact:* the Church has changed, and changed
'most profoundly,' on that fact we agree—everybody agrees.
But we need to know how deep that profound change goes:
or better, what is the nature of the change.

It was in 1950 that Teilhard de Chardin wrote to a priest
who had left the Church: 'Essentially I think as you do that
the Church (like any living reality after a certain time) comes
to a period of "moulting" or "necessary reform." After two
thousand years it is inevitable. Humanity is in process of
moulting. How can Christianity avoid doing the same? More

precisely, I think that the Reform in question (much more profound than that of the 16th century) *is no longer a simple matter of institution and morals, but of Faith . . . .*'

That conviction of Teilhard's is now widespread. Officially it is rejected, but semi-officially it is propagated in theology, liturgy, catechism, and the Catholic press, with an ambiguity less and less ambiguous—why bother, when you have the 'machine' under your control? There is no need to recall the most striking examples: they have appeared time and time again in the *Courrier de Rome*, *La Pensée catholique*, *Itinéraires*, the *Courrier de Pierre Debray*, and many other publications. That the *Histoire des crises du clergé français contemporain* of Paul Vigneron should, in spite of its moderation, have been passed over in silence or merely mentioned in the semi-official Catholic press, while *Le christianisme va-t-il mourir?* of Jean Delumeau, which condemns 1500 years of the Church's history and announces, as the Good News, the era of the Liberal Evangelical Church, should have received the Catholic *Grand Prix de Littérature*, is a 'sign of the times' of tragic dimensions. It is indeed a New Religion which the innovators are promising us. Fr. Cosmao bears witness to the *fact*. It is a pity he has not told us clearly what he thinks of it."

Vatican II and Retirement

Mgr. Lefebvre was appointed to the Central Preparatory Commission of the Second Vatican Council in 1960 by Pope John XXIII—proof that the confidence placed in him by Pope John was no less than that of Pope Pius XII.

On 23 January 1962 he resigned his archbishopric in favor of a native African, now His Eminence Cardinal Hyacinthe Thiandoum, who had been ordained by Mgr. Lefebvre, who regards himself as his spiritual son, and who did all in his

power to effect a reconciliation between the Archbishop and
Pope Paul VI.

On 23 January 1962 Mgr. Lefebvre was appointed Bishop
of Tulle in France, upon the personal insistence of Pope
John XXIII, despite opposition from the already Liberal-
dominated French hierarchy. Then, in July 1962, he was
elected Superior-General of the Holy Ghost Fathers (the
world's leading missionary order). After some hesitation he
accepted this post upon the insistence of the General Chapter
and the advice of Pope John. It involved him in travelling
all over the world to visit the various branches of the order.
There were few other prelates on the eve of the Council with
his first-hand experience of the state of the Church throughout the world.

A series of draft documents for the Council Fathers to
discuss had been drawn up by scholars selected from the entire world. These draft documents *(schemata)* were the fruit
of an intensive two year effort by 871 scholars ranging from
cardinals to laymen. Mgr. Vincenzo Carbone, of the General
Secretariat, was able to claim with perfect accuracy that no
other Council had had a preparation "so vast, so diligently
carried out, and so profound."* Mgr. Lefebvre writes:

I took part in the preparations for the Council as a member of the
Central Preparatory Commission. Thus, for two years I was present at
all its meetings. It was the business of the Central Commission to check
and examine all the preparatory *schemata* issued by all the committees.
Consequently I was well placed for knowing what had been done, what
remained to be examined and what was to be put forward during the
Council.

This work was carried out very conscientiously and with a concern
for perfection. I possess the seventy-two prepatory *schemata* and can
state, speaking generally, in these seventy-two *schemata* the doctrine of
the Church was absolutely orthodox and there was hardly any need for

*See *The Rhine Flows into the Tiber*, p. 22.

retouching. There was, therefore, a fine piece of work for presentation to the Council—*schemata* in conformity with the Church's teaching, adapted to some extent to our era, but with prudence and wisdom.

Now you know what happened at the Council. A fortnight after its opening not one of the prepared *schemata* remained, not one! All had been turned down, all had been condemned to the wastepaper basket. Nothing remained, not a single sentence. All had been thrown out.*

During the course of the Second Vatican Council (1962-1965), Mgr. Lefebvre was one of the leaders of the International Group of Fathers *(Coetus Internationalis Patrum)* which sought to uphold the traditional Catholic faith. The role of Mgr. Lefebvre during the Council will not be discussed in this book as it is fully documented in his own book, *A Bishop Speaks,* and in my own account of Vatican II, *Pope John's Council.* The texts of Mgr. Lefebvre's interventions, and a good deal of supplementary information, are now available in French in his book, *J'Accuse le Concile.* An English translation of this book is pending. All that needs to be stated here is that Mgr. Lefebvre, in his criticisms of the reforms which have followed the Council, and of certain passages in the documents themselves, is not being wise after the event. He was one of the very few Fathers of Vatican II who, while the Council was still in progress, had both the perspicacity to recognize deficiencies in certain documents and the courage to predict the disastrous results to which these deficiencies must inevitably give rise.

By 1968 the General Chapter of the Holy Ghost Fathers had become dominated by a Liberal majority which was determined to reform the Order in a sense contrary to Catholic tradition. Mgr. Lefebvre resigned in June of that year rather than collaborate in what would be the virtual destruction of

---

* *A Bishop Speaks,* p. 131. The story of how the Liberals managed to consign a preparation "so vast, so diligently carried out, and so profound" to the wastepaper basket is told in detail in Chapter V of *Pope John's Council.*

the Order as it had previously existed. He retired to Rome
with a modest pension which was just sufficient to rent a
small apartment in the Via Monserrato from some nuns.
After a full and active life devoted to the service of the
Church and the glory of God he was more than content to
spend his remaining years in quietness and prayer. In the light
of subsequent events, Mgr. Lefebvre's unobtrusive retirement
is a fact upon which considerable stress must be laid. Some of
his enemies have accused him of being proud and stubborn, a
man who could not accept defeat. He is portrayed as a pro-
ponent of an untenable theological immobilism totally unre-
lated to the age in which we are living. Although this untenable theology was defeated, discredited even, during the
Council, Mgr. Lefebvre's pride would not allow him to admit
defeat. The Seminary at Ecône, it is maintained, is his means
of continuing the fight which he waged so unsuccessfully
during the conciliar debates.

But Mgr. Lefebvre's retirement proves how baseless, ma-
licious even, such suggestions are. Those who have met him
know that he is not a man who will fight for the sake of
fighting—he has always been a realist. No one could have
compelled him to resign as Superior-General of the Holy
Ghost Fathers—he had been elected for a term of twelve
years. But he could see quite clearly that the Liberals dominated the General Chapter; that they were determined to get
their way at all costs; that resistance on his part could only
lead to unedifying division. *"Je les ai laissés à leur collégial-
ité,"* he has remarked. "I left them to their 'collegiality'."*

---

*J. Hanu, *Non, Entretiens de José Hanu avec Mgr. Lefebvre* (Editions Stock,
1977), p. 189 (161). Now available in English as *Vatican Encounter* (Kansas City,
1978), available from the Angelus Press and Augustine Publishing Co. Wherever
this book is referred to the page reference will be to the French edition with the
equivalent page in the English translation following in parentheses.

II

A New Apostolate

ARCHBISHOP LEFEBVRE would have earned a distinguished and honored place in the history of the Church even if he had retired finally from public life in 1968, as he had intended. No one had done more for the Church in Africa in this century; no one had done more to uphold the true faith during Vatican II. But the most important task for which God has destined him had not even begun. When he retired in 1968 he could not have imagined that God had reserved for him what was possibly the most important role assigned to any prelate during this century. An exaggeration? Mgr. Lefebvre was to be given the task of preserving the Catholic priesthood in the West during what is proving to be a period of universal apostasy. But he did not seek to undertake this task. He was sought out by the young men who proved to be the first seminarians of Ecône—but when they came they were quite unknown to him and, as for Ecône, he did not know of its existence.

The young men had been sent to the Archbishop because they wished to become priests but could find no seminary offering a truly traditional Catholic formation. They had asked older priests for advice and had been told to go to Mgr. Lefebvre. He was reluctant at first but they insisted. He told them that if he undertook their direction their studies would be long and intense and they would lead a life of prayer and sacrifice, the formation necessary to prepare them for the priesthood in these times. They insisted that this was what they wanted. But where could they study? Unfortunately, nowhere suitable could be found in Rome itself; but an old friend, Mgr. Charrière, Bishop of Lausanne, Geneva, and Fribourg, suggested that the students pursue their studies at the University of Fribourg. The *Fraternité Sacerdotale de Saint Pie X* was established in his diocese on All Saints' Day, 1970, with all the necessary canonical formalities. *

Alas, it soon became clear that this university was infected with Modernism and Liberalism. With the approval of Mgr. Nestor Adam, Bishop of Sion, Mgr. Lefebvre obtained a large house which had belonged to the Canons of St. Bernard in this diocese. The house was at Ecône, no more than a hamlet near the small town of Riddes in the Catholic Canton of Valais. The name of Ecône is now known throughout the world, and thousands of visitors from all over the world come there each year. But until the foundation of the Seminary of St. Pius X it is doubtful whether the name would have meant anything to anyone not living in the immediate vicinity.

The Seminary was formally opened on 7 October 1970. A fascinating account of the events leading up to its acquisition by Mgr. Lefebvre was provided by Father Pierre Epiney, Parish Priest of Riddes, in an address which he gave at the opening of the Priory of St. Pius V at Shawinigan-Sud, Quebec, on 19 March 1977. Father Epiney spoke from his heart as a

---

*The text of the Decree of Erection is contained in Appendix V.

priest and pastor.* The circumstances in which this saintly young priest was deprived of his parish are described under the date 15 June 1975. Father Épiney's account follows:

The Beginning of Ecône

My dear colleagues and Canadian friends, I am not going to talk abstractions. All I want to do is give my own testimony, for Providence willed that I should be the first eyewitness of what happened at Ecône.

Ecône will soon be known throughout the world

Ten years ago I was appointed parish priest of Riddes, in which Ecône is situated. That was in 1967. At that time Ecône was nothing in particular. Only one Canon of the Grand-Saint-Bernard remained, and he just looked after some dogs and a few calves. The place was up for sale. In 1968, on 31 May, the Feast of the Queenship of the Blessed Virgin Mary, one of my parishioners, M. Alphonse Pedroni (he has already been to Canada with me and also with Mgr. Lefebvre) overheard a member of the Communist Party say in a local café: "Ecône is for sale: we're buying it. And the first thing we'll do is destroy the chapel." Alphonse went home, took up the telephone, and called the Canon:

"Is it true that Ecône is for sale?"

"Yes, it's true."

"I'll buy it at the price you have been offered."

He found four friends to help him buy that house and insure that it kept its religious character. The property had belonged to the Canons of Saint-Bernard for over 600 years.

*Father Épiney's account was published in the French-Canadian traditionalist journal *Le Doctrinaire*, No. 30, April 1977.

These five men improved the land (in our country it is all vineyards) and waited for the providential moment.

Then one day Mgr. Lefebvre appeared. He was in touch with some young men who wanted to become priests. He had tried opening a house in Fribourg, in Switzerland, but it had become too small. Providence led him to a meeting with these men who were happy to put the house they had bought at his disposal.

I shall always remember that visit of Mgr. Lefebvre's. We had a meal together in a local restaurant. He did not know us. He seemed perplexed at the attitude of M. Pedroni, who said not a word all during the meal. In the end Mgr. Lefebvre urged him to say something.

"Listen, Monseigneur. We are happy to entrust that house to you. I should just like to say this: Ecône will soon be known throughout the world."

During the difficult summer we have just lived through at Ecône, Mgr. Lefebvre reminded me of that: "Alphonse was a true prophet."

"No" to retraining

As for me, what opened my eyes was a retraining course for priests ten years ordained, at Montana in Switzerland. It was to last fifteen days, I stuck it for ten! Then I left and went on a pilgrimage to Fatima. Back home, I told myself I must do something: things could not go on as they were. The theories taught in the retraining were not the Catholic faith we were taught in the seminary. They were hazy theories leading nowhere.

So I thought: "You are no theologian; you are not going to write articles for the papers; you are just a parish priest. You must try to adopt at least two supernatural means to stem the damage and to restore to the parish—with the smallest proportion of practicing Catholics in the whole country—

some enthusiasm and a little more love of God."

I decided to begin with the Rosary: the Rosary every day, and on Thursday evenings before the Blessed Sacrament. I decided to go back to the traditional Mass, but with the Epistle and Gospel in French, and every Friday to hold catechism classes for adults. I was astonished at the graces received. The people came. I had a hundred to a hundred and fifty at catechism. I was amazed; and preparing catechism did me a lot of good, because it made me go back over the whole of traditional doctrine. People came to say the Rosary, including a good pagan.

I had to build a church, but I had nothing. I turned to St. Joseph. (I thanked him specially this morning, on his feast day: he has given me such help.) We managed to overcome all difficulties so well that the bishop himself, the day he came to consecrate the church, said to me: "You can thank God. I know this parish—there were not even two men who came to Mass." (He was himself a Canon of Saint-Bernard, and had been parish priest at Ecône. He knew the people.) "You can thank God. What I have seen this morning is beyond anything I could have imagined."

The Seminary at Ecône: What will happen?

So I am telling you that I have been well rewarded spiritually and materially. And then Providence pitched the Ecône Seminary into my parish. You can imagine how interested I was, seeing what was going on (for these newcomers do exactly the opposite of what the retrainees are doing). Mgr. Adam, my bishop, was also interested. He twice asked me to pick him up and bring him to the Seminary. He was delighted with what he saw there. Of course there were others, incited by the French progressives, who took a poor view of it. But at last the enterprise started, and I saw the seminarians arriving one by one.

The first week at Ecône they had nothing, so they came to eat at my table. For example, I witnessed the arrival of Denis Roch, a converted Protestant, an engineer. I shall not forget his first visit. After we had talked for an hour he said to me: "Father, Providence arranged for us to meet today. If you please, shall we say a decade of the Rosary together?" We knelt down in the room. It is not every day that you meet a young man like that, a convert from Protestantism, who says to his parish priest after a conversation: "Shall we say a decade of the Rosary?"

So, I witnessed the birth and the growth of this great work. I had the good fortune to be close to Mgr. Lefebvre and to learn much from him. I can therefore tell you without fear of being mistaken: He is truly a man of God; he is a good and a great missionary. Someone said to me one day: "He makes me think of Saint Pius X." Yes, that is so. He has only one desire: that Our Lord Jesus Christ shall reign over all hearts, over all families, over all nations, and that souls shall be saved—for he is a missionary. He does not theorize; he can talk very simply to people because his purpose is the conversion of people: he wants all souls to go to heaven.

I remember one day, a year ago, Cardinal Thiandoum, Archbishop of Dakar, was with me. He had come to topple me into the New Mass. I let him talk; and then I said:

"Listen, Eminence. Do you know who Mgr. Lefebvre is? Must I, a simple parish priest, remind you what he has done for you in Dakar? Eminence, who made you a priest?

—Mgr. Lefebvre.

—Eminence, who founded the major seminary?

—Mgr. Lefebvre.

—Eminence, who made the Archdiocese of Dakar?

—Mgr. Lefebvre.

—Eminence, who made the Dakar Carmel?

—Mgr. Lefebvre.

—Eminence, who made the monastery of Vieta in Dakar?

—Mgr. Lefebvre. He is my father, I am his son. You are right.

—Well then, Eminence, now that Mgr. Lefebvre finds himself in a situation like this, attacked, calumniated, ridiculed, dare you let your father be so defamed, and say nothing?

(That made him weep.)

Then it is your duty to defend your father and to defend Holy Church. You are too afraid. You must not be afraid, especially when you are invested with authority. What do you risk? — losing your position? losing your life? Good! you will go to heaven."

As for Mgr. Lefebvre, he has no fear. Yet his temperament is very gentle. There is nothing swaggering or bellicose about him. But I have rarely in my life met a man with such courage, such strength of will, such firmness in decision, such persistence and perseverance. And I can say—for I lived with him, at his side, this difficult summer—that he has come to the fight, this year, with redoubled courage. Providence has blessed him with extraordinary powers, for, humanly speaking, he should have been crushed. That proves we have to do with a man of God. I think Providence has made us a great present in giving us this missionary.

That is just what the opposition is now most afraid of, for the missionary in Mgr. Lefebvre has set about "having children." You may laugh at that, but it is true. It was thought that "Vatican II" had won. A few old priests were still resisting, but they would die off. The matter was clear: the whole post-conciliar renewal would be put into effect, as well in the great cities as in the African bush. Fine! — and they were already rubbing their hands. Then, all of a sudden, in a tiny corner of Switzerland, an Archbishop appears who sets about "having children," giving to the Church priests who celebrate the traditional Mass. So the enemy, occupying a strong position in the Vatican, saw red and trained all its guns on Ecône; and Ecône, till then unknown, became famous the world over.

Last year, because of the ordinations, the Vatican launched a press campaign to discredit Mgr. Lefebvre and his young priests, to have them taken for schismatics and rebels. But that very press campaign turned against the Vatican; for when people have been able to see and hear Mgr. Lefebvre their Catholic Faith has revived, and they have said: "He is the one who is right. He, at least, can be known for what he is. We can see that he is an archbishop and that his priests are priests. As for the others, we just do not know what they are." So a large part of public opinion turned in favor of Mgr. Lefebvre and his work. ✑

The Seminary Expands

It soon became known that there was an orthodox seminary in Switzerland. More young men with vocations came forward and financial support began to arrive, first from Switzerland and France, then Germany, then Britain, Australia, the U.S.A. and now from all over the world. Mgr. Lefebvre has rejected as totally false the claims that Ecône relies for its support on rich European industrialists or American millionaires. There are a few large donations (which are very welcome, and why not?) but the major part of the financial support for Ecône is made up of tens of thousands of small gifts, the sacrifices mainly of Catholics of modest means or even the very poor.* The Archbishop has made St. Joseph responsible for the financial support of the Seminary —and has had no cause for complaint. The number of vocations was so great that an ambitious building program was undertaken. Three new wings have been added and the Seminary is now able to house 140 seminarians and their pro-

*Hanu, p. 194 (165-166).

fessors in accommodation of high quality—in fact all the facilities of the Seminary, lecture hall, kitchen, dining hall, and living accommodation are almost certainly of a far higher standard than those of any other seminary in Europe. This was, to a certain extent, a matter of necessity as the standards demanded by the Swiss planning authorities are very high. It was even necessary to incorporate—at very great cost—an atomic bomb proof shelter, a feature which is obligatory in all new public buildings in Switzerland.

I have tried to evoke the spirit of the Seminary, and life there, in Chapter VI, which includes an account of my first visit to Ecône in 1975.

In its early years the Seminary received the enthusiastic support of at least some sections of the Vatican, that of Cardinal Wright, Prefect of the Congregation for the Clergy, in particular. A letter which he wrote in 1971, expressing his satisfaction at the progress of the Seminary, is reproduced in Appendix V. He was still recommending young men with vocations to apply for admission to Ecône as late as 1973. I possess the written testimony of one of the seminarians to this effect.

Houses have also been opened in a number of other countries, one of them at Albano, near Rome. This house at Albano was obtained with all the authorization required by Canon Law. It is being used at present for the religious order for women founded by the Archbishop but will eventually be used for sixth year training for the newly ordained priests of the Society. This will not only free accommodation at Ecône for new entrants but, in Mgr. Lefebvre's own words, will also "enable our young priests to draw upon all the resources of the eternal Rome, its Tradition, its martyrs, its magisterium, its monuments, and also to deepen their attachment to the Bishop of Rome, the successor of Peter."*

*See Ecône Newsletter No. 5.

The aim of the Seminary is to form good and true priests, devoted to Our Lord, to Our Lady,to the Church, and to the Mass; men burning with pastoral zeal.

The Archbishop is convinced that such a formation can be achieved only by means of a traditional seminary formation based, above all, on Thomism and the traditional Latin Liturgy.

This view certainly seems to be confirmed by the position in France, where half of the major seminaries have already been closed. In France, between 1963 and 1973 there was an 83 per cent drop in the number of men studying for the priesthood. In 1963 there were 917 seminary entrants. In 1973 there were only 151.* So great indeed is the excess of priests who die or abandon the priesthood over the number of new ordinations to replace them that a spokesman for the French Bishops' Conference has gone so far as to suggest the ordination of married men as a possible solution.

There is, incidentally, a very high "drop-out" rate in the remaining French seminaries, 422 students having "dropped-out" in 1973.**

Should this trend continue it is quite within the bounds of possibility that within ten years the Society of St. Pius X could be ordaining more priests than all the seminaries in France put together.

There can be no doubt that it was the escalating success of Ecône in the face of the accelerating decline in the French seminary system which initiated the campaign against Ecône.

---

*Report issued by the French National Center for Vocations and cited in the *Irish Catholic*, 20 March 1975.

**The Tablet, 27 January 1973 and 1 June 1974. The same reports reveal that in 1971, for example, the excess of deaths over ordinations was 465 and that in the same year almost 200 priests left the priesthood. In 1967 there were 40,994 priests in France. The French Bishops' Conference estimated that by the end of 1975 there would be only 21,820. The number of actual ordinations has declined as follows; 1966-566, 1970-284, 1973-219, 1976-136.

It will be shown in Chapter III that Mgr. Lefebvre was far from popular with the more Liberal French bishops even before the Council. As Appendix VIII to *Pope John's Council* makes clear, the post-conciliar "renewal" in France had proved to be a *débâcle* almost as catastrophic in its dimension as that in Holland. The success of Ecône provided so dramatic a contrast to this *débâcle* that its very existence became intolerable for some French bishops. They referred to it as *Le Séminaire Sauvage*—the Wildcat Seminary—giving the impression that it had been set up illegally without the authorization of the Vatican. This appellation was seized upon gleefully by the Liberal Catholic press throughout the world and soon the terms "Ecône" and "Wildcat Seminary" became synonymous.

The Canonical Status of Ecône

In view of the frequency of the allegation that Mgr. Lefebvre established his seminary without canonical authorization, the canonical status of the Seminary at Ecône is examined in some detail in Appendix V. At this point I will refer briefly to some of the evidence which makes it quite clear that the Seminary was established legally. Firstly, at no stage in the campaign against Ecône did any Vatican spokesman ever allege that the canonical basis of the Seminary was in doubt. Had there been any weakness in the canonical status of Ecône the Vatican would certainly have used this in its campaign to discredit the Archbishop. On the contrary, in 1974 two Apostolic Visitors were dispatched by the Vatican to conduct an official inspection of the Seminary (see the entry for 11-13 November 1974). The letter of condemnation sent to Mgr. Lefebvre by the Commission of Cardinals stated that the Society "no longer having a juridical basis, its foundations, and notably the Seminary at

Ecône, lose by the same act the right to existence." Obviously, the Vatican would not conduct an official inspection of
an unofficial seminary nor would it withdraw the right to
exist from a seminary which had never possessed such a right.
(The Cardinals' letter is included under the date 6 May 1975.)

Definite proof that the Society of St. Pius X and the
Seminary enjoyed Vatican approval well after the foundation
of Ecône is provided by the fact the members of three religious orders were transferred from their own orders to the
Society of St. Pius X by the Sacred Congregation for Religious. I have documentary proof that this was done in 1972
before me as I write. The Vatican would hardly have allowed
members of religious orders to be transferred to a Society
which had established a "wildcat seminary." Again, in
February 1971, Cardinal Wright wrote to Mgr. Lefebvre expressing his pleasure at the progress and expansion of the
Society and mentioning that it was receiving praise and approval from bishops in various parts of the world (this letter
is reproduced in full in Appendix V). It has been alleged that
this letter could not have involved praise for the Seminary as
it had not yet been founded in February 1971.* On the contrary, it was formally opened on 7 October 1970. On 6 June
1971 the Archbishop blessed the foundation stone of the
new buildings, an event which some of his opponents have
confused with the foundation of the Seminary.

Finally, bishops from a number of countries incardinated
priests from Ecône into their dioceses, observing all the required canonical procedure. This could not have taken place
had the canonical basis of the Seminary not been sound.

The Importance of Cardinal Villot

The French bishops held what they believed to be a

*See Father Milan Mikulich's *Orthodoxy of Catholic Doctrine*, April 1977, p. 4.

trump card—Cardinal Villot, Secretary of State and the most powerful man in the Vatican, in *de facto* terms probably even more powerful than Pope Paul VI himself. As well as holding the all-powerful office of Secretary of State, Cardinal Villot controlled twelve other key Vatican positions.* Ecône could not be allowed to survive if the French bishops were to retain any credibility. They could count on Cardinal Villot— and with his support there was no hope for the Seminary. It had been sentenced to death. Before examining the campaign designed to implement this death sentence it will be of considerable value if readers are enabled to form an impression of Mgr. Lefebvre for themselves. Ideally they should meet him, but short of doing this the best alternative is to read what he has to say about himself. Chapter III is an account of his life given in his own words—but this should obviously be supplemented by reading his book *A Bishop Speaks.*** Indeed, it is presumed throughout the present work that the reader already has a copy of this fundamental text.

---

*Hanu, p. 238 (204).

** Available from The Angelus Press

III

Archbishop Lefebvre
in His Own Words

THE ADDRESS given by His Grace, the Most Reverend Marcel Lefebvre, Titular Archbishop of Synnada in Phrygia and Superior General of the Society of St. Pius X, on the occasion of the community celebration of his seventieth birthday, 29 November 1975, at the International Seminary of Saint Pius X, Ecône, Switzerland:

"During the course of my life, I have had many consolations, in every position given to me, from young curate at Marais-de-Lomme in the Diocese of Lille, to the Apostolic Delegation of Dakar. I used to say when I was Apostolic Delegate that, from then on, I could only go downwards, I could go no higher; it was not possible. Obviously, they could still have given me a cardinal's hat! Probably God wanted me to do something else . . . to prepare His ways.

And if in the course of my missionary life I had real consolations, God always spoiled me . . . always. He spoiled me in my parents, first of all, I must say, who suffered greatly from the war of 1914-18. My mother died from it, in fact. And my father, having helped Englishmen, especially, to escape from the zone occupied by the Germans, had his name put on the German lists, and when the last war came, his name having been carefully recorded, he was arrested and died in a German jail. Both my parents were models for me and certainly I owe much to their virtue. If five out of eight children in the family are religious priests or sisters, it is not without reason.

So I was spoiled in my parents; spoiled also in my studies at the French Seminary, in having as Superior and Director of the French Seminary the venerated Père Le Floch, who was a man of great kindness and of great doctrinal firmness, to whom I owe much for my formation as a seminarian and as a priest. They reproached me for having spoken of Père Le Floch at my consecration. It seemed to me that I could not do otherwise than to thank those who had formed me and who were, in fact, indirectly the cause of my nomination and my selection as a bishop.

But I was openly reproached with that simply because Père Le Floch was a traditionalist. I was not supposed to speak of this man, who had even been discussed by the French Parliament, because he wanted to form his seminarians in complete conformity to Tradition and to truth. He too was accused of being an 'integrist.' He was accused of involving himself in politics. He was accused of being with *Action française*, whereas never, in any of his spiritual conferences, had Père Le Floch spoken to us of *Action française*. He spoke to us only of the encyclicals of the Popes; he put us on our guard against Modernism; he explained to us all the encyclicals and especially those of Saint Pius X; and thus he formed us very firmly in doctrine. It is a curious thing—those who were on the same benches as myself, many of whom later became bishops of France, did not follow the doctrine that Père Le Floch had taught them, although it was the doctrine of the Church.

So I was spoiled during my seminary training, then spoiled even as curate at Marais-de-Lomme, where I spent only one year, but where I had such joy in taking care of a working-class parish, and where I found so much friendliness. Then I spent fifteen years in the missions in the bush, as well as at the mission seminary for six years, then again in the bush in Gabon. I became so attached to Africa that I had indeed resolved never to return to Europe. I liked it so well there and was so happy—a missionary in the midst of the Gabonese jungle—that the day I learned that they were recalling me to France to be Superior of the seminary of philosophy at Mortain, I wept, and I would indeed have disobeyed, but that time my faith was not in danger!*

I was obliged to obey and to return, and it was at Mortain, after two years as Superior of the seminary of philosophy, that I was called to be Vicar Apostolic of Dakar. I spent very happy years at Mortain. I have the best memories of the seminarians of that time and I think that they too, many of whom are still living, those who are now priests and missionaries, also have happy memories of that period. When I learned that I was named to Dakar, it was a heavy blow for me, for I knew nothing of Senegal, I knew none of the Fathers there, and I did not know the language of the country, while in Gabon, I knew the language of the country, I knew all the Fathers, and I would certainly have felt much more at home. Perhaps I would even have been capable of a better apostolate toward the missionaries and the Africans of Senegal.

I did not know that a year later yet another nomination awaited me, which was that of Apostolic Delegate. That increased the crosses a little, but at the same time the consolations, because I must say that, during the eleven years from 1948 to 1959 that I was Apostolic Delegate, God filled

*Every Catholic, including priests and members of religious orders, must refuse to obey even the order of a lawful superior if complying with that order could endanger his faith.

me with joy in visiting all those dioceses with which I had been charged by the Holy Father. I had to visit them, send reports to Rome, and prepare the nomination of bishops and Apostolic Delegates.

The dioceses confided to me at that time numbered thirty-six, and during the years that I was Apostolic Delegate they increased to sixty-four. What I mean is that it was necessary to divide the dioceses, to name bishops, to name Apostolic Delegates, and then to visit the dioceses, to settle the difficulties that might exist in those territories, and at the same time to get to know the Church. This missionary Church was represented by her bishops, who accompanied me on all the journeys that I made in their dioceses. I was received by the Fathers, and by those who were in contact with the apostolate, with the natives, with the different peoples, and with the different mentalities, from Madagascar to Morocco, because Morocco was also dependent upon the Delegation of Dakar; I travelled from Djibouti to Pointe Noire in Equatorial Africa.

All these dioceses that I had the occasion to visit made me conscious of the vitality of the Church in Africa, for this period between 1948 and 1960 was a period of extraordinary growth. Numerous were the congregations of Fathers and the congregations of Sisters that came to help us. That is why I also visited Canada at that time, and many of the countries of Europe, to attempt to draw men and women religious to the countries of Africa to aid the missionaries, and to make the missions known.

And each year I had the joy of going to Rome and approaching Pope Pius XII. For eleven years I was able to visit Pope Pius XII, whom I venerated as a saint and as a genius— a genius, humanly speaking. He always received me with extraordinary kindness, taking an interest in all the problems of Africa. That is also how I got to know very closely Pope

Paul VI, who was at that time the Substitute* of Pope Pius XII and whom I saw each time that I went to Rome before going to see the Holy Father.

So I had many consolations, and was very intimately involved, I would say, in the interests of the Church—at Rome, then in all of Africa, and even in France, because by that very fact, I had to have relations with the French government, and thus with its ministers. I was received several times at the Elysée, and several times I was obliged to defend the interests of Africa before the French government. I should also say that at that time the Apostolic Delegate, of whom I was the first in the French colonies, was always considered as a Nuncio, and thus I was always given the privileges that are given to diplomats and to ambassadors. I was always received with great courtesy, and they always facilitated my journeys in Africa.

Oh, I could well have done without the detachments of soldiers who saluted me as I descended from the airplane! But if it could facilitate the reign of God, I accepted it willingly. But the African crowds who awaited the Delegate of the Holy Father, the envoy of the Holy Father—in many regions it was the first time that they had received a delegate of the Holy Father—now that was an extraordinary joy. And the fact that the government itself manifested its respect for the representative of the Pope increased still more, I would say, the honor given to the Pope himself and to the Church. All that was, as you can imagine, a great source of joy for me, to see the Church truly honored and developing in an admirable manner.

At that time the seminaries were filling and religious congregations of African Sisters were being founded. I regret that the Senegalese Sister is not here today. She is at St-Luc, but she was unable to come. I know that she would certainly

---

*The assistant to the Vatican Secretary of State is known as the "Substitute".

have been happy to take part in this celebration. Yes, the number of Sisters multiplied throughout Africa. All this is to show you once more how God spoiled me during my missionary life.

And then there was the Council, the work of the Council. Certainly it is there, I should say, that the suffering begins somewhat. To see this Church which was so full of promise, flourishing throughout the entire world . . . I should also add that, from 1962 on, I passed several months in the Diocese of Tulle, which were not useless for me because I was able to become familiar with a diocese of France and to see how the bishops of France reacted and in what environment they were.

I must say that often I was somewhat hurt to see the narrowness of mind, the pettiness of their problems, the tiny difficulties which they considered enormous problems, after returning from the missions where our problems were on a much greater scale, and where the relations between the bishops were much more cordial. In the least matters, you could sense how touchy they were; that was something which caused me pain.

And I was also surprised at the manner in which I was received into the French episcopate. For it was not I who had asked to be a bishop in France. It was Pope John XXIII at that time who obliged me to leave. I begged him to leave me free, to leave me in peace and to let me rest for a while after all those years in Africa. But he would hear nothing of it and he told me, 'An Apostolic Delegate who returns to his country should have a diocese in his country. That is the general rule. So you should have a diocese in France.' So I accepted since he imposed it upon me, and you know what restrictions were placed upon me by the bishops of France and particularly the assembly of Archbishops and Cardinals, who asked that I be excluded from the assembly of Archbishops and Cardinals, althought I was an archbishop, that I should not have a big diocese, that I should be placed in a small diocese, and that this would not be considered a precedent. This is one of the things that I found very painful, for why should a *confrère* be received in such a way, with so many restrictions?

No doubt the reason was because I was already considered a traditionalist, even before the Council. You see, that did not begin at the Council! So in 1962 I spent some time in Tulle. I was received with great reserve; with cordiality, but they were also afraid of me. The Communist newspapers already spoke of me obviously in somewhat less than laudatory terms. And even the Catholic papers were very reserved: what is this traditionalist bishop coming to do in France? What is he going to do at Tulle? But after six months, I believe that I can say that the priests whom I had the occasion to see, to meet . . . I had the occasion to give Confirmation in almost all the parishes, and our relations were truly excellent. I admired the clergy of France, who were often living in poverty, but who constituted a fervent, a devoted, a zealous clergy, really very edifying.

Then I was named Superior General of the Holy Ghost Fathers, and there again, I had occasion to travel, this time not only to Africa, but South America, North America, and everywhere where there were Holy Ghost Fathers . . . the Antilles, all the English territories of Africa and all the English-speaking territories; the Belgian Congo; South Africa; and so on—all of which obviously permitted me to become more familiar with all these missions, and I really believed that God was everywhere pouring forth extraordinary graces on His Church. At that time the effects of the Council, and all this degradation, had not yet begun. So it was a very happy period, very consoling.

Then came the Council and the results of the Council, and, I must say, it was an immense pain for me to see the decline of the Church, so rapid, so profound, so universal, that it was truly inconceivable. Even though we could foresee it, and those who worked with me in the famous *Coetus Internationalis Patrum* (the International Group of Fathers) did foresee it, the assembly of two hundred and fifty Fathers who strove to limit the damage that could be foreseen during the Council, none of us, I think, could have foreseen the rapidity with which the disintegration of the Church would take place.

It was inconceivable, and it obliged us to admit in a few years how much the Church was affected by all the false principles of Liberalism and of Modernism, which opened the door to practically every error, to all the enemies of the Church, considering them as brothers, as people with whom we had to dialogue, as a people as friendly as ourselves, and thus to be placed on the same footing as we, in a theoretical manner, and even in practice. Not that we do not respect their persons; but as for their errors, we cannot accept them. But you have all been familiar with this portion of history for some time now.

Indeed, I suffered terribly. Imagine if I had remained with the Holy Ghost Fathers where, in theory, I should have stayed until 1974. I could have stayed until 1974 as Superior General. I had been named for twelve years in 1962. But I submitted my resignation in 1968 and, in fact, I was glad to do so, because I did not want to collaborate in the destruction of my congregation. And had I remained Bishop of Tulle, I cannot very well imagine myself at present in a diocese of France! In an environment like that, I should probably have had a nervous breakdown!

It seemed that God intended my apostolic life to end in 1968, and I foresaw nothing else than simply to go into retirement at Rome; indeed, I rented a small apartment at Rome from some Sisters in Via Monserrato, and I was very happy there. But I think that God decided that my work was not yet finished. I had to continue. Well, I could never have imagined—because there I was in a small apartment, which M.

Pedroni and M. Borgeat know well—I could never have imagined at that time that God was reserving for me such profound joys and such immense consolations.

For could there be, in my last years, a consolation greater than to find myself surrounded by such faithful collaborators, faithful especially to the Church and to the ideal which we must always pursue; than to find myself surrounded by such devoted, such friendly, and such generous lay people, giving their time and their money and doing all that they can to help us? And besides them, I should recall, we must think of the tens of thousands of benefactors who are with us and who write to us—we receive their letters all the time. Now that is obviously for us and for myself an immense consolation. It is truly a family that has been created around Ecône.

And then, to have such good seminarians! I did not expect that either. I could never imagine or really believe that, in the age in which we live, in the environment in which we live, with all this degradation that the Church is undergoing, with all this disorganization, this confusion everywhere in thought, that God would still grant the grace to young men of having this desire, a profound desire, a real desire, to find an authentic priestly formation; to search for it, to leave their countries to come so far, even from Australia, even from the United States, to find such a formation; to accept a journey of twenty thousand kilometers to find a true Seminary. It is something I could never imagine. How could you expect me to imagine such a thing? I like the idea of an international Seminary and I am very happy with it, but I could never imagine that the Seminary would be what it is and that I would find young men with such good dispositions.

I believe that I can say, without flattering you and without flattering myself, that the seminary strangely resembles the French Seminary that I knew, and I believe that I can even say that it is of a quality even more pleasing to God . . . more spiritual, especially, and it is that which makes me very happy, because it is the character that I very much desire to give to the Seminary It is not only an intellectual character, a speculative character—that you should be true scholars . . . may you be so, certainly, it is necessary—but especially that you should be saints, men filled with the grace of God, filled with the spiritual life. I believe that it is even more essential than your studies, although the studies are indispensable.

For this, then, and for all the good that you are going to do, how can you expect me not to thank God? I ask myself why God has thus heaped His graces upon me. What have I done to deserve all these graces and blessings? No doubt God wished to give me all these graces and blessings so that I could bear my cross more easily.

Because the cross is heavy, after all . . .heavy in the sense to which I made allusion this morning. For it is hard, after all, to hear oneself called, and to be obliged in a way to accept that people call you, disobedient. And because we cannot submit and abandon our faith. It is a very painful thing, when you love the Church, when you love obedience, when for your entire life you have loved to follow Her leaders and Her guides. It is painful to think that our relations are so difficult with those who ought to be leading us. And all that is certainly a heavy cross to bear. I think that God gives His blessings and graces in compensation, and to strengthen us in our work.

For all this, then, I thank God, first of all, and I thank all of you, and may God do as He pleases. If He wishes me to be at your service yet for some time, let it be so. *Deo gratias!* If on the other hand He wishes to give me a small reward somewhat sooner, more quickly, well, let it be *Deo gratias* also. As He wishes. I have worked only in His service and I desire to work to the end of my days in His service and in yours also. So thank you again and let us ask God to grant that this seminary may continue for His glory and for the good of souls.''

IV

The Campaign against Ecône

THE CAMPAIGN against Ecône is documented here in chronological order. The source of most of the information in this chapter is *La Documentation Catholique* No. 1679 but Mgr. Lefebvre's account of his "trial" is taken from *Itinéraires* of July 1975.

On 26 March 1974 a meeting was convened in Rome to discuss the Priestly Fraternity of St. Pius X (which will be referred to hereafter simply as the Society of St. Pius X) and its principal foundation, the Seminary at Ecône.

Present at this meeting were Cardinal Garrone, Prefect of the Congregation for Catholic Education; Cardinal Wright, Prefect of the Congregation for the Clergy; Mgr. Mayer, Secretary of the Congregation for Religious; Mgr. Mamie, Bishop of Lausanne, Geneva, and Fribourg—the diocese in which the Society first obtained canonical authorization; Mgr. Adam, Bishop of Sion—the diocese in which Ecône is located. It was decided that a report on the Society and Seminary should be compiled.

With surprising speed the requested report was dispatched within four days, on 30 March 1974. It had been compiled by Mgr. Perroud, Vicar-General of the diocese of Lausanne, Geneva, and Fribourg. This report, accompanied by a letter from Bishop Mamie, was sent to Cardinal Garrone.

On 30 April 1974 Mgr. Lefebvre and Mgr. Mamie met at Fribourg.

At some time in June 1974, Pope Paul is alleged to have convoked the *ad hoc* Commission of Cardinals. While it cannot be claimed with certainty that this is untrue, it is certain that the document convoking the Commission has never been produced. As will be shown later, this document was one of the items which Mgr. Lefebvre's advocate would have demanded to see had not the Archbishop's appeal been blocked. It is not unreasonable to presume that one reason why the Archbishop was denied due legal process was that a number of serious irregularities would have been brought to light. It can hardly be a coincidence, in view of the criticisms aroused by the doubtful legality of the proceedings against Mgr. Lefebvre, that when a Commission of Cardinals was convoked to examine the case of Fr. Louis Coache, a traditionalist priest who had been deprived of his parish for his defense of the traditional Mass and catechism, great care was taken to leave no legal loopholes. The text of this document will be cited under the date of 10 June 1975. It will also be made clear that not one shred of evidence proving that the Pope had approved of the action taken against the Archbishop and his Seminary was produced until 29 June 1975. Pope Paul stated in a letter of this date, which is included in its chronological order, that he had approved of the action taken against the Archbishop *in forma specifica* (this term will also be explained under the same date). It is not unreasonable to conclude that this was an attempt to give retrospective legality to what must certainly be one of the greatest travesties of justice in the history of the Church.

On 23 June 1974 the Commission of Cardinals met and decided upon a canonical visitation of the Seminary.

The Apostolic Visitation of the Seminary at Ecône took place from 11-13 November 1974. The two Visitors were both Belgians: Mgr. Descamps, a biblical scholar, and Mgr. Onclin, a canonist. The Apostolic Visitation was carried out with great thoroughness. Professors and students were subjected to searching and detailed questions concerning every aspect of life in the Seminary. However, considerable scandal was occasioned by opinions which the two Roman Visitors expressed in the presence of the students and staff. For, according to Mgr. Lefebvre, these two Visitors considered it normal and indeed inevitable that there should be a married clergy; they did not believe there was an immutable Truth; and they also had doubts concerning the traditional concept of our Lord's Resurrection.*

On 21 November 1974, in reaction to the scandal occasioned by these opinions of the Apostolic Visitors, Mgr. Lefebvre considered it necessary to make clear where he stood in relation to the Rome represented by this attitude of mind. "This," he said, "was the origin of my Declaration which was, it is true, drawn up in a spirit of doubtlessly excessive indignation."

In this Declaration he rejected the views expressed by the Visitors, even if they were currently acceptable in the Rome which the Visitors represented in an official capacity.

In this Declaration, he stated:

. . . we refuse . . . and have always refused to follow the Rome of Neo-Modernist and Neo-Protestant tendencies . . . .

No authority, not even the highest in the hierarchy, can compel us to abandon or diminish our Catholic faith, so clearly expressed and professed by the Church's Magisterium for nineteen centuries.

*See p. 46.

It is difficult to see how any orthodox Catholic could possibly disagree with Mgr. Lefebvre concerning this. It is all the more significant, therefore, that the Commission of Cardinals subsequently stated that the Declaration "seemed unacceptable to them on all points."

It is also important to note that this Declaration was not intended as a public statement, let alone as a Manifesto defying the Holy See. It was intended to be a private statement solely for the benefit of the members of the Society of Saint Pius X.

However, the Declaration was leaked without Mgr. Lefebvre's permission, and because the text, or extracts from it, were being used in a manner which he could not condone, he authorized *Itinéraires* to publish the full and authentic French text in January 1975. An English translation of this Declaration was published in *Approaches* 42-3 and *The Remnant* of 6 February 1975.

It is particularly significant that the Commission of Cardinals persistently refused to view this Declaration in the context of its origin: as a private reaction of righteous indignation to the scandal occasioned by the views propagated by the two Apostolic Visitors who had been sent to Ecône by the Commission of Cardinals.

The full text of the Declaration follows.

The Declaration of 21 November 1974

We hold firmly with all our heart and with all our mind to Catholic Rome, Guardian of the Catholic Faith and of the traditions necessary to the maintenance of this faith, to the eternal Rome, mistress of wisdom and truth.

We refuse on the other hand, and have always refused, to follow the Rome of Neo-Modernist and Neo-Protestant tendencies which became clearly manifest during the Second

Vatican Council, and after the Council, in all the reforms which issued from it.

In effect, all these reforms have contributed and continue to contribute to the destruction of the Church, to the ruin of the priesthood, to the abolition of the Sacrifice of the Mass and the Sacraments, to the disappearance of the religious life, and to a naturalistic and Teilhardian education in the universities, in the seminaries, in catechetics: an education deriving from Liberalism and Protestantism which had been condemned many times by the solemn Magisterium of the Church.

No authority, not even the highest in the hierarchy, can compel us to abandon or to diminish our Catholic Faith, so clearly expressed and professed by the Church's Magisterium for nineteen centuries.

"Friends," said St. Paul, "though it were we ourselves, though it were an angel from heaven that should preach to you a gospel other than the gospel we have preached to you, a curse upon him" (Gal. 1:8).

Is it not this that the Holy Father is repeating to us today? And if there is a certain contradiction manifest in his words and deeds as well as in the acts of the dicasteries,* then we cleave to what has always been taught and we turn a deaf ear to the novelties which destroy the Church.

It is impossible to profoundly modify the *Lex Orandi* without modifying the *Lex Credendi*. To the New Mass there corresponds the new catechism, the new priesthood, the new seminaries, the new universities, the "Charismatic" Church, Pentecostalism: all of them opposed to orthodoxy and the never-changing Magisterium.

This reformation, deriving as it does from Liberalism and Modernism, is entirely corrupted; it derives from heresy and results in heresy, even if all its acts are not formally heretical.

---

*I.e. the Roman Congregations (Departments) presided over by cardinals which govern the life of the Church, e.g. the Congregation for the Clergy.

It is therefore impossible for any conscientious and faithful Catholic to espouse this reformation and to submit to it in any way whatsoever.

The only attitude of fidelity to the Church and to Catholic doctrine appropriate for our salvation is a categorical refusal to accept this reformation.

That is why, without any rebellion, bitterness, or resentment, we pursue our work of priestly formation under the guidance of the never-changing Magisterium, convinced as we are that we cannot possibly render a greater service to the Holy Catholic Church, to the Sovereign Pontiff, and to posterity.

That is why we hold firmly to everything that has been consistently taught and practiced by the Church (and codified in books published before the Modernist influence of the Council) concerning faith, morals, divine worship, catechetics, priestly formation, and the institution of the Church, until such time as the true light of tradition dissipates the gloom which obscures the sky of the eternal Rome.

Doing this, with the grace of God, the help of the Virgin Mary, St. Joseph, and St. Pius X, we are certain that we are being faithful to the Catholic and Roman Church, to all of Peter's successors, and of being the *Fideles Dispensatores Mysteriorum Domini Nostri Jesu Christi In Spiritu Sancto.*

† Marcel Lefebvre

Public Defamation

A statement condemning those who adhere to the Old Mass made by the French episcopate on 14 November 1974 was certainly aimed against Ecône, for at the same time the bishops let it be known that they would not accept any priests from Ecône in their dioceses.*

---

*Courrier de Rome, No. 140, February 1975, p. 4.

A campaign against the Seminary was then launched laying great stress on the Archbishop's refusal to use the New Mass. He, on the other hand, is adamant that no legal obligation to do so exists.

Examples of this preparatory stage of the offensive can be found in *La Croix* of 17, 18, 21, and 22 January and 1 February 1975. A change of tactics can be discerned from 8 February onwards, clearly resulting from a realization that proving the Archbishop wrong with regard to the legal position of the Mass would not be easy. From 8 February 1975, the charge against Ecône was one of a "Refusal of the Council and the Pope." Mgr. Lefebvre's Declaration of 21 November 1974 was cited in order to try to justify this charge.

The Commission of Cardinals met on 21 January 1975 to discuss the Report of the Apostolic Visitors.

However, the Report of the Visitors (who seem to have been honest men though far from impeccably orthodox) was not only favorable to the Seminary but even flattering. It was therefore quite unusable as a basis for the condemnation of Ecône.

In the words of Mgr. Lefebvre:

After telling me of the favorable impression the Seminary had made on the Apostolic Visitors no further reference was made to the Society or to the Seminary either on 13 February or 3 March. It was exclusively a question of my Declaration of 21 November 1974, which had been made as a result of the Apostolic Visitation.

The Commission of Cardinals therefore seized upon the only supposed evidence to hand—the Declaration of 21 November 1974.

In this connection, it is important to repeat that, in the opinion of most well-informed commentators, the action taken against Ecône by the Swiss bishops, in conjunction with Rome, had been instigated by the French hierarchy, with the

Vatican Secretary of State, Cardinal Villot, acting as its instrument.*

As Mgr. Lefebvre points out, the Apostolic Visitation was the first step towards the suppression of the Seminary. And this action was taken only after a prolonged press campaign in which the Seminary had been subjected to the most odious calumnies, which had been taken up first by the French bishops and then by the Swiss episcopate. One French Archbishop had indeed been reported as stating that he would have "the scalp of the Seminary" before 1975 was out.**

But the most convincing evidence that the Commission of Cardinals was determined at all costs to close the Seminary was the fact that nothing more was heard of the Apostolic Visitation after its report was found to be favorable.

In a letter dated 21 May 1975, accompanying his appeal which was lodged at the Apostolic Signature on 5 June, Mgr. Lefebvre demanded that, if there was anything in his Declaration which should be condemned, the Commission of Cardinals should condemn him personally rather than suppress the Society of St. Pius X, the Seminary, and the other houses which had been founded by the Society.

The Archbishop has yet to be given one word from the Commission specifying anything in the Declaration which is alleged to deviate from orthodoxy. He insists that should such an allegation be made he must be tried by the Congregation for the Doctrine of the Faith, the only tribunal competent to decide in such a matter.

Certainly to close down the most flourishing and the most orthodox seminary in the West on the basis of alleged but unspecified unorthodoxy found in a single document is an unprecedented enormity. It is all the more outrageous, given

* *Vide* Mgr. Lefebvre's letter of 15 July 1975 to the editor of *Approaches*. It is reproduced below under this date.

** *Courrier de Rome*, No. 146, p. 1.

the total inactivity (if not the connivance) of the Vatican concerning the travesty of the Catholic Faith and priestly formation that has for long been perpetrated in so many other seminaries, above all in French seminaries.

Indeed, one would have to go to Soviet Russia to discover a comparable caricature of justice. But concerning even the worst travesties of justice behind the Iron Curtain, it can at least be said that they are not perpetrated in the name of Christ's Church, let alone during a Holy Year of Reconciliation!

On 24 January 1975, Mgr. Mamie, Bishop of Lausanne, Geneva, and Fribourg, wrote to Cardinal Tabera, Prefect of the Congregation for Religious. In this letter he stated that, following the meeting of 21 January and having made a careful study of Mgr. Lefebvre's Declaration, he considered it a sad but urgent necessity to withdraw the approval given by his predecessor to the Society of St. Pius X. More and more people, he said, were refusing the Mass of Paul VI throughout French and German Switzerland and it had even been alleged that Mgr. Adam (Bishop of Sion) was mistaken in claiming that Pope Paul had abrogated the Missal of Pius V. In such a situation the Seminary could do no good.

At the same time he felt bound to admit the existence of certain unlawful aberrations instigated by those who used the Council as an excuse for withdrawing themselves from the Hierarchy, the Magisterium, and the Truth. This problem was preoccupying the Swiss bishops as gravely as the question of Ecône. They were working daily to rectify what needed rectifying. They also encouraged those who needed encouraging.

There are several points in this letter to which attention should be drawn.

Firstly, its date, 24 January 1975, and Mgr. Mamie's admission that he had been present at the meeting on 21 January when the Cardinals decided to invite Mgr. Lefebvre to Rome. It is quite clear that Mgr. Mamie's letter of 24 January had been decided upon during the 21 January meeting. In other words, the suppression of Ecône was agreed upon on 21 January 1975, more than three weeks *before* the discussion with Mgr. Lefebvre took place.

Secondly, however sincere Mgr. Adam and Mgr. Mamie might be in their belief that the Pope had abrogated the Old Mass with all the necessary legal formalities, they both refrain from stating when and in what terms this abrogation was made public.

Thirdly, while Mgr. Mamie concedes that, in Switzerland as elsewhere, many of those responsible for grave aberrations use the Council to justify their defiance of the Magisterium, documented evidence of sanctions being taken against such people by the Swiss (or any other) Hierarchy is very hard to come by. The frequent references to the existence of such abuses and the insistence that steps are being taken to correct them, included (even by Pope Paul VI himself) in public attacks upon Mgr. Lefebvre, indicate the unease felt by the Archbishop's critics in the face of their evident observance of double standards. There are in the Church today two weights, two measures—one for Mgr. Lefebvre and other traditionalists who wish to uphold the Faith and one for the Liberals who wish to destroy it.

On 25 January 1975, Cardinal Garrone, Prefect of the Congregation for Catholic Education, sent the following letter to Mgr. Lefebvre on behalf of the Commission of Cardinals. All three signed the letter. A close study of this letter reveals how carefully the Cardinals have concealed the fact that Archbishop Lefebvre is being convoked before a tribunal which, it would be claimed later, had been constituted by express mandate of the Holy Father. Nor does the letter give the least indication that it is the Declaration of 21 November 1974 which is in question. It is simply a request for a discussion with the Archbishop— *"Nous voudrions maintenant nous entretenir avec vous . . ."* The text of the letter follows:

Your Excellency,

Their Excellencies Cardinal Wright, Cardinal Tabera and I have studied the result of the visit to the Ecône Seminary by His Excellency Mgr. Descamps. We are grateful to you for having given him every facility to accomplish the mission on behalf of the Holy See.

We would now like to discuss with you some points which leave us somewhat bewildered following his visit, and concerning which, among others, we must report to the Holy Father.

Can you arrange to be free for this meeting at 10:00 a. m.* on the morning of 13 February next in the premises of our Congregation?

Thanking you in anticipation in the name of the three Cardinals entrusted with this question and assuring you of my respectful and fraternal sentiments.

On 13 February, Mgr. Lefebvre met the Commission of Cardinals as arranged.There was a further session on 3 March.

The following is Mgr. Lefebvre's own account of the methods adopted by the Commission of Cardinals in their search for an excuse to suppress the Society of St. Pius X and its various establishments including the Ecône Seminary. This statement was published in *Itinéraires* No. 195, July-August 1975.

The Statement of Mgr. Lefebvre

It should be remembered that even before the proceedings opened, the Seminary of the Society, from the moment of its very foundation, had been the victim of a campaign of denigration in the press, more especially when its attraction for the young and its world-wide reputation became evident. This campaign of denigration included the odious calumny

*The time of the meeting was later changed to 9:00 a.m.

that Ecône was a wild-cat seminary.* Calumnies such as these
were re-echoed first by the French episcopate, in spite of the
fact that the Bishop of Fribourg knew perfectly well that
they had no foundation in fact.

It was obvious that steps had been taken in Rome to obtain our suppression. On 9 November we received a letter
from a Nunciature of Berne, informing us that a Commission,
nominated by the Pope, and consisting of three Cardinal
Prefects of the Congregations involved—Religious, Catholic
Education, Clergy—was sending us two Apostolic Visitors:
His Excellency Mgr. Descamps and Mgr. Onclin.

The two Visitors arrived at 9:00 a. m. on Monday, 11 November. For three days they questioned 10 professors, 20 of
the 104 students, and myself. They left at 6:00 p. m. on 13
November without having signed any Protocol of Visit. We
have never been given any information concerning the con-
tents of their Report.

Convinced that this was the first step towards the suppression of our Seminary, which for long had been the aim of
the progressives, and realizing that the Visitors had come
with the aim of bringing us into line with the changes that
had taken place within the Church since the Council, I decided to make my position clear to the entire Seminary.

I could not adhere to the Rome represented by Apostolic
Delegates who considered the ordination of married men
both normal and inevitable; who could not accept the idea of
immutable Truth, and who expressed doubts concerning the
traditional concept of Our Lord's Resurrection.

This was the origin of my Declaration, which was, it is
true, drawn up in a spirit of doubtless excessive indignation.

---

*This was also the description used in the headline above a most misleading and
slanted report in the English Catholic weekly *The Universe* of 6 June 1975. This
report would have disgraced any newspaper, let alone a "Catholic" paper which,
boasts on its masthead of Pope Paul's prayerful concern for its efficacy as an instrument of truth. Moreover, even when the false nature of the entire report was
drawn to the editor's attention, *The Universe* refused to print any correction.

Two and a half months passed without any news. Then on 30 January 1975, I received a letter, signed by the members of the Commission, inviting me to Rome "to discuss" with them "some points which leave us somewhat bewildered."

Accepting this invitation, I went to Rome, to the Congregation for Catholic Education, on 13 February 1975. Their Eminences Cardinals Garrone, Wright, and Tabera, accompanied by a secretary, invited me to join them at a conference table. His Eminence Cardinal Garrone asked me whether I had any objection to the discussion being recorded and the secretary proceeded to install a recording machine.

After telling me of the favorable impression received by the Apostolic Visitors, no further reference was made either to the Society or to the Seminary either on 13 February or on 3 March. It was exclusively a question of my Declaration of 21 November 1974, which had been made as a consequence of the Apostolic Visit.

Cardinal Garrone vehemently reproached me on account of this, even going so far as to imply that I was a "lunatic," that I imagined myself to be an Athanasius.* This tirade lasted for some 25 minutes. Cardinal Tabera, going one better, said: "What you are doing is worse than what is being done by all the progressives." He also said that I had severed communion with the Church, etc.

Was I taking part in a discussion? Or was I rather facing judges? What was the competence of this Commission? I had merely been told that it had been mandated by the Holy Father and that it was he who would judge. But it was clear that judgment had already been passed.

I tried in vain to formulate arguments or explanations giving the true meaning of my Declaration. I made it clear that I respected and would always respect the Pope and the Bishops but added that to me it was not an evident fact that to

---

*Mgr. Lefebvre has never, at any time, compared himself with St. Athanasius. The fact that a sound basis for such a comparison exists is made clear in Appendix I.

criticize certain texts of the Council and the Reforms which derived therefrom was equivalent to breaking with the Church. I said that I was making every effort to discover the deeply rooted causes of the present crisis in the Church and that everything I had done proved that my desire was to build the Church, not to destroy it. But not one of my arguments was taken into consideration. Cardinal Garrone insisted that the cause of the crisis lay in the media of social communications.

At the end of the meeting of 13 February as at the end of that of 3 March, my impression was that I had been deceived. Whereas I had been invited to a discussion, in fact I was facing a tribunal which had already decided to condemn me. Nothing was done to help me towards a compromise or towards an amicable solution. Nothing in writing was given to me specifying the accusations; no written monition. Nothing but the argument of authority, accompanied by invective and threats, was presented to me in the course of five hours of discussion.

After the end of the second session, I asked for a copy of the recording. Cardinal Garrone replied that it was only right that I should have a copy, that I had a right to it, and he informed his secretary accordingly.

That very evening I sent a man with all the necessary equipment to make a recording from the original tape. But the secretary stated that there was no question of my having more than a transcription. I went myself next day to ask for a copy (of the recording). The secretary went to consult the Cardinal and returned to inform me that it was indeed a transcription I was to get. This was promised for the following evening. To be certain that it would be ready I telephoned the following morning. The secretary then told me that there was no question of my being given a transcription, but that I could call between 5:00 p. m. and 8:00 p. m. to see it. Faced with this kind of behavior I let the matter drop.

So then, after this mockery of a trial concerning a supposedly favorable Visitation about which there were only some slight reservations, and after two sessions which concentrated exclusively on my Declaration in order to condemn it totally, without reservation or nuance whatsoever, without its being concretely examined and without my being given anything in writing, one after the other I received first a letter from His Excellency Mgr. Mamie suppressing the Society and the Seminary with the approval of the Commission of Cardinals, and then a letter from the Commission confirming Mgr. Mamie's letter. All this without the formulation of a formal and precise accusation concerning what had been discussed. And this decision, declared Mgr. Mamie, came into effect immediately (*"immédiatement exécutive"*).

I was therefore expected immediately to dismiss from the Seminary 104 seminarians, 13 professors, and other personnel. And this, two months before the end of the scholastic year! One requires only to write all this down in order to know the reactions of anyone who still retains a little common sense and honesty. And all this on 8 May of the Year of Reconciliation!

Does the Holy Father really know of these things? We find it difficult to believe he does.

† Marcel Lefebvre

On 15 April 1975, through the medium of *Itinéraires*, Mgr. Lefebvre published the text of his reply to the Abbé de Nantes concerning two articles in the February and March issues of the Abbé de Nantes' newsletter, *La Contre-Réforme Catholique*, which appeared to implicate him.* All tradition-

---

*"*Abbé*" is a common title given to the clergy in France. Father Georges de Nantes is one of the best known figures in the French traditionalist movement. He has been much criticized by other traditionalists in recent years due to his public criticism of Mgr. Lefebvre. He is mentioned in *Pope John's Council*, (pp. 187-188). He is referred to incorrectly in *Vatican Encounter* as "the abbot of Nantes."

alists would do well to emulate Mgr. Lefebvre's exemplary restraint and his respectful attitude to the Holy Father, as well as his uncompromising fidelity to the Eternal Rome, as expressed not only in the following letter but also in his Declaration of 21 November 1974.

Dear Father,

You will admit, I think, that it is not I who wished that our correspondence should become public. I have already told you so in writing. Controversy such as this cannot but weaken the spiritual forces which we require to combat error and heresy.

The indelicacy of your action is such that I would have kept silent if you had not written most insidious articles prejudicing me personally in your last two issues (of *La Contre-Réforme Catholique*).

The first concerned a Bishop's breaking with Rome—which you deemed to be desirable. Undoubtedly, no explicit allusion was made. However, in the next few lines you mentioned my name in connection with the *Credo* Pilgrimage (to Rome), and uninformed readers automatically linked the person named with the preceding lines. This kind of thing is odious. I would have you know that if a Bishop breaks with Rome it will not be me. My Declaration (of 21 November) stated this explicitly and emphatically enough.

And it is in this connection that I must also tell you of my utter disagreement with the commentaries further to this in your last issue, which say what you wish, what you would like to see, but not what is.

We think that when the Apostle Paul reproached Peter he kept and even showed towards the head of the Church the affection and respect due to him. St. Paul was at one and the same time with Peter, head of the Church, who at the Council of Jerusalem had given clear directions, and against Peter, who in practice acted contrary to his own instructions. Are we not sometimes tempted to feel similarly today? But this does not authorize us to despise the successor of Peter. It must make us pray for him with ever increasing fervor.

With Pope Paul VI, we denounce Neo-Modernism, the self-destruction of the Church, Satan's smoke in the Church, and consequently we refuse to co-operate in the destruction of the Church by the propagation of Modernism and Protestantism, by involvement in the reforms which are inspired by these errors, even if they come to us from Rome.

As I had occasion to say recently in Rome concerning the Second Vatican Council: Liberalism has been condemned by the Church for a century and a half. It has found its way into the Church via the Council. The Church is dying of the practical consequences of this Liberalism. We must therefore do everything to help the Church and those who govern it to free themselves from this Satanic influence.

That is the significance of my Declaration.

As for your illogicalities and the fact of your not having met me at Ecône, I shall not speak of these. They are trifles compared with the main problem to which I have just referred.

Please accept, dear Father, my respectful and cordially devoted greetings in Christ and Mary.

† Marcel Lefebvre
19 March 1975
The Feast of Saint Joseph.

In a letter to Mgr. Mamie dated 25 April 1975, Cardinal Tabera stated that the Commission of Cardinals not only agreed with the request made by Mgr. Mamie in his letter of 24 January (to withdraw canonical approval from the Society of St. Pius X), but also urged him to do so without further delay. Mgr. Mamie was assured by Cardinal Tabera that his invaluable collaboration in the service of the Lord and His Church was greatly appreciated.

On 6 May 1975 Mgr. Mamie wrote to Mgr. Lefebvre stating that after long months of prayer and reflection he had reached the sad but necessary decision that he must withdraw all the acts and concessions granted by his predecessor to the Society of St. Pius X. He also stated that Mgr. Lefebvre would soon receive a letter from the *ad hoc* Commission of

Cardinals confirming that this action had been taken in full
agreement with the Holy See. It was the Declaration of 21
November 1974, he said, which had finally confirmed him
in this course of action. Mgr. Mamie considered the Archbishop to be manifestly opposed not only to Vatican II but
also to the person and the acts of the successor of St. Peter,
His Holiness Pope Paul VI, and he therefore could not allow
him to continue to claim that the Society had the support of
the Bishop of Fribourg. He therefore could no longer allow
the authority of the Bishop of Lausanne, Geneva, and Fribourg to continue to provide the canonical basis of Mgr.
Lefebvre's institutions.

This decision (he said) took effect immediately and he
had informed the relevant Roman Congregations of his
action by the same post, as well as the Apostolic Delegate
and Mgr. Adam, President of the Swiss Episcopal Conference.

The two concluding paragraphs of his letter read as follows:

As for us, we shall continue to demand that the faithful as well as
the clergy accept and apply all the orientations and decisions of the
Second Vatican Council, all the teachings of John XXIII and of Paul VI,
all the directives of the secretariats instituted by the Council, including
the new liturgy. This we have done and this we shall continue to do,
even in the most difficult of days and with the grace of God, because
for us it is the only way to edify the Church.

It is therefore with great sadness, Monseigneur, that I assure you of
my prayers and most fraternal sentiments, in union with Christ Jesus,
His Church, and the one who has received the divine powers of confirming his brothers, the Sovereign Pontiff, the Successor of Peter.

The penultimate paragraph of this letter merits particularly
careful study.

Why this exclusive preoccupation only with all of the orientations and decisions of Vatican II and the teachings of Popes

John XXIII and Paul VI?

Does Mgr. Mamie have no interest in previous Councils? After all, they were of far greater status than Vatican II. For whereas they were dogmatic, Vatican II was merely pastoral— whatever pastoral may mean.*

And what about Pope Pius XII? Is he already forgotten in Lausanne, Geneva, and Fribourg?

It is not difficult to understand why Mgr. Mamie prefers not to remember Pope Pius XII, who would certainly not have permitted a Roman Congregation to issue directives permitting laywomen to give Communion in the hand to standing communicants. In fairness to Pope John, it must be stressed that neither would he have tolerated such practices. Did he not dismiss Mgr. Bugnini, who, more than anyone else, has been responsible for stage-managing the liturgical revolution which the Congregation for Divine Worship proceeded to impose on the Church?

It is also not difficult to see why Mgr. Mamie is so determined to condemn Mgr. Lefebvre's Declaration, which insists that the only attitude which a faithful Catholic can possibly have to this kind of Reformation is to refuse categorically to accept it.

It is true that not even the most ardent Liberal would dare to suggest that any previous Pope would have tolerated the kind of directives now being issued by some of the secretariats instituted in the wake of Vatican II. It is interesting to note that in the very year when the New Order of the Mass was foisted on the Church in the name of the Pope by the Congregation for Divine Worship, even Cardinal Gut, the then Prefect of that Congregation, admitted that the Holy Father had frequently yielded against his own better judgment in sanctioning various kinds of unlawful liturgical initiatives

---

*The authority of the documents of Vatican II is explained in Chapter 14 of *Pope John's Council*.

undertaken by priests determined to impose their will on the Church.*

It is also relevant to note that Mgr. Bugnini is reported to have told one of his friends that "he had all the difficulty in the world" in getting Pope Paul to authorize the New Mass.** It must also be noted that a mere two months after Cardinal Villot had successfully contrived to have Ecône suppressed, Pope Paul VI at long last dismissed Archbishop Bugnini, the moving spirit behind the New Mass, by suppressing the Congregation for Divine Worship, merging it with the Congregation for the Sacraments, and excluding Mgr. Bugnini from any position in the new Congregation.***

As for Mgr. Mamie's much vaunted loyalty to Pope John and Pope Paul, this is, to say the least, of a very selective nature.

Mgr. Mamie has no right whatsoever to claim that he implements all the teachings of John XXIII and Paul VI. For example, in his encyclical *Veterum Sapientia* (1962) on the importance and value of Latin in the life of the Church, Pope John stated, *inter alia*, that the major sacred sciences must be taught through the medium of Latin in Catholic universities and seminaries.

Pope John insisted that bishops and superiors-general of religious orders "shall studiously observe the Apostolic See's decision in this matter and obey these our prescriptions most carefully", and added:

In the exercise of their paternal care they shall be on their guard lest

La Documentation Catholique, No. 1551, (16 November 1969), p. 1048.

**Rev. L.M. Barielle, *La messe catholique, est-elle encore permise?* (Editions Saint-Gabriel)

***The background to Archbishop Bugnini's dismissal is explained in *Pope John's Council*, Chapter XII. A more detailed treatment will appear in *Pope Paul's New Mass*.

anyone under their jurisdicition, being eager for innovation, writes against the use of Latin in the teaching of the higher sacred studies or in the liturgy, or through prejudice makes light of the Holy See's will in this regard or interprets it falsely.

Needless to say, Mgr. Mamie's zeal to crush the Seminary at Ecône, where Latin textbooks are still used, is not matched by an equivalent zeal to insure that this particular teaching of Pope John is observed in the seminaries of which he approves.

As for Mgr. Mamie's obedience to Pope Paul, although it was made clear in *Memoriale Domini* that the Holy Father wished the traditional method of receiving Communion to be maintained, Communion in the hand is now widespread throughout Switzerland, not excluding the Diocese of Lausanne, Geneva, and Fribourg.

The liturgy provides yet another example of Mgr. Mamie's selective obedience. In 1974, the Holy Father sent a copy of *Jubilate Deo*, a book containing all the more common Latin chants, as a personal gift to every bishop in the world. He did so in the hope that this would impress upon them his concern that the specific teaching of Vatican II concerning the liturgical use of Latin should be implemented. At the same time he made it clear that he wanted all the faithful to be familiar with these Latin chants. Yet despite Mgr. Mamie's professed loyalty to the teaching of Paul VI, it would be difficult to find many parishes in his diocese where the Holy Father's wishes have been respected.

Clearly, it is to Mgr. Mamie rather than to Mgr. Lefebvre that the Commission of Cardinals should have addressed the words: "It is inadmissible that each individual should be invited to submit papal directions to his private judgment and decide for himself whether to accept or reject them."

As for the specific teachings of the promulgated documents of Vatican II—which must not be confused with the innumerable orientations imposed on the Church in the name of Vatican II, as is made clear in pages 68-70, the specific teaching of the Council is probably observed more faithfully at Ecône than any other seminary in the Western world.

V

The Condemnation

ON THE SAME DAY that Mgr. Mamie wrote to Mgr. Lefebvre, 6 May 1975, the Commission of Cardinals also pronounced their condemnation.

The complete text of this condemnation is as follows:

Your Excellency,

It is in the name of the Commission of Cardinals and by the express mandate of the Holy Father that we write to you.

We remain deeply grateful to you for enabling our recent discussions to take place in such a fraternal atmosphere that on no occasion did our differences of opinion compromise the profound and serene communion which exists among us.   But this only increases our sorrow at the apparent intransigence of your views, with the consequences that cannot but derive from them.

Our discussions were concerned principally with your public Declaration published in the review *Itinéraires*. It could not be otherwise in view of the fact that the Declaration stated explicitly what the Visitor to Ecône (Mgr. Descamps) had been unable to bring to light. He suggested that we clear this up in a discussion with you.

Now such a Declaration appears unacceptable to us on all points. It is impossible to reconcile most of the affirmations contained in this document with authentic fidelity to the Church, to the one who is responsible for Her, and to the Council in which the mind and will of the Church were expressed. It is inadmissible that every individual should be invited to submit papal directives to his own private judgment and decide for himself whether to accept or reject them. This is nothing less than the customary language of those sects which appeal to the popes of yesterday in order to refuse obedience to the Pope of today.

Throughout our conversations, our desire was to lead you, Your Excellency, to recognize the cogency of such objections and to withdraw your own affirmations. You told us that you found this impossible. "If I had to rewrite this text," you said, "I would write the same things."

Under such circumstances the Commission was left with no alternative but to pass on its absolutely unanimous conclusions to the Pope together with the complete dossier of the affair so that he could judge for himself. It is with the entire approval of His Holiness that we communicate the following decisions to you:

1) "A letter will be dispatched to Mgr. Mamie according him the right to withdraw the approval which his predecessor gave to the Fraternity and to its statutes." This has been done in a letter from His Excellency Cardinal Tabera, Prefect of the Congregation for Religious.

2) Once it is suppressed, the Society "no longer having a juridical basis, its foundations, and notably the Seminary at Ecône, lose by the same act the right to existence."

3) It is obvious—we are invited to notify it clearly— "that no support whatsoever can be given to Mgr. Lefebvre as long as the ideas contained in the Manifesto of 21 November continue to be the basis for his work."

We cannot communicate these decisions to you without profound sadness. We know the generous perseverance with which you have worked and the good which in consequence has been accomplished.

We can well imagine what a cruel predicament you will find yourself in. But we are sure that all those who have read or wish to read your Declaration, without gratuitously suspecting any motives other than the Declaration itself for the actions which have been taken, will concede that, in the face of the evidence, matters could not have been resolved differently, given your refusal to withdraw this text. No Church institution, no priestly formation can be built upon such a foundation.

We hope, Your Excellency, that the Lord will give you the light and enable you to find the path that conforms with His will, in the confidence of the one to whom as bishops we owe a sincere and effective obedience.

As for us, we can only assure you of our fraternal attachment and our prayers.

Gabriel-Marie Cardinal Garrone,
Prefect of the Sacred Congregation for Catholic Education
President of the Commission of Cardinals

John Cardinal Wright,
Prefect of the Sacred Congregation for the Clergy

Arturo Cardinal Tabera,
Prefect for the Sacred Congregation for Religious
and for Secular Institutes

This letter is being sent to Their Excellencies Mgr. Mamie and Mgr. Adam.

As an exercise in public relations on behalf of Mgr. Lefebvre's persecutors, the Cardinals' letter is indeed a superb performance. The image it evokes is clear. It is of three very moderate, reasonable, and supremely charitable cardinals doing everything in their power to save a well-intentioned but hopelessly intransigent and unenlightened pre-Vatican II Archbishop from the tragic consequences of his own invincible folly. But he refused to be saved!

The crucial phrase in this letter reads as follows, and its significance could not possibly be overstressed:

. . . the Declaration stated explicitly what the Visitor to Ecône (Mgr. Descamps) had been unable to bring to light.

The Cardinals admit quite openly that the Apostolic Visitation had been unable to bring to light any excuse for closing the Seminary—and, as was stated earlier, it was clearly to find an excuse that the Visitors were sent in the first place. It will be necessary for the reader to pause for a few moments and consider the precise import of what the Cardinals are actually saying here if its full enormity is to be appreciated. When carefully analyzed the following conclusions are not simply obvious but inescapable.

1) The Visitors were sent to the Seminary to find a pretext for closing it but could not do so.
2) During their Visitation they made statements which outraged the Catholic sensibilities of the seminarians.
3) In order to insure that the scandal caused did not result in any seminarians confusing Rome itself with the persons of the Visitors representing it, Mgr. Lefebvre made his Declaration affirming his faith in the Eternal Rome.
4) This Declaration, provoked by the Visitors, is now to be used as the sole, I repeat, the sole justification for closing the Seminary in place of the evidence the Visitors could not find because it did not exist. This is the "Conciliar Church" with a vengeance!

In order to alienate traditionally-minded Catholics from Mgr. Lefebvre it was necessary to invoke papal authority for the action taken against him. But in their anxiety to involve the Pope the three Cardinals only succeed in contradicting themselves and adding to the confusion and legitimate suspicion surrounding the whole process against the Archbishop. Firstly, they claim that their unanimous conclusions (not decisions) and the complete dossier have been passed to the Pope so that he can "judge for himself."

Secondly, they claim that "it is with the entire approval of His Holiness that we communicate the following decisions to you." This makes it clear that the decisions are not those of the Pope; they are the decisions of an unspecified authority which the Pope is alleged to have approved. The obvious solution would be that the decisions are those of the three Cardinals themselves but this possibility is ruled out by an explicit statement referring to the third decision: "we are invited to notify it clearly."

It will also be noted that the three decisions are included within quotation marks and so the cardinals are definitely communicating a decision of someone other than themselves who is not the Pope. Thus, the dubious legality of the procedure used against Mgr. Lefebvre is highlighted by the fact that he has been condemned by an anonymous judge.

Another significant point is that when quoting the decisions of this anonymous judge within the quotation marks, the Declaration of Mgr. Lefebvre is misrepresented by the use of the term "Manifesto." The Cardinals themselves use the same term as Mgr. Lefebvre—"Declaration." "Manifesto" is also the term used in a contentious report which appeared in *L'Osservatore Romano* two days later, 8 May 1975, which will be discussed in chronological sequence under that date. As *L'Osservatore Romano* traditionally reflects the mind of the Secretary of State it is at the very least a reasonable hypothesis that the anonymous judge of Mgr. Lefebvre was none other than Cardinal Villot himself. It is also of very great significance that when the Cardinals' letter appeared in the official French Catholic daily, *La Croix*, on 5 June 1975, the tell-tale quotation marks had conveniently vanished.

Nor can it be concluded with any certainty that these decisions were approved by the Pope simply on the word of the Cardinals concerned. As the case of Father Coache, cited on pp. 108-109 proves, it can no longer be presumed that any statement coming from the Vatican is true. In this case, it will be noted that in the letter they refer to their discussions with Mgr. Lefebvre taking place "in such a fraternal atmosphere that on no occasion did our difference of opinion compromise the profound and serene communion which exists among us." Yet, as Mgr. Lefebvre's account of the discussions revealed, Cardinals Garrone and Tabera treated him with considerable acrimony and even accused him of being a lunatic.

Further, when considering the integrity of these Cardinals it must be noted that in 1976 the transcript of the discussions which had been refused to Mgr. Lefebvre was leaked to the press in what Mgr. Lefebvre claims is definitely a "doctored" version.*

The first documentary evidence of papal approval of the action taken against Mgr. Lefebvre was the letter from the Pope of 29 June 1975, which will be discussed under that date, and which appears suspiciously like an attempt to impart retroactive legality to a totally illegal process.

One thing is at least certain:

It is obvious that Mgr. Lefebvre and the three Cardinals do not seem to be speaking of the same Church. As the French canonist, Fr. E. des Graviers, said in the 1 July 1975 issue of the *Courrier de Rome*, with reference to Mgr. Lefebvre's Declaration:

> **What reproach can be made against such a text, against such a declaration of fidelity to the Catholic faith and to the Church? In our view none at all. . . .And yet our three Cardinals find such a declaration unacceptable on all points! They must therefore be opposed to the Tradition of the Church, to Her traditional teaching and to the Councils. It is not Mgr. Lefebvre who should be criticized but rather the letter of the three Cardinals—and if it expresses their innermost convictions, one has a right to ask if they are worthy to wear the purple. . . . "**

Finally, it is necessary to point out that much of Mgr.

*Hanu, p. 214 (183).

Lefebvre's Declaration is concerned with judgments on the present state of the Church. These are statements of fact and must be accepted or refuted on empirical grounds. The Archbishop alleges that the present reforms "have contributed and continue to contribute to the destruction of the Church, to the ruin of the priesthood, etc. etc." It is ludicrous to claim that such statements cannot be reconciled with "an authentic fidelity to the Church." Pope Paul VI himself admitted that the Church was undergoing a process of "self-destruction" as early as 1968.* Was Pope Paul's assessment accurate or not? Are the reforms which have followed Vatican II contributing to this process or not? These are not questions of doctrine but questions of fact which the Cardinals and all the other opponents of Archbishop Lefebvre did not dare to answer.

On 8 May 1975 it became clear that the campaign against Ecône was moving to a climax when *L'Osservatore Romano* intervened with an unsigned article, *A proposito di un Manifesto,* indicating its origination in the Secretariat of State.**

The Secretary of State in question was Cardinal Villot, who exemplified, and exercised continual pressure on behalf of, episcopal Neo-Modernist influences within France.

In his book, *Catholiques et Socialistes* (Editeur: Grasset), Georges Hourdin, the doyen of French Neo-Modernism, has publicly boasted:

Paul VI would indeed be astonished, perhaps even shocked, if he were told that he is the Pope of the transition to Socialism. Yet this statement may well prove to be historically true. In any case he is certainly the Pope who recognized the legitimacy of the transition.

---

*"*La chiesa si trova in un momento . . . si potrebbe dire di autodistruzione.*" L'Osservatore Romano,* 8 December 1968.

**This article was reproduced under the title *Concerning a Manifesto* in the 12 June issue of the English edition of *L'Osservatore Romano.*

Many of the texts he has written or signed prove this. These texts can be said to be French in inspiration.

The dishonesty of the *L'Osservatore Romano* article of 8 May 1975 can be seen from the following facts:

First, the article was tendentiously entitled "Concerning a Manifesto." Thus what had been essentially a declaration of basic principles was subtly presented as though it were something in the nature of a defiant political program.

This impression was reinforced by stating in the text of the article simply that it had been published by the French review *Itinéraires*, without any indication that its author was Mgr. Lefebvre and that he had signed the Declaration. To still further emphasize this impression, the article appeared on page two, which in the daily Italian edition, is where the editor customarily takes issue with the press or publishes *mises au point* of this kind directed against publications of one kind or another.

Secondly, although *L'Osservatore Romano* published most of the Declaration, it omitted the key paragraph at the very end where Mgr. Lefebvre made clear his fidelity "to the Catholic and Roman Church" and "to all of Peter's successors."

Thirdly, although Mgr. Lefebvre had made his attitude to Rome and to the Holy Father clearer still in his further statement of 19 March 1975 (see pp. 49-51) which was published in the 15 April *Supplément-Voltigeur* of *Itinéraires* and published once again in the May 1975 issue of *Itinéraires*, the readers of *L'Osservatore Romano* were kept in total ignorance of this further clarification of Mgr. Lefebvre's position.

Fourthly, although *L'Osservatore Romano* admitted that there have been all kinds of abuses and excesses, that "it has been possible to speak of the 'decomposition' of the Church," and that "defensive measures have not been in proportion to the dangers" (which is precisely what Mgr. Lefebvre has been saying all along). The article then proceeded, not to suggest that certain measures should be taken without delay to remedy this catastrophic state of affairs, but to suggest that the (apparently anonymous) author of the Declaration was objectively schismatic and in revolt against the authentic Magisterium of the Church.

Towards the end it asked the following questions (which are numbered here for ease of reference):

1. Under such conditions, is there still any real, and not just verbal communion with the living Church?

2. Whom will they obey, ultimately, those who recognize themselves in this document? Who will be the interpreter of this Tradition to which reference is made, when the interpretation of the living Magisterium is suspected *a priori*?

3. What are we to think of those who will be formed in this spirit?

4. How is it possible, without an extraordinary presumption, to conceive such a completely negative appreciation of the Episcopate and of all those working in the service of Christ in Seminaries and Universities?

Immediately afterwards there followed the insinuation:

5. One hesitates to speak of a sect, but how can one avoid thinking of it at least?

That such attitudes can develop in the Church today, that they can be publicly expressed and sweep along people in good faith, cannot but make us reflect seriously. The appearances must be grave indeed for people to be able to lose the sense of the Church to such an extent, on the pretext of saving her.

The significance of these questions and insinuations can be properly appreciated only when one asks what "Living Church," what "Living Magisterium" is under suspicion? For whereas one must indeed be uncompromisingly respectful towards the authentic Magisterium of the living Church, this certainly does not mean that one must accept heresy simply because it has been proposed for acceptance by false shepherds of episcopal rank.

And this is precisely what is being done by the French Hierarchy (not that it is alone by any means), with the connivance of the Secretariat of State, which acts in the name of the Pope but in effect is an instrument of French Neo-Modernism.

How indeed could anyone *not* suspect the orthodoxy of the French Hierarchy when, in addition to having been a party to the falsification of Scripture in its catechetical texts and also in its Lectionary for Sunday Masses, it has gone so far as to define the Mass in the very terms anathematized by Trent (stating in the Sunday Missal that "at Mass it is simply a question of commemorating the unique sacrifice already accomplished"), and even to encourage Sunday assemblies without a priest, justifying this (in the words of Mgr. Derouet, Bishop of Sées) on the pretext that "the Christian Sunday is not primarily a gathering around a priest. It is the meeting of Christians who wish to celebrate together the Resurrection of their Lord, to nourish themselves with His word and His body."*

There are two points concerning this stage of the anti-Ecône campaign which are particularly worthy of attention.

Firstly, the 8 May 1975 article in *L'Osservatore Romano* was simply the opening salvo of a press barrage which had been carefully prepared and directed by the Secretariat of State.**

---

*In the absence of the priest, there can of course be no Sacrifice of the Mass, no Real Presence and consequently no Body (of Christ) with which the faithful can nourish themselves. This can be seen to be particularly ominous when it is borne in mind that the original Article 7 of the *Institutio Generalis* defined the Mass as "a sacred meeting or assembly of the People of God, met together under the presidency of the priest, to celebrate the memorial of the Lord." For with the function of the priest thus presented by the authors of the New Mass as being essentially *presidential*, his role as *priest* was already implicitly dispensable.

**Consider for example the *Report from Rome* dated 11 May 1975, obviously based on briefing by a spokesman of the Secretariat of State, which appeared in the Milan newspaper *Corriere Della Sera* under the headline, CONSERVATIVE BISHOP NEAR TO EXCOMMUNICATION.

Secondly, the basic theme of the campaign was that Mgr. Lefebvre's Declaration and Ecône's existence represented "a considered and explicit rejection of the decisions of the Second Vatican Council and of the authority of Pope Paul VI."

This was made particularly obvious when on 9 May 1975, the day after the publication of the *L'Osservatore Romano* article, Mgr. Mamie announced that he had withdrawn episcopal approval from the Priestly Society of St. Pius X with the agreement of the three Roman Congregations (Clergy, Religious and Secular Institutes, and Catholic Education).* Mgr. Mamie explained:

> Behind the very pronounced attachment of this fraternity (and in particular of the Seminary at Ecône) to the traditional liturgy and the Latin language, and its determination to defend tenets of faith and discipline which are essential to the Church against certain current fashions of thought and action, lay in actual fact a considered and explicit rejection of the decisions of the Second Vatican Council and of the authority of Pope Paul VI. This became evident soon enough. A declaration by Mgr. Lefebvre dated 21 November 1974, and widely circulated since, provided clear expression of this rejection and gave us the painful evidence that it was henceforth impossible to approve this institution and its orientations.

It was subsequently revealed that on 6 May 1975 a commission composed of Cardinals Garrone, Wright, and Tabera had informed Mgr. Lefebvre "by express mandate of the Holy Father" that it had authorized Mgr. Mamie to withdraw the approval granted by his predecessor to the Society of St. Pius X, and that its various establishments, in particular the Ecône Seminary, had no longer any right to exist.

There were two significant omissions in Mgr. Mamie's

---

*Since the Society had been established canonically outside Mgr. Mamie's diocese it could not be suppressed without the approval of Rome.

statement.

Although the Old Mass could almost be said to be Ecône's *raison d'être*, there was no reference by Mgr. Mamie to Ecône's refusal to use the New Order of the Mass. This would seem to have been an implicit admission that fidelity to the Old Mass cannot be called in question canonically, or be cited to justify disciplinary action.

It was no less significant that the Report of the Apostolic Visitation of the Seminary by two representatives of the Holy See in November 1974 was not mentioned. This, however, was scarcely surprising, for as Mgr. Lefebvre had stated on 16 April 1975:

> **In the midst of the trials which the Church is undergoing today, our modest initiative pursues its course with the blessing of God and even with a flattering report from the Visitors sent by Rome last November.**

The fact that the only evidence that Mgr. Mamie could adduce was Mgr. Lefebvre's Declaration demonstrated that there was in fact no case whatsoever against Ecône. For Mgr. Mamie's statement distorts Mgr. Lefebvre's 21 November 1974 Declaration and also entirely ignores his supplementary statement of 19 March 1975 in the same way as did the *L'Osservatore Romano* of 8 May 1975.

Who Is Rejecting Vatican II?

The injustice of the attack against Mgr. Lefebvre and Ecône is made very clear when some examination is made of precisely what is meant by a "rejection of the decisions of the Second Vatican Council." I have provided considerable documentation in my book *Pope John's Council* to prove that what are often passed off as decisions of the Council are, in fact, aberrations emanating from the post-conciliar commissions invested with the power to implement the conciliar documents. Only too often it will be found that not a single word can be quoted from any Council document authorizing these aberrations, which are justified by the commissions either on the grounds that the Council did not actually forbid them or by a very liberal interpretation of one of the ambiguous phrases which had been inserted in the documents precisely to justify such aberrations after the Council. In the Constitution on the Liturgy, for example, there is not a single word ordering the use of the vernacular. The celebration of Mass facing the people is not even mentioned. Nor does it anywhere recommend Communion in the hand, Lay Ministers of Communion, or the composition of new Canons. But the Constitution does specifically state that "there must be no innovations unless the good of the Church genuinely and certainly requires them."

However, there were some specific instructions in the Constitution. For example, it was insisted that Gregorian chant should be "given pride of place in liturgical services."

This instruction is obeyed in Ecône. But how many other seminaries obey it?

The same Constitution ordered that "in accordance with the centuries-old tradition of the Latin rite, the Latin language is to be retained by clerics in reciting the Divine Office."

This instruction is obeyed in Ecône. But how many other seminaries obey it?

The Council also ordered members of religious orders to wear their habit; it also recommended a year of spirituality at the commencement of seminary studies; it demanded that a key place should be given to the teaching of St. Thomas during seminary training.

Ecône obeys the Council faithfully in all these respects. But how many other seminaries do?

It is indeed no exaggeration to claim that the Holy See's

Basic Norms for Priestly Training, issued in 1970 along the lines suggested by Vatican II, are observed more faithfully at Ecône than at almost any other seminary in the West.

The fact of the matter is that there is not one hierarchy in the West which is making any attempt to enforce the teaching of Vatican II, even where this teaching is quite unequivocal and explicit.

As for the sudden concern on the part of the Secretariat of State for "the authority of Pope Paul VI" —where was this concern at the time of *Humanae Vitae?* It is worthwhile examining the statements of the Western Hierarchies and seeing just how many have honestly attempted to insist upon the clear and uncompromising condemnation of contraception demanded by the Pope. There were a few which did so in words (e.g., India, Ireland, and Scotland), but they were very few. And even in Ireland there has been a notorious refusal by Authority to discipline rebellious theologians and academic clerics who have continued to defy the Church's authoritative teaching on marriage and the family with impunity.

It may also be asked how many hierarchies have attempted to enforce the Eucharistic teaching given by Pope Paul VI in *Mysterium Fidei,* or to insure that catechetics in Catholic schools are based on Pope Paul's *Credo of the People of God.*

How many hierarchies take any action to discipline priests and institutions which do not simply ignore but even ridicule the authoritative teaching of the Holy Father? To ask such questions is also to answer them. It can thus be seen that the alleged respect for the decisions of Vatican II and for the authority of the Holy Father professed by Mgr. Mamie, the Commission of Cardinals, and the Secretariat of State is hypocrisy of the most blatant variety.

The true significance of the action taken against Ecône was given in an article by Edith Delamare in the French daily *L'Aurore* on 14 May 1975, in which she said:

The action taken by Rome against a flourishing Seminary, which is flourishing because it is traditional, is an historic act in the already two-centuries-old struggle between Liberal and conservative Catholicism.

In his Encyclical *Pascendi Dominici Gregis,* Saint Pius X, the Patron of Archbishop Lefebvre's Society and Seminary, pointed out that the conserving force in the Church is Tradition and that Tradition is represented by religious authority. But the appalling seriousness of the present crisis can be gauged from the fact that religious authority is being used to suppress those who uphold Tradition, not those who have contempt for Tradition.

Saint Pius X wrote:

There is little reason to wonder that the Modernists vent all their bitterness and hatred on Catholics who zealously fight the battles of the Church. There is no species of insult which they do not heap upon them, but the usual course is to charge them with ignorance or obduracy.

That, alas, is what was being done by the Vatican Secretariat of State in the name of Pope Paul VI.

Reaction to the Condemnation

Following the withdrawal of canonical recognition from the Society of Saint Pius X (and from its establishments, which include Ecône) there was much sympathy expressed for the Seminary and for Archbishop Lefebvre in both Switzerland and France.

In Switzerland, the news of the action taken by Mgr. Mamie with the support of Cardinals Wright, Garrone, and Tabera was reported in the press of 10 May. On the following day, 11 May, the Sunday after the Ascension, the number of layfolk at the principal Mass at the Seminary rose from 150 to 300, despite Mgr. Mamie's insistence that no faithful Catholic could continue to support the Seminary.

The congregation could not but feel that the Gospel for the day was particularly appropriate, especially the passage (St. John 16: 1-2):

> I have told you this so that your faith may not be taken unawares. They will forbid you the synagogue; nay, the time is coming when anyone who puts you to death will claim that he is performing an act of worship to God.

A number of Swiss papers published a statement by leading personalities in Valais, the Canton in which Ecône is located. This statement, which had been issued earlier with a view to preventing the action since taken, was the reproduction of a letter to Pope Paul in which these leading public figures affirmed their total support for the work for the renewal of the priesthood being accomplished at Ecône. They insisted that the Seminary had brought honor to their country and they deplored the campaign of denigration against it by all kinds of subversive elements.

They stated:

> We admire this Seminary because of its fidelity to the doctrine of the Church, to the Chair of Peter, and to the totality of Catholic Tradition to which you so often draw our attention, most Holy Father.

The signatories included a recent President of Switzerland.

On 15 May 1975, Mgr. Mamie wrote to the priests of his diocese. His aim was obviously to reconcile his failure to discipline his own refractory clergy (concerning whom he complained at some length) with his suppression of Ecône, which exemplified obedience to Tradition.

It was a singularly unconvincing exercise. Its most bizarre feature was the contrast between his call for unbounded charity, his recognition of the difficulties felt by those who preferred the Old Mass and his response—an absolute prohibition of the public celebration of the Old Mass in his diocese!

21 May 1975
Letter to Cardinal Staffa from Archbishop Lefebvre

Eminence,

Please find herewith the documents which support, or which are the cause of, my appeal to your Department.

I am drawing up an appeal:

1. Against the form in which the decisions were taken expressed in the letter of the 6 May 1975 as well by His Excellency Monseigneur Mamie, Bishop of Fribourg, as by the three Cardinals who signed the letter addressed to me from Rome.

This form of procedure is contrary to Canon 493 of the *Codex Juris Canonici.* *

2. Against the competence of the Commission of Cardinals which condemns me on a matter of faith, because of my Declaration which appeared in the review *Itinéraires* and which I wrote on 21 November 1974. I demand to be judged by the only Tribunal competent in these matters, the Sacred Congregation for the Doctrine of the Faith.

3. Against the sentence pronounced by Monseigneur Mamie and approved by the Cardinals of the Commission: in fact, my Declaration, if it deserves condemnation, should condemn me personally and not destroy the Fraternity, nor the Seminary, nor the houses that have been erected, the more so as the Cardinals assured me that the Apostolic Visitation had passed a favorable judgment on the work of the Seminary, the Visitation which took place on 11, 12, 13 November 1974.

---

*Canon 493 stipulates that canonical authorization given by a bishop for a foundation cannot be withdrawn except by the Holy See (and not by that bishop or his successors).

In virtue of this appeal, and in virtue of the law (this appeal being suspensive), I consider that, until proof to the contrary, my Fraternity and all that depends on it keep their canonical existence.

I remain at the disposal of your Eminence for further information, and I beg you to accept the expression of my respect in Our Lord and Our Lady.

† Marcel Lefebvre

VI

The Credo Pilgrimage

O N 25 MAY 1975, Mgr. Lefebvre, the Seminary Professors, and the students of Ecône went to Rome to lead
the *Credo* Holy Year Pilgrimage. The account of this Pilgrimage which follows was orginally printed in *The Remnant*
of 23 June 1975. It was entitled *"Lauda Sion."*

"The Pilgrimage to Rome in May, 1975, led by Archbishop
Marcel Lefebvre, is of such historic significance in so many
respects that it appears almost impossible to present any of
them adequately. There are four major basilicas in Rome at
which pilgrims for the Holy Year of 1975 can gain their indulgence—St. Peter's, St. John Lateran, St. Mary Major, and
St. Paul's Without-the-Walls. During the week-end of 24-26
May, Holy Year pilgrims from all over the world were astoun-
ded to see an event which took place at each of these basilicas in almost identical circumstances. A venerable prelate in
full episcopal robes, a prelate whose very being radiated holiness, serenity, and Christian joy, entered each basilica followed by a procession of a nature sufficient to convince any
spectator that far from being in a process of self-destruction

or 'auto-demolition' as Pope Paul has expressed it, the Church must be entering upon a period of renewed vigor, the kind of second Spring which Cardinal Newman had promised. The prelate, Archbishop Lefebvre, was followed by what seemed an endless double file of priests and seminarians. There were, in fact, about 120, but they seemed to be far more. Behind the seminarians came a group of nuns in an unfamiliar habit, the postulants of the new order founded by the Archbishop. Then came the faithful in their thousands, faithful Catholics from countries as far apart as Australia and Argentina—and as they entered the basilicas, they sang.

> *Lauda Sion Salvatorem,*
> *lauda ducem et pastorem,*
> *in hymnis et canticis.*

This sublime hymn of praise to Christ our God, present in the Blessed Sacrament, surged up to the bright blue sky above the basilicas as the pilgrims filed in, and then filled the basilicas with praise after they entered. Pilgrims with other groups and the Roman clergy as well were quite overwhelmed by the scale and fervor of this Pilgrimage. Nothing like it had been seen before during this Holy Year, nothing like it will be seen again. It had not been the largest pilgrimage to come—although it would seem blasphemous to describe the group which had taken over St. Peter's exactly one week before as a pilgrimage. Indeed, the appearance in St. Peter's Basilica of about 9,000 charismatics, some of whom danced and some of whom gibbered, brings immediately to mind St. Matthew's warning concerning the 'abomination of desolation which was spoken of by Daniel the prophet, standing in the holy place.' Indeed, if the Mass concelebrated by Cardinal Suenens and five hundred Pentecostal priests was valid, then the passing of Hosts from hand to hand, to be broken in pieces by the congregation and offered even to tourists of any belief or none, was in truth an abomination!

Here then is one aspect of great significance: the Pentecostals received special papal authorization to use the Main Altar of the Confession of St. Peter; Cardinal Suenens was warmly embraced by the Pope; and the Pope addressed the charismatics—certainly with some words of caution and admonition, but also with a great deal of warmth and praise. There was, on the other hand, no papal welcome for Archbishop Lefebvre; he would not have been given the High Altar to celebrate Mass for his Pilgrimage, because the Mass he would have celebrated would have been the Mass codified by Pope Saint Pius V, Mass as it was said in Rome during his pontificate, virtually the only form of Mass to be celebrated in St. Peter's Basilica from the time it had been built. But such is the state of the Church today that it is this form of Mass, arguably the supreme achievement of Western Christianity, which is now regarded, practically speaking, as an abomination. The Pentecostals with their guitars, their dancing, their gibberish, are acceptable. The age-old Mass is not.

Thus the presence of the Archbishop and his pilgrims in Rome so soon after the Pentecostals both symbolized and manifested the two-centuries-old struggle between Liberal and traditional Catholicism, which reached its climax on the ninth of May in this Holy Year of 1975, when canonical approval was withdrawn from his Society of St. Pius X and the Seminary at Ecône.

Here, then, is the next aspect of great significance with regard to this Pilgrimage: it was remarked above that anyone seeing the great procession led by the Archbishop entering one of the Roman basilicas would have concluded that the Church could not be undergoing a process of self-destruction or 'auto-demolition.' When it is realized that those in authority in the Church at present are intent upon destroying the Seminary which is forming such holy and such fervent young priests, then self-destruction is the only term applicable. It is no wonder that, as the great procession entered St. Peter's Basilica, it sang the *Parce Domine*.

Traditional Catholic devotions took place in all the basilicas visited by the *Credo* pilgrims—and, in addition to the
four major basilicas mentioned, these included St. Sebastian,
St. Lawrence, and the ruins of Maxentius. The traditional
Roman Mass was sung for huge congregations in St. Mary
Major, Maxentius, and St. Lawrence. At least one hundred
more must have been said during the course of the Pilgrimage
by the many priests who took part, from both the Ecône
Seminary and the groups which came from different countries. Some of these Masses were offered at side altars in St.
Peter's, including that of St. Pius X. *L'Osservatore Romano*
had published an expression of 'pained surprise' at the fact
that all the Masses for the *Credo* pilgrims were to be Tridentine Masses and thought this inappropriate in a year of 'reconciliation.'

The fact of the matter is that precisely in this year of
'reconciliation' the prime aim of the Church ought to be to
reconcile Herself with Her own traditions—the abandoning
of which has caused nothing but disaster. Veneration for Her
traditions was once the prime characteristic of the Church of
Rome, yet today the official Vatican newspaper can express
regret at the celebration of the Mass of St. Pius V—the greatest of these traditions. However, with or without the approval
of the Vatican, the Mass which had been the only Mass for
Roman-rite pilgrims in the Holy Year 1950, and for its predecessors for centuries before, was celebrated with due ceremony and due honor once again in this Holy Year of 1975.
It was the fervent prayer of all present that it will be the only
Mass permitted for Roman-rite pilgrims in the year 2,000.

Most of the pilgrims considered the Pontifical High Mass
sung in the ruins of the ancient Basilica of Maxentius to have
been the most memorable of the entire Pilgrimage. Loud
speakers insured that the words and music of this ancient
Mass echoed across Rome, the Mass whose origins reach back
to the time of the martyrs with whom this basilica has such

poignant associations, and so many of whom lie buried in its precincts. Many pilgrims and citizens who were not taking part in the *Credo* Pilgrimage were overjoyed to discover a celebration of the traditional Mass and swelled the ranks of a congregation which certainly exceeded three thousand in number. The Mass ended with the singing of the *Te Deum*, and all knelt on the stony ground while His Grace passed along giving his blessing.

The Mass which ended the 'official' Pilgrimage in the Basilica of St. Lawrence was equally impressive. The great basilica was literally packed to the doors and, despite the fact that a good number of priests helped to distribute Holy Communion, this still took almost twenty-five minutes, during which time the pilgrims waited with patience and sang with devotion. Archbishop Lefebvre preached very important sermons during Mass in the basilicas of Maxentius and St. Lawrence.

The all-night vigil for this Pilgrimage was held in the Church of San Girolamo della Carità. Some of those who had been on previous traditionalist pilgrimages regretted the fact that it was not held in St. Peter's Square, and indeed those who have had the grace to take part in these vigils had good reason for doing so. However, the fact that this Pilgrimage was led by the Archbishop made it necessary to make its essentially religious character clear throughout—anything which could give the appearance of a demonstration or a confrontation had to be avoided. It is likely that the timing for the withdrawal of canonical approbation from the Society of St. Pius X was designed to provoke some form of violent or intemperate reaction during the Pilgrimage. There was no such incident; the dignity and restraint shown by all present was as remarkable as their fervor. It would, of course, be argued by the Liberal establishment that the celebration of the traditional Mass was in itself an act of provocation, hence the admonition in *L'Osservatore Romano*. But any Catholic,

whatever his position or rank, who would consider the celebration of the traditional Mass 'provocative' has reached a
stage where we can only say, 'God help and forgive him',
and breathe a prayer on his behalf.

During the all-night vigil, an unceasing stream of hymns
and prayers was offered up to God, above all for the restoration to our altars of the traditional Mass, which was celebrated every two hours throughout the night by one of the
priests present. One of the most impressive sights was the
entry of the pilgrims into the indescribably beautiful Basilica
of St. Paul's Without-the-Walls on Monday morning. The
clergy of the Basilica gave their fullest cooperation and put
every facility at the disposal of the pilgrims, including their
loudspeaker equipment. As in all the basilicas, the three
Paters, Aves, and *Glorias* necessary for gaining the indulgence
were recited, and *Credo* was sung and the general atmosphere was such that it really did seem hard to believe that
anything had changed since 1950—that these fine young seminarians, who are the pride and joy of hundreds of thousands of the faithful, will never be ordained if the present
'parallel magisterium' has its way.

During the week-end innumerable prayers and acts of
penitence were offered up by the pilgrims, in groups or as
individuals. Some made the ascent of the Scala Santa on their
knees on three or more occasions—not the least among them
being the English-speaking pilgrims. It seems permissible to
wonder whether, if the New Mass should be abolished and
the old one restored, a single Catholic would ever get down
on his knees and make the slow and painful journey up the
Scala Santa in the interests of Archbishop Bugnini's *Novus
Ordo Missae.*

The traditionalist Pilgrimage for the Holy Year of 1975
was, then, a great success in every way. It was a success for
the honor and glory offered to Almighty God and the graces
it brought down on the pilgrims; it was a success for the way

in which the strength and resilience of the traditional Faith were made clear to the Vatican and, equally important, to the traditionalists themselves. There was not one who did not leave full of hope and encouragement.''

The sermon which Mgr. Lefebvre preached in the Basilica of Maxentius on 25 May 1975 was published in *The Remnant* of 6 March 1976. It was entitled "The One True Religion."

The One True Religion

My dear brethren:

If there is one day on which the Church's liturgy affirms our Faith, that day is the Feast of the Blessed Trinity. This morning, in the breviary which the priest formerly had to recite, he had to add to the psalms of Prime the Creed of St. Athanasius. This is the creed which affirms clearly, serenely, but perfectly, what we are bound to believe concerning the Blessed Trinity, and also concerning the divinity and the humanity of Our Lord Jesus Christ. Indeed, all our faith is summed up in our belief in the Most Holy Trinity and in Our Lord Jesus Christ, God made Man. The whole of our Creed, which we shall sing in a few minutes, is focused, as it were, on the very person of Our Lord Jesus Christ. He it is who is our God, He our Savior; it is through Him that we shall enter Heaven. He is the door of the sheep-fold, He is the Way, the Truth, the Life. There is no other name on earth by which we may be saved: the Gospels tell us all this.

Therefore, when our Faith is being attacked from all sides we must hold steadfastly and firmly to it. We must never accept that there can be any compromise in the affirmation of our Faith. Herein, I think, lies the drama through which we have lived for the last ten, perhaps fifteen years. This drama, this tragic situation we are going through, lies in seeing that our Faith is no longer affirmed with certainty: that through a false ecumenism we have, as it were, reached the point of putting all religions on the same footing, of granting what is called "equal rights" to all religions. This is a tragedy because it is all entirely contrary to the truth of the Church. We believe that Our Lord Jesus Christ is our God, our Saviour, our Redeemer; we believe that the Catholic Church alone has the Truth, thus we draw the proper conclusions, by respecting in our personal lives the Religion which Our Lord Jesus Christ founded. For, if other religions are quite prepared to admit that there can be other beliefs and other religious groups, we cannot do so. Why do other religions admit this? Because their religions are religions which have been founded by men and not by God. Our holy and beloved Religion has been founded by God Himself, by Our Lord Jesus Christ.

He it is who has given us the Holy Sacrifice of the Mass, He who died upon the Cross. Already on the day of the Last Supper He wished, in a certain manner, to enact in advance what was to take place on the Cross, commanding us to do likewise continually to the end of time, thus making priests of those to whom He gave the power to consecrate the Eucharist. He did this by His own Will, His Will as God, because Jesus Christ is God; He has, thus, given us the Holy Sacrifice of the Mass, which we love so much, which is our life, our hope, and our salvation. This Sacrifice of Calvary cannot be transformed, the Sacrifice of the Last Supper cannot be transformed—for there *was* a Sacrifice at the Last Supper—we cannot transform this Sacrifice into a simple commemorative meal, a simple repast at which a memory is recalled, this is not possible. To do such a thing would be to destroy the whole of our Religion, to destroy the most precious thing which Our Lord has given us here on earth, the immaculate and divine treasure which He put into the hands of His Church, which He made a priestly Church. The Church is essentially priestly because she offers the redemptive Sacrifice which Our Lord made on Calvary, and which she renews upon our altars. For a true Catholic, one who is truly faithful to Our Lord Jesus Christ, anything which touches what He Himself established moves him to the very depths of his heart, for he loves it as the apple of his eye. So, if it comes, in any way, to the point of destroying from within what Our Lord Jesus Christ gave to us as the source of life, as the source of grace, then we suffer, we suffer dreadfully, and we demand absolutely that this spring, this fountain of life, this fountain of eternal life, this fountain of Grace be preserved for us whole and entire.

And if such is true of the Holy Sacrifice of the Mass, it is also true of the Sacraments. It is not possible to make any considerable changes in the Sacraments without destroying them, without running the risk of rendering them invalid, and consequently without running the risk of drying up the grace, the supernatural and eternal life which they bring to us. It is again Our Lord Jesus Christ Himself who established the Sacraments; it is not for us, we are not the masters of the Sacraments: even the Sovereign Pontiff cannot change them. Without doubt he can make changes in the rites, in what is accidental in any Sacrament; but no Sovereign Pontiff can change the substance of a Sacrament, for that was established by Our Lord Jesus Christ. It is Our Lord Jesus Christ Himself who took such care in the founding of our holy Religion, Who left us directions as to what we must do, Who gave Himself to us in the Holy Eucharist through the Holy Sacrifice of the Mass. What more could we ask? What other religion can lay claim to possess such a thing? And why? Because the only true religion is that of the Catholic Church.

This is a matter of fundamental importance, fundamental for our behavior, fundamental for our religion, and fundamental also for the way we should behave towards those people who do not believe in our holy Religion. This is extremely important, because it is precisely towards those who do not believe, those who do not have our Faith, that we must have immense charity, the *true* charity. We must not deceive them by telling them that their religion is as good as ours—that is a lie, that is selfishness, that is not true charity. If we consider what profound riches have been given to us in this Religion of ours, then we should have the desire to make it known to others, and share these riches and not say to them: "But you already have all you need! There is no point in your joining us, your religion is as good as ours." See how this matter is one of paramount importance, for it is precisely such false ecumenism which makes the adherents of all the other religions believe that they have certain means of salvation. Now this is *false*. Only the Catholic Religion, and only the Mystical Body of Christ, possesses the means of salvation. We cannot be saved without Jesus, and we cannot be saved without grace. "He who does not believe," said Our Lord, "will be condemned." We must believe in Our Lord Jesus Christ in order to be saved. "He who believes shall be saved; he who obeys My commandments shall have eternal life; he who eats My Flesh and drinks My Blood shall have eternal life." Here is what Our Lord taught us. Therefore, we should have a tremendous desire, a really *tremendous* desire, to communicate our Faith to others. And this is exactly what made the missionary spirit of the Church. If the strength, the certainty, of our faith is weakened, then the missionary spirit of the Church also diminishes, since it is no longer necessary to cross the seas, to cross the oceans, to go and preach the Gospel, for what is the good of it? Let us leave each man to his own religion, if that religion is going to save him.

Therefore, we must hold fast to our Faith, we must adhere strictly to its affirmation, and we must not accept this false ecumenism which makes all religions into sister-religions of Christianity, for they are nothing of the kind. It is very important to state this nowadays, because it is precisely this false ecumenism which had too much influence after the Council. False ecumenism is the reason why the seminaries are empty. Why is this so? Why are there no more vocations for the missionary orders? Precisely because young men no longer feel the need to make the Truth known to the whole world. They no longer feel the need to give themselves completely to Our Lord Jesus Christ simply because Our Lord Jesus Christ is the only Truth, the only Way, the only Life. What attracts the young to preach the Gospel is that they know they have the Truth. If vocations are withering away, it is due to this false ecumenism. How we suffer at the thought that, in certain countries, people speak of "eucharistic hospitality," of "inter-communion"—as if one could give the Body and Blood of Our Lord Jesus Christ to those who do not believe in the Body and Blood of Our Lord Jesus Christ, consequently to those who do not adore the Holy Eucharist, because they do not believe in it! Without sacrilege, without blasphemy, the Body and Blood of Our Saviour cannot be given to a person who denies His Real Presence in the Eucharist. On this point, therefore, we must have a firm and solid faith, a faith which does not compromise. This is entirely in keeping with the tradition of the Church.

Thus the martyrs believed who lie buried everywhere in this basilica, and in all the churches of Rome, who suffered here in this forum of Augustus, who lived among pagans for three centuries and were persecuted as soon as they were known to be Christians. They were thrown into prison . . . our thoughts turn to the Mamertine prison, so close to us here, where Peter and Paul were put in chains because of their faith. And shall we be afraid to affirm our faith? We would not in that case be the true descendants of the martyrs, the true descendants of those Christians who shed their blood for Our Lord Jesus Christ in affirmation of their faith in Him. They, too, could indeed have said, "But, since all religions are of equal value, if I burn a little incense before an idol, what does that matter? My life will be saved." But they preferred to die, they preferred to be thrown to the beasts in the Colosseum, quite close to us here. So many, many martyrs were thrown to the beasts, rather than offer incense to pagan gods!

So, may our presence here in Rome be an occasion for us to strengthen our faith, to have, if necessary, the souls of martyrs, the souls of witnesses (for a martyr is a witness), the souls of witnesses of Our Lord Jesus Christ, witnesses of the Church. Here is what I wish you, my most dear brethren, and in this we must be unflinching, whatever happens. We must never agree to diminish our faith; and if by misfortune it were to happen that those who ought to defend our Faith came to tell us to lessen or diminish it, then we must say: "NO." Saint Paul put this very well: "Though we, or an angel from heaven, preach a gospel to you besides that which we have preached to you, let him be anathema." Well, that, I think, sums up clearly what I wanted to say to you, so that when you return to your homes you may have the courage, the strength, despite difficulties, despite trials, to remain true to your Faith, come what may, to uphold it for yourselves, your children and future generations, the Faith which Our Lord Jesus Christ gave to us; so that the pathway to heaven may still have many pilgrims, that it may still be crowded with people on their journey upwards, that it may not be a deserted byway, while on the other hand, the road leading to hell is filled with those who did not believe in Our Lord Jesus Christ, or who rejected Him. We must think on these things, because it is what Our Lord told us: "If we do not believe, we shall be condemned."

A Visit to Ecône

After the *Credo* Holy Year Pilgrimage I returned to Ecône with the seminarians, travelling on the all-night train from Rome and arriving on the morning of Tuesday, 27 May. The account which follows is my personal impression of Ecône. It will, I hope, convey however inadequately something of the spirit of the Seminary. The train in which we were travelling continued on to France with large numbers of French pilgrims on board.

Tuesday, 27 May.

The train stops at about 10:00 a. m. The whole platform is soon full of seminarians in their long black soutanes. Their fellow pilgrims lean from every window in the train laughing, talking, shouting, gesticulating—some are weeping and smiling at the same time. Everyone seems in the best of good humor —and what a lot of young girls there are! One might imagine that there was a pcp-group on the platform! The train begins to move. The passengers lean even further out. *"Adieu! Au revoir!"* They wave. They smile. They weep. *"Merci pour tout—* Thank you for everything!" cries one of the girls. *"Merci pour tout!"* Her farewell is echoed from other windows. Some of the seminarians watch the train as it vanishes from sight; others begin stacking the luggage. I have the feeling I am back in the army again and have just piled out of a troop train; the atmosphere is almost identical. There is a great deal of laughter, and a tremendous atmosphere of comradeship; but, unlike the army, there is no one giving orders. In fact, no one ever appears to give any orders. The seminarians and their professors seem to form a corporate entity—an impression that will be strengthened throughout my stay at the Seminary. Everyone knows what he should be doing, how he should be doing it, and when.

"Come along, we've been invited for a beer." We all troop

out of the station to a local restaurant. The seminarians are tremendously popular wherever they go. We can't all fit inside. There are more than a hundred seminarians, about twenty priests, myself, and a young American who will be entering the Seminary in September. Some of us sit at the tables on the pavement. Everything is "on the house."

It is soon time to take another train along the branch line to Riddes; then follows a walk of several kilometers to the Seminary at Ecône. Fortunately a Volkswagen bus is available to take the luggage. We approach the Seminary through extensive vineyards which belong to it and are tended by the students. Manual work forms an important item in their training. Ecône is situated among scenes of breath-taking natural beauty. Great snow-capped mountains rise up on every side. A gigantic waterfall tumbles down the mountainside behind the Seminary. The buildings themselves consist, firstly, of a large and very Swiss-looking house—formerly belonging to the Canons of St. Bernard and about three hundred years old. Archbishop Lefebvre had begun his work of priestly formation with a few students in Fribourg. The numbers expanded immediately and this building with the surrounding land was put at his disposal. The influx of new seminarians was soon so great that it was inadequate almost at once. New wings stretch off in all directions and their effect upon the visitor, the British visitor at least, is staggering. I would not have believed that any Catholic institution could be so ultramodern. Truly, where the buildings are concerned, it is the space-age seminary. But there is no time to look around; lunch is being served immediately. I am taken to the bursar together with my American friend and we are shown to guest rooms in the old house. The rooms are furnished comfortably but simply; nothing useful is missing and everything works perfectly—and what a view from the window! We are asked to come down for lunch at once. The refectory is a huge room, clean, cheerful, and full of light; for there are large windows looking out onto the mountains on one side, and the other wall, alongside which there is a corridor, is made entirely of great glass bricks. I am astonished to find a case for my table-napkin with my name typed on a card inserted into a plastic socket—and I can scarcely have been in the building for five minutes! When I return to my room after lunch there is an identical card on the door. I had heard of Swiss efficiency—but really!

Every meal begins with a short grace (in Latin, naturally). There is reading from the Bible (which is always in French) and this is heard throughout the refectory by means of a superb amplification system which functions faultlessly. The same is true of a loudspeaker system which reaches every part of the building and the grounds. This is all operated by nuns in the most traditional habits who sit in a room surrounded by the most sophisticated electronic equipment, from which they summon "Monsieur the Abbé This" to answer a telephone call from Germany or "Monsieur the Abbé That" to come to Parlor Number Two where a visitor awaits him. The same system is used to rouse the community each morning in a very gentle manner with a series of soothing chimes. Similar chimes indicate the beginning or end of a lecture, a service in the chapel, or a mealtime.

The meals are simple but nourishing. The food is cooked by brothers of the order in a kitchen that looks like something out of the twenty-first century. It is served by the seminarians, who take it in turns to wait at table. Almost all the work in the Seminary is carried out by the seminarians, including such tasks as cleaning the corridors and stairs; but as these are all covered in thick hard-wearing carpet it is easily done.

When lunch is over it is announced that the community Mass will be at 17:00. In view of the exacting pilgrimage they have just completed, the afternoon will be free. During this time I am shown around the Seminary. My stock of superla-

tives is inadequate to express the impression it makes on me.
The light and airy lecture rooms, the large and comfortable
study-bedrooms for the students (the professors have a study, a separate bedroom, and a private bathroom). The library
in the newest wing is already well stocked but with row after
row of new and empty shelves to allow for expansion.
There is a music room with the latest stereo equipment and
an extensive collection of religious and classical music: I am
pleased to see that someone has been playing Byrd's *Mass for
Five Voices*. There is no television and the students are not
allowed radios; nor is smoking permitted in the Seminary.

There are a good number of chapels and oratories but the
main chapel is a recently converted barn—a massive structure
with walls at least three feet thick. It is divided into two
sections, one for the community and one for visitors. The
number of visitors wishing to attend the Seminary Masses had
grown so much that this new chapel was necessary—the previous one could hardly accommodate the seminarians. At
least one hundred and fifty visitors had been attending the
community Mass each Sunday. On 9 May, the Swiss bishops
had withdrawn their canonical authorization from the Seminary. Canonically it had ceased to exist—in the language of
Orwell's *Nineteen Eighty-four* it could now be described as an
"unseminary." The announcement had appeared in the Swiss
press on Saturday, 10 May. The bishops had said that, as a
result of their decision, no faithful Catholic could continue
to support the Seminary (*"aucun fidèle n'a plus le droit de
lui accorder son appui"*). There was some speculation in the
Seminary as to how many, if any, visitors would come for
the Mass on Sunday, 11 May. Over three hundred crammed
themselves into the chapel—double the normal number and
this figure increased the next week.

Just before 17:00 the seminarians file in for their community Mass. I have already referred to my impression of
their forming a corporate entity: it is during the liturgy that

this impression becomes most manifest. All stand as the celebrant and servers enter. As the Mass begins a sharp tap is
heard. All kneel as if one person. *Introibo ad altare Dei—
Ad Deum qui laetificat juventutem meam—*it is as if one person is responding, half speaking, half chanting. I soon discover that Ecône has a liturgical style of its own. *Judica me
Deus, et discerne causam meam de gente non sancta . . .* It
is impossible not to apply these words to those who are per-
secuting the Seminary; to those who will allow practically
any abomination to take place during the celebration of Mass,
but who are adamant that to begin it with Psalm 42 is a crime
crying out to heaven for vengeance! (As the celebrant is now
encouraged to add some words of his own at the beginning of
Mass, why should he not choose Psalm 42? and if the congregation wishes to say some of the verses, is this not a dialogue?
and surely nothing is more praiseworthy than a dialogue in
the renewed Church?)

It is not simply the seminarians who seem to be an entity—everything in the chapel blends into an organic whole:
the dignified and beautiful altar; the priest with his quiet
words, his slow and deliberate gestures; the acolytes whose
movements must surely be synchronized, the words of the
Mass; the seminarians who have been absorbed into the liturgy, who are simply part of what is happening. And what is
happening? The Sacrifice of Calvary is being rendered present
in our midst. There is indeed but one entity here—and that
entity is Christ. *Hoc est enim Corpus Meum.* Christ is present
upon the altar, present physically, present in person. The
priest raises Christ's true Body for our adoration—the same
Body Which was born of the Virgin, Which hung on the Cross
as an offering for the salvation of the world, and Which is
seated at the right hand of the Father. The priest who elevates the Host is also Christ, and how easy it is to believe this
at Mass at Ecône. And the Congregation is Christ too, His
Body on earth to build up His kingdom and, when they re-

ceive Holy Communion, they are united with Him and with each other as fully and perfectly as it is possible to be. This then is the secret of Ecône, this is the aim and the effect of the formation given there, the complete incorporation into Christ of these young men whose vocation it is to bring Christ to others.

In the pew in front of me there is a young couple with three children. The older girls use their missals with complete facility and make the responses with scarcely a glance at the page. The youngest child, about six years old, has a little book with a simple text and pictures of the action of the Mass. From time to time her sister checks to see that the picture corresponds with what the priest is doing at the altar.

Ite Missa Est says the priest. *Deo Gratias* comes the response; and what grace and blessings those who have been present at the Mass have to thank God for. Yet this is the Seminary which the French bishops, the Swiss bishops, and now the Vatican are trying to suppress. *In principio erat Verbum. . . .*Once again the reason why is clear. We are in the midst of a "renewal" which forbids the reading of the Last Gospel of St. John. *Et lux in tenebris lucet, et tenebrae eam non comprehenderunt.* Ecône is a light, a light shining in the darkness that is now enveloping the Church, a light which reveals the hollowness of a renewal about which much is spoken but of which nothing is seen, a light which must be extinguished if the shallowness of this renewal is to remain hidden.

Wednesday, 28 May.

Today I am to follow the seminarians throughout their normal program. They rise at 6:00. At 6:30 there is Prime followed by meditation. The Community Mass takes place at 7:15 and breakfast is at 8:00. Lectures begin at 9:00. The next is at 10:00 and the third at 11:00. Each lasts about forty-five minutes. They begin and end with prayer, they are very intensive and demand a high degree of attention. A large proportion of the students are graduates of secular universities and are able to cope with the demanding curriculum without great difficulty. Some of the younger seminarians find it requires an enormous effort—particularly those whose French is not too good when they arrive, as the teaching is conducted through this medium. There are several dozen students whose mother tongue is not French—Germans, Italians, Spaniards, English, Scottish, Australian, and above all American. There are also students from Africa and Asia. The title "International Seminary of St. Pius X" is well merited. I notice that an English student sitting next to me, now in his second year, makes his notes in French. In the Canon Law lecture the subject is that of the Oath. There is a great deal to condense into one lecture and the professor expounds the subject at great speed. The students open their Latin Codes of Canon Law at Canon 316. The difference between an oath and a vow is explained. We soon learn the difference between a *iuramentum assertorium* and a *iuramentum promissorium.*   Canon follows canon as information is given on witnesses worthy of confidence, when oaths are binding on heirs, licitness, validity, obligation, annulment, dispensation, commutation, complications arising from possible conflicts with civil law. From time to time my eyes wander to the window through which I can see the great waterfall gleaming and shimmering in the bright sun. Soon the sun becomes too bright and the curtains are drawn. The loudspeaker summons an Abbé with a German name to the telephone. The professor is explaining how two apparently contradictory canons are not contradictory at all. Then chimes are heard over the loudspeaker announcing the end of the lecture. After the lecture the students crowd round the professor in friendly and animated conversation. During the lecture the atmosphere was formal and businesslike—afterwards it is all friendliness and informality.

At 12:10 there is Sext and the Angelus followed by lunch. Lunch is followed by recreation and the manual work —which can be synonymous if necessary. All students are asked to report to the *vigneron,* who has some urgent tasks to be done in the vineyard. There must have been some who when they answered a call to become laborers in the vineyard of the Lord had not expected to do so in quite such a literal manner. But the work is done with a great deal of gusto and a great deal of laughter, and the *vigneron* seems well pleased as he reappears with wine for those who want it.

Manual work is followed by two hours private study by the students in their rooms or the library—and study they do and study they must. If there is any feeling of anxiety among the seminarians during my visit it concerns their forthcoming examinations rather than the campaign to have the Seminary closed.

At 16:00 *Goûter* is available for those who want it—a cup of tea or coffee and a piece of bread and jam. Every weekday there is a plainchant practice at 18:00 —which explains the exceptionally high standard of chant in the Seminary. This is followed at 18:30 by a spiritual conference and at 19:00 by one of a variety of spiritual exercises, the Rosary, Benediction, Way of the Cross. Dinner is at 19:30, after which a period of recreation follows until Compline at 20:45. At 22:00 hours lights must be put out and strict silence observed.

It is impossible in any written account even to begin to convey any adequate impression of the atmosphere of Ecône. Serenity is perhaps the best word to describe it. This serenity derives in part from order and from discipline, but it is a discipline which comes from within, a discipline that is freely and consciously accepted, but which is practiced unconsciously and naturally. Above all, the atmosphere comes from the spirit of prayer which pervades the community. If asked to describe Ecône in one phrase there could be no other answer but "a community of prayer." This prayer springs from and is fostered by the deep spirituality evoked by the sublime liturgical worship which permeates the life of the Seminary. Whenever there are no lectures, there are students praying in the chapel or one of the many oratories. Look from any window in the Seminary and you will see soutane-clad figures walking in the vineyards and along the mountain paths saying the rosary. In the long corridors of the Seminary there are some very fine examples of baroque statuary— Our Lady, St. Joseph, the Sacred Heart. Strangely enough they appear in complete harmony with their very modern setting. Votive lights burn before them continually and in the evening there is almost invariably one young man kneeling in prayer before each statue. There is a particularly strong devotion to St. Pius X—the patron of the Seminary—before whose picture, beneath which there is a relic in the wall, a stream of prayers is offered for his intercession. However, although the atmosphere of Ecône is one of sanctity it is certainly not sanctimonious; there is no affectation, no conscious attempt to appear pious. The spirituality is natural and spontaneous and certainly accounts for the cheerfulness, the feeling of joy, which is equally evident and a real indication of true holiness.

Thursday, 29 May.

Thursday, 29 May, is the Feast of *Corpus Christi* which is prepared for by solemn Vespers on the Wednesday evening. I will not even attempt to describe the beauty, the dignity, the perfection of this service. There is all-night exposition of the Blessed Sacrament and, during the night, I have the good fortune to make a visit to the chapel just before Matins are sung. I am not normally at my most receptive at 3:00 a. m., but I can state in all honesty that the only question I ask myself is not, "When will it end?" but, "Why must it end?" At about 4:00 a. m. I go outside for a few minutes to see the dawn appearing. The mountains are clearly visible, their snow-capped peaks turning red with the first rays of the sun. A chorus of innumerable birds has burst into its own version of Matins, almost drowning the rush of the great waterfall and blending with the sound of the eternal chant which filters through the windows of the chapel. At that moment, the brave new Church of Vatican II seems quite remote, quite unreal, and quite irrelevant with its dialogues and discussions, its committees and commissions, its political priests and emancipated nuns, its smiles and goodwill to all who are not of the Household of the Faith, its harshness and vindictiveness towards any Catholic who is less than enthusiastic about being updated. The great renewal with all its works and pomps seems no more than a memory now of a distant and unpleasant dream. Here is the eternal and unchanging Church. I turn to the ancient house of the Canons of St. Bernard. I would not be surprised to see one or more of them come down the steps at any moment; and should any do so and enter the chapel, then, no matter whether they had returned from fifty, a hundred, two hundred or three hundred years before, they could take their places beside the seminarians and begin singing Matins just as they had done when they lived at the foot of these same mountains.

At about 8:30 on the Feast of *Corpus Christi* we all leave for the parish church at Riddes. The parish priest has invited all the seminarians to take part in his *Corpus Christi* procession—a courageous gesture as the Swiss bishops have said there can no longer be any support for the Society of St. Pius X. Fr. Épiney, the Curé, is a very dynamic young priest. He has just built a very large and very modern church constructed of grey concrete. I must confess that I do not much like it, either the exterior or the interior. The church is packed to the doors for Mass with one empty section of seats reserved for the seminarians and their professors. Outside there is an atmosphere of great excitement and anticipation. Two bands are waiting—the Socialist band in blue uniforms and the *Fanfare indépendante* in crimson: this, I am told, is the "Radical" band and has Masonic ties. Both are anti-clerical and the *Fanfaristes* manifest this by remaining outside the church. But virtually everyone in Riddes is devoted to the Curé—and the bandsmen will manifest this devotion by playing in his procession. My friends at the Seminary told me I was in for a surprise. They were correct. The young Curé celebrates a Solemn High Tridentine Mass. The deacon and sub-deacon are seminarians who will be ordained on June 29th. The seminarians sing the Proper—many of the congregation join in. I notice that a good number of the young people present have very new missals—the Daily Missal which is on sale at the Seminary. The Curé gives a passionate sermon on devotion to the Blessed Sacrament which is listened to with rapt attention. He deplores the fact that there are even those who call themselves Catholics but do not kneel to receive their Lord and some who have the temerity to hold out their hands for the Host. The Blessed Sacrament is God; there is no honor, no devotion, no praise too great to offer to Him. We must be prepared to endure any humiliation, persecution even, rather than diminish our reverence for the Blessed Sacrament by one iota. In this sermon and in another when the procession halts for Benediction in the Town Square, he expresses his complete solidarity with the Seminary. He and the people of Riddes know what value to put on the calumnies used against it, no matter from what level they come. Our religion is a religion of love, and in the service of love malice and calumny have no part. There are reporters present. Cameras flash. I learn later that informed opinion is certain that the revenge of the bishops will be swift and severe. The Curé may not even last a week—he will certainly be out within a month. It is a humbling experience to see a young man prepared to make any sacrifice for a matter of principle, a young man who considers that truth

takes priority over expediency. My mind immediately turns
to another young man who took such a stand nearly 2,000
years ago; and it is this very Man, God the Son made Man,
whom the Curé elevates in the Monstrance for our adoration
at the start of the procession. Truly, here is Christ carried in
the arms of an *alter Christus.*

The procession is a never to be forgotten event. There
were clouds in the sky before Mass; these have vanished now
and the sun is blazing down. The *Pange Lingua* surges upwards. The procession seems to go on for ever. There are the
two bands. There are this year's first communicants—the
little boys in their long white robes looking as charming as
the girls. There is another group of children with baskets of
rose petals which they scatter on the road along which God
the Son will pass. The children of the village are present in
their different age groups. A Marian group carries a statue of
Our Lady of Fatima. The seminarians file past together with
their professors; their number seems almost endless. An
elderly and very poor lady is overcome with emotion. She
begins to ask me something. I explain that I am only a visitor.
She is delighted to learn that Ecône is known in Britain and
that there are five British seminarians there now; and even
more delighted to know that this number will be increased
in the autumn. "Monsieur," she says, "Monsieur, the seminarians. How they sang at Mass. It was heaven come down to
earth." "Heaven come down to earth"—this is it precisely.
That is what Ecône is.

Behind the Blessed Sacrament walk the civic dignitaries—
they are all there including the Socialist mayor whose devotion to the Curé equals that of any of the Catholic parishioners. Then come the ordinary Faithful—first the men and
then the women; thousand upon thousand of them. Many
must have come from outside this little town. All ages and
all social classes walk together reciting the Rosary as they
pass along the streets between houses decorated in honor of

the Feast while the bands play and the sun shines. There are practically no spectators—almost everyone is walking in the procession. My American friend and I decide that it is about time we do so too and we join the men. He is a young convert who, after graduating at an American University, has been working for a doctorate in Spain. He must return that night to defend his thesis. He will be entering the Seminary in September. He has only one regret and that is that he cannot enter now.

Eventually the procession returns to the church. There is Benediction yet again. The service ends with the *Te Deum* during which the seminarians file out. The great hymn of praise continues with almost undiminished vigor. I have to follow it from my missal (to my shame). I notice that most of the congregation know it by heart and sing it from their hearts. *Salvum fac populum tuum Domine, et benedic haereditati tuae. . .* We all go out to where the bands are playing and an unlimited supply of wine is available to all. The Curé moves among his people, a true father in God, laughing, smiling, joking, listening. The seminarians are surrounded by admirers and well-wishers. This has been a revelation of what Catholicism can be—how Belloc would have approved! And not least of the laughter and the wine.

I must leave the Seminary after Compline that night to take the train for London. The thought of leaving is painful. My own spiritual life has not simply been deepened and strengthened; it seems to have only just begun. I am just beginning to learn the true meaning of prayer and worship. Compline draws to an end. The lights are extinguished for the *Salve Regina.* The chant rises effortlessly up to the Blessed Lady who will certainly act as the gracious advocate for the hundred and more young men who are placing their hope in her—*exsules filii Evae.* Exiles indeed, exiles because their hopes and their beliefs are anathema to the forces holding effective power in the Church today. If they belonged to any of a thousand and one heretical sects they would be smiled upon; if they professed Judaism, the Islamic or the Hindu faith they would be welcomed with open arms; if they were Marxist politicians, then red carpets would be laid before their feet. But they are young men who believe in the traditional and unchanging Catholic Faith; they are young men filled with a burning love for Our Lord and Our Lady; they are young men who have no other desire in life than to bring Christ upon the altar in the sublime setting of the Mass codified by St. Pius V and which has nourished the Faith of so many saints and countless millions of faithful Catholics throughout the centuries. But this rite of Mass is inimical to Protestants. It enshrines and proclaims so clearly the doctrines of the Real Presence and the Real Sacrifice which they do not believe in and will not accept. The Tridentine Mass is an obstacle to Ecumenism. Ecumenism is the new god of the new Church and Ecumenism is a jealous god. The young men who kneel in the shadows before me, pouring out their prayer to the Blessed Virgin Mary, evoke the memory of St. Ignatius and his tiny band of followers, who eventually grew into a great army of soldiers of Christ who not only halted the progress of the Protestant heresy but won back millions of souls to God. The forces of Modernism realize too clearly that unless something can be done to prevent these young men from being ordained and going out into the world then the victory of Modernism, which had seemed so secure for a time, will be in serious doubt. The Faithful will rally to these young men, the young in particular, and there will indeed be a renewal; but a Catholic renewal built on the sound basis of the traditional liturgy, traditional teaching, and traditional spirituality of the Church.

Calumny is the weapon which will be used in an attempt to destroy it. More often than not the Society of St. Pius X will be unable to refute these calumnies, but truth is great and must prevail. For those who might be tempted to believe the calumnies I know that every member of this Society, from Archbishop Lefebvre to the youngest seminarians, would have only one answer: "Come and see." Ecône has no secrets, as any visitor will soon find out. If there is anything to be discovered there it is the secret of holiness. I would be surprised to learn of any man of good will who could visit the Seminary and think otherwise.

The Seminary
at Ecône, Switzerland

Daily life at
the Seminary

His Grace with Professors of the Seminary

*Archbishop Lefebvre,
with three of the
author's children,
Adrian, Owen,
and Adrienne*

*Archbishop Lefebvre
visiting at St. Mary's
in the United States
of America*

*Archbishop Lefebvre visiting Padre Pio
while Superior General of the Holy Ghost Fathers*

Archbishop Lefebvre with Fr. Denis Roch, Econome General of the Society, and Fr. Paul Aulagnier, District Superior of France

His Grace with three of his American priests.

The Credo Pilgrimage to Rome, May 1975

The newly ordained priests—29 June 1976

Archbishop Lefebvre with Pope Pius XII

À Monsieur le Cardinal Jean Villot,
    Notre Secrétaire d'État,

Nous avons pris connaissance de l'interview demandée à Monseigneur Marcel Lefebvre par l'hebdomadaire "France Catholique - Ecclesia" (N° 1322 du 13 février 1976). Parmi les erreurs contenues dans cette interview il en est une que Nous voulons rectifier Nous-même : vous seriez un écran placé entre le Pape et Monseigneur Lefebvre, un obstacle à la rencontre qu'il désire avoir avec Nous. Cela n'est pas exact.

Nous estimons qu'avant d'être reçu en audience, Monseigneur Lefebvre doit revenir sur sa position inadmissible à l'égard du Concile œcuménique Vatican II et des mesures que Nous avons promulguées ou approuvées, en matière liturgique ou disciplinaire (et, par conséquent, aussi doctrinale). Cette position, il ne cesse malheureusement de l'affirmer par sa parole et par ses actes. Un réel changement d'attitude est donc nécessaire, pour que l'entretien souhaité puisse avoir lieu dans l'esprit de fraternité et d'unité ecclésiale, que Nous désirons tant depuis le début de cette pénible affaire et surtout depuis que Nous avons personnellement, à deux reprises, écrit à Monseigneur Lefebvre.

Nous continuons à espérer qu'il Nous donnera bientôt, dans les faits, la preuve concrète de sa fidélité à l'Église et au Saint-Siège, dont il a reçu tant de marques d'estime et de confiance. Nous savons que Vous partagez cet espoir ; c'est pourquoi que Nous Vous autorisons à rendre publique cette lettre, conforme à la bienveillance et à l'affection que Nous éprouvons pour Vous, Notre collaborateur dans la charge apostolique.

    Avec Notre paternelle Bénédiction.

Du Vatican 21 février 1976.   Paulus P.P. VI

The handwritten letter from Pope Paul VI to Cardinal Villot, dated 21 February 1976 (see pp. 163-166).

A Notre Frère dans l'Épiscopat
Marcel Lefebvre
Ancien Archevêque - Évêque de Tulle.

8-IX-1975

Paulus PP. VI

The handwritten letter from Pope Paul VI to Mgr. Lefebvre, dated 8 September 1975 (see pp. 134-135)

✠ ÉVÊCHÉ ✠ DE LAUSANNE GENÈVE ET ✠ FRIBOURG ✠

Décret d'érection

de la "Fraternité Sacerdotale Internationale Saint Pie X"

————

Etant donné les en__uragements exprimés par le Concile Vatican II, dans le décret "Optatum totius", concernant les Séminai____ internationaux et la répartition du clergé;

étant donné la nécessité urgente de la formation de prêtr__ zélés et généreux conformément aux directives du décret suscité;

constatant que les statuts de la Fraternité Sacerdotale correspondent bien à ces buts :

Nous, François Charrière, Evêque de Lausanne, Genève et Fribourg, le Saint Nom de Dieu invoqué, et toutes prescriptions canoniques observées, décrétons ce qui suit :

1) Est érigée dans notre diocèse au titre de "Pia Unio" la Fraternité Sacerdotale Internationale Saint Pie X.

2) Le siège de la Fraternité est fixé à la Maison Saint Pie X, 50, route de la Vignettaz, en notre ville épiscopale de Fribour_

3) Nous approuvons et confirmons les statuts ci-joints de la Frate__ pour une période de six ans "ad experimentum", période qui pour__ être suivie d'une autre semblable par tacite reconduction; aprè__ quoi, la Fraternité pourra être érigée définitivement dans notre diocèse ou par la Congrégation Romaine compétente.

Nous implorons les Bénédictions divines sur cette Fraterni__ Sacerdotale afin qu'elle atteigne son but principal qui est la forme__ tion de saints Prêtres.

Fait à Fribourg en notre Evêché le 1er novembre ____, en la fête de la Toussaint.

+ François Charrière, évêque

+ François Charrière, Evêque de Lausanne, Genève et Fribourg

The Decree of Erection establishing the Priestly Fraternity of Saint Pius X, dated 1 November 1970 (see Appendix V).

SACRA CONGREGATIO
PRO CLERICIS
———

Prot. N. 133515/I.
(In responso hic numerus referatur)

Exc.me Domine,

Magno cum gaudio litteras tuas recepi, quibus
Excellentia Tua notitias et statuta Operae vulgo dictae:
"Fraternité Sacerdotale" mihi nota facit.

Ut Excellentia tua exponit, Associatio, cura
eiusdem Excellentiae tuae ab Episcopo Friburgensi D.no
Francisco Charrière adprobata die 1 novembris 1970, iam
fines evasit nationis Helveticae, et plurimi Ordinarii
ex diversis orbis partibus, ipsam laudant et adprobant.
Haec omnia et speciatim sapientes normae, quibus Opera
informatur et regitur, bene sperare faciunt de eadem as-
sociatione.

Ex parte igitur huius Sacrae Congregationis,
quod attinet, "Fraternitas Sacerdotalis" multum conferre
poterit ad finem adipiscendum Consilii, in hoc S. Dica-
stero constituti, pro Cleri in mundo distributione.

Omni quo par est obsequio me profiteor
Excellentiae Tuae Rev.mae

addictissimum in Domino

J. Card. Wright
Praef.

Exc.mo ac Rev.mo Domino
D.no Marcello LEFEBVRE
Archiepiscopo tit. de Synnada in Phrygia
Via Casalmonferrato, n. 33
              R O M A E
              ℓCerr.

*Letter from Cardinal Wright expressing his pleasure at the progress
of the Fraternity, dated 18 February 1971 (see Appendix V).*

VII

Rejection of the Appeals

IN A LETTER to Mgr. Mamie dated 31 May 1975, Cardinal Tabera reaffirmed his approval and support for Mgr. Mamie's action in withdrawing recognition from the Society of St. Pius X.

Within a few days of writing this letter, Cardinal Tabera died suddenly. Let us pray that God may have mercy on him.

31 May 1975
Letter of Mgr. Lefebvre to Pope Paul VI

Most Holy Father,

Prostrate at the feet of Your Holiness, I assure you of my entire and filial submission to the decisions communicated to me by the Commission of Cardinals in what concerns the Fraternity of St. Pius X and its Seminary.

However, Your Holiness will be able to judge by the enclosed account* if, in the procedure, Natural and Canon Law have been ob-

* The Letter to Cardinal Staffa of 21 May 1975.

served.* When I think of the toleration Your Holiness shows with regard to the Dutch bishops and theologians like Hans Küng and Cardonnel, I cannot believe that the cruel decisions taken in my regard come from the same heart.

If it is true that the only ground of accusation against me that is retained is my Declaration of 21 November 1974, I beg Your Holiness to refer me to the competent Congregation: the Sacred Congregation for the Doctrine of the Faith.

Oh, how I wish Your Holiness would deign one day to welcome the members of the Sacerdotal Fraternity of Saint Pius X and its seminarians, with their poor superior! Your Holiness would see at once their deep devotion to, and veneration of, the Successor of Peter and their unique desire to serve the Church under his shepherd's crook.

There is no doubt that their concern to preserve a pure and full faith in the midst of the confusion of this world's ideas joins us with Your Holiness's concern, and if, at times, they express it in a somewhat impassioned way, I ask Your Holiness to pardon a zeal which is excessive but which comes from generous souls ready to give even their blood in defense of the Church and her Head, like the Machabees and all the martyrs.

May Mary the Queen, whose feast we keep today, bring Your Holiness the assurance of our filial affection.

And may God . . .

† Marcel Lefebvre.

On 2 June 1975, Mgr. Mamie published the Cardinals' letter of 6 May to Mgr. Lefebvre.

On 5 June Mgr. Lefebvre's lawyer lodged his appeal with the Court of the Apostolic Signature in Rome, listing serious breaches of Canon Law in the action taken against him and demanding the production of evidence that the Pope had in fact authorized the Cardinals to take their quite unprecedented action against the Society of St. Pius X. The text of

* Non-observance of Natural and Canon Law which evidently annuls the preceding paragraph.

the appeal is entered under 21 May 1975.

Bulletin No. 17 of the International Federation *Una Voce,* published 6 June 1975, included a comment by its distinguished president, Dr. Eric M. Saventhem, concerning the action taken against Mgr. Lefebvre. His remarks included the following:

With Mgr. Lefebvre's reply to the Abbé de Nantes known in Rome, the article in *L'Osservatore Romano* stands revealed as a deliberate calumny.* By this "Reply," Mgr. Lefebvre had given an answer to all *L'Osservatore Romano's* rhetorical questions even before they were formulated. To raise them all the same, in the Vatican's official newspaper, and without breathing a word about the "Reply," is rank dishonesty.

The Cardinals' letter shows the sanctions now imposed on Mgr. Lefebvre to be based solely on the accusation that his Declaration is "incompatible with authentic fidelity to the Church, the Pope and the Council." Implied in this reproach is the accusation of a schismatic intent. It is not suggested that the Declaration is in any way incompatible with the "authentic doctrine concerning the Church, the Pope and the Council"—the Cardinals *know* that they cannot fault the text of the Declaration on doctrinal grounds. And no proof is offered for the "schismatic intent" other than that strange reference to the "traditional language of the sects." One would like to know what sects the Cardinals were thinking of and one would ask them the following question: what about those who invoke the "Church of today" in order to shirk obedience to the "Church of all the ages"? Is that not much more typically a sectarian line of thought and argument?

More profoundly though: what are the criteria for "authentic fidelity"? Surely the chief criterion is that of total acceptance and public profession of the Church's own doctrine concerning Herself and particularly Her supreme hierarchical authority, i. e. the Pope and any legitimate council whose decisions the Pope has endorsed? In that case the

* The article of 8 May 1975.

accusation of "lack of authentic fidelity" would have to be made in the
first place against those who, like Professor Küng, have openly attacked
this doctrine. And if the Cardinals have found it necessary, in the case
of Mgr. Lefebvre, to withdraw the ecclesiastical approbation which
makes Ecône a proper "seminary," then Professor Küng should have
long since been deprived of his *missio canonica,* i.e. the authority by
virtue of which he instructs future priests in fundamental theology.

Nothing can be more arbitrary than the Cardinals' decision—and this
notwithstanding the fact that it is said to be fully endorsed by the Holy
Father himself. There is no evidence of this endorsement, to begin with.
Moreover, it is unheard of that a senior member of the episcopal hierarchy (Mgr. Lefebvre has been a bishop for nearly 30 years and has held
high Curial offices as Apostolic Delegate for the French-speaking parts
of Africa) should be "disciplined" without due process—before either
the Congregation for Bishops or the Congregation for the Faith—and
that sentence should be passed in the name of the Holy Father without
the "accused" having appeared before his judge: since he founded the
Fraternity in 1969 Mgr. Lefebvre has twice made a formal request to be
received in audience by His Holiness and in both cases no audience was
in fact granted.

Suffering from so many defects, both as regards form and equity,
the decisions of the Cardinals' Commission cannot bind anyone in conscience—least of all the Archbishop himself. Life at Ecône is continuing
without change and Mgr. Lefebvre is consulting his many friends in
Rome as to the proper procedure with which to appeal against the Roman judgment.

On 10 June 1975 Mgr. Lefebvre's appeal was rejected on
the grounds that the condemnation of the three Cardinals
had been approved *in forma specifica* by the Pope and that
therefore no appeal was admissible. Had this appeal gone forward it would have been necessary to produce the "express
mandate" of the Holy Father authorizing the three Cardinals
to act against Mgr. Lefebvre and also the approbation *in forma specifica* of the action which they took. There is every

reason to believe that no such documents exist and that therefore the action taken against Mgr. Lefebvre was un-canonical and automatically void. Had these documents existed there is not the least doubt that the Commission of Cardinals would have produced them. The decision against Mgr. Lefebvre could then have been set out, as was that against Fr. Coache, which, although unjust, at least denoted an observance of the correct legal procedure. The decision against Fr. Coache was phrased as follows:

On 1 March 1975 there was a meeting of the Commission of Cardinals which the Holy Father had designated by a letter of the Secretariat of State No. 265 485 of 4 November 1974 to re-examine *ex novo*, etc. The above-mentioned decree was submitted to the consideration of Pope Paul VI who, *re mature pensa*, approved it *in omnibus et singulis* on 7 June 1975, and ordered that it should be notified as soon as possible to all the parties concerned.*

It is quite clear that the Pope's letter to Mgr. Lefebvre of 29 June 1975 (which will be found in its chronological order) was an attempt to give retroactive legality to a manifestly illegal process. This letter, far from allaying doubts concerning the regularity of the procedure against the Archbishop, constituted the clumsiest of possible public admissions that it had been irregular. This *a posteriori* legalization of an illegal act will certainly scandalize anyone in the least familiar with the most elementary principles of jurisprudence. As Mgr. Lefebvre expressed it himself:

Has anyone ever seen, in Canon Law, or in other legal systems, a law, a decree, a decision endowed with a retroactive effect? One condemns and then judges afterwards.**

*Hanu, pp. 222-223 (191).
**Hanu, p. 223 (191).

A final point with regard to Mgr. Lefebvre's appeal—it was rejected in only five days whereas such appeals normally involve months or even a year or more of study.

On 14 June 1975, Mgr. Lefebvre's lawyers lodged an appeal with the Supreme, Tribunal of the Apostolic Signature. He did not even receive a reply to this appeal, and in fact he discovered that Cardinal Staffa had been threatened with dismissal if he so much as examined any appeal coming from Mgr. Lefebvre.*

There may be readers who find it impossible to believe that those charged with governing the Church founded by Christ could behave in such a manner. It will suffice to cite the case of Father Coache once more to dispel their illusions. Among the many invaluable historical documents published by *Itinéraires* is its Dossier: *The Unjust Condemnation of Fr. Coache* (160 pages in length) in its issue of January 1976. It includes numerous letters to and from Fr. Coache, his Bishop, and various Vatican departments. Fr. Coache had incurred the displeasure of his Bishop for the crime of organizing a procession of the Blessed Sacrament, and he was to be deprived of his parish. He informed his Bishop that he would appeal to Rome against the decision and duly wrote his appeal. But learning there was a postal strike in Italy, he delayed posting it. Some days later the Vicar General arrived with a telegram from the Vatican announcing that his appeal had been rejected. Fr. Coache opened the drawer containing the envelope with his appeal in it, showed it to the Vicar General and said: "Here's my appeal. I haven't posted it yet!" Exit the Vicar General in confusion. A few days later, the postal strike being over, a letter from the Vatican confirming the rejection of his appeal arrived. The Latin text and translation are set out below. This letter proves that no Catholic today can presume that any statement coming from the Vati-

*Hanu, p. 216, 223 (185, 191).

can is true. The same goes for the "establishment" of the
"Conciliar Church" in any country. I have a number of ex-
amples on record of straightforward lies told by prominent
Liberal clerics in England.

The text of the letter from the Sacred Congregation for
the Clergy is taken from the January 1976 issue of *Itinéraires*.

SACRA CONGREGATIO
PRO CLERICIS
Prot. 124205   Romae, 6 Junii 1969.

    Excellentissime Domine,
    **Examini subiecto recursu Reverendi sacerdotis Coache Aloisii, istius
dioeceseos, haec Sacra Congregatio respondit: "Recursum esse reicien-
dum."**

    **Velit Excellentia Tua de hac responsione certiorem facere recurren-
tem, qui pareat praeceptis Ordinarii sui.**

    **Dum haec Tecum communico cuncta fausta Tibi a Domino adprecor
ac permanere gaudeo.**

    Excellentiae Tuae Rev. mae addictissimus.

                             P. Palazzini, a Secretis.

Excellentissimo ac Rev. mo Domino,
D. NO STEPHANO DESMAZIÈRES
Episcopo
Bellovacen.

A translation of this letter follows.

    Excellentissime Domine,
    **Having examined Fr. Coache's Appeal, our Sacred Congregation has
decreed: "The Appeal is rejected."**

    **Please have the goodness to communicate this decision to the plain-
tiff in order that he may obey the orders of his Bishop, etc. etc.**

An Editor Silenced

There was considerable sympathy for Ecône and the Old Mass in England. Particularly significant in this connection was the editorial of the *Catholic Herald* of 13 June 1975 (the issue which reported the suppression of Ecône).

It began by admitting that most of the letters received by the editor concerned the liturgy, and that most of these letters were against the reforms. It went on to refer to the recent episcopal *pronunciamento,* which was simply a restatement of the October 1974 renewed proscription of the Old Mass by the Congregation for Divine Worship. Describing this as "a landmark in ecumenical history," the editorial stated:

The present position of the Catholic seems to be this: If he wants to attend a Tridentine Mass, the priest who proposes to say the Mass has first to receive permission from a bishop; if, on the other hand, the Catholic wishes to attend a non-conformist service, at the heart of which may be a denial of the Real Presence, he does not have to seek permission at all. Indeed, some priests positively encourage the faithful to attend the services of other denominations. This may be a good thing. At the same time it adds up to a nice irony.

Those who wish to attend the Tridentine Mass as a matter of course —while not wishing to deprive others of the New Order—do not do so necessarily because they love Latin. Many of them, for instance, find the new Latin Mass tiresome. And many of those who wish to see a return of the Tridentine rite cannot utter a word of Latin (though they are perfectly capable of reading the crib in their missals). They wish merely to see the old Order permitted because it had a dignity and beauty they find lacking in the New Order.

Clearly, at any rate, the reforms have gone far enough. The time has come for Catholics to cry: "An end to it." Perhaps then the bickering will stop.

It is hardly surprising that the present Liberal establishment could not countenance the prospect of an offical Catholic weekly presenting the news objectively and commenting upon it in balanced editorials. It was soon made clear to Stuart Reid, the newly appointed editor, that although he had been guaranteed editorial freedom, this meant only freedom to write what was acceptable to the Liberal establishment. He was told that he must either submit his editorials to censorship or have them written for him by someone who could be guaranteed not to deviate from the party line. Under these circumstances he felt that he had no honorable option but to resign.

A Priest Dismissed

On 15 June 1975, Fr. Pierre Épiney, the young parish priest of Riddes, the nearest parish to the Seminary at Ecône, was summarily deprived of his parish by Mgr. Adam, because of his "refusal to submit to the Sovereign Pontiff and to Vatican II."

In an open letter to Fr. Epiney, Mgr. Adam stated that this was the most cruel decision in his 23-year episcopate but that he would be failing in his duty if "by my silence, I were to collude with your disobedience." Within a few days of the Bishop's decision being known over 800 of the adult parishioners had signed a petition in support of Fr. Épiney and more have since been added. This represents almost all the adult practicing Catholics in the parish. An earlier petition to have Fr. Épiney removed attracted only 12 signatures. Fr. Épiney complied with Mgr. Adam's order to vacate his parish church on 15 June but conducted an evening vigil before the Blessed Sacrament which concluded exactly at midnight, when he left the Church which had been packed to the doors for the vigil.

Evidently, there is only one serious sin in the contemporary Church—"to refuse to submit to Vatican II." One of the grounds for the dismissal of Fr. Épiney was that he had returned to the celebration of the Tridentine Mass. As, to the certain knowledge of Mgr. Adam, he has been saying only this form of Mass for several years, the Bishop's sudden pangs of conscience are curious to say the least.

Needless to say, the real reason for Fr. Épiney's dismissal was his refusal to obey the *diktat* of the faceless Roman authority who insisted that "no support whatsoever must be given to Mgr. Lefebvre."

On 29 June 1975, Pope Paul VI dispatched his first letter to Archbishop Lefebvre. This letter was made public in a dossier on Ecône published in the *Nouvelliste* of Sion on 12 December 1975. (Sion is the diocese in which Ecône is situated.)

29 June 1975
Letter of Pope Paul VI
to Archbishop Marcel Lefebvre

To Our Brother in the Episcopate, Marcel Lefebvre
Former Archbishop—Bishop of Tulle.

Dear Brother,

It is with sorrow that We write to you today. With sorrow because We appreciate the interior anguish of a man who sees the annihilation of his hopes, the ruin of the initiative which he believes he has taken for the good of the Church. With sorrow because We think of the confusion of the young people who have followed you, full of ardor, and now find themselves in a blind alley. But Our grief is even greater to note that the decision of the competent authority—although formulated very clearly, and fully justified, it may be said, by your refusal to modify your public and persistent opposition to the Second Vatican Council, to the post-conciliar reforms, and to the orientations to which the Pope himself is committed—that this decision should still lend itself to discussion even to the extent of leading you to seek some juridical possibility of invalidating it.

The precise reason for the Pope's "grief" at Mgr. Lefebvre's attempt to "invalidate" the action taken against him is that he has had the temerity to resort to the standard legal procedure and lodge an appeal to the competent tribunal. As, according to the Commission of Cardinals and stated expressly in its letter of 6 May 1975 (see p. 59), the sole motive for the action taken against Mgr. Lefebvre was the Declaration of 21 November 1974, the competent authority to decide upon the orthodoxy of this letter was the Congregation for the Doctrine of the Faith. Mgr. Lefebvre has asked that his Declaration be examined by this Congregation, the "competent authority," but this request has been denied.

Careful note should also be taken of the manner in which no distinction is made between "opposition to the Second Vatican Council, to the post-conciliar reforms, and to the orientations to which the Pope himself is committed." All must be accepted together as a strict package.

Although, strictly speaking, it is not necessary to recapitulate, We do however deem it opportune to confirm to you that We have insisted on being informed concerning the entire development of the inquiry concerning the Priestly Fraternity of St. Pius X, and from the very beginning the Cardinals' Commission, which We set up, regularly and most scrupulously rendered an account of its work. Finally, the conclusions which it proposed to Us, We made all and each of them Ours, and We personally ordered that they be immediately put into force.

This is the first documentary evidence to support the claim that the Pope had given approval to the action taken against

Mgr. Lefebvre *in forma specifica.* Papal approval is normally given to acts of the Curia *in forma communi.* This simply gives the necessary legal status to the curial act in question when such approval is necessary. A decree which has received such approbation still remains the decree of those who enacted it—it is an act of the Holy See rather than a specifically papal act. If such an act contained legal irregularities sufficient to invalidate it, then it would be invalid despite having received papal approval *in forma communi.* Without proof to the contrary, papal approbation should always be presumed to have been given *in forma communi.* The special approbation known as *in forma specifica* is granted only after the Pope has given the matter his close personal attention in every aspect and possibly made changes in the text submitted to him. Such approval is indicated by such formulas as *ex motu proprio, ex scientia certa, de apostolicae auctoritatis plenitudine.* This manner of approbation transforms the act into a specifically papal one and the steps leading up to it are considered as having only consultative status. Normally, even if there had been legal irregularities in the preliminary stages, these could not affect the juridical validity of a decision which the Pope had made his own. Up to the publication of this letter there had been no more than a gratuitous affirmation by Cardinal Villot that the Pope had approved the steps taken against Mgr. Lefebvre *in forma specifica,* thus blocking the appeal which could have revealed, *inter alia,* that no such approval had been given up to that point. The question that must be asked is whether this letter from the Pope is an attempt to give approval *in forma specifica* retrospectively. If it is not, why can no earlier document be produced?

Thus, dear Brother, it is in the name of the veneration for the successor of St. Peter that you profess in your letter of 31 May, more than that, it is in the name of the Vicar of Christ that We ask of you a public act of submission, in order to make amends for the offense which your writings, your speeches, and your attitudes have caused with regard to the Church and its Magisterium.

Mgr. Lefebvre's profession of veneration for the successor of St. Peter is the only point in his letter of 31 May to which specific reference is made. No answer is made to his claim that Natural and Canon Law have been violated or that his Declaration should be submitted for judgment to the Congregation for the Doctrine of the Faith.

Such an act necessarily implies, among other things, the acceptance of the measures taken concerning the Priestly Fraternity of St. Pius X and all the practical consequences of these measures. We beseech God that He may enlighten you and lead you thus to act, despite your present disinclination to do so. And We appeal to your sense of episcopal responsibility that you may recognize the good that would thereby result for the Church.

Certainly, problems of another order entirely preoccupy Us equally —the superficiality of certain interpretations of conciliar documents, of individual or collective initiatives deriving sometimes rather from arbitrary wilfulness *(libre arbitre)* than from confident adhesion to the teaching of Scripture and Tradition, of initiatives which arbitrarily evoke the faith to justify them. We know them, We suffer because of them, and for Our part, We strive in season and out of season to remedy them.

Pope Paul VI thus shows himself to be aware of the abuses which are widespread in every aspect of the Church's life, in doctrine, in the liturgy, in morality. He returns to this theme on future occasions, most notably in his Consistorial Address of 24 May 1976 and in his long letter to Mgr. Lefebvre dated 11 October 1976, which can be found under this date. In this letter Pope Paul even concedes that these abuses are going to the extent of sacrilege. He invariably

stated that he was taking action to remedy these abuses, but
it must be stated, with all the respect due to the Holy Father, that the anguished faithful in many countries saw no
sign at all of any action being taken to correct abuses during
his pontificate, particularly in the liturgy. To give just one example, Pope Paul himself made it quite clear that he wished
the traditional manner of receiving Holy Communion to be
adhered to in his Instruction *Memoriale Domini* of 29 May
1969. But since this Instruction was published he has legal-
ized the abuse of Communion in the hand throughout the
West. A detailed examination of the manner in which one liturgical abuse after another has spread throughout the world,
with the acquiescence of the Vatican, will be provided in
my book *Pope Paul's New Mass*. The beginning of the story
has already been documented in *Pope John's Council*.

**But how can one use things such as these to justify oneself in com-
mitting excesses which are gravely harmful?**

This is truly an astonishing statement. How is it possible
to condemn as harmful excesses the training of priests in the
traditional manner, and in almost total conformity to the
norms laid down during and subsequent to Vatican II; in
continuing to teach traditional doctrine and morality in total
conformity with the acts of the Magisterium dating back
2,000 years, and in conformity with such documents of
Pope Paul VI himself as *Mysterium Fidei,* his *Credo,* or his
Humanae Vitae; and in continuing to offer Mass in accordance with the Missal of Saint Pius V, a Missal which has provided the source of the spiritual life of so many saints in so
many countries, and to which Pope Paul himself paid tribute
in his Apostolic Constitution *Missale Romanum?*

**Such is not the right way to do things, since it makes use of ways
comparable to those which are denounced. What can one say of a mem-**

ber who wishes to act alone, independently of the Body to which he belongs?

It also quite astonishing to find Mgr. Lefebvre's "faults" equated with the abuses he denounces. His "faults" are to continue teaching the traditional faith, using the traditional liturgy, and forming seminarians in the traditional manner even if this involves disobeying the Vatican and even the Pope himself. How can such devotion to the traditional faith be compared with the abuses mentioned by the Archbishop in his letter of 31 May where he refers to the Dutch Bishops who have publicly questioned the virginal conception of Our Lord—a doctrine fundamental to our entire faith? Pope Paul VI did not denounce the Dutch hierarchy.

You permit the case of St. Athanasius to be invoked in your favor.

If some Catholics claim that there is a parallel between the case of Archbishop Lefebvre and that of St. Athanasius, what can the Archbishop do about it? Appendix I shows that a good case can be made for invoking such a parallel.

It is true that this great Bishop remained practically alone in the defense of the true faith, despite attacks from all quarters. But what precisely was involved was the defense of the faith of the recent Council of Nicea. The Council was the norm which inspired his fidelity, as also in the case of St. Ambrose.

St. Athanasius defended not so much the Council of Nicea as the traditional faith which this very important dogmatic council taught. Mgr. Lefebvre would certainly defend any of the traditional articles of faith restated in the documents of Vatican II, as, indeed, some of them are.

How can anyone today compare himself to St. Athanasius in daring

to combat a council such as the Second Vatican Council, which has no less authority, which in certain respects is even more important than that of Nicea?

Within the space of a few lines the charge against Mgr. Lefebvre has been changed from allowing himself to be compared to St. Athanasius to actually comparing himself with the great saint—something that he has neither done nor would ever contemplate doing! There is, in fact, a very striking comparison between Archbishop Lefebvre and St. Athanasius. Pope Liberius subscribed to one of the ambiguous formulae of Sirmium, which seriously compromised the traditional faith, and he confirmed the excommunicaton of St. Athanasius. It is true that Liberius acted under pressure and later repented—but it is equally true that it was Athanasius who upheld the faith and was canonized. The story of Liberius and Athanasius is told in some detail in Appendix I.

It is really hard to believe that Pope Paul VI could claim seriously that Vatican II is equal in authority and in some respects more important than the Council of Nicea. The Council of Nicea, the first Ecumenical Council, promulgated infallible teaching concerned with the divinity of Christ—nothing could be more fundamental or more important. Vatican II deliberately refrained from utilizing that assistance of the Holy Ghost which would have enabled it to promulgate infallible teaching. The teaching of Nicea belongs to the Extraordinary Magisterium and those who deny it are anathematized. The teaching of Vatican II belongs to the Ordinary Magisterium and no such sanction is applied to anyone rejecting it. There is thus no possible way in which the teaching of Vatican II could be considered equal in authority to Nicea, still less more important. When the Pope makes such claims he is expressing his personal opinion and his views in no way demand our assent. The question of the relative status of the two councils is considered in Appendix III.

We beg you therefore to meditate concerning the warning which We address to you with firmness and in virtue of Our Apostolic authority. Your elder (brother) in the faith, He Who has received the mission of confirming His brothers, addresses you, His heart full of hope.

He wishes He could already rejoice in being understood, heard and obeyed. He awaits with impatience the day when He will have the happiness to open to you His arms, to make manifest a refound communion, when you will have replied to the demands He has just formulated. At present He confides this intention to the Lord, Who rejects no prayers.

In veritate et caritate,
Paulus PP VI
The Vatican 29 June 1975

The Significance of Pope Paul's Letter

Jean Madiran, editor of *Itinéraires,* considers that the personal intervention of the Pope marks a second and tragic phase in the campaign against the Archbishop. In the issue dated February 1976 he writes (pp. 122-123):

What is most tragic, in the second phase of this deplorable business, is that the Pope has been prevailed on to condemn the one bishop who is a genuine defender of pontifical authority, and to condemn him precisely for that.

Mgr. Lefebvre's Declaration of November 1974, which is in all points Catholic, has been condemned by the Holy See "in all points," including the first.

"We cleave with all our heart and soul to Catholic Rome, guardian of the Catholic faith and of the traditions necessary to maintain that faith, to eternal Rome, mistress of wisdom and truth."

To succeed in getting the Pope to condemn the only bishop in Europe, as far as we know, who speaks publicly in such terms, and to condemn him precisely for that, is indeed a masterpiece of *self-destruction* of the Church.

On the other hand, those who make themselves out to be supporters of "obedience"—and who practice it now and then—destroy authority when they preach and put into effect an arbitrary, blind, and servile concept of obedience. Those who "obey the Church" when she condemns Joan of Arc, those who "obey the Pope" when he signs and promulgates the first version, unacceptable, of Article 7, destroy, by making a hateful caricature of it, the very authority to which they pretend to appeal. It is only the Catholic idea of obedience which gives a safe and legitimate foundation for pontifical authority. They are not defending pontifical authority but destroying it—those who say Paul VI must be obeyed because he is a man of progress, a truly modern pope, a progressive democrat, an open and collegial spirit, and the like: for those standards are matters of opinion, debatable, changeable, and at the mercy of the manipulators of public opinion with their subjective evaluations and their presentation of them on radio and televsion.

Today Mgr. Lefebvre is the only bishop in Europe and perhaps in the whole world who proclaims aloud, and openly preaches, the true doctrine of authority in the Church. He is disowned and attacked by the present holders of that authority: which amounts to attempted suicide.

Pontifical authority has only one foundation: Catholic tradition, the first monument of which is the New Testament. All motives for obeying the Pope which are outside Catholic tradition are false, deceptive and fragile. Servile obedience seems for a time to insure for those who benefit from it the enjoyment of a comfortable despotism. But it is only an artificial construction, which sows disorder and is doomed to destruction.

In any case, we are not taken in! Most of those who demand from us unconditional obedience to the spirit of the Council and to the Pope who appeals to it are just those who, until the Council, provided the theory and gave the example of systematic non-obedience. Those Modernists and progressives, the theorists and practiced exponents of disobedience to the Church, are suspect when they start crying up obedience; and it is at once likely that the obedience they recommend is not good.

And when the disobedience they promote is an obedience at one and the same time unconditional and based on worldly motives ("Paul VI is a modern Pope, a true democrat who understands his times and is open to evolution"), evidently that is not Catholic.

Mgr. Lefebvre states in his Declaration that: "If there is a certain contradiction manifest in his words and deeds (the Pope's) as well as in the acts of his dicasteries,* then we cleave to what has always been taught and we turn a deaf ear to the novelties which destroy the Church."

That is Catholic truth, immediately recognized as such, with no hesitation or uncertainty, by any heart inhabited by theological faith.

Moreover, Mgr. Lefebvre has proclaimed that truth with great moderation, considering the circumstances, and with great delicacy towards the very controversial figure of the reigning pontiff.

The Issues Made Clear

With the Pope's letter of 29 June 1975, the issues at stake have been made quite clear. Our attitude to subsequent events will be governed by our reaction to the manner in which the Society of St. Pius X and its Seminary at Ecône were suppressed. Given that the Pope's letter of 29 June is legally acceptable as approval of this suppression *in forma specifica,* it would be technically correct to concede that the Archbishop is being disobedient. Let it be noted here that he and his legal advisers do not accept that even in the light of the Pope's letter of 29 June 1975 the decision against him can be considered as legally valid. Could it be proved that the decision conformed with the strict legal requirements of Canon Law, it was clearly an outrage against the Natural Law, and a Catholic would be entitled to resist such a decision.

*The Roman Congregations

As will be shown in Appendix II, *The Right to Resist an Abuse of Power,* Bishop Grosseteste was certainly resisting a perfectly legal papal command in 1253—but it would surprise me if a single reader of this book would say that this great English Bishop was wrong. What every theologian of repute would certainly accept is that resisting the Pope is not *ipso facto* wrong, what matters is the reason for resistance. What has never ceased to astonish me from the beginning of the whole affair is not the manner in which Catholic Liberals pour invective upon the Archbishop—this is only to be expected—but the manner in which self-proclaimed champions of orthodoxy condemn him for the sin of disobedience with an alacrity which would have left the most accomplished pharisee at a loss for words, and the manner in which they issue their condemnations without even a pretense of taking into consideration the reasons which have prompted Mgr. Lefebvre to make his stand. The case can be summarized as follows:

1. The Society of Saint Pius X was established according to all the requirements of Canon Law, with the approval of the Vatican and the active encouragement of the Congregation of the Clergy and its Prefect, Cardinal Wright.

2. The Society soon established the most flourishing and orthodox Seminary in Europe at enormous financial cost, borne by thousands of faithful Catholics all over the world.

3. An Apostolic Visitation of the Seminary brought to light no reason for complaint.

4. Mgr. Lefebvre was summoned to appear before three Cardinals for a discussion which turned out to be a trial.

5. The entire case against him was based on a statement provoked by unorthodox opinions expressed by the Apostolic Visitors to Ecône.

6. The entire Society was suppressed as the result of a single statement made by only one of its members.

7. The Archbishop rightly insisted that if the statement was

alleged to be unorthodox the only tribunal competent to assess it was the Congregation for the Doctrine of the Faith. He asked to have his Declaration considered by this Congregation. His request was refused.

8. Up to this point, no public statement had been issued quoting a specific passage in this Declaration which was alleged to be unorthodox.

9. Not one iota of evidence has ever been produced to prove that the Commission of Cardinals had been constituted by the Pope according to the required canonical norms or that the Pope had approved its decisions *in forma specifica.*

10. However, even had this Commission of Cardinals formed a legally constituted tribunal with the authority to try and condemn Mgr. Lefebvre (without considering it necessary to mention this fact to him), it has been shown on p. 61 that the decisions taken against Mgr. Lefebvre were not those of the tribunal, still less of the Pope, but of some anonymous authority.

11. At the moment when it would have been necessary to produce the relevant documents in response to the Archbishop's appeal, it was stated that his appeal could not be heard as the Pope had approved the decisions of the Commission of Cardinals *in forma specifica*—the very point which the Archbishop disputed and for which his lawyer would have required proof.

12. On this basis the Archbishop was expected to close his Seminary in mid-term and send professors and seminarians home.

Mgr. Lefebvre claims that this constituted an abuse of power. The reader must decide whether he is justified in making this claim. The question at issue is this: Is it outrageous that the Archbishop should have refused to submit to the Pope, or is it outrageous that the Pope should have demanded that the Archbishop should submit to such a travesty of justice?

On 22 October 1976, *The Cambridge Review,* a non-

Catholic publication, included an article on the legal aspects of the treatment accorded to Mgr. Lefebvre, part of which is reproduced below.

The Cambridge Review Speaks Out

Archbishop Marcel Lefebvre's stand against the new form of the Roman Mass has finally assured full publicity to the arguments of the Catholic traditionalists. There is one aspect of his position, however, that has received almost no attention from the press, and which is, of course, determinedly played down by his ecclesiastical opponents: and that is the strength of his position in Canon Law. In what follows we shall investigate some of the legal arguments, and in so doing we shall notice that the vaunted "reforms" of the Second Vatican Council have done almost nothing to reduce the Vatican's preference for administrative despotism over legal procedures.

Let us take, in the first place, the attempt by the Bishop of Fribourg to suppress Lefebvre's Fraternity of St. Pius X and hence, of course, the famous seminary at Ecône. The position in Canon Law is this: A Bishop has authority to suppress a religious house when it is one that he has erected within his own diocese. But if the order to which the house belongs extends beyond the boundaries of his own diocese, he has no such authority, since he would be trespassing on the jurisdiction of other bishops. Only the Holy See can suppress a congregation that exists in more than one diocese. In fact, the Bishop of Fribourg erected Lefebvre's Fraternity in his own diocese at Lefebvre's request. The Fraternity is now a religious congregation, duly set up, existing in a number of countries. In Canon Law this makes it a *persona moralis,* that is to say, a legal person or corporation—similar in this respect to an Oxford or Cambridge College.

But although the Bishop had no authority himself to suppress the order, he was given Vatican permission to revoke the decrees by which the order had been established. Does this mean that the Vatican empowered the Bishop to use the full authority of the Holy See to suppress the Fraternity *in toto*—or only as it existed in his diocese? The words of the Vatican decree leave it ambiguous. Such (no doubt deliberate) ambiguity, and the fact that the Bishop was merely *empowered* and not instructed to carry out the act of suppression indicates that the Vatican does not wish to take responsibility for an act which it instigated. Furthermore, according to canon lawyers, ambiguity in such a case usually allows of a strict construction of the decree—i.e., that only the order within the diocese of Fribourg was allowed to be suppressed. Such shiftiness on the part of the Vatican is not attractive.

The point of investigating the legality of the purported suppression of Lefebvre's order is that it illuminates the whole course of subsequent events. What was the Archbishop to do faced with his suppression? Since the Roman Church does, in fact, possess legal procedures, the proper and normal course was for him to appeal against the decision to the Administrative Section of the *Signatura Apostolica*—the highest Papal court. This he duly did, after taking legal advice. Yet while his appeal was actually before the court, a letter arrived from the Secretariat of State which announced that the decision taken against Lefebvre was a Papal one, against which no appeal was possible. Hence every legal recourse by the Archbishop was blocked, and he had been denied any hearing. The Papal action was, of course, valid in law, given the ample authority of the Roman Pontiff; but it can be considered illicit in its violation of natural justice, which is, after all, supposed to be one of the foundations of Canon Law. Morally such an attempt to deny a man's rights and frustrate his life's work, while refusing him any legal recourse, is (to an

Englishman at least) appalling.

But these legal questions raised in the treatment of Lefebvre are of secondary interest. What really matters is his refusal to accept the New Mass. Here again, the press have laid heavy stress upon his "defiance of the Pope", etc., and no doubt the average English Catholic, brought up on exaggerated notions of the deference due to all Papal acts, however foolish, assumes that that is the end of the matter. Indeed, Catholic newspapers have already resorted to the formula that Lefebvre has "placed himself outside the Church even without being formally excommunicated"—which neatly avoids the embarrassment of finding grounds on which he could properly be excommunicated. In fact the misrepresentation has been almost scandalous; and of course the strength of Lefebvre's case in Canon Law has gone entirely unnoticed.

It is remarkable that many Catholics are under the impression that the Second Vatican Council went some way towards abrogating the Latin Mass, merely tolerating it in certain circumstances. The words of Hans Küng are relevant here:

"It could and should be recognized that Mgr. Lefebvre is right in one aspect. There is no doubt that post-conciliar development in a number of cases has gone far beyond what was agreed at the Council, not only *de facto* but also *de jure,* with the agreement of the Church leaders. According to Vatican II, for example, Latin was to be retained in principle as the language of the Church of what is known as the Latin rite; the vernacular was permitted only exceptionally in individual parts of the Church. Today with Rome's consent the whole Catholic liturgy, even in Rome itself, is overwhelmingly in the vernacular."

The proponents of the new forms never tire of asserting—quite falsely—that this is somehow an outcome of the Council. This falsehood is encouraged by no less a body than the Sacred Congregation of Rites. This body—the supreme authority, under the Pope, in liturgical matters—has been issuing legislation enforcing the new rite, and regularly claiming that its decrees embody the "norms" of the Council. It has, for instance, authorized Bishops to *prescribe* a purely vernacular Mass on Sundays. This is completely opposed to the decision of the Council that the vernacular may be *permitted* in certain parts of the Mass, and that "*in ritibus latinis usus linguae Latinae servetur*". The claim of the Sacred Congregation of Rites to be carrying out decisions of the Council in thus allowing Bishops to force priests to say vernacular Masses is entirely spurious.

But the Catholic traditionalists can derive further support from Canon Law. It is almost universally assumed that the Tridentine Mass has been abolished and that Lefebvre and his followers are acting illegally in continuing to celebrate it. But is this so? Here again the legal position is extremely interesting, and provides support for Lefebvre.

The Tridentine rite was not invented by Pius V. It is rather the freezing of the Roman rite at one particular stage of its development. This rite, which was the "local" rite of the whole Western Church (with some variants, like the Ambrosian and Sarum rites) was in immemorial use in the Roman Church: what is called a *consuetudo immemorabilis et particularis.* This ancient *consuetudo* was given the force of law by Pius V after the Council of Trent; and he decreed that his law must never be abrogated. It is worth noting that Pius V's legislation was the first such interference in the Liturgy by a Pope in the whole history of the Church. Hitherto a rite was deemed to derive its legitimacy from its "immemorial" use as a particular tradition. Tradition, not legislation, was the claim to legitimacy—as it still is in the Eastern Orthodox Church.

Now according to almost all canon lawyers, if a piece of Papal legislation enforcing an already existing rite (like Pius V's enforcement of the Tridentine rite) is subsequently abrogated, then the rite itself reverts to its former status: it remains a valid and licit rite *unless it is itself specifically abro-*

gated. (An analogy would lie in the relation of Common Law
to Statute Law.) And in fact the Pope did *not* abrogate the
consuetudo immemorabilis of the Latin Church, but only
Pius V's legislation. Therefore the Tridentine Mass remains
entirely licit, and no Bishop, of Northampton or elsewhere,
can properly dismiss a priest for saying it.

These are juridical arguments, and they help one to see
that the Vatican has been behaving evasively and (one is
tempted to say) dishonestly towards the traditionalists. They
do not touch those features of the new rite that for many
Catholics made their remaining in the Church merely a matter of grim loyalty. For them the loss of any numinous quality in favor of a superficial notion of "participation" has been
most painful. Then there are the many absurdities of the new
arrangements—the handshake which is supposed to be the
equivalent of the Kiss of Peace, a liturgical form found previously only amongst the Mormons; the odd gesture of consecration made by priests "concelebrating" Mass—a sort of
Fascist salute at half-cock. These and other attempts to adapt
the liturgy to a bourgeois imagination have wrought a serious
impoverishment.

But of course the objections of the traditionalists are not
fundamentally "aesthetic" (if that is the right word for their
sense of such impoverishment). Lefebvre's final objection to
the new rite is that its formulations are ambiguous, that it
makes a heterodox interpretation of the doctrine possible.
(An heretical interpretation of the Tridentine rite would require the ingenuity of the Newman of Tract XI). Contrary to
popular impression, Lefebvre has never denied the validity of
the new rite itself.

For the Archbishop and his followers, the changes in the
Mass are central examples of what they see as stealthy attempts to alter doctrine. Indeed the offense which brought
down the whole apparatus of Vatican censure upon Lefebvre
was his famous Declaration that he and his seminarians were

loyal to Rome, "but to the Rome of tradition, not the Rome of Modernists." It is asserted by Ecône seminarians that this Declaration was provoked by an address that one member of an Apostolic Visitation delivered to the Ecône students, in which he was understood to deny both the Virgin Birth and the immortality of the soul.

This Declaration led to Lefebvre's being interrogated by an *ad hoc* committee of three Cardinals (Garrone, Wright, and Tabera). Partial·transcripts of these strange proceedings have been published, and make it clear what a travesty of any judicial proceeding it was. Garrone, who emerges as an unintelligent man lacking self-control, hectors and shouts down the Archbishop. At the same time it emerges that he is judge, prosecuting counsel, and tale-bearer to the Pope. During this interrogation Lefebvre asks that he be judged by the Holy Office, which is alone authorized to pronounce that his declaration was heretical. This request is, of course, refused, since no grounds could possibly be found for an adverse judgment. Once again an avenue of appeal is blocked; the Vatican is clearly determined that there shall be no legal process. All this is done in the name of the Pope, and through his authority.

29 June 1975
The Ordinations at Ecône

The Feast of SS. Peter and Paul, 29 June 1975, was celebrated at Ecône with the ordination to the priesthood of three deacons. The necessary legal procedure for their incardination in the dioceses of bishops sympathetic to Archbishop Lefebvre had already been completed. Approximately a thousand of the faithful were present and hundreds were unable to find a place inside the chapel. Subject to the approval of the civil authorities, a new and much larger chapel will eventually be built at Ecône.

In July 1975, Mgr. Lefebvre's second appeal was rejected. Technically, as from July 1975, the Society of St. Pius X and its foundations no longer existed. In the language of George Orwell's *Nineteen Eighty-four*, the Seminary at Ecône, the most flourishing and most orthodox seminary in the West, then became an unseminary. The most serious aspect of this situation was that some members of religious orders teaching at Ecône had to leave, as their superiors would not allow them to remain in an institution which had no legal existence.

About a dozen students did not return in September as a result of the changed situation. But given the enormous pressure brought to bear upon the students and their families, this is a significantly small proportion.

However, the number of young men seeking to enter Ecône was still so high that dozens had to be refused even after filling the vacancies caused by those who had left.

15 July 1975

On 15 July 1975, Mgr. Lefebvre wrote to thank Hamish Fraser for devoting an entire issue of *Approaches* to the campaign against Ecône. This letter is significant for its affirmation of the Archbishop's belief that Cardinal Villot was the moving spirit behind the campaign.

Dear Mr. Hamish Fraser,

I have read with much interest your brochure on the war against Ecône and I thank you for it with all my heart, for it indeed throws light on our problems and you do so dispassionately and with an exactitude that I like very much. It is my wish that this brochure may have a really wide distribution.

For the moment, I have been refused an audience with the Holy Father.

It is Cardinal Villot himself who intervened and it is he also who nullified the appeal to the Apostolic Signature. It is he, personally, who took things in hand and who seems determined to encompass our disappearance.

But we have such a volume of support from thousands and thousands of people that we have decided to continue despite everything, persuaded as we are that we are doing the work desired by the Church and by the Pope himself.

Thanking you again for your faithful friendship, I assure you of mine and of my prayers.

† Marcel Lefebvre

The *Catholic Herald* (London) of 25 July 1975 carried an N. C. Report stating that Mgr. Mamie had invited the students from Ecône to contact Mgr. Adam (Bishop of Sion) or himself in order that arrangements could be made for them to continue their studies for the priesthood at the University of Fribourg. Cardinal Marty, Archbishop of Paris, had associated himself with this invitation and the bishops promised that any student who wished could be incardinated into his original diocese or into a religious order.

The French daily, *L'Aurore*, reported on 21 July that Cardinal Garrone had offered to arrange for the French-speaking seminarians to enter the Pontifical French Seminary in Rome. The enemies of Ecône were clearly distressed that, notwithstanding their machinations, the Seminary still existed.

VIII

The War of Attrition

UNDER THE HEADING "Official Information of the Conference of Swiss Bishops concerning Mgr. Lefebvre's Foundations," the 12 December 1975 issue of the *Nouvelliste* (of Sion, Switzerland) reproduced a Dossier concerning Ecône which had just been released for publication by the Swiss Bishops' Conference.

This Dossier comprised the following documents:

1. A letter from Cardinal Villot dated 27 October 1975 addressed to the Presidents of Episcopal Conferences.
2. The text of a typewritten letter signed by His Holiness Pope Paul VI dated 29 June 1975 addressed to Mgr. Lefebvre.
3. The text of an entirely handwritten letter dated 8 September 1975, from His Holiness Pope Paul VI to Mgr. Lefebvre.
4. The text of the handwritten reply from Mgr. Lefebvre to His Holiness Pope Paul VI dated 24 September 1975.
5. In addition to these documents the *Nouvelliste* also pub-

lished a commentary on them by Mgr. Pierre Mamie, the Bishop of Lausanne, Geneva, and Fribourg.

These documents are included here in their chronological order, with the exception of the papal letter of 29 June, which has already been included under that date.

8 September 1975
Letter of Pope Paul VI
to Archbishop Lefebvre

To Our Brother in the Episcopate, Marcel Lefebvre
Former Archbishop-Bishop of Tulle

Awareness of the mission with which the Lord has entrusted Us led Us on 29 June last to address to you an exhortation that was both urgent and fraternal.

Since that date, We have waited each day for a sign on your part expressing your submission—or better than that, your attachment and unreserved fidelity—to the Vicar of Christ. Nothing has yet come. It seems that you have not renounced any of your activities and, even, that you are developing new projects.

Do you perhaps consider that your intentions have been badly understood? Do you perhaps believe the Pope to be badly informed, or subject to pressure? Dear Brother, your attitude in Our eyes is so serious that—We tell you again—We have Ourselves attentively examined it in all aspects, Our primary concern being for the good of the Church and a particular concern for persons. The decision which We confirmed to you in Our previous letter was taken after mature reflection and before the Lord.

The time has now come for you to declare yourself clearly. Despite the grief We feel in making public Our interventions, We can no longer delay doing so if you do not soon declare your complete submission. We implore you to force us neither to take such a step nor afterwards take sanctions against a refusal of obedience.

Pray to the Holy Spirit, dear Brother. He will show you the necessary renunciations and help you to re-enter in the path of a full communion with the Church and with the successor of Peter. We Ourselves invoke Him on your behalf while telling you once more of Our affection and Our affliction.

8 September 1975

Paul PP VI

24 September 1975
Letter of Mgr. Marcel Lefebvre
to Pope Paul VI

Dear Holy Father,

If my reply to the letter of Your Holiness is belated, it is that it was repugnant to me to make a public act that could have led people to think that I had the pretension of treating the successor of Peter on a footing of equality.

On the other hand, on the advice of the Nunciature, I hasten to write these few lines to Your Holiness in order to express my unreserved attachment to the Holy See and to the Vicar of Christ. I very much regret that my feelings in this regard could have been called in question and that certain of my expressions may have been wrongly interpreted.

It is to His Vicar that Jesus Christ confided the responsibilities of confirming his brethren in the faith and whom He asked to watch that each Bishop should faithfully guard the deposit of faith, in accordance with the words of Paul to Timothy.

It is this conviction which guides me and has always guided me throughout the whole of my priestly and apostolic life. It is this faith which I endeavour with God's help to inculcate in the youth who are preparing themselves for the priesthood.

This faith is the soul of Catholicism affirmed by the Gospels: "on this Rock I shall build my Church."

With all my heart, I renew my devotion towards the Successor of Peter, "The Master of Truth" for the whole Church, *"columna et firmamentum Veritatis."*

† Marcel Lefebvre

27 October 1975
Letter from Cardinal Villot to
the Presidents of Episcopal Conferences

Your Eminence, Your Excellency,

On 6 May last, in full agreement with the Holy See, Mgr. Pierre Mamie, Bishop of Lausanne, Geneva, and Fribourg, withdrew canonical approval from the Priestly Fraternity of St. Pius X, directed by Mgr. Marcel Lefebvre, former Archbishop-Bishop of Tulle.

The foundations of this Fraternity, and particularly the Seminary of Ecône, by this same action lost the right to exist. Thus a particularly complex sad affair was settled from the juridical point of view.

What point have we reached in this matter six months afterwards? Mgr. Lefebvre has not yet accepted in deeds the decision of the competent authority. His activities continue, his projects tend to assume concrete form in various countries, his writings and talks continue to lead astray a certain number of confused Catholics. It is alleged here and there that the Holy Father has allowed himself to be influenced or that the development of the procedure has been vitiated by formal defects.

It is not simply alleged "here and there" that there were formal defects in the legal proceedings against Mgr. Lefebvre, it is Mgr. Lefebvre himself who makes the claim, and his advocate was prepared to prove it if granted a proper legal hearing. The fact that the Archbishop was denied the right to appeal certainly gives credence to his allegation.

Fidelity to the Church of yesterday is invoked in order to disassociate oneself from the Church of today as though the Church of the Lord could change in nature or in form.

In view of the harm done to Christian people by the continuation of such a situation and only after having utilized all the resources of charity, the Sovereign Pontiff has ordered that the following information, which should contribute towards dispelling remaining doubts, be communicated to all Episcopal Conferences.

The Priestly Fraternity of St. Pius X was instituted on 1 November 1970 by Mgr. Francois Charriere, the then Bishop of Lausanne, Geneva, and Fribourg. A diocesan pious union, it was destined in the mind of Mgr. Marcel Lefebvre to be subsequently transformed into a Religious Community without vows. Until its recognition as such — which recognition morever was not given — it consequently continued to be subject to the jurisdiction of the Bishop of Fribourg and to the vigilance of the dioceses in which it carried on its activities. Such is the position according to law.

However, it became apparent soon enough that those responsible refused all control by the legitimate authorities. . .

This is a straightforward calumny. The letter from Cardinal Wright cited under the date 18 February 1971 proves that Archbishop Lefebvre was keeping the appropriate Vatican departments acquainted with the progress of the Fraternity—and that this progress was regarded with warm approbation by Cardinal Wright. The only attempt by "legitimate authority" to exercise "control" was the Apostolic Visitation of November 1974. In his letter of 25 January 1975 (cited in full under that date), Cardinal Garrone thanked Mgr. Lefebvre for the total cooperation which he had given to the Apostolic Visitor. "We are grateful to you for having given him every facility to accomplish the mission on behalf of the Holy See."

. . . remaining deaf to their warnings . . .

This is another calumny. As no such warnings from "the legitimate authorities" were received by Mgr. Lefebvre (and not even one is cited by Cardinal Villot), the Archbishop can hardly be accused of remaining deaf to them!

. . . persevering against the whole world in their chosen direction: systematic opposition to the Second Vatican Council and to post-conciliar reform.

This is a very vague and sweeping allegation. It should be noted that opposition to the Council itself and to the reforms claiming to implement it are bracketed together. Throughout the entire campaign against the Archbishop he is invariably ordered to accept the Council and the Reforms—it is never conceded that a distinction can be made between them. In this respect I must ask readers to refer to my book *Pope John's Council,* where I provide ample documentation to prove that a good number of the reforms claiming to implement the Council cannot possibly be justified by specific reference to a Council document. I also demonstrate that there are, as Mgr. Lefebvre claims, some badly worded passages in the actual documents which have been utilized by the Liberals in their efforts to undermine the Church. Now either these ambiguous passages exist or they do not. If they do exist, then Mgr. Lefebvre clearly has a duty to draw attention to them; if his criticisms are unfounded, then this should be pointed out. At the moment his opponents are not prepared to discuss, let alone attempt to refute, his criticisms. Their invariable attitude is that anyone who criticizes the documents of Vatican II is *ipso facto* in the wrong.

It was not acceptable that candidates for the priesthood should be trained in a spirit of hostility towards the living Church, towards the Pope, towards the Bishops, and towards the priests with whom they were asked to collaborate.

Not one word is adduced to prove that the seminarians were trained in this spirit. Quite clearly, the testimony of the Apostolic Visitors gave no such impression or it would have been used against the Archbishop.

It became urgent to help the seminarists who had thus been train-ed. Finally, it appeared necessary to remedy the increasing trouble in several dioceses in Switzerland and other nations.

In view of the gravity of this matter and anxious that the inquiry should be conducted quite dispassionately, the Holy Father therefore set up a Commission of Cardinals composed of three members: Cardinal Gabriel-Marie Garrone, Prefect of the Congregation for Catholic Education (who was President of the Commission); Cardinal John Wright, Prefect of the Congregation for the Clergy; and Cardinal Arturo Tabera, Prefect of the Congregation for Religious and Secular Institutes. This Commission had as its task, first to collect the fullest possible information and to proceed to an examination of all aspects of the problem, and then to propose its findings to the Sovereign Pontiff.

The first phase of its work lasted approximately a year. That is to say that, contrary to certain allegations, it was done without any haste and time was taken for profound reflection. The evidence of a very large number of witnesses was received. An Apostolic Visitation of the Fraternity was effected at Ecône (11-13 November 1974) by Mgr. Albert Descamps, Rector Emeritus of the University of Louvain, and Secretary of the Pontifical Biblical Commission, assisted by Mgr. Guillaume Onclin, in the capacity of canonical adviser. Mgr. Mamie and Mgr. Adam, Bishop of Sion (the diocese in which Ecône is situated), were heard on several occasions and Mgr. Lefebvre was twice called to Rome, in February and March 1975. The Pope himself was frequently and scrupulously kept informed of the development of the inquiry and its results, which he had to confirm in the course of the summer to Mgr. Lefebvre (cf. the two Pontifical letters which will be referred to later).

The second phase resulted in the decision which is known, a decision made public by order of His Holiness communicated to the Cardinals' Commision, and a decision without right of appeal since each of its points was approved *in forma specifica* by the Supreme Authority.

Once again it must be stated that not one shred of documentary evidence of the Pope's approval *in forma specifica* can be produced dated earlier than his letter of 29 June 1975. It is reasonable to presume that Cardinal Villot forbade Cardinal Staffa to examine the Archbishop's second appeal in order to prevent this serious irregularity from being brought to light.

I shall not deal any further with the history of what happened. If you consider it useful, you can in effect ask for details from the Pontifical Representative in your country. He has been instructed to give you such information should it be needed.

It is therefore now clear that the Priestly Fraternity of St. Pius X has ceased to exist, that those who still claim to be members of it cannot pretend—*a fortiori*—to escape the jurisdiction of the diocesan Ordinaries, and, finally, that these same Ordinaries are gravely requested not to accord incardination in their dioceses to the young men who declare themselves to be engaged in the service of the Fraternity.

This paragraph makes clear the true purpose of Cardinal Villot's letter. In order to be ordained, a priest must be accepted (incardinated) into either a diocese or a religious order. By instructing the world's bishops to refuse to incardinate the students from Ecône, Cardinal Villot imagined that he had signed the death-warrant of Ecône, since students would not go there to study for the priesthood when there was no possibility of their being ordained. Up to this point the priests ordained at Ecône had all been regularly incardinated into dioceses in accordance with the requirements of Canon Law.

It remains for me to present to you the enclosed documents, two letters addressed by the Holy Father to Mgr. Lefebvre, and a reply from the latter. Their publication had been delayed until now: the Gospel teaches that fraternal correction must first be attempted with discretion. This is also the reason why the Holy See has abstained from all kinds of polemic from the beginning of this affair and has never sought to react to the insinuations, lying manipulation of the facts, and personal accusations so liberally diffused in the press. But there sometimes comes a moment when silence can no longer be kept and when it is necessary for the Church to know (cf. Mt. 18: 15-17).*

There had indeed been a press campaign based on "insinuations, lying manipulation of the facts, and personal accusations"—but it was in operation against Mgr. Lefebvre rather than on his behalf. As the entry for 8 May 1975 makes clear, a lead was given in this campaign by an article in *L'Osservatore Romano*, probably written by Cardinal Villot himself:

The first letter dated 29 June 1975 had been taken to Ecône on 8 July. It has never been answered. You will read in it, as in the second (8 September) the grief of the Common Father and the hope he still entertains, even if no sign of real good will has yet been given him. You will see that his dearest wish is to receive his Brother in the Episcopate whenever he submits.

The letter from Mgr. Lefebvre certainly shows evidence of personal devotion with regard to the Pontiff, but unfortunately nothing authorizes one to think that the author is resolved to obey. It cannot therefore itself alone be considered a satisfactory reply.

Your Eminence/Your Excellency, if circumstances are such that the problem affects you in one way or another, you yourself or other Bishops of your country, you will have it at heart in this Holy Year to work for peace and reconciliation. The hour is not one for polemics, it is rather one for charity and for examination of conscience. Excesses often call forth other excesses. Vigilance in doctrinal and liturgical

---

* "If thy brother does thee wrong, go at once and tax him with it, as a private matter between thee and him; and so, if he will listen to thee, thou hast won thy brother. If he will not listen to thee, take with thee one or two more, that the whole matter may be certified by the voice of two or three witnesses. If he will not listen to them, then speak of it to the Church; and if he will not even listen to the Church, then count him all one with the heathen and the publican." The scriptural text is not given in Cardinal Villot's letter, which includes merely the scriptural reference.

matters, clear-sightedness in discerning the reforms which require to be undertaken, patience and tact in the guidance of the People of God, solicitude for priestly vocations and an exacting preparation for the tasks of the ministry, all that is undoubtedly the most effective manner in which a Pastor can bear witness.

I am sure you will understand this appeal and, with you, I desire that the unity of the members of the Church may shine forth still more in the future.

† Jean Cardinal Villot

3 September 1975
Letter to Friends and Benefactors*
(No. 9)

Dear Friends and Benefactors,

It seems to me that the moment has come to bring to your knowledge the latest events concerning Ecône, and the attitude which in conscience before God we believe we must take in these grave circumstances.

As far as the appeal to the Apostolic Signature is concerned: the last attempt on the part of my lawyer, to find out from the Cardinals forming the Supreme Court exactly how the Pope intervened in the proceedings being brought against us, was stopped in its tracks by a hand-written letter from Cardinal Villot to Cardinal Staffa, President of the Supreme Court, ordering him to forbid any appeal.

As for my audience with the Holy Father, it has likewise been refused by Cardinal Villot. I shall obtain an audience only when my work has disappeared and when I have con-

---

*The Ecône Newsletter No. 9 has been included at this point (not in chronological order) because it was referred to by Mgr. Mamie in a commentary published in the *Nouvelliste* of 12 December 1975. Readers would not have been able to form a balanced judgment of Mgr. Mamie's commentary without reading the Newsletter first. The commentary follows immediately after Newsletter No. 9.

formed my way of thinking to that which reigns supreme in today's reformed Church.

However, the most important event is undoubtedly the signed letter from the Holy Father (of 29 June) presented as the Pope's own handwriting by the Papal Nuncio in Bern, but in fact typewritten, and which takes up again in a new form the arguments or rather the statements of the Cardinal's letter. This I received on 10 July last. It calls on me to make a public act of submission "to the Council, to the post-conciliar reforms, and to the orientations to which the Pope himself is committed (*orientations qui engagent le pape lui-même*)."

A second letter from the Pope which I received on 10 September urgently required an answer to the first letter.

This time, through no desire of my own, my only aim being to serve the Church in the humble and very consoling task of giving Her true priests devoted to Her service, I found myself confronted with the Church authorities at their topmost level on earth, the Pope. So I wrote an answer to the Holy Father, stating my submission to the successor of Peter in his essential function, that of faithfully transmitting to us the deposit of the faith.

If we consider the facts from a purely material point of view, it is a trifling matter: the suppression of a Society which has barely come into existence, with no more than a few dozen members, the closing down of a Seminary—how little it is in reality, hardly worth anyone's attention.

On the other hand if for a moment we heed the reactions stirred up in Catholic and even Protestant, Orthodox and atheist circles, moreover throughout the entire world, the countless articles in the world press, reactions of enthusiasm and true hope, reactions of spite and opposition, reactions of mere curiosity, we cannot help thinking, even against our will, that Ecône is posing a problem reaching far beyond the modest confines of the Society and its Seminary, a deep and unavoidable problem that cannot be pushed to one side with a sweep of the hand, nor solved by any formal order, from whatever authority it may come. For the problem of Ecône is the problem of thousands and millions of Christian consciences, distressed, divided and torn for the past ten years by the agonizing dilemma: whether to obey and risk losing one's faith, or disobey and keep one's faith intact; whether to obey and join in the destruction of the Church, whether to accept the reformed Liberal Church, or to go on belonging to the Catholic Church.

It is because Ecône is at the heart of this crucial problem, seldom till now posed with such fullness or gravity, that so many people are looking to this house which has resolutely made its choice of belonging to the eternal Church and of refusing to belong to the reformed Liberal Church.

And now the Church, through her official representatives, is taking up a position against Ecône's choice, thus condemning in public the traditional training of priests, in the name of the Second Vatican Council, in the name of post-conciliar reforms, and in the name of post-conciliar orientations to which the Pope himself is committed.

How can such opposition to Tradition in the name of a Council and its practical application be explained? Can one reasonably oppose, should one in reality oppose, a Council and its reforms? What is more, can one and should one oppose the orders of a hierarchy commanding one to follow the Council and all the official post-conciliar changes?

That is the grave problem, today, after ten post-conciliar years, confronting our conscience, as a result of the condemnation of Ecône.

One cannot give a prudent answer to these questions without making a rapid survey of the history of Liberalism and Catholic Liberalism over the last centuries. The present can only be explained by the past.

Principles of Liberalism

Let us first define in a few words the Liberalism of which the most typical historical example is Protestantism. Liberalism pretends to free man from any constraint not wished or accepted by himself.

First liberation: frees the intelligence from any objective truth imposed on it. The Truth must be accepted as differing according to the individual or group of individuals, so it is necessarily divided up. The making of the Truth and the search for it go on all the time. Nobody can claim to have exclusive or complete possession of it. It is obvious how contrary that is to Our Lord Jesus Christ and His Church.

Second liberation: frees the faith from any dogmas imposed on us, formulated in a definitive fashion, and which the intelligence and will must submit to. Dogmas, according to the Liberal, must be submitted to the test of reason and science, constantly, because science is constantly progressing. Hence it is impossible to admit any revealed truth defined once and for all. It will be noticed how opposed such a principle is to the Revelation of Our Lord and His divine authority.

Lastly, *Third liberation:* frees us from the law. The law, according to the Liberal, limits freedom and imposes on it a restraint first moral and then physical. The law and its restraints are an affront to human dignity and human conscience. Conscience is the supreme law. The Liberal confuses liberty with license. Our Lord Jesus Christ is the living Law, as He is the Word of God; it will be realized once more how deep runs the opposition between the Liberal and Our Lord.

Consequences of Liberalism

The consequences of Liberal principles are to destroy the philosophy of being and to refuse all definition of things, so as to shut oneself into nominalism or existentialism and evolutionism. Everything is subject to mutation and change.

A second consequence, as grave as the first, if not more so, is to deny the supernatural, and hence original sin, justification by grace, the true reason for the Incarnation, the Sacrifice of the Cross, the Church, the Priesthood. Everything Our Lord accomplished gets falsified; which works out in practical terms as a Protestant view of the Liturgy of the Sacrifice of the Mass and the Sacraments whose object is no longer to apply the merits of the Redemption to souls, to each single soul, in order to impart to it the grace of divine life and to prepare it for eternal life through its belonging to the Mystical Body of Our Lord, but whose central purpose from now on is the belonging to a human community of a religious character. The whole liturgical Reform reflects this change of direction.

Another consequence: the denying of all personal authority as sharing in the authority of God. Human dignity demands that man submit only to what he agrees to submit to. Since, however, no society can live without authority, man will accept only authority approved by the majority, because that represents authority being delegated by the largest number of individuals to a designated person or group of persons, such authority being never more than delegated.

Now these principles and their consequences, requiring freedom of thought, freedom of teaching, freedom of conscience, freedom to choose one's own religion, these false freedoms which presuppose the secular state, the separation of Church and State, have been, ever since the Council of Trent, steadily condemned by the successors of Peter, starting with the Council of Trent inself.

Condemnation of Liberalism
by the Magisterium of the Church

It is the Church's opposition to Protestant Liberalism which gave rise to the Council of Trent, and hence the considerable importance of this dogmatic Council in the struggle against Liberal errors, in the defense of the Truth and the Faith, in particular in the codifying of the Liturgy of the Mass and the Sacraments, in the definitions concerning justification by grace.

Let us list a few of the most important documents, completing and confirming the Council of Trent's doctrine:

—The Bull *Auctorem fidei* of Pius VI against the Council of Pistoia.

—The Encyclical *Mirari vos* of Gregory XVI against Lamennais.

—The Encyclical *Quanta cura* and the *Syllabus* of Pius IX.

—The Encyclical *Immortale Dei* of Leo XIII condemning the secularization of states.

—*The Papal Acts of Saint Pius X* against the Sillon and Modernism, and especially the Decree *Lamantabili* and the Anti-Modernist Oath.

—The Encyclical *Divini Redemptoris* of Pius XI against Communism.

—The Encyclical *Humani generis* of Pius XII.

Thus Liberalism and Liberal Catholicism have always been condemned by Peter's successors in the name of the Gospel and apostolic Tradition.

This obvious conclusion is of capital importance in deciding what attitude to adopt in order to show that we are unfailingly at one with the Church's Magisterium and with Peter's successors. Nobody is more attached than we are to Peter's successor reigning today when he echoes the apostolic Traditions and all his predecessors' teachings. For it is the very definition of Peter's successor to guard the deposit of Faith and hand it faithfully down. Here is what Pope Pius IX proclaimed on the subject in *Pastor aeternus:*

For the Holy Spirit was not promised to the successors of Peter, that by His revelation they might make known new doctrine, but that

by His assistance they might individually keep and faithfully expound the revelation or deposit of faith delivered through the Apostles.

Influence of Liberalism on Vatican II

Now we come to the question which so concerns us: How is it possible that anyone can, in the name of the Second Vatican Council, oppose the centuries-old apostolic traditions, and so bring into question the Catholic Priesthood itself, and its essential act, the Holy Sacrifice of the Mass?

A grave and tragic ambiguity hangs over the Second Vatican Council which is presented by the Popes themselves* in terms favoring that ambiguity: for instance, the Council of the *aggiornamento*, the "bringing up-to-date" of the Church, the pastoral non-dogmatic Council, as the Pope again called it just a month ago.

This way of presenting the Council, in the Church and the world as they were in 1962, ran very grave risks which the Council did not succeed in avoiding. It was easy to interpret these words in such a way that the Council was opened wide to the errors of Liberalism. A Liberal minority among the Council Fathers, and above all among the Cardinals, was very active, very well organized and fully supported by a constellation of Modernist theologians and numerous secretariats. Take for example the enormous flow of printed matter from the IDOC, subsidized by the Bishops' Conferences of Germany and Holland.

Everything was in their favor, for their demanding the instant adaptation of the Church to modern man, in other words man who wishes to be freed from all shackles, for their presenting the Church as out of touch and impotent, for their saying "*mea culpa*" on behalf of their predecessors. The Church is presented as being as guilty as the Protestants and

*Popes John XXIII and Paul VI.

Orthodox for the divisions of old. She must ask present-day Protestants for forgiveness.

The Traditional Church is guilty in Her wealth, in Her triumphalism; the Council Fathers feel guilty at being out of the world, at not belonging to the world; they are already blushing at their episcopal insignia, soon they will be ashamed of their cassocks.

Soon this atmosphere of liberation will spread to all fields and it will show in the spirit of collegiality which will veil the shame felt at exercising a personal authority so opposed to the spirit of modern man, let us say Liberal man. The Pope and Bishops will exercise their authority collegially in Synods, Bishops' Conferences, Priests' Councils. Finally the Church is opened wide to the principles of the modern world.

The Liturgy too will be Liberalized, adapted, subjected to experiments by the Bishops' Conferences.

Religious liberty, ecumenism, theological research, the revision of Canon Law will all soften down the triumphalism of a Church which used to proclaim Herself the only ark of salvation! The Truth is to be found divided up among all religions, joint research will carry the universal religious community forward around the Church.

Geneva Protestants, Marsaudon in his book *Ecumenism as Seen by a Freemason*, Liberals like Fesquet are triumphant. At last the era of Catholic states will disappear. All religions equal before the Law! "The Church free in the free State," Lamennais' formula! Now the Church is in touch with the modern world! The Church's privileged status before the Law and all the documents cited above turn into museum pieces for an age that has out-grown them! Read the beginning of the Schema on The Church in the Modern World (*Gaudium et Spes*), the description of how modern times are changing; read the conclusions, they are pure Liberalism. Read the Declaration on Religious Freedom and compare it with the Encyclical *Mirari vos* of Gregory XVI, or with *Quanta cura* of

Pius IX, and you can recognize the contradiction almost word for word.*

To say that Liberal ideas had no influence on the Second Vatican Council is to fly in the face of the evidence. The internal and external evidence both make that influence abundantly clear.

Influence of Liberalism on the post-conciliar reforms and trends

And if we pass on from the Council to the reforms and changes of direction since the Council the proof is so clear as to be blinding. Now, let us take careful note that in the letters from Rome calling upon us to make a public act of submission, the Council and its subsequent reforms and orientations are always presented as being three parts of one whole. Hence all those people are gravely mistaken who talk of a wrong interpretation of the Council, as though the Council in itself was perfect and could not be interpreted along the lines of the subsequent reforms and changes.

Clearer than any written account of the Council, the official reforms and changes that have followed in its wake show how the Council is officially meant to be interpreted.

Now on this point we need not elaborate: the facts speak for themselves, alas all too eloquently.

What still remains intact of the pre-conciliar Church? Where has the self-destruction (as Pope Paul called it) not been at work? Catechetics—seminaries—religious congregations—liturgy of the Mass and the Sacraments—constitution of the Church—concept of the Priesthood. Liberal ideas have wrought havoc all round and are taking the Church far beyond Protestant ideas, to the amazement of the Protestants and to the disgust of the Orthodox.

*See Appendix IV for a discussion of the Declaration on Religious Freedom.

One of the most horrifying practical applications of these Liberal principles is the opening wide of the Church to embrace all errors and in particular the most monstrous error ever devised by Satan: Communism. Communism now has official access to the Vatican, and its world revolution is made markedly easier by the official non-resistance of the Church, nay, by her regular support of the revolution, in spite of the despairing warnings by cardinals who have been through Communist jails.

The refusal of this pastoral Council to issue any official condemnation of Communism alone suffices to disgrace it for all time, when one thinks of the tens of millions of martyrs, of people having their personalities scientifically destroyed in the psychiatric hospitals, serving as guinea-pigs for all sorts of experiments. And the pastoral Council which brought together 2,350 Bishops said not a word, in spite of the 450 signatures of Fathers demanding a condemnation, which I myself took to Mgr. Felici, Secretary of the Council, together with Mgr. Sigaud, Archbishop of Diamantina.

Need the analysis be pushed any further to reach its conclusion? These lines seem to me to be enough to justify one's refusing to follow this Council, these reforms, these changes in all their Liberalism and Neo-modernism.

We should like to reply to the objection that will no doubt be raised under the heading of obedience, and of the jurisdiction held by those who seek to impose this Liberalization. Our reply is: In the Church, law and jurisdiction are at the service of the Faith, the primary reason for the Church. There is no law, no jurisdiction which can impose on us a lessening of our Faith.

We accept this jurisdiction and this law when they are at the service of the Faith. But on what basis can they be judged? Tradition, the Faith taught for 2,000 years. Every Catholic can and must resist anyone in the Church who lays hands on his Faith, the Faith of the eternal Church, relying on his childhood catechism.

Defending his Faith is the prime duty of every Christian, all the more of every priest and bishop. Wherever an order carries with it a danger of corrupting Faith and morals, it becomes a grave duty not to obey it.

It is because we believe that our whole Faith is endangered by the post-conciliar reforms and changes that it is our duty to disobey, and to maintain the traditions of our Faith. The greatest service we can render to the Catholic Church, to Peter's successor, to the salvation of souls and of our own, is to say "No" to the reformed Liberal Church, because we believe in our Lord Jesus Christ, Son of God made Man, Who is neither Liberal nor reformable.

One final objection: the Council is a Council like the others, therefore it should be followed like the others. It is like them in its ecumenicity and in the manner of its being called, yes; like them in its object, which is what is essential, no. A non-dogmatic Council need not be infallible; it is only infallible when it repeats traditional dogmatic truths.

How do you justify your attitude towards the Pope?

We are the keenest defenders of his authority as Peter's successor, but our attitude is governed by the words of Pius IX quoted above. We applaud the Pope when he echoes Tradition and is faithful to his mission of handing down the deposit of the Faith. We accept changes in close conformity with Tradition and the Faith. We do not feel bound by any obedience to accept changes going against Tradition and threatening our Faith. In that case, we take up position behind the papal documents listed above.

We do not see how, in conscience, a Catholic layman, priest or bishop can adopt any other attitude towards the grievous crisis the Church is going through. *Nihil innovetur nisi quod traditum est*—innovate nothing outside Tradition.

May Jesus and Mary help us to remain faithful to our episcopal promises! "Call not true what is false, call not good what is evil." That is what we were told at our consecration.

On the Feast of Saint Pius X, 1975

† Marcel Lefebvre

A few lines added to the above document will inform you of how our work is progressing.

A dozen seminarians left us at the end of the academic year, some of them because of the repeated attacks on us by the hierarchy. Ten more have been called up for military service. On the other hand, we have 25 new seminarians entering at Ecône, 5 at Weissbad in the Appenzell Canton, and 6 at Armada in the USA.

Moreover, we have five postulant brothers and eight postulant sisters. You can see that young people, by their sense of the Faith, know where to find the sources of the graces necessary for their vocation. We are preparing for the future: in the United States by building a chapel at Armada with 18 rooms for seminarians; in England by buying a larger house for the four priests now dispensing true doctrine, the true Sacrifice and the Sacraments. In France, we have acquired our first Priory, at St. Michel-en-Brenne. These priories, including one house for priests and brothers, another for sisters and a house of 25 to 30 rooms for the spiritual exercises, will be sources of prayer-life and sanctification for layfolk and priests, and centers of missionary activity. In Switzerland at Weissbad, a Society of St. Charles Borromeo is putting rooms at our disposal in a rented building in which private lessons are being organized for German-speaking students.

That is why we are counting on the support of your prayers and generosity in order to continue, despite the trials, this training of priests indispensable to the life of the Church. We are being attacked neither by the Church nor by the Successor of Peter, but by churchmen steeped in the errors of Liberalism and occupying high positions, who are making use of their power to make the Church of the past disappear, and to

install in its place a new Church which no longer has anything to do with Catholicism.

Therefore we must save the true Church and Peter's successor from this diabolical assault which calls to mind the
prophecies of the Book of Revelation.

Let us pray unceasingly to the Blessed Virgin Mary, St.
Joseph, the Holy Angels, St. Pius X, to come to our help so
that the Catholic Faith may triumph over errors. Let us remain united in this Faith, let us avoid disputations, let us
love one another, let us pray for those who persecute us and
let us render good for evil.

And may God bless you.
† Marcel Lefebvre

A Commentary by Mgr. Mamie, published in
the *Nouvelliste* of Sion of 12 December 1975

In a letter to friends and benefactors of the Priestly Fraternity of
St. Pius X (No. 9, dated the Feast of St. Pius X, 1975)—which has been
widely diffused—Mgr. Lefebvre writes:

"It seems to me that the moment has come to bring to your knowledge the latest events concerning Ecône, and the attitude which in conscience before God we believe we must take in these grave circumstances."

In the same letter he also states:

"It is because we believe that our whole Faith is endangered by the
post-conciliar reforms and changes that it is our duty to disobey, and to
maintain the traditions of our Faith. The greatest service we can render
to the Catholic Church, to Peter's successor, to the salvation of souls
and of our own, is to say "No" to the reformed Liberal Church, because we believe in Our Lord Jesus Christ, Son of God made Man, Who
is neither Liberal nor reformable."

On November 6 last, on Swiss Television there was a program dealing with *intégrisme*. * In this program prominence was given to liturgical initiatives in the form of Masses celebrated according to the rite of St. Pius V.

The journal *Le Monde,* in its issue of 27 November 1975, gives some information on the same question and in particular publishes a letter from the Superior General of the Holy Ghost Congregation which publicly disowns the positions taken by Mgr. Lefebvre.

The journal *La Croix,* in its issue of 27 November 1975, also informs its readers in an article entitled "Mgr. Lefebvre Refuses Obedience to Paul VI."

In accord with the Conference of Swiss Bishops, we have on our part decided to publish the letters which compose this new dossier. Some comments are necessary:

1. It is surprising that Mgr. Lefebvre had not replied to the first clear and paternal letter from the Sovereign Pontiff.

2. It was therefore necessary for the Pope to write a new letter in his own hand in order that Mgr. Lefebvre could acknowledge the authenticity of the first letter.

3. In his reply, Mgr. Lefebvre expresses his "unreserved attachment to the Holy See and to the Vicar of Christ."

4. However, as I see it, there is a contradiction between this affirmation on the one hand, and on the other the continued activities of the Ecône Seminary, the establishment of new institutions, certain positions taken against the Second Vatican Council and the Letter to Friends and Benefactors we have already cited, for this letter speaks of a "right to disobey."

It is with great sorrow that we communicate this information. We were so hopeful that Mgr. Lefebvre would have accepted the de-

---

Intégrisme is a very much misused word. However by *intégrisme* properly so called is meant the spirit of those who refuse to accept any changes whatsoever. It is not be be confused with Tradition which is the handing on of essential values, not accretions which have long since ceased to be relevant. Mgr. Mamie implicitly suggests that the traditional Mass exemplifies *intégrisme*-in other words, that it was so overburdened with historical accretions as to be no longer a vehicle of Tradition.

mands of the Sovereign Pontiff. It is more urgent than ever to intensify our prayers that the faithful, priests, and bishops remain attached by their actions to the Successor of Peter, for without attachment and submission to the Pope there is no longer a Catholic Church.

We recall:

a. That His Holiness Pope Paul wrote to Mgr. Lefebvre (in his letter of 29 June 1975): "Certainly, problems of another order entirely preoccupy Us equally—the superficiality of certain interpretations of conciliar documents, of individual or collective initiatives deriving sometimes rather from arbitrary wilfulness *(libre arbitre)* than from confident adhesion to the teaching of Scripture and Tradition, of initiatives which arbitrarily evoke the faith to justify them. We know them, We suffer because of them, and, for Our part, We strive in season and out of season to remedy them.

But how can one use things such as these to justify oneself in committing excesses which are gravely harmful? Such is not the right way to do things, since it makes use of ways comparable to those which are denounced."

b. That His Eminence Cardinal Villot, Secretary of State, wrote to us (in his letter of 27 October 1975):

"Vigilance in doctrinal and liturgical matters, clear-sightedness in discerning the reforms which require to be undertaken, patience and tact in the guidance of the People of God, solicitude for priestly vocations and an exacting preparation for the tasks of the ministry, all that is undoubtedly the most effective manner in which a Pastor can bear witness."

c. That we wrote (on 7 June last):

"However, we remain sad (but confident) because we have had to speak publicly of dissensions in the family of the children of God and of the sons of the Church. We should have loved to resolve our problems among ourselves in discretion and silence. We did not succeed in doing so. Let us pray very much that peace and confidence may be restored.''

May God enable us to remain faithful to the Truth with constant Charity.

Fribourg, 6 December 1975
† Pierre Mamie
Bishop

13 February 1976
Report of an interview granted by Mgr. Lefebvre
to Louis Salleron and published in
La France Catholique-Ecclesia

Louis Salleron: Monseigneur, not only in France, but throughout the entire world, there is an immense number of Catholics who have placed their trust in you because the Seminary of Ecône seems to them the rampart of their faith during what Father Bouyer has described as "the decomposition of Catholicism." However, many today are troubled because the information they read in the newspapers presents you as disobedient to the Pope.

Mgr. Lefebvre: It seems to me that, on the contrary, my Seminary is the clearest expression of an attitude of obedience to the Pope, successor of Peter and Vicar of Jesus Christ.

L. Salleron: You have however spoken of the "duty to disobey."

Mgr. Lefebvre: Undoubtedly. It is a duty to disobey the prescriptions of those who themselves constitute disobedience to the doctrine of the Church. You have a family. If your children receive in the catechism an official teaching, authorized or imposed, which either distorts or is silent with regard to the truths one must believe, your duty is to disobey those who presume to teach this new catechism to your children. In so doing, you obey the Church.

L. Salleron: Cardinal Villot has stated in writing that you refused to accept control by the competent ecclesiastical authorities. Is that true?

Mgr. Lefebvre: It is absolutely false. Besides, I have several times had the pleasure of a visit from Mgr. Adam (Bishop of Sion) and I have explicitly invited Mgr. Mamie (Bishop of Lausanne, Geneva and Fribourg) who has always refused to come, because he considered my Seminary illegal, although he declared in his letter suppressing it that the Seminary had (as from that moment only) *lost* its legal status.

L. Salleron: Cardinal Villot also says that you are systematically opposed to the Council. Is that true?

Mgr. Lefebvre: It is equally false (to say) that I am systematically opposed to the Second Vatican Council. But I am convinced that a Liberal spirit was active at the Council and became apparent frequently in conciliar texts, particularly in certain declarations such as that on religious freedom, the one on non-Christian religions and on the Church in the world. That is why it seems to me very legitimate to have considerable reservations concerning these texts.

Since authorized theological research calls in question veritable dogmas of our faith, I cannot understand why I should be condemned for discussing certain texts of a council which even the Pope himself has recently affirmed to be non-dogmatic. I am accused of infidelity to the Church while none of these theologians engaged in research is condemned. There are truly two weights and two measures.

L. Salleron: However, it is the Pope himself who seems to

think that you do not obey the Church.

Mgr. Lefebvre: Then there has been a misunderstanding. My thoughts and my will in this matter have always been entirely free from any ambiguity. One day I had occasion to write to the Abbé de Nantes: "I want you to know that if a Bishop breaks with Rome, it will not be me."

L. Salleron: Have you had some discussion with the Pope about this question?

Mgr. Lefebvre: No. It is precisely that which I deplore.

L. Salleron: He has not summoned you in order to let you know his mind on this question?

Mgr. Lefebvre: Not only have I not been invited, but I have never been able to obtain an audience with him, and for that reason I have been wondering if my request for an audience had been presented to him. Recently a Bishop whom I very much esteem has seen the Holy Father in order to tell him of the upset in his diocese caused by all measures taken against me which seems to represent a condemnation of my work. And he asked him to receive me. The Holy Father begged him to discuss this with Cardinal Villot, who told him: "There can be no question of this. The Pope could change his mind and there would be confusion." You see therefore that there is a screen between the Holy Father and me.

L. Salleron: In his second letter, the Pope told you that he is perfectly well informed concerning you.

Mgr. Lefebvre: Since I cannot have an audience with him I have a right to think that he is not "well informed."

L. Salleron: He is probably basing this on the Report of the two Apostolic Visitors who had been to Ecône and on the Report of the three Cardinals who interviewed you by express command of the Holy Father.

Mgr. Lefebvre: I don't know what was in these documents. As for the Report of the two Apostolic Visitors, it was not communicated to me. . .

L. Salleron: It is said to have been favorable to the Seminary at Ecône.

Mgr. Lefebvre: So they say, and I am happy because of that. But in fact I know nothing, since this report was not communicated to me. As for my discussions with Cardinals Garrone, Wright and Tabera, I can tell you the following fact: Cardinal Garrone most courteously asked me if I had any objection to the discussion being recorded. I willingly agreed and after the discussion I asked for a copy of the recording to be given to me. Cardinal Garrone agreed, saying it was my right. When I came to ask for the promised recording I was told that it would only be a typed transcript. That wasn't the same thing because there could be suppressions and modifications on the typed copy.

I was in Rome for several days. The promised copy should have been delivered to me. Seeing no sign of it, I telephoned to speed things up—only to be told that it wasn't possible for me to be given this copy but that I could come and see it on such and such a day at such and such an hour. I refused to be a party to this farce. And consequently, just as I don't know what was in the Apostolic Visitors' Report, neither do I know what was contained in the Report of the Cardinals' Commission. If the recording has been neither destroyed nor cut, I can assure you that it would be interesting to listen to. But, obviously, the Holy Father has been given only such reports as were prepared for him, and of which I am totally ignorant.

L. Salleron: In short, you have been condemned in a trial without your having been given the evidence.

Mgr. Lefebvre: It wasn't even a trial, for the Cardinals' Commission wasn't a tribunal and had never been presented to me as such. I have been condemned, as you say, in so irregular a manner that I can't see what the word "condemnation" can mean.

And this, be it noted, at a moment when we are told that the Church no longer condemns, and without having been able to be heard by the Holy Father, who has made dialogue the mark of his government. That is why I think that all this has been contrived behind his back.

L. Salleron: But what difficulty do you find in making the public act of submission that is being asked of you: i. e. "to the Council, to the post-conciliar reforms and to the orientations to which the Pope himself is committed"?

Mgr. Lefebvre: I find a diffculty in the equivocation which borders on falsehood. From the "Council" one proceeds to "post-conciliar reforms" and from there to the "orientations to which the Pope himself is committed." One no longer knows what precisely is involved. What is to be understood by the "orientations to which the Pope himself is committed"? Must we understand it to mean such of the orientations as involve the Pope personally (and what are these?), or the *actual* orientations of the Church, to all of which the Pope is committed?

When one sees what is happening in France—to speak only of our own country—am I to think that, in its collegiality, the episcopate has submitted "to the Council, to post-conciliar reforms, and to the orientations to which the Pope himself is committed"?

Logically, I must think so, since no public act of submission has been asked of the French Episcopate by Cardinal Villot or the Sovereign Pontiff. Is it therefore to the destruction of the priesthood, to the changing or the negation of the Holy Sacrifice of the Mass, to the abandonment of moral values, to the politicization of the Gospel, and to the constitution of a national Church centered on the episcopal conference and the secretariat of the episcopate that I must subscribe to bear witness to my communion with the Catholic Church and the Vicar of Christ? It is absurd. My Catholic faith and my duty as a bishop forbid me to do so.

L. Salleron: I believe that what you are being asked to do is simply to close the Seminary of Ecône.

Mgr. Lefebvre: But why? It is perhaps the only one that corresponds not only to the tradition of the Church but also to the Decree of Vatican II concerning the training of priests. Moreover, I had occasion one day to say so to Cardinal Garrone, who did not deny it.

L. Salleron: If, instead of asking you to make a badly defined act of submission, the Pope were to give you an express order by a new letter, to close the Seminary of Ecône, would you close it?

Mgr. Lefebvre: After a trial carried out in a proper way according to the elementary norms of natural law and ecclesiastical law, yes, I would agree to close my Seminary.

Let me be told in an explicit and concrete manner what I am being reproached with in my activities and in my writings, and let me be given the elementary right to defend myself with the help of an advocate.

L. Salleron: Despite everything, then, you are an optimist?

Mgr. Lefebvre: It isn't a question of optimism. I don't know what will happen, and sufficient unto the day is the evil thereof. But I have confidence however because, being supported by the millenary tradition of the Church, which cannot possibly have been mistaken, I cannot see how, this being so, I can be the subject of condemnation.

The ordeal which the Church is undergoing can be ended only by a return to the principles which make her continuous and everlasting.

21 February 1976
Letter from Pope Paul VI to Cardinal Villot

(The following is a translation of the text of an entirely hand-written letter, dated 21 February 1976, from Pope Paul to Cardinal Villot. It was reproduced photographically in *La France Catholique-Ecclesia* of 5 May 1976.)

To: Jean Villot, Our Secretary of State

We have taken notice of an interview requested of Mgr. Marcel Lefebvre by the weekly *France Catholique-Ecclesia* (No. 1322, of 13 February 1976).

Among the errors contained in this interview there is one which We wish to rectify Ourself: you would seem to be a screen placed between the Pope and Mgr. Lefebvre, an obstacle to the meeting which he wishes to have with Us. That is not true.

It is particularly significant that although the Holy Father does not say what other "errors" are contained in the interview, concerning the only one he does refer to specifically he confines himself to denying that Cardinal Villot acts as a screen between him and Mgr. Lefebvre. He does not deny that, having been begged to see Mgr. Lefebvre by an African Bishop-friend of Mgr. Lefebvre, he urged the Bishop to see Cardinal Villot, who promptly told him that this was out of the question since it might induce the Holy Father to change his mind.

If this is not "screening" the Holy Father it is only in the sense that to use the word "screen" in that context constitutes understatement.

We consider that before being received in audience Mgr. Lefebvre must renounce his inadmissible position concerning the Second Ecumenical Vatican Council and measures which We have promulgated or approved in matters liturgical and disciplinary (and by consequence, also doctrinal).

It has hitherto always been generally understood, and taught, that, far from being synonymous, the two terms were clearly distinguished. It would have been different had it been a case of insisting that what was essentially doctrinal was therefore also a matter of discipline. But to state the contrary, particularly with reference to post-conciliar reforms, is ominous indeed since it has hitherto been insisted with wearying monotony that these were of exclusively pastoral significance and did not imply any doctrinal change.

This position alas! he does not cease to affirm by words and deeds. A real change of attitude is therefore necessary, in order that the desired interview may take place in the spirit of fraternity and ecclesial unity which We have desired so much since the beginning of this painful affair, and above all since We have personally and on two occasions written to Mgr. Lefebvre.

In *Itinéraires* of April 1976, Jean Madiran adds this footnote:

"One asks why . . . it is only of Mgr. Lefebvre that these conditions are demanded: Paul in effect receives all kinds of people (abortionists, libertines, stars in immoral shows, free-masons, communists, terrorists, etc.) whose attitude is quite unsatisfactory, without 'a real change of attitude' being demanded of them before being received in audience . . . It seems increasingly obvious that this inequality of treatment is neither accidental nor arbitrary; it is an inevitable practical consequence of the axiom according to which Vatican II has more importance than the Council of Nicea.*

The theoretical prior importance accorded Vatican II . . . has given rise to a new form of communion. Those who approve or at least applaud the Council belong to this new communion and are fraternally received by Paul VI, even if they reject or know nothing of the preceding 20 Councils and the defined dogmas.

By contrast, those who remain faithful to the defined dogmas and to the entire apostolic tradition, but have reservations concerning the Council and the circumstantial reforms deriving from it, they alas! are considered as out of communion and find the door shut against them so long as they have not changed their attitude.

Thus the Council has the ambition of summarizing and the function of replacing everything that preceded it. It becomes the principal criterion of true and false, of good and evil.

It is only conciliar evolution which in turn has as much authority as and more importance than the Council itself.

One has a right to be more conciliar than the Council; one has no right to be less. It is only in this perspective that the official attitude with regard to Mgr. Lefebvre finds coherence, and explanation. But what a frightening coherence, what a terrible explanation."

*See Appendix III.

Pope Paul's letter continues:

We continue to hope that he will soon give Us, in deeds, the concrete proof of his fidelity to the Church and to the Holy See, from
which he has received so many marks of esteem and confidence.
We know that you share this hope ; that is why We authorize you to
make this letter public, in accordance with the good wishes and affection which We feel for you, Our collaborator in the apostolic charge.
With Our personal benediction.

Paulus PP VI
The Vatican, 21 February 1976.

27 March 1976
Letter to Friends and Benefactors
(No. 10)

Dear Friends and Benefactors,

Amidst trials and opposition our Work goes serenely ahead,
trusting in God and based on the Faith which does not
change and cannot be shaken.

On April 3rd there will be 11 more deacons at Ecône, and
many seminarians will on the same day be receiving Minor
Orders. Together with the dozen seminarians doing military
service, Ecône now counts 110 seminarians. We already have
some 40 applications for next October.

In Weissbad, as in Armada in the United States, applications are so numerous that both houses will soon be filled.

Our Sisters in Albano include four Novices and five Postulants. The latter will receive the habit on Easter Sunday,
and if one counts the four Americans who will be joining
them soon, plus the ten or so applicants for October, then
the House where they train will already be gathering together some 23 aspirants to the religious life.

They will be moving to France in October because the house at Albano, originally intended for young priests, will be occupied by the newly ordained sixth-year students.

Our Brothers have two Novices and seven Postulants. They will be gladly received in our various houses, increasing in number: four in the USA (Armada, New York, San José and Houston); two in England (Highclere and Sanderstead); one in Brussels; five in France, one in Germany (Munich); three in Switzerland; one in Italy (Albano).

It is thanks to your prayers and your generosity that in a year's time we shall be able, please God, to have 26 priests at your disposal: 13 are already at work training students or ministering to souls.

How does it come about that a Work thus resembling all those of its kind existing before the Second Vatican Council should be harshly and pitilessly hounded down by the Roman Authorities, unjustly and illegally suppressed, accused of breaking off communion with Rome, etc.?

The reason is precisely that we are continuing to believe and act as the Church always has believed and acted. Hence the truth is that modern Rome has changed. And yet it was clear to see where the novelties already repeatedly condemned by the Magisterium of the Church would lead.

The balance-sheet for the ten years following the Council is catastrophic in all departments. Churchmen, herein following numerous bad examples, thought that they could replace what Our Lord instituted with institutions better suited to the modern world, forgetting that Jesus Christ is God "yesterday, today and for ever" (Heb. 13:8), and that His Work is suited to all times and to all men.

Saint Pius X condemned them in his masterly Encyclical *Pascendi.* Such innovators pervert the faith, bring supernatural means down to the level of man and destroy the hierarchical constitution of the Church.

For a long time now we have been warned by the Popes.

Pius IX had the Documents of the *Alta Vendita* of the Carbonari published in which we read: "In a hundred years' time . . . bishops and priests will think they are marching behind the banner of the keys of Peter when in fact they will be following our flag." (*Masonic Infiltrations in the Church*, Barbier.) Fogazzaro at the beginning of the century, founder of the Modernist lodge of Milan, used to say: "The Reform will have to be brought about in the name of obedience." (*The Church under Occupation*, Ploncard d' Assac.)*

Now, when we hear in Rome that he who was the heart and soul of the liturgical reform is a Freemason, we may think that he is not the only one. The veil covering over the greatest hoax ever to have mystified the clergy and baffled the faithful is doubtless beginning to be torn asunder.

Now is the time then to hold more faithfully than ever to Tradition and the unchanging Church, and to pray to God, to the Blessed Virgin Mary, and to St. Michael the Archangel to free the Church from the scandalous occupation of which She is victim.

"This is the victory that overcomes the world, our faith." (1 John 5:4.)

May God bless you through the intercession of His Holy Mother, and I wish you all a Holy Eastertide!

† Marcel Lefebvre

21 April 1976
**Letter from Archbishop Benelli
to Archbishop Lefebvre**

This letter is important because it states precisely, in wri-

---

*The full text of the Documents of the *Alta Vendita*, and much other useful information on the Carbonari, is published in *Grand Orient Freemasonry Unmasked* by Mgr. G. Dillon. (Augustine Publishing Company)

ting, for the first time the real conditions of the submission demanded of Mgr. Lefebvre. The author of the letter, Mgr. Benelli, who has the title of "Substitute"* in the Vatican Secretariat of State, was its most notable personage after Cardinal Villot until he was created a Cardinal and appointed Archbishop of Florence in May 1977.

Monseigneur,

It is now a month since we met. As I offer you my best wishes for the Easter feast, I should like to repeat how happy I am that our meeting was so frank, and also how, every day, the expectation grows keener that you will return to that effective communion with Pope Paul VI which the celebration of the Resurrection required and of which our conversation had given hope.

The meeting took place in Rome, on 19 March 1976, on Mgr. Benelli's initiative (he was reviving a request for an audience by Mgr. Lefebvre which, the year before, had been left unanswered).

Indeed, you certainly remember the step envisaged as most suitable for arriving at that happy result.

"Envisaged"? Not at all; imposed in the name of the Pope by Mgr. Benelli, but he had sent Mgr. Lefebvre nothing in writing.

After reflecting, alone and before God, you will write to the Holy Father informing him of your acceptance of the Council and of all its documents, affirming your full attachment to the person of His Holiness Pope Paul VI and to the totality of his teaching . . .

A Pope who thus wishes to impose a *full* attachment to

---

*Assistant to the Secretary of State.

the *totality* of *his own* teaching—that makes a double difficulty. 1^{O} As is known, or as should be known, the totality
of the teaching of a Pope (especially of a modern Pope,
speaking much and often) does not involve papal authority
in the same degree in all its parts; it can often happen that
that authority is not involved at all, when he speaks as a
private doctor. *Full* attachment to the *totality* of the teaching is an exorbitant demand; it is a form of unconditional
submission. That is the first anomaly, and it is serious. 2^{O}
The second anomaly, no less serious; the question is of the
teaching of Paul VI, by itself; of his personal teaching. The
head of a school can so speak. A Pope does not speak in that
way. All pontifical documents prior to Paul VI attest the
fact: they refer constantly to the teachings of predecessors,
and they confirm, repeat, develop and apply them, and they
never seek to distinguish themselves from them as individuals. Shall we suppose that this is a stupidity of Mgr. Benelli's? Not at all. He is faithfully reproducing the thought of
Paul VI. For   it is the same thought which Paul VI himself
expresses in his consistorial discourse of 24 May 1976, showing plainly that his own teaching has a distinct individuality:
"We think that no one can be in doubt of the meaning of the
orientations and the encouragements that, in the course of
Our pontificate, We have given to pastors and to the people
of God, and even the whole world. We are grateful to those
who have made a program of the teaching given with a purpose which has always sustained with a lively hope, etc".
Where his predecessors used to speak of the teaching of the
Popes, of the Holy See, or of the Church, Paul VI speaks of
his personal teaching. Just as Vatican II is presented to us as
the Council, abstracting from previous councils, so Paul VI
presents his teaching as something separate and particular, so
that in isolation it can be taken as a program, and he expresses his gratitude to those who have so taken it. On those who
have not taken it so, he will impose it: Mgr. Benelli's phrase

about full attachment to the totality of the teaching of Paul VI is perfectly consistent with the passage quoted from the Consistorial allocution.

> . . . and undertaking, as concrete proof of your submission to the Successor of Peter, to adopt and to get adopted in the houses dependent on you, the Missal which he himself promulgated in virtue of his supreme apostolic authority.

Enter the new Missal! Until this date, nothing had been said to Mgr. Lefebvre of this obligatory adoption. It constitutes the real condition. This new Mass of which not a word had been whispered in the whole business during a year—the silence on the subject was trickery. Now the veil is removed from it, and it is indeed the essential. More than that, it is not at all a matter of a simple "step that has been envisaged." It might have been that, in the form of a hypothesis, in an explanatory conversation and a fraternal dialogue; but, as indicated on p. 169, the matter is the notifications of conditions imposed by the Pope: that will be confirmed in Mgr. Benelli's letter of 12 June 1976.

> I can fully understand how costly such a step must be. That, perhaps, is why you hesitate to take it. Yet, can there be any other way? I address myself to you as a brother, with hope and confidence: this step is possible; it must be taken for the good of the whole Church and for those outside it who are looking at us; and I desire to do everything to help you take it.
>
> A few days ago we celebrated Easter. Christ the Saviour points the way. To be united with Him there is no other road than to put everything into His hands. I pray with all my heart that you may reach Him, and thus give to His Vicar on earth the profound joy that he awaits with impatience.
>
> Be assured, Monseigneur, of my devoted fraternal feelings.
>
> † J. Benelli.

IX

The Consistory Allocution

The Allocution of Pope Paul VI to the
Consistory of Cardinals on 24 May 1976

Only those parts of the allocution concerning Mgr. Lefebvre and the Tridentine Mass are reproduced here. The text is that published in the English edition of *L'Osservatore Romano* of 3 June 1976.

The Pope's Allocution

On the one hand there are those who, under the pretext of a greater fidelity to the Church and the Magisterium, systematically refuse the teaching of the Council itself, its application and the reforms that stem from it, its gradual application by the Apostolic See and the Episcopal Conferences, under Our authority, willed by Christ.

In this passage the Pope fails to make a crucially important distinction between the teaching of the Council itself and reforms claiming to interpret that teaching—reforms which in many cases cannot be justified by reference to so much as a single sentence in a conciliar document. See again the comment regarding the Seminary at Ecône in the light of the specific teaching of the Council, p. 68-70.

This sentence also contains an extremely serious doctrinal error on the part of the Pope or whoever wrote this speech for him. This error is not apparent in the English translation and reference must be made to the official Latin text published in *L'Osservatore Romano* (Italian edition) of 24 May 1976. The phrase "the Episcopal Conferences, under Our authority, willed by Christ" is rendered in Latin as follows: *"Conferentiarum episcopalium sub Nostra auctoritate, quae a Christo originem ducunt."* The use of the plural *ducunt* means that the Pope is claiming that it is not simply his Apostolic Authority but the National Episcopal Conferences which have their origin in Christ. This is totally untrue. The authority of the Pope and the worldwide episcopal college have their origin in Christ—but there is no warrant in Scripture or Tradition for National Episcopal Conferences to be invested with doctrinal or disciplinary teaching authority. This is still true in the strictly legal sense today. National Episcopal Conferences are able to authorize or even recommend a course of action, but each individual bishop is at liberty to decide whether or not to implement these decisions in his diocese. The National Episcopal Conference, having no legal status, has no authority to impose its decisions. But what happens in practice is that individual bishops feel unable to oppose the majority decision and submit to it despite their personal misgivings. Thus one English bishop whom I reproached for allowing Communion to be given in the hand in his diocese, following a decision of the English and Welsh Episcopal Conference to permit this, replied that, although he personally deplored the practice and had done all he could to prevent its acceptance, he now had no practical option but to go along with the majority. This is precisely what Mgr. Lefebvre had forecast during the collegiality debate, warning that collegiality would not give the bishops more power but that the individual bishop would no longer be the ruler in his own diocese.

Returning to the subject of the doctrinal error in the Pope's allocution, the unorthodoxy of this statement was quickly exposed in traditionalist journals (e.g., the *Courrier de Rome*, No. 159 of 15 July 1976). When the allocution was reprinted in the *Acts of the Apostolic See* (AAS 68, 1976 (6), p. 375) the error was corrected. The plural *ducunt* had been changed to the singular *ducit*, referring solely to the Pope's authority as having its origin in Christ. This provides another instance of the fact that simply because the Pope has stated something it does not follow that it is certainly orthodox.

Discredit is cast upon the authority of the Church in the name of a Tradition to which respect is professed only materially and verbally. The faithful are drawn away from the bonds of obedience to the See of Peter and to their rightful Bishops; today's authority is rejected in the name of yesterday's.

The Pope here is presupposing that anyone invested with authority *must* be obeyed simply because he possesses authority. As Appendix II will show, it is the traditional Catholic teaching that even legitimate authority need not be obeyed (and that obedience might be sinful) if it abuses its power or commands anything contrary to or compromising the faith. Thus, according to Pope Paul's thinking as expressed here, when he made the erroneous statement that Episcopal Conferences had their origin in Christ, the faithful had no right to question it. Similarly, the Pope had to correct that notorious Article 7 of the General Instruction to the New Mass which he had approved, and he was also compelled to revise the new rite of Baptism which he had previously approved. In Britain and the USA the bishops have ordered priests to give Communion in the hand to anyone demanding it—in this case it is clear that priests would not sin by refusing to obey their lawful bishops.

And the fact is all the more serious in that the opposition of which We are speaking is not only encouraged by some priests, but is led by a Prelate, Archbishop Marcel Lefebvre, who, nevertheless, still has Our respect.

This allegation is quite untrue. The opposition to the post-conciliar reforms existed long before most Catholics, particularly in the English-speaking world, had ever heard of the name of Archbishop Lefebvre. The only authority exercised by Mgr. Lefebvre is over the Fraternity of St. Pius X. He and the Fraternity enjoy the support of hundreds of thousands of faithful Catholics because it is Mgr. Lefebvre and the Fraternity who uphold both Tradition and the many traditions to which Catholics are so attached and which, in some cases, could not be abolished or radically modified without compromising Tradition itself. Thus, while it is true to state that Mgr. Lefebvre enjoys the support of the majority of traditionalists, it is not correct to describe him as their leader—a title which he himself has repudiated on many occasions as for example his sermon at Lille on 29 August 1976.

It is so painful to take note of this: but how can We not see in such an attitude—whatever may be these people's intentions—the placing of themselves outside obedience and communion with the Successor of Peter and therefore outside the Church?

Thus it is now possible to deny any and every fundamental dogma of the faith; to disobey any and every disciplinary law of the Church, even the "Conciliar Church"; to be guilty even of sacrilege; and still not be told that communion with the Successor of Peter has been broken—but remain true to the traditional faith, and one is considered "outside the Church."

For this, unfortunately, is the logical consequence, when, that is, it is held as preferable to disobey with the pretext of preserving one's faith intact, and of working in one's own way for the preservation of the Catholic Church, while at the same time refusing to give her effective obedience. And this is said openly.

The use of the word "pretext" here is very unjust. A pretext (Latin, *praetextu)* is an ostensible reason given to hide the true one; in other words, it denotes a lack of sincerity, and while it is legitimate to argue that traditionalists may be mistaken in their attitude, there is no justification for claiming that they are insincere. It is also unfair and inaccurate to claim that they are working for the preservation of the Church in their own way—they are attempting to preserve the faith in a form which has a tradition of centuries behind it.

It is even affirmed that the Second Vatican Council is not binding . . .

This is a difficult statement upon which to comment. Who had affirmed this and in precisely what terms? And what does the Pope mean by "the Second Vatican Council"? Presumably he is referring to the doctrinal teaching of the Council. I have discussed the authority of the Documents of Vatican II in detail in Chapter XIV of *Pope John's Council.* Briefly, the position is that they are not binding in the same way as the documents of previous General Councils, which were promulgated with the authority of the Church's extraordinary Magisterium, under pain of anathema. As the Pope himself has stated specifically on a number of occasions, the documents of the Council come to us with the authority of the Ordinary Magisterium of the Church. The teaching of the Ordinary Magisterium does not at all carry the same authority. It is explained excellently in the *Approaches* supplement by Dom Paul Nau, *The Ordinary Magisterium of the Church Theologically Considered*. This study shows clearly that the authority of the Ordinary Magisterium increases even to the point of infallibility depending upon the frequency with which a particular teaching has been repeated. But the author also cites the opinion that a novelty taught by the Ordinary Magisterium could be erroneous if it conflicted with previous teaching. This certainly seems to be the case with certain passages in the Declaration on Religious Liberty, which contradict previous authoritative (and possibly infallible) teaching (see Appendix IV). As Mgr. Lefebvre made clear in an interview which he granted me on 16 November 1976, and in his letter to the Pope dated 3 December 1976 (which will both be found in their correct chronological sequence), he accepts everything in the teaching of the Council which is in conformity with Tradition. This is the correct Catholic attitude to the teaching of the Ordinary Magisterium, bearing in mind that the normal presumption must be that the teaching of the Ordinary Magisterium will be in conformity with Tradition and that instances where it is not will be rare in the extreme.

. . . that the faith would also be in danger because of the reforms and post-conciliar directives; that one has the duty to disobey in order to preserve certain traditions.

It is quite clear that any faithful Catholic who understands the nature of certain post-conciliar directives and the manner in which they have been implemented must certainly repudiate them not simply to preserve his faith but to show that he takes his faith seriously.

What traditions? Is it for this group, not the Pope, not the College of Bishops, not the Ecumenical Council, to decide which among the innumerable traditions must be considered as the norm of faith!

The unfortunate truth is that it became clear in practice that neither Pope Paul VI nor the Bishops were prepared to take practical steps to uphold the basic norms of faith, apart from issuing pious exhortations which they made no effort to implement. Even those many orthodox Catholics who feel unable to support Mgr. Lefebvre must testify to the truth of this. Instead of prohibiting publication of that veritable textbook of Modernism, the Dutch Catechism, Pope Paul VI allowed it to be circulated with the addition of an appendix which no one need read. This is equivalent to the father of a family allowing his children to drink poison providing an antidote of doubtful efficacy is ready. Where is there a country in the West in which priests who have publicly dissented from the Encyclical *Humanae Vitae* do not occupy important teaching posts in Catholic education institutes? What could possibly be a greater cause of a diminution in reverence to the Blessed Sacrament, and an occasion of sacrilege, than the practice of Communion in the hand? It was condemned by Pope Paul himself in *Memoriale Domini.* Nonetheless, he authorized its introduction into almost every country in the West. With all the respect due to a Vicar of Christ, it must be said that the faithful could not assume that Pope Paul VI and his Bishops could be relied upon to uphold those traditions necessary for the preservation of the faith.

As you see, Venerable Brethren, such an attitude sets itself up as judge of that divine will which placed Peter and his lawful Successors at the head of the Church to confirm the brethren in the faith, and to feed the universal flock, and which established him as the guarantor

and custodian of the deposit of faith.

This again is quite untrue—Mgr. Lefebvre does not challenge the nature of papal authority (no one has done more to uphold it) or question the fact that it exists by divine will. What he has done is to question certain specific acts of a particular Pope, and, equally important, the failure of this Pope to *act* in defense of the Faith. In doing this the Archbishop is acting in accordance with approved theological principles (cf. Appendix II).

And this is all the more serious in particular, when division is introduced precisely where *congregavit nos in unum Christi amor,* **in the Liturgy and the Eucharistic Sacrifice, by the refusing of obedience to the norms laid down in the liturgical sphere.**

This is perhaps the most astonishing statement in the entire allocution. It is the post-conciliar liturgical reform which has totally destroyed the unity of the Roman rite. We have been presented not so much with a new form of Mass (however inferior to the old) but with an ongoing liturgical revolution, in which anything is tolerated but the traditional Mass. In the face of this liturgical anarchy, traditionalists wish to adhere to a form of Mass which in all essentials dates back more than a millennium, for which they are accused of promoting liturgical disunity!

It is in the name of Tradition that We ask all Our sons and daughters, all the Catholic communities, to celebrate with dignity and fervor the renewed liturgy.

In practice, where the New Mass is celebrated strictly in accordance with what rubrics there are, it is so oppressively dull and insipid that no one could possibly participate in it with fervor. This explains the increase in the so-called Folk

Masses, the introduction of dancing and audio-visual effects, and the liturgical antics of the Pentecostals, as an effort to infuse some form of life (however depraved) into what is no more than the corpse of the vibrant, noble, and dignified liturgy of the Roman Mass. Pope Paul must have realized that the liturgy in its present form is a source of misery and even revulsion to countless thousands of the faithful, and that even where they accept it as an act of obedience to expect them to do so with fervor is to ask the impossible.

> The adoption of the new *Ordo Missae* is certainly not left to the free choice of priests or faithful. The Instruction of 14 June 1971 has provided, with the authorization of the Ordinary, for the celebration of the Mass in the old form only by aged and infirm priests, who offer the divine Sacrifice *sine populo*.

It is extremely significant that Pope Paul makes no reference at all to his Apostolic Constitution *Missale Romanum* of 3 April 1969 which authorizes the introduction of the New Mass. If the traditional Mass has been prohibited this is the only document which could have done so. Not even the most fervent apologists for the New Mass have ever claimed *Missale Romanum* contains one word explicitly prohibiting the old one; the most they dare claim is that it is prohibited implicitly or that the Old Mass lapsed automatically with the introduction of the new one. A comprehensive summary of the legal position of the traditional Mass is available in Father Bryan Houghton's book *Mitre and Crook*.* The In-

---

*Published in 1978 by Arlington House (USA), also available from The Angelus Press. Available in Britain from Augustine Publishing Co. This is certainly one of the most important books written on the liturgical revolution and, although in the form of a novel, contains much factual information. A summary of all the legislation relative to the traditional Mass is available on pages 87-101.

Two very useful articles by the French canonist, Father Raymond Dulac, *Does the Novus Ordo Have the Strict Force of Law?* and *The Legal Status of Quo Primum* are available from the Remnant Press in the USA and Augustine Publishing Co. in Great Britain. See also footnote to p. 447.

struction of 14 June 1971 was, in fact, a *Notificatio* originally published without either date or the author's name and
of very dubious authority. It was examined in detail in
Itinéraires, No. 159 of January 1972 (p. 16 ff.) and in *The
Remnant.* The claim that a form of Mass which has provided
the basis for Catholic spirituality for a thousand years can
now be celebrated only by aged and infirm priests, and then
only if they do it behind closed doors as if they were celebrating a Black Mass, is a fitting epitomization of the "Spirit
of Vatican II."

   **The new *Ordo* was promulgated to take the place of the old, after
mature deliberation, following upon the requests of the Second Vatican
Council.**

   At no time did the Fathers of Vatican II ever authorize
the composition of a new order of Mass, *Novus Ordo Missae,*
"to take the place of the old"! They did no more than authorize minor modifications to the existing Mass and insisted
that no changes should be made unless the good of the
Church genuinely and certainly required them and that all
existing rites were to be preserved. I have demonstrated in
Chapters XV and XVI of *Pope John's Council* that there is no
relationship whatsoever between the reform which the Council authorized and that which has been imposed upon the
faithful in practice.

   **In no different way did Our Holy Predecessor Pius V make obliga-
tory the Missal reformed under his authority, following the Council of
Trent.**

   This attempt to compare the reform undertaken by Saint
Pius V and that authorized by Pope Paul VI is so totally incredible that it could not possibly be dealt with within the

context of this commentary.*

The official Latin text of Pope Paul's allocution, published in *L'Osservatore Romano* of 24-25 May 1976, does not refer to the Missal "reformed" under the authority of St. Pius V but of the Missal "recognized" by his authority (*"Missale auctoritate sua recognitum"*). The Latin verb *recognosco* can have a stronger sense than simply to "recognize." With regard to a written document it means that it has been examined with respect to its genuineness and value and is certified or authenticated as genuine.** This is precisely the action taken by St. Pius V with respect to the existing Roman Mass which was examined diligently by the best scholars and then codified in its existing form with a few modifications which would not have been noticed by the ordinary worshipper.

An Italian translation of this allocution which appeared in the same edition of *L'Osservatore Romano* translated *recognitum* as *riformato*, "reformed"—a mistranslation carried over into the English edition. Leaving aside the question of this mistranslation, Pope Paul's claim that what he had done in his reform was what "in no different way" (*"haud dissimili ratione"*) St. Pius V had done, is so at variance with historical fact that it forfeits all claim to credibility. If something is untrue the fact that it is stated to be true by the Pope cannot alter the fact that it is untrue. The Pope is not inerrant, he can be mistaken on matters of fact. It is probable (though not certain) that if pressed, the editor of *The Wanderer* or the President of Catholics United for the Faith would admit that the Church does not require us to believe

---

*I must refer readers to my pamphlet *The Tridentine Mass*, which describes the reform of Pope Saint Pius V, and my pamphlets *The New Mass* and *The Roman Rite Destroyed*, which describe the reform of Pope Paul VI, and suggest that they decide for themselves whether there is any difference in the nature of the reforms enacted by the two pontiffs. This has been dealt with in greater detail in my book *Pope Paul's New Mass*. Available from the Angelus Press in the USA.

**"*Haec omnia summa cura et diligentia recognita.*" Cicero.

that the Pope is inerrant. On a practical level, they insist that he is and accuse any Catholic who points out papal errors of being schismatic.

With the same supreme authority that comes from Christ Jesus, We call for the same obedience to all the other liturgical, disciplinary and pastoral reforms which have matured in these years in the implementation of the Council decrees. Any initiative which tries to obstruct them cannot claim the prerogative of rendering a service to the Church: in fact it causes the Church serious damage.

Once again, anyone with experience of the new liturgy in practice will know that a faithful Catholic who loves the Mass and loves the Church has no alternative but to try to obstruct a reform which, with all due respect to Pope Paul VI, does *not* proceed from mature deliberation. Communion in the hand is now part of this official reform in dozens of countries where it has been sanctioned by Pope Paul himself, even though it began not as a result of mature deliberation but as an act of calculated rebellion against papal authority. The Pope consulted the Bishops of the world, who voted overwhelmingly against the innovation; it is still prohibited in Italy. The Pope insisted upon the retention of the traditional method but has none the less given way before the *fait accompli* technique of the Liberals. Yet where it has been made official, Catholics who oppose the abuse are classed among those who "cause the Church serious damage." By asking us not to oppose innovations which our personal experience has proved to be harmful, the Pope is asking us to dehumanize ourselves, to become robots. It is not a case of opposing something simply because it conflicts with personal taste or established habits. In this instance it is the honor and reverence due to the Blessed Sacrament, the avoidance of sacrilege which is at stake. Our objections to the innovation, and our adherence to the traditional practice, are based on the very reasons put forward by Pope Paul VI himself in *Memoriale Domini*. With all due respect, it must be said that as Christ's Vicar upon earth it was his duty to safeguard the Blessed Sacrament from the sacrilege to which this practice inevitably leads. He failed to do so and, not for the first time in the history of the Church, the faithful found that their Catholic duty was *not* to follow the example of the Pope.

Various times, directly and through Our collaborators and other friendly persons, We have called the attention of Archbishop Lefebvre to the seriousness of his behavior, the irregularity of his principal present initiatives, the inconsistency and often falsity of the doctrinal positions on which he bases this behavior and these initiatives, and the damage that accrues to the entire Church because of them.

If such admonitions have been made they have not been made public. The first admonition of a genuinely doctrinal nature given by the Pope to Mgr. Lefebvre was that he should accept the totally false proposition that Vatican II has as much authority as Nicea, and more importance in some respects (the letter of 29 June 1975).

It is with profound sadness but with paternal hope that We once more turn to this confrère of Ours, to his collaborators and to those who have let themselves be carried away by them. Oh, certainly, We believe that many of these faithful—at least in the beginning—were in good faith: We also understand their sentimental attachment to forms of worship or of discipline that for a long time had been for them a spiritual support and in which they had found spiritual sustenance. But We are confident that they will reflect with serenity, without closed minds, and they will admit that they can find today the support and sustenance that they are seeking in the renewed forms that the Second Vatican Ecumenical Council and We Ourself have decreed as being necessary for the good of the Church, Her progress in the modern world, and Her unity.

Firstly, does this imply that traditionalists are no longer in good faith? Secondly, while traditionalists naturally look to the traditional liturgy and devotional practices with a nostalgia which is both right and fitting, their opposition to the "Conciliar Church" and to the liturgical reform in general is based not upon sentiment but on a determination to uphold the faith which these reforms compromise. Examine the prayers which Cranmer removed from the traditional Mass (set out in detail in *Cranmer's Godly Order)* and compare these with the prayers removed from the Mass with the authority of Pope Paul VI. By what possible stretch of the imagination can it be claimed that it was absolutely essential to remove these prayers "for the good of the Church, Her progress in the world, and Her unity"? And can it truly be possible that Pope Paul VI really believed that the Church is making progress in the modern world—the devastation which has followed in the wake of the conciliar reform must surely have been evident even from the windows of the Vatican? And as for the unity of the Church, what has done more to destroy that unity than the post-conciliar liturgical reform?

We therefore exhort yet once again all these brethren and sons and daughters of Ours; We beseech them to become aware of the profound wounds that they otherwise cause to the Church, and We invite them again to reflect on Christ's serious warnings about the unity of the Church and on the obedience that is due to the lawful Pastor placed by Him over the universal flock, as a sign of the obedience due to the Father and the Son.

On the contrary, the wounds in the Church and the damage to her unity have not been caused by the stand made by the traditionalists. The traditionalists have taken their stand as a reaction to these wounds and this disunity.

We await them with an open heart, with arms ready to embrace

them: may they know how to rediscover in humility and edification, to the joy of the whole People of God, the way of unity and of love.

In other words, traditionalists will only become accept-able if they abandon all that they most love and revere and believe to be essential to the well-being of the Church and accept the entire post-conciliar revolution without reserva-tion. The price is unacceptable.

The Pope then goes through the motions of what has be-come a standard procedure whenever traditionalists are at-tacked, and delivers generalized admonitions to those at the opposite end of the spectrum who are guilty of doctrinal and liturgical error. These individuals are never named nor are these admonitions ever reinforced with action. Referring to these Liberal Catholics, the Pope makes yet another aston-ishing statement:

Such Christians are not very numerous, it is true, but they make much noise, believing too easily that they are in a position to interpret the needs of the entire Christian people or the irreversible direction of history.

Virtually every position of importance in the entire Cath-olic establishment throughout the West is in the hands of these Liberals; they control all the official commissions, catechetical, liturgical, and ecumenical; all too frequently Episcopal Conferences serve only to act as their mouthpieces, and yet Pope Paul himself claimed that they are few in num-ber but make much noise.

Outside of Which Church?
by Jean Madiran

As a reaction to the papal allocution of 24 May 1976,

Jean Madiran wrote the following article which first appeared in the *Supplément-Voltigeur* of *Itinéraires* of 15 June 1976. The following translation was made by Father Urban Snyder and appeared in *The Remnant* of 21 July 1976.

"In his allocution to the Consistory of 24 May 1976, where he mentions Archbishop Lefebvre several times by name, Paul VI seems to cut him off and yet he doesn't. He accuses the Archbishop of 'putting himself outside the Church.' But which Church? There are two. And Paul VI has not renounced being the Pope of these two Churches simultaneously. Under such conditions, 'outside the Church' is equivocal and does not cut off anything.

That there are now two Churches, with one and the same Paul VI at the head of both, is not our doing, we are not making it up, but simply stating the way things are.

Many episcopates, which declare themselves to be in communion with the Pope, and whom the Pope does not reject from his communion, are objectively outside the Catholic communion.

The episcopate of Holland, in an official document, has explicitly called into doubt the virginal conception of Our Lord, but they have not been summoned by the Pope to retract or to resign. On the contrary—they have spread throughout the whole world their 'Dutch Catechism' which doesn't contain the things necessary to know for salvation, and which inspires all the new catechisms.

The French episcopate since 1969 subjects the faithful, 'as a reminder of faith', to the false teaching that in the Mass 'there is question simply of a memorial.' None of our protestations or supplications has succeeded in bringing them to deny or even explain this. It is in the name of the Council, of the Pope, and of the bishops in communion with him that now, for ten years or more, and without any efficacious denial, there is imposed on us all the discourses and decisions which install the immanent apostasy, the permanent auto-demolition, the capitulation before the world, the cult of man, the opening to Communism. There is no question here of some handful of marginal dissidents, as the Pope insinuates in his allocution. There is question of the greater part of the actual holders of the apostolic succession. Legitimate holders? Yes, but prevaricators, deserters, impostors. Paul VI remains at their head without either disavowing or correcting them. He keeps them in his communion, he presides over their Church also.

Archbishop Lefebvre is not in his present situation through any fault of his own. He didn't innovate anything, he didn't invent anything, he didn't overturn anything; he has simply preserved and transmitted the deposit which he received. He has kept the promises of his baptism, the doctrine of his catechism, the Mass of his ordination, the dogmas defined by Popes and Councils, the theology and the traditional ecclesiology of the Church of Rome. Just by his existence, by his very being, and without having willed it, he is thus the witness of a crisis which is not of his making, but that of an uncertain Pope at the head of two Churches at the same time.

Cardinal Suenens declared in 1969: 'We could draw up an impressive list of theses, taught in Rome yesterday and before yesterday as sole truths (*seules valables*), and which were eliminated by the Council Fathers.' A formidable doctrinal revolution! Cardinal Suenens is happy about it. The greater part of the actual holders of the apostolic succession think and speak on this point like Cardinal Suenens. Neither he nor they are disavowed. Paul VI remains at their head and keeps them in his communion; a communion where they profess that the Church, yesterday and before yesterday, was mistaken. But on all these points where they teach that the Church was mistaken, who or what can guarantee to us that it is not they themselves who, today, are mistaken and are misleading us?

It doesn't help at all to reassure us that the Council is

badly interpreted and the Pope badly understood. If the Council has been constantly interpreted the way it has, it is with the active or passive consent of the bishops in communion with the Pope. Thus there is established a Conciliar Church, different from the Catholic Church. And no bishop, however scandalous his post-conciliar excesses, has received from Paul VI the severe public rebukes which he has reserved for Archbishop Lefebvre alone, and for the sole reason that the Archbishop remains unshakeably faithful to the Catholic religion such as it was until 1958.

If the Catholic religion, such as it was in 1958 at the death of Pius XII, contained some things optional, variable, which (let us suppose) have become anachronistic in 1976, to remain attached to them does not, all the same, constitute a crime. Anachronism is not necessarily in itself something which puts you 'outside the Church.' If we are going to talk about anachronisms, pure, simple, and unlimited, they are in the new catechisms from which the things necessary for salvation have been excised; they are in the vernacular Masses, accompanied by Marxist chants and erotic dances; they are in the falsification of Scripture imposed by the episcopate, such as where a (French) liturgical reading proclaims that 'to live holily it is necessary to marry'; they are in all the other infamous things of like kind of which none, for the past ten years, has been either retracted by those guilty, or condemned by higher authority. There are indeed crimes really going on in the Church, those just mentioned, but they are considered less criminal than preserving the Catholic religion such as it was in 1958 at the death of Pius XII.

All this presupposes a new religion, another ecclesial community, which nevertheless is installed in the posts of command of Church administration, and boasts of communion with Pope Paul, having at the same time, to put it mildly, the consent of Pope Paul.

Archbishop Lefebvre 'outside the Church'? Out of the

one just mentioned, certainly. But it surpasses belief that a person 'puts himself outside' the *Catholic* Church, without budging, or by simply remaining in the Catholic religion such as it was at the death of Pius XII in 1958.

There are two Churches under Paul VI. Not to see that there are two, or not to see that they are strangers the one to the other, or not to see that Paul VI thus far is presiding over both, partakes of blindness and in some cases perhaps of invincible blindness. But when one has once seen it, not to say it would be to add complicity by silence to an enormous monstrosity.

Gustav Corcao in the review *Itinéraires* for November, 1975, and then Father Bruckberger in *L'Aurore* for 18 March 1976, remarked in print: The religious crisis is not like that in the 14th century, when you had, for one single Church, two or three Popes simultaneously; today, rather, there is question of one single Pope for two Churches, the Catholic and the post-conciliar.

But to belong simultaneously to two such contrary Churches is impossible. It is impossible even for a Pope, by the very definition of his office. If Paul VI doesn't disengage himself, there is going to be an inevitable blow-up *(choc en retour)* as a result.''

X

The War of Attrition Continues

12 June 1976
Letter from Mgr. Benelli
to the Apostolic Nuncio in Berne

Official letter from the Vatican Secretariat of State,
Registered under the number 307,554,
and addressed to Mgr. Ambrogio Marchioni,
Nuncio at Berne.

Monseigneur,

On the subject of Monseigneur Marcel Lefebvre, the Sovereign Pontiff asks me to communicate to you the three following points, and I ask you to bring them without delay to the knowledge of the prelate, at the same time giving him a copy of this letter:

1º You will hand over officially to Mgr. Lefebvre—who seemed to be absent from Switzerland on the 24 May—the Latin text and the French translation of the allocution given by His Holiness on the occasion of the recent secret Consistory of Cardinals, which all the bishops have already had opportunity of knowing.

The *official* presentation of the Latin text *and its French translation:* it is not that Mgr. Lefebvre is suspected of not understanding Latin. It is the effect of the tendency to "officialize" as "French translation" a version which is manifestly translated not from the Latin text but from the Italian, which is the original version. This new Vatican practice, which is a source of defects, confusion, and anarchy, has been progressively extended and imposed since the death of Pope Pius XII in 1958.

2⁰ You should, at the same time, inform Mgr. Marcel Lefebvre that, *de mandato speciali Summi Pontificis,* in the present circumstances and according to the prescriptions of canon 2373, 1⁰, of the Code of Canon Law, he must strictly abstain from conferring orders from the moment he receives the present injunction.

This reference to Canon Law indicates suspension for a year from the administration of the sacrament of Holy Order, suspension reserved to the Holy See, and incurred *ipso facto* by one who ordains a priest without authorization from the former's Ordinary: in precise terms, without the "dimissorial letters" by which a bishop "refers" one of his subjects to another bishop to receive from him the sacrament of Holy Order.

3⁰ In the discourse to the Consistory on 24 May 1976, the Holy Father was at pains to recall, himself, the fraternal approaches he had several times tried to make to Mgr. Lefebvre. He has said repeatedly, and now says again, that he is ready to receive him as soon as he has given public testimony of his obedience to the present successor of Saint Peter and of his acceptance of Vatican Council II. The conditions are well known to Mgr. Lefebvre:

they are still those which I specified to him, in the name of His
Holiness, when we met on 19 March, and of which I reminded
him in my letter of 21 April last.

There had been approaches by Pope Paul VI, all mentioned in the preceding pages: not one was fraternal; not one
was paternal. It is not enough to say it has been done for it
to become true. Paul VI had refused to take into consideration the letter that Mgr. Lefebvre sent him on 31 May 1975;
he has acted as though he did not know of this recourse to
him put into his hands.

So there is indeed question of *conditions* which had been
made known by Mgr. Benelli *in the name of His Holiness*. If
one refers to Mgr. Benelli's letter of 21 April, it can be seen
that there was no explicit question of conditions made
known in the name of the Pope, but of "a step envisaged,"
which suggests the idea of a friendly conversation rather than
that of an ultimatum. It is in euphemisms of this sort that
the whole "fraternal" character of Vatican approaches to
Mgr. Lefebvre consists.

Well, the Holy Father has confirmed that no such testimony has
yet reached him, in spite of the promises about it made several times.

Mgr. Benelli no doubt means the promises that he himself
had several times made to Pope Paul VI. Mgr. Lefebvre, for
his part, has never, at any moment, promised to adopt the
Mass of Article 7 nor to profess that Vatican II has as much
authority as Nicea, and more importance.

The public scandal continues to be such that the Sovereign Pontiff
could wait no longer before asking the Sacred College to take notice of
the continuance of this non-ecclesial attitude. Today, also, he can wait
no longer. He therefore adjures Mgr. Lefebvre not to harden himself in
a position which would lead him further and further into a blind alley,

when he can still, "in humility and edification," make the gesture which His Holiness awaits "with paternal hope."

Accept, Monseigneur, with my thanks for your mediation in this grave matter, the assurance of my faithful and cordial devotion in Our Lord.

† J. Benelli
subst.

22 June 1976
Letter of Mgr. Lefebvre to Pope Paul VI

This letter was made public by Mgr. Lefebvre on 12 July 1976. He added a "preliminary note" which will be found below, in its chronological place.

Most Holy Father,

Will Your Holiness please fully understand the sorrow which grips me, and my stupefaction, on the one side at hearing the paternal appeals Your Holiness addresses to me, and on the other the cruelty of the blows which do not cease striking us, the latest of them striking worst of all my dear Seminarians and their families on the eve of their priesthood for which they have been preparing for five or six years.

Your Holiness has known me since 1948, and you know perfectly well what the faith is that I profess, the faith of your *Credo,* and you know equally my profound submission to the Successor of Peter which I renew into the hands of Your Holiness.

The trouble and the confusion spread in the Church these last years, which Your Holiness denounces in your last discourse to the Consistory, are precisely the reason for the serious reserves I make about the perilous adaptation of the Church to the modern world.

But I am deeply convinced that I am in full communion with the thought and the faith of Your Holiness. I implore Your Holiness, therefore, to allow me to have a dialogue with envoys chosen by you from among the Cardinals who have known me for a long time,* and, with the help of God's grace, there is no doubt that the difficulties will be smoothed out.

Hoping that this suggestion will be acceptable to Your Holiness, I assure you of my entire availability, and of my respectful and filial affection in Christ and Mary.

† Marcel Lefebvre

25 June 1976
Letter from Mgr. Benelli to Mgr. Lefebvre

Monseigneur,

The Holy Father has received your letter of 22 June. He desires me to inform you of his mind on this subject. Certainly as I myself said to you last April in a fraternal letter, what is asked of you calls for courageous obedience on your part, the more so as you have voluntarily pursued your course in what was manifestly a blind alley. But you cannot describe as cruelty the attitude of the Holy See, which is only registering your conduct and taking the measures it calls for.

On 19 March, I told you quite frankly what, in your negative judgments on the Council, in your frequent statements on the offices of the Holy See and their directives applying the Council, in your way of acting counter to the responsibility of other bishops in their respective dioceses, was inadmissible for His Holiness, contrary to ecclesial communion, and damaging for the unity and peace of the Church. All that was required of you was a clear admission that you were wrong on those points necessary for every Catholic spirit, and after that one could have considered the best way of facing the remaining problems arising from your acts.

---

*Since Paul VI had constantly refused to give him a personal hearing, Mgr. Lefebvre proposes that the dialogue shall take place with Cardinals chosen from among those who have known him for a long time (and not any more in the scandalous conditions of 1975, with the three Cardinals of unworthy behavior).

The "wrong" which is Mgr. Lefebvre's, and which he is "asked only to admit," thus becomes almost imperceptible. It is limited to speaking freely—supposedly too freely—too "negatively." Is that how he has left the "communion" of Paul VI? Here, once more, one sees the inability of the Holy See to state precisely with what Mgr. Lefebvre is reproached. This imprecision in the complaints contrasts with the precision of the conditions imposed for his submission in the preceding letter of Mgr. Benelli (dated 21 April). It is likewise remarkable that, in enumerating "what is inadmissible for His Holiness," Mgr. Benelli does not mention the celebration of the traditional Mass. If that Mass is validly forbidden, why this off-hand silence about a grave fault, the most grave?

But, not only have you not done that during more than three months, in spite of your promises, but you have continued on the same line, even taking new initiatives in several parts of Europe and America. This public scandal could not but draw on you a public admonition from the Holy Father, on 24 May last. You could see, moreover, that the Holy Father attacks with the same firmness abuses committed in the other sense, outside or contrary to the true sense of the Council, which you claim is the origin of your attitude.

A flagrant untruth! In the other sense the "same firmness" of Paul VI demands no public submission, names no one, notably no bishop, and declares no one to be "outside the Church."

But after this summons, severe but paternal and hopeful, you remain obstinate and propose to ordain priests in the same spirit, on your own responsibility, independently of the Ordinaries, within the framework of a Society which the competent ecclesiastical authority has juridically suspended.

The Holy Father charges me this very day to confirm the measure of which you have been informed in his name, *de mandato speciali:* you are to abstain, now, from conferring any order. Do not use as a pretext the confused state of the seminarians who were to be ordained: this is just the opportunity to explain to them and to their families that you cannot ordain them to the service of the Church against the will of the supreme Pastor of the Church. There is nothing desperate in their case: if they have good will and are seriously prepared for a presbyteral ministry in genuine fidelity to the Conciliar Church.

Here we have it, then. Everything is clear at last. The only priests acceptable to the Vatican are priests prepared to make an act of "genuine fidelity to the Conciliar Church." It is, therefore, not traditionalists who are making a distinction between the Catholic Church, the eternal Church, and the Church of Vatican II. This distinction is made by an official spokesman for the Conciliar Church. Since the seminarians at Ecône have already promised their fidelity to the Catholic Church they cannot transfer it to the Conciliar Church.

Those responsible will find the best solution for them, but they must begin with an act of obedience to the Church.

To the Church? Yes, but Mgr. Benelli has already given the game away. It is to the *Conciliar* Church that they must make this act of obedience. Here before our eyes is the drama of the occupation of the Church Militant by an alien power. In the name of the *Catholic* Church, Catholics are required to subject themselves to the *Conciliar* Church.

They were informed in good time. In case of transgression, they should know that they expose themselves to the canonical penalty provided in canon 2374;* and if, temerariously, they disregard it, they

---

* i.e. the penalty of suspension.

expose themselves to irregularity* (cf. canon 985, 7), while the one
who ordains them would incur suspension for a year *ab ordinum col-
latione*, according to can. 2373, paras 1 and 3, independently of the
order recently communicated to him by the mediation of the Apostolic
Nuncio.

Rev. Father Dhanis, Consultor of the Congregation for the Doctrine of the Faith and professor at the Pontifical Gregorian University,
will bring you this letter. So that everything shall be perfectly clear, it
goes without saying that he is ready to give whatever explanations you
may want.

Accept, Monseigneur, the assurance of my prayer for your intentions in these grave circumstances, and of my devotion in Our Lord.

† J. Benelli
subst.

---

*"Irregularity" is the perpetual canonical impediment to the reception and exer-
cise of Holy Orders. The impediment can be removed only by dispensation, as
distinct from impediments called simple, which cease with the cessation of their
cause.

XI

The Ordinations of 29 June 1976

THOSE WHO ARE ordained to Holy Orders, whether to the diaconate or the priesthood, must first be accepted by a diocesan bishop or a religious order. The technical term for this acceptance is "incardination." It is not permitted to ordain men who will simply be wandering priests not subject to any competent authority. A diocesan bishop who has accepted a candidate for Holy Orders does not necessarily have to carry out the actual ordination himself. He can authorize another bishop to conduct the ordination on his behalf (by sending dimissorial letters). Up to and including the ordinations of 1975, all those ordained at Ecône had been properly incardinated into the dioceses of bishops sympathetic to Mgr. Lefebvre. The Vatican has not suggested that there was anything in the least illicit or irregular about these ordinations.

Once it became clear that Mgr. Lefebvre could not be browbeaten into closing his Seminary a new tactic was devised by Cardinal Villot. He decided to make it impossible for the seminarians to be ordained by intimidating those bishops sympathetic to Mgr. Lefebvre to the extent that they would decline to incardinate any seminarians from Ecône into their dioceses. Young men would clearly have little incentive to enroll in, or remain in, a seminary from which they could not be ordained. Thus in his letter of 27 October 1975 to the hierarchies of the world, Cardinal Villot stated:

> **It is therefore now clear that the Priestly Fraternity of St. Pius X has ceased to exist, that those who still claim to be members of it cannot pretend—*a fortiori*—to escape the jurisdiction of the diocesan Ordinaries (bishops), and, finally, that these same Ordinaries are gravely requested not to accord incardination in their dioceses to the young men who declare themselves to be engaged in the service of the Fraternity.**

Mgr. Lefebvre was thus faced with the dilemma of having either to incardinate his seminarians directly into the Fraternity itself or to close down the Seminary. There would have been no point in continuing it if the students were not to be ordained. He opted for the former course having taken legal advice from competent canon lawyers who advised him that, despite the letter from Pope Paul dated 29 June 1975, the entire legal process taken against the Fraternity had been so irregular that it could not be considered as having been legally suppressed. The Archbishop was further advised that, as the Vatican had permitted priests to be incardinated directly into the Fraternity on three separate occasions, it could be considered that the privilege of incardinating priests directly into the Fraternity now existed.

It is only fair to point out that canonists who are by no means unsympathetic to the Archbishop take a contrary viewpoint and accept that, from a strictly legal standpoint, the Fraternity had been legally suppressed and that the privilege of incardinating priests into it had not been adequately established.

It would be possible to devote endless pages to discussing the merits of each position but even it if is conceded, for the sake of argument, that the Vatican had the law upon its side it did not follow that the Archbishop was necessarily in the wrong. There are many orthodox Catholics who evade the necessity of considering the Archbishop's case on its merits by reducing the entire question to one of legality. "Archbishop Lefebvre is in breach of Canon Law," they argue, "therefore he is wrong."

At the risk of laboring a point which has probably been made sufficiently clear already, the Law is at the service of the Faith. It is intended to uphold the Faith and not to undermine it. Given that the manner in which the case against the Archbishop was conducted constituted an abuse of power, then he was entitled to resist.

Archbishop Lefebvre decided that he could best serve the Church by ordaining his seminarians and incardinating them into the Society of St. Pius X. The question which no Catholic of integrity can evade trying to answer honestly, is whether this decision constitutes inexcusable defiance of papal authority or a legitimate act of resistance to an abuse of power. The subsequent action taken against the Archbishop must be assessed in the light of the answer given to this question. Sanctions were imposed upon him by the Vatican; they will be detailed in their chronological sequence. Once again, the Archbishop decided to ignore them as they were simply a consequence of his refusal to accept the original command to close his Seminary. Even his worst enemies cannot accuse Mgr. Lefebvre of a lack of logic or consistency. His position is based upon one fundamental axiom: the action taken against him violates either Ecclesiastical or Natural Law, possibly both. If he is correct then his subsequent actions can be justified and the legality or illegality of subsequent Vatican decisions is irrelevant. Those who condemn the Archbishop invariably ignore this fundamental axiom and concentrate upon the legal *minutiae* of the subsequent sanctions. Those who support the Archbishop will do so most effectively by continually redirecting attention to this axiom rather than allowing themselves to be diverted into futile and endless discussion on these legal *minutiae*. It is also essential to cite the controversy within the context of the entire "Conciliar Church" where not simply any and every ecclesiastical law can be defied with impunity by Liberals but any and every article of the Catholic Faith can be denied with equal impunity. Reduced to its simplest terms, the true problem posed by the drama of Ecône is not whether Archbishop Lefebvre is right to defy the Vatican and continue ordaining priests but whether the Vatican is right to order the most orthodox and flourishing Seminary in the West to close.

The Ordination Ceremony

In its issue of 30 June 1976, the *Nouvelliste,* a Swiss secular paper, carried a front page report which included the following:

Yesterday morning at Ecône, in an atmosphere of faith and spiritual radiance, there assembled, in a meadow prepared for the ceremonies, 1,500 recollected and visibly moved Catholics. There were Romans, Turinese, French from numerous provinces and also from Paris, Germans, citizens of Lichtenstein and, arriving at the very last moment, some Americans; there was an equally impressive number of Valaisians (the canton in which Ecône is situated) and, most impressive of all, a very large number of priests from different orders.

There was no great pomp or ceremony: a tent to shelter the altar, Mgr. Lefebvre and his concelebrants (i. e. the newly ordained priests), and a large red carpet before the tent.

. . . When the time came for his sermon, Mgr. Lefebvre, obviously

moved, explained that for him this day was an exceptional feast and a
dramatic moment.

The full text of the sermon follows. During the sermon the
Archbishop refers to the arrival, the day before, of a representative of the Vatican who had placed a new Missal into his
hands and promised all the difficulties between the Archbishop and the Vatican would be straightened out if he
would use this Missal the next day. This emissary was the
Senegalese Cardinal Hyacinthe Thiandoum who had been
ordained a priest and consecrated as a bishop by Mgr. Lefebvre. The Cardinal's interview with the Archbishop lasted
until the early hours of the morning of 29 June and in consequence Mgr. Lefebvre had very little rest before the arduous ceremonies which faced him on the Feast of Saints Peter
and Paul.

It is of some significance that despite all the invective it
had poured upon the Archbishop and his Seminary, the Vatican was prepared to normalize relations at the price of the
Archbishop's celebrating just one New Mass.

29 June 1976
Sermon delivered by Archbishop Lefebvre at the
Ordination of thirteen priests and thirteen sub-deacons
on the Feast of Saints Peter and Paul, 1976

In the name of the Father, and of the Son, and of the Holy
Ghost. Amen.

My dear friends, dear confrères, dear brethren . . . who
have come from every country, from all horizons: It is a joy
for us to welcome you and to feel you so close to us at this
moment so important for our Fraternity and also for the
Church. I think that, if the pilgrims have permitted themselves to make this sacrifice, to journey day and night, to

come from distant regions to participate in this ceremony, it is because they had the conviction that they were coming to participate in a ceremony of the Church, to participate in a ceremony which would fill their hearts with joy, because they will now have the certitude in returning to their homes that the Catholic Church continues.

Ah, I know well that the difficulties are numerous in this undertaking which we have been told is foolhardy. They say that we are in a deadlock. Why? Because from Rome have come to us, especially in the last three months, since 19 March in particular, the Feast of Saint Joseph, demands, supplications, orders, and threats to inform us that we must cease our activity, to inform us that we must not perform these ordinations to the priesthood. They have been pressing these last few days. In the last twelve days in particular, we have not ceased to receive messages and envoys from Rome enjoining us to refrain from performing these ordinations.

But if in all objectivity we seek the true motive animating those who ask us not to perform these ordinations, if we look for the hidden motive, it is because we are ordaining these priests that they may say the Mass of all time.* It is because they know that these priests will be faithful to the Mass of the Church, to the Mass of Tradition, to the Mass of all time, that they urge us not to ordain them.

In proof of this, consider that six times in the last three weeks—*six* times—we have been asked to re-establish normal relations with Rome and to give as proof the acceptance of the new rite; and I have been asked to celebrate it myself. They have gone so far as to send me someone who offered to concelebrate with me in the new rite so as to manifest that I accepted voluntarily this new liturgy, saying that in this way

---

*The Archbishop's frequently repeated expression, '*la Messe de toujours,*' has no suitable English equivalent. In translating it as 'the Mass of all time,' the translator has attempted to render the literal sense without losing the flavor of the original French expression.

all would be straightened out between us and Rome. They put a new Missal into my hands, saying "Here is the Mass that you must celebrate and that you *shall* celebrate henceforth in all your houses." They told me as well that if on this date, today, this 29th of June, before your entire assembly, we celebrated a Mass according to the new rite, all would be straightened out henceforth between ourselves and Rome. Thus it is clear, it is evidence that it is *on the problem of the Mass* that the whole drama between Ecône and Rome depends.

Are we wrong in obstinately wanting to keep the rite of all time? We have, of course, prayed, we have consulted, we have reflected, we have meditated to discover if it is not indeed we who are in error, or if we do not really have a sufficient reason not to submit ourselves to the new rite. And in fact, the very insistence of those who were sent from Rome to ask us to change rite makes us wonder.

And we have the precise conviction that this new rite of Mass expresses a *new* faith, a faith which is not ours, a faith which is not the Catholic Faith. This New Mass is a symbol, is an expression, is an image of a new faith, of a *Modernist* faith. For if the most holy Church has wished to guard throughout the centuries this precious treasure which She has given us of the rite of Holy Mass which was canonized by Saint Pius V, it has not been without purpose. It is because this Mass contains *our whole faith,* the *whole* Catholic Faith: faith in the Most Holy Trinity, faith in the Divinity of Our Lord Jesus Christ, faith in the Redemption of Our Lord Jesus Christ, faith in the Blood of Our Lord Jesus Christ which flowed for the redemption of our sins, faith in supernatural grace, which comes to us from the Holy Sacrifice of the Mass, which comes to us from the Cross, which comes to us through all the Sacraments.

This is what we believe. This is what we believe in celebrating the Holy Sacrifice of the Mass of all time. It is a lesson of faith and at the same time a *source* of our faith, *indispensable* for us in this age when our faith is attacked from all sides. We have *need* of this true Mass, of this Mass of all time. of this Sacrifice of Our Lord Jesus Christ really to fill our souls with the Holy Ghost and with the strength of Our Lord Jesus Christ.

Now it is evident that the new rite, if I may say so, supposes another conception of the Catholic religion—another religion. It is no longer the priest who offers the Holy Sacrifice of the Mass, it is the assembly. Now this is an entire program—an entire program. Henceforth it is the assembly also that replaces authority in the Church. It is the assembly of bishops that replaces the power of (individual) bishops. It is the priests' council that replaces the power of the bishop in the diocese. It is numbers that command from now on in the Holy Church. And this is expressed in the Mass precisely because the assembly replaces the priest, to such a point that now many priests no longer want to celebrate Holy Mass when there is no assembly. Slowly but surely the Protestant notion of the Mass is being introduced into the Holy Church.*

And this is consistent with the mentality of modern man—absolutely consistent. For it is the democratic ideal which is the *fundamental* idea of modern man, that is to say, that the power lies with the assembly, that authority is in the people, in the masses, and not in God. And this is most grave. Be-

---

*It should be noted that the Archbishop is not denying the validity of the New Mass; for an explicit statement of his views on this point see pp. 348-349. He is pointing out the manner in which the New Mass can be made to accord with Protestant belief. Protestants deny that there is any distinction in essence between priest and layman. The President, who presides over the Eucharist, possesses no powers not possessed by the rest of the congregation. He acts as their representative. In the Roman Canon there are prayers which make explicit the distinction between priest and congregation. The priests are referred to as God's servants and the congregation as His family or people, e.g. the *Hanc igitur, unde et Memores*, and *Nobis quoque*. With Eucharistic prayer No. II in particular, it is possible for the priest to appear as no more than the President of a concelebrating congregation.

cause we believe that God is all-powerful; we believe that God has all authority; we believe that all authority comes from God. *"Omnis potestas a Deo."* All authority comes from God. We do not believe that authority comes from below. Now that is the mentality of modern man.

And the New Mass is not less than the expression of this idea that authority is at the base, and no longer in God. This Mass is no longer a hierarchical Mass; it is a democratic Mass. And this is most grave. It is the expression of a *whole new ideology*. The ideology of modern man has been brought into our most sacred rites.

And this is what is at present corrupting the entire Church. For by this idea of power bestowed on the lower rank, in the Holy Mass, they have destroyed the priesthood! They are destroying the priesthood, for what is the priest, if the priest no longer has a personal power, that power which is given to him by his ordination, as these future priests are going to receive it in a moment? They are going to receive a character, a character which will put them *above* the people of God! Nevermore shall they be able to say after the ceremony about to be performed, they shall never be able to say: "We are men like other men." This would not be true.

They will no longer be men like other men! They will be men of God. They will be men, I should say, who almost participate in the divinity of Our Lord Jesus Christ by His sacerdotal character. For Our Lord Jesus Christ is Priest for eternity, Priest according to the Order of Melchisedech, because He *is* Jesus Christ; because the divinity of the Word of God was infused into the humanity which He assumed. And it is at the moment that He assumed this humanity in the womb of the Most Blessed Virgin Mary that Jesus became Priest.

The grace in which these young priests are going to participate is not the sanctifying grace in which Our Lord Jesus Christ gives us to participate by the grace of baptism; it is the grace of *union*—that grace of union unique to Our Lord Jesus

Christ. It is in this grace that they are going to participate, for it is by His grace of union with the divinity of God, with the divinity of the Word, that Our Lord Jesus Christ became Priest; that Our Lord Jesus Christ is King; that Our Lord Jesus Christ is Judge; that Our Lord Jesus Christ ought to be adored by all men: by His grace of union, sublime grace! grace which no being here below could ever receive—this grace of the divinity itself descending into a humanity which is Our Lord Jesus Christ, anointing Him, after a fashion, like the oil that descends on the head and consecrates him who receives this oil. The humanity of Our Lord Jesus Christ was penetrated by the divinity of the Word of God, and thus He was made Priest. He was made Mediator between God and men.

It is in this very grace, which will place them above the people of God, that these priests are going to participate. They too will be the intermediaries between God and God's people. They will not merely be the representatives of the people of God; they will not be the functionaries of the people of God; they will not merely be 'presidents of the assembly.' They are priests for eternity, marked by this character for eternity, and no one has the right not to respect them; even if they themselves did not respect this character—they have it always in themselves, they will always have it in themselves.

This is what we believe, this is our faith, and this is what constitutes our Holy Sacrifice of the Mass. It is the *priest* who offers the Holy Sacrifice of the Mass; and the faithful *participate* in this offering, with all their heart, with all their soul, but it is not they who offer the Holy Sacrifice of the Mass. As proof, consider that the priest, when he is alone, offers the Holy Sacrifice of the Mass in the same manner and with the same value as if there were a thousand people around him. His sacrifice has an infinite value: the sacrifice of Our Lord Jesus Christ offered by the priest has an infinite value.

This is what we believe. This is why we think that we cannot accept the new rite, which is the work of *another* ideology, or a new ideology. They thought that they would attract the world by accepting the ideas of the world. They thought they would attract to the Church those who do not believe by accepting the ideas of these persons who do not believe, by accepting the ideas of modern man—this modern man who is a Liberal, who is a Modernist; who is a man who accepts the plurality of religions, who no longer accepts the social Kingship of Our Lord Jesus Christ. This I have heard twice from the envoys of the Holy See, who told me that the social Kingship of Our Lord Jesus Christ was no longer possible in our time; that we must accept definitely the pluralism of religions. That is what they told me. That the Encyclical *Quas Primas*, which is so beautiful, on the social Kingship of Our Lord Jesus Christ, which was written by Pope Pius XI, would never be written today by the Pope. This is what they said to me—the official envoys of the Holy See.

Well, we are not of this religion. We do not accept this new religion. We are of the religion of all time; we are of the Catholic religion. We are not of this 'universal religion' as they call it today—this is not the Catholic religion any more. We are not of this Liberal, Modernist religion which has its own worship, its own priests, its own faith, its own catechisms, its own Bible, the 'ecumenical Bible'—these things we do not accept. We do not accept the 'ecumenical Bible.' There is no 'ecumenical Bible.' There is only the Bible of God, the Bible of the Holy Ghost, written under the influence of the Holy Ghost. It is the Word of God. We do not have the right to mix it with the words of men. There is no 'ecumenical Bible' which could possibly exist. There is only one Word—the Word of the Holy Ghost. We do not accept the catechisms which no longer uphold our Creed. And so on and so forth.

We cannot accept these things. They are contrary to our Faith. We regret infinitely, it is an immense, immense pain for us, to think that we are in difficulty with Rome *because of our faith*! How is this possible? It is something that exceeds the imagination, that we should never have been able to imagine, that we should never have been able to believe, especially in our childhood—then when all was uniform, when the whole Church believed in Her general unity, and held the same Faith, the same Sacraments, the same Sacrifice of the Mass, the same catechism. And behold, suddenly all is in division, in chaos.

I said as much to those who came from Rome. I said so: Christians are torn apart in their families, in their homes, among their children; they are torn apart in their hearts by this division in the Church, by this new religion now being taught and practiced. Priests are dying prematurely, torn apart in their hearts and in their souls at the thought that they no longer know what to do: either to submit to obedience and lose, in a way, the faith of their childhood and of their youth, and renounce the promises which they made at the time of their ordination in taking the anti-Modernist oath; or to have the impression of separating themselves from him who is our father, the Pope, from him who is the representative of Saint Peter. What agony for these priests! Many priests have died prematurely of grief. Priests are now hounded from their churches, persecuted, because they say the Mass of all time.

We are in a truly dramatic situation. We have to choose between an appearance, I should say, of disobedience—for the Holy Father cannot ask us to abandon our faith. It is impossible, impossible—the abandonment of our faith. We choose *not* to abandon our faith, for in that we cannot go wrong. In that which the Catholic Church has taught for two thousand years, the Church *cannot* be in error. It is absolutely impossible, and that is why we are attached to this tradition which is expressed in such an admirable and definitive manner, as Pope Saint Pius V said so well, in a definitive manner in the Holy Sacifice of the Mass.

Tomorrow perhaps, in the newspapers, will appear our condemnation. It is quite possible, because of these ordinations today. I myself shall probably be struck by suspension. These young priests will be struck by an irregularity which in theory should prevent them from saying Holy Mass. It is possible. Well, I appeal to Saint Pius V—Saint Pius V, who in his Bull said that, in perpetuity, no priest could incur a censure, whatever it might be, in perpetuity, for saying this Mass. And consequently, this censure, this excommunication, if there was one, these censures, if there are any, are absolutely *invalid*, contrary to that which Saint Pius V established in perpetuity in his Bull: that *never* in any age could one inflict a censure on a priest who says this Holy Mass.

Why? Because this Mass is canonized.* He canonized it definitively. Now a Pope cannot remove a canonization. The Pope can make a new rite, but he cannot remove a canonization. He cannot forbid a Mass that is canonized. Thus, if he has canonized a Saint, another Pope cannot come and say that this Saint is no longer canonized. That is not possible. Now this Holy Mass was canonized by Pope Saint Pius V. And that is why we can say it in all tranquillity, in all security, and even be certain that, in saying this Mass, we are professing our faith, we are upholding our faith, we are upholding the faith of the Catholic people. This is, indeed, the best manner of upholding it.

And that is why we are going to proceed in a few moments with these ordinations. Certainly we should desire to have a blessing as was given in the past by the Holy See—a benediction came from Rome for the newly-ordained. But we be-

---

*The Mass is 'canonized' in the sense that Pope Saint Pius V with all his authority established it as the official *rule* or manner of saying Mass for all priests of the Roman Rite for all time.

lieve that God is here present, that He sees all things, and that He also blesses this ceremony which we are performing; and that one day He will certainly draw from it the fruits which He desires, and will aid us in any case, to maintain our Faith and to serve the Church.

We ask this especially of the Most Blessed Virgin Mary and of Saints Peter and Paul today. Let us ask the Most Blessed Virgin, who is the Mother of the Priesthood, to give these young men the true grace of the priesthood; to give them the Holy Ghost in Whose giving she was intermediary the day of Pentecost.

Let us ask Saint Peter and Saint Paul to maintain in us this faith in Peter. Ah, yes, we believe in Peter, we believe in the Successor of Peter! But as Pope Pius IX says well in his dogmatic constitution, the Pope has received the Holy Ghost, not to make new truths, but to maintain us in the Faith of all time. This is the definition of the Pope made at the time of the First Vatican Council by Pope Pius IX. And that is why we are persuaded that, in maintaining these traditions, we are manifesting our love, our docility, our obedience to the Successor of Peter.

In the name of the Father, and of the Son, and of the Holy Ghost. Amen.

XII

The Suspension

1 July 1976
Declaration at a Press Conference

Father Romeo Panciroli, spokesman of the Press Bureau
of the Holy See, made the following declaration on 1 July
1976, which was published on 8 July in the diocesan bulletin of Mgr. Mamie and reproduced in *La Documentation
Catholique* of 1 August:

According to information from Switzerland, Mgr. Lefebvre has actually gone ahead with the ordination of a certain number of priests and
deacons. According to the same information, the candidates were not
provided with dimissorial letters from their Ordinary or with a valid
canonical title.

In that case, the following rules of the Code of Canon Law apply:

1° Mgr. Lefebvre has automatically incurred suspension for a year from
the conferring of orders, a suspension reserved to the Apostolic See.
The same is true of earlier ordinations which may have taken place

under the same conditions, with the aggravating circumstance, in this case, of irregularity linked with repetition of the offense. This suspension is in addition to the prohibition of conferring orders pronounced by the Holy Father and transgressed by Mgr. Lefebvre, but which obviously is still valid and operative.

2º Those who have been ordained are *ipso facto* (automatically) suspended from the order received, and, if they were to exercise it, they would be in an irregular and criminal situation. The priests who may have been already suspended for a preceding irregular promotion to the diaconate could be punished with severe penalties according to the circumstances, in addition to the fact that they have put themselves in an irregular situation.

3º The Holy See is examining the special case of the formal disobedience of Mgr. Lefebvre to the instructions of the Holy Father who, by the documents of 12 and 25 June 1976, expressly forbade him to proceed with the ordinations. Even fraternal interventions these last days, started by the Holy Father to get Mgr. Lefebvre to abandon his project, could not prevent the interdiction being violated.

4 July 1976
The Mass in Geneva

On 4 July 1976, Mgr. Lefebvre preached at a Solemn High Mass celebrated in Geneva by Father Denis Roch, a convert from Calvinism who had been ordained on 29 June. This Mass is of particular interest for two reasons. Firstly, it provided an opportunity of assessing the reaction of the ordinary faithful to the Archbishop's decision to ordain his seminarians in defiance of the Vatican. The importance of this reaction was heightened by the fact that Mgr. Mamie, Bishop of Lausanne, Geneva, and Fribourg went to exceptional lengths to make use of this Mass as a trial of strength between himself and Mgr. Lefebvre. Father Roch was denied

access to all the Catholic churches in Geneva, he was forbidden to celebrate Mass in Geneva, and Mgr. Lefebvre was
forbidden to preach. Furthermore, Mgr. Mamie commanded,
in a statement published in the *Nouvelliste* on 2 July, that:

> The Catholics of this diocese, and those who are visiting it, must be
> warned: no Catholic is authorized to take part in the first Mass (of
> Father Roch) to be celebrated on 4 July.

La Tribune de Genève (a secular Swiss paper) gave considerable coverage to the Mass in its 5 July 1976 issue. The
paper noted that the Mass was celebrated in the *Palais des
Expositions:*

> More than 2,000 people assembled in this vast hall despite the inter-
> diction of Mgr. Mamie . . . The congregation manifested great fervor.
> Hundreds of the faithful received Holy Communion. Men, women,
> adolescents and young children knelt and prayed with devotion . . . no
> Catholic church in Geneva would have been large enough to welcome
> such a vast number of believers.

Subsequent Masses celebrated by the Archbishop in France
and elsewhere proved that, despite the Vatican sanctions, a
Mass celebrated by him will attract a congregation of several
thousand almost anywhere in Catholic Europe. In most dioceses he can certainly attract a larger congregation than the
diocesan bishop—particularly in France. It is not intended to
suggest that the rightness or wrongness of Mgr. Lefebvre's,
or any other, case can be assessed by the extent of support
for it. If rightness depended on numbers, the persecuted
Catholics of Elizabethan England would have had a very poor
case. But as the Archbishop's enemies are trying continually
to minimize the extent of support for him it is worth taking
note of the attendance at these Masses. The support for Mgr.
Lefebvre is an excellent example of the true *sensus fidelium.*

The second reason for the significance of this Mass is the very fine sermon preached by the Archbishop. He does go over some points made in other sermons but, as it has not been published in English, it is included here as a useful exposition of Mgr. Lefebvre's attitude immediately following the ordinations of 29 June, a period during which he certainly underwent great emotional and physical strain.

4 July 1976
Sermon by Mgr. Lefebvre at Geneva

My Dear Monsieur l'Abbé,
My Dear Friends,
My Dear Brothers,

It is not in this Exhibition Hall that your first Mass should have taken place, you being a child of this city. It is in a large and beautiful church of the City of Geneva that you should have celebrated this ceremony so dear to the hearts of all the Catholics of Geneva. But, as Providence has decided otherwise, here you are before the crowd of your friends, of your relatives, of those who want to share your joy and the honor which God has done you of being His priest, a priest for ever.

This history of your vocation is the implementation of a plan.

And I shall say what our plan is.

You were born of Protestant parents in this City of Geneva, and in childhood and youth you followed the teaching of the Protestant religion. You were well educated, and you had a profession which gave you all the world can hope for here below. Then, all of a sudden, touched by the grace of God through the intercession of the Blessed Virgin Mary, you abruptly decided, under the influence of that grace, to direct yourself to the true Church, the Catholic Church; and you desired not only to become a Catholic but also to become a priest. I can still see you arriving for the first time at Ecône; and I confess that it was not without a certain apprehension that I received you, asking myself if so rapid a passage from Protestantism to the desire of becoming a Catholic priest was not an inspiration with no future. That is the reason why you stayed some time at Ecône reflecting more deeply on the desire within you, your aspiration to the priesthood. We all admired your perseverance, your will to reach that goal, despite your age, despite a certain weariness of ecclesiastical studies, of the study of philosophy, theology, Scripture, Canon Law—for you were a scientist. And now, by God's grace, after those years of study at Ecône you have received the grace of sacerdotal ordination. It seems to me to be difficult for anyone who has not received that grace to realize what the grace of priesthood is. As I said to you a few days ago at the time of the ordination: You can no longer say that you are a man like other men; that is not true. You are no longer a man like other men: henceforward you are marked with the sacerdotal character which is something ontological, which marks your soul and puts it above the faithful. Yes, whether you are a saint, or, which God forbid, whether you are like priests who are, perhaps, alas, in hell: they still have the sacerdotal character. This sacerdotal character unites you to Our Lord Jesus Christ, to the priesthood of Our Lord Jesus Christ in a very special way, a participation which the faithful cannot have; and that is what permits you, which will permit you in a few moments, to pronounce the words of consecration of Holy Mass, and in a way to make God obey your order, your words. At your words Jesus Christ will come personally, physically, substantially under the species of the bread and wine; He will be present on the altar, and you will adore Him; you will kneel to adore Him, to adore the presence of Our Lord Jesus Christ. That is what the priest is. What an extraordinary reality! We need to be in heaven—and even in heaven shall we understand what the priest is? Is it not St. Augustine who says: "Were I to find myself before a priest and an angel, I should salute the priest first, before the angel"?

So, then, here you are, become a priest. I said that the history of your vocation is a whole plan, it is our plan. That is profoundly true, because we have the Catholic Faith and are not afraid to affirm our faith; and I know that our Protestant friends, who are perhaps here in this assembly, approve of us. They approve of us: they need to feel the presence amongst them of Catholics who are Catholics, and not Catholics who appear to be in full accord with them on points of faith. One does not deceive one's friends; we cannot deceive our Protestant friends. We are Catholics; we affirm our faith in the divinity of Our Lord Jesus Christ, we affirm our faith in the divinity of the Holy Catholic Church, we think that Jesus Christ is the sole way, the sole truth, the sole life, and that one cannot be saved outside Our Lord Jesus Christ and consequently outside His Mystical Spouse, the Holy Catholic Church. No doubt, the graces of God are distributed outside the Catholic Church; but those who are saved, even outside the Catholic Church, are saved by the Catholic Church, by Our Lord Jesus Christ, even if they do not know it, even if they are not aware of it, for it is Our Lord Jesus Christ Himself who has said it: "You can do nothing without me—*nihil potestis facere sine me.*" You cannot come to the Father without going by me, so you cannot come to God without going by me. "When I shall be lifted up from the earth, " says Our Lord Jesus Christ, meaning He will be on His cross, "I shall draw all souls to me." Only Our Lord Jesus Christ, being God, could say such things: no man here below can speak as Our Lord Jesus Christ has spoken, because He alone is the Son of God, He is our God—*Tu solus altissimus, tu solus Dominus.* He is Our Lord, He is the Most High, Our Lord Jesus Christ.

It is for that that Ecône remains in being, it is for that that Ecône exists, because we believe that what the Catholics have taught, what the Popes have taught, what the Councils have taught for twenty centuries, we cannot possibly abandon. We cannot possibly change our faith: we have our *Credo*, and we will keep it till we die. We cannot change our *Credo*, we cannot change the Holy Sacrifice of the Mass, we cannot change our Sacraments, changing them into human works, purely human, which no longer carry the grace of Our Lord Jesus Christ. It is because, in fact, we feel and are convinced that in the last fifteen years something has happened in the Church, something has happened in the Church which has introduced into the highest summits of the Church, and into those who ought to defend our faith, a poison, a virus, which makes them adore the golden calf of this age, adore, in some sense, the errors of this age. To adopt the world, they wish to adopt also the errors of the world; by opening on to the world, they wish also to open themselves to the errors of the world, those errors which say, for example, that all religions are of equal worth. We cannot accept that, those errors which say that the social reign of Our Lord Jesus Christ is now an impossibility and should no longer be sought. We do not accept that. Even if the reign of Our Lord Jesus Christ is difficult, we want it, we seek it, we say every day in the Our Father: "Thy kingdom come, thy will be done on earth as it is in heaven." If His will were done here below as it is done in heaven—imagine what it would be like if God's will were really done here below as it is done in heaven: it would be paradise on earth! That is the reign of Our Lord which we seek, which we desire with all our strength, even if we never achieve it; and, because God has asked that from us, even if we have to shed our blood for that kingdom we are ready. And that is what the priests are whom we form at Ecône, priests who have the Catholic faith, priests such as have always been formed.

Do you not think there is something inconceivable, unbelievable? Take my example, which is like yours. I have now been a priest for fifty years and a bishop for thirty. That means I was a bishop before the Council, a priest before the Council. In my career as priest and bishop I was made responsible for the formation of priests. In the beginning when I went as a missionary to Gabon I was appointed to the seminary of Gabon in Equatorial Africa. I formed priests, one of whom became a bishop. I was recalled to France, and again I was appointed to form seminarians in the seminary of Mortain with the Holy Ghost Fathers. I then went back as bishop of Dakar, in Senegal. I set myself again to form good priests of whom two are bishops and one has just been named Cardinal; and when I was at Mortain in France I formed seminarians, one of whom is now Bishop of Cayenne; so amongst my pupils I have four bishops, one of them a cardinal. I form my seminarians at Ecône exactly as I have always formed my seminarians for thirty years; and now, all of a sudden, we are condemned, almost excommunicated, thrown out of the Catholic Church, in disobedience to the Catholic Church, because I have done the same thing that I have done for thirty years. Something has happened in Holy Church. It is not possible! I have changed not one iota in my formation of seminarians, on the contrary I have added a deeper and stronger spirituality, because it seemed to me a certain spiritual formation was lacking in young priests, as, in fact, many have abandoned the priesthood, many, alas, have given the world appalling scandal in their leaving of the priesthood. So it seemed to me necessary to give these priests a deeper, stronger, more courageous spiritual formation to enable them to face difficulties. . . *

So, something has happened in the Church: the Church since the Council, already some time before the Council, during the Council, and throughout the reforms, has chosen

*Some words are missing on the tape recording.

to take a new direction, to have Her new priests, Her new priesthood, a new type of priest as has been said; She has chosen to have a new sacrifice of the Mass, or rather let us say a new eucharist; She has chosen to have a new catechism, She has chosen to have new seminaries, She has chosen to reform Her religious congregations. And what have we now come to? A few days ago I read in a German paper that in the last few years there are three million fewer practicing Catholics in Germany. Cardinal Marty himself, he who also condemns us, Cardinal Marty, Archbishop of Paris, has said that Mass attendance is down fifty per cent in his diocese since the Council.

Who will say that the fruits of that Council are marvelous fruits of holiness, fervor, and growth of the Catholic Church?

They have chosen to embrace the errors of the world, they have chosen to embrace the errors which come to us from Liberalism, and which come to us—alas, it must be said—from those who lived here four centuries ago, from those reformers who have spread Liberal ideas throughout the world; and those ideas have at last penetrated to the interior of the Church. This monster which is at the interior of the Church must disappear, so that the Church may find Her own nature again, Her own authenticity, Her own identity. That is what we are trying to do, and it is why we continue: we do not want to be destroyers of the Church. If we stop, we shall be certain, convinced, that we are destroying the Church, as those are engaged in destroying Her who are steeped in that false idea. And so we wish to go on with the construction of the Church; and we cannot do better to get the Church built than to make these priests, these young priests—showing always the example of a deep Catholic faith, of an immense charity. I think I can say that it is we who have a true charity towards Protestants, towards all those who do not have our faith. If we believe our Catholic faith, if we are convinced that God has really given His graces to the Catholic Church, we have the desire of sharing our riches with our friends, giving them to our friends. If we are convinced that we have the truth, we should exert ourselves to make it known that that truth can benefit our friends as well. It is a failure in charity to hide one's truth, to hide one's personal riches and not let those profit from them who do not have their own. Why have missions, why set off to distant countries to convert souls, if not because one is certain of having the truth and desirous of sharing the graces received with those who have not yet received them? It is indeed Our Saviour who said: "Go and teach all nations, baptizing them in the name of the Father and of the Son and of the Holy Ghost. He that believeth shall be saved, he that believeth not shall be condemned." That is what Our Saviour said. Strengthened by these words, we continue our apostolate, trusting in Providence: it is not possible that this condition of the Church should remain indefinitely.

This morning, in the lessons which Holy Church has us read, we read the story of David and Goliath, and I thought to myself: Should we not be the young David with his sling and a few stones which he found in the stream to strike down Goliath clad in special armour and with a sword capable of splitting his enemy in two? Well, who knows if Ecône is not the little stone which will finish by destroying Goliath? Goliath believed in himself; David believed in God and invoked God before attacking Goliath. That is what we are doing. We are full of confidence in God, and we pray God to help us to strike down this giant who believes in himself, who believes in his armour, his muscles, and his weapons. That means the men who believe in themselves, who believe in their science, who believe that by human means we shall succeed in converting the world. As for us, we put our trust in God, and we hope that this Goliath who has penetrated into the interior of the Church will one day be struck down, and that the Church will truly discover Her authenticity, Her truth such as She has always had. Oh, the Church always has it; She does not will to perish; and we hope, precisely, to cooperate with that vitality of the Church and that continuity of the Church. I am convinced that these young priests will continue the Church. That is what we ask them to do, and we are sure that with the grace of God and the help of the Blessed Virgin Mary, Mother of the Priesthood, they will succeed.

In the name of the Father and of the Son and of the Holy Ghost. Amen.

6 July 1976
Letter of Cardinal Baggio to Mgr. Lefebvre

Cardinal Sebastiano Baggio wrote this official letter (numbered 514/76) in his capacity as Prefect of the Roman Congregation responsible for bishops and by order of Pope Paul.

Monseigneur,

It is the Holy Father who desires me to send you this letter. It is intended above all, on the part of His Holiness and in the name of Jesus Christ, to be a new expression of the most earnest desire, and of the ardent hope felt for a long time, of seeing you finally, after a renewal of your espiscopal and ecclesial conscience, retrace your steps and re-establish that communion which, by your attitude, you have again broken more openly, and in fact on the Feast of the Holy Apostles Peter and Paul.

I do not wish to touch here on the question of the non-observance of the conditions to which a bishop should keep who is proceeding to the ordination of subjects not his own, non-observance for which the Code of Canon Law itself provides, in canons 2373, 2374 and 985 n. 7, appropriate sanctions.

On the other hand, it is incumbent on me, in execution of a duty coming to me from above, to state that, in ignoring the express prohibition by the Holy Father, clearly and lawfully manifested in the documents of 12 and 23 June last, and with fraternal interventions by qualified persons, you have publicly disobeyed the prohibition by proceeding to the ordination of several priests and of some "subdeacons."

Cardinal Baggio writes subdeacons within quotation marks because the subdiaconate has been suppressed in the "Conciliar Church."

Also, by this present monition, I implore you to change your attitude, to ask pardon humbly of the Holy Father, and to repair the spiritual damage inflicted on the young men ordained and the scandal caused to the people of God.

I cherish the hope that you will not refuse to take the hand which His Holiness holds out to you yet again.

When the Vatican gives notice of a new threat or a new sanction it describes this as "holding out a hand yet again"!

If, however, the invitation were to prove vain, and if a proof of recognition of error did not arrive at this Congregation within ten days of your receipt of my letter,* you must know that, basing itself on a special mandate of the Sovereign Pontiff, it will be the duty of this Congregation to proceed against you by inflicting the necessary penalties, in conformity with canon 2331, para. 1.**

I beg you to believe that it is with great pain that I have written this letter to a confrère in the episcopate, and I assure you, Monseigneur, of my respectful devotion in Our Lord.

Sebastiano Card. Baggio
Prefect

---

*I. e. ten days from Sunday, 11 July 1976.

**The canon mentioned does not specify the penalties: *congruis poenis, censuris non exclusis, pro gravitate culpae puniantur.*

8 July 1976
The Chronicle of Father Bruckberger

Father Henri Bruckberger is one of the leading men of letters among the French clergy today. He was a chaplain to the Resistance during the war and was forced to escape to the U.S.A. in order to evade the Gestapo. He writes a weekly column in the French daily *L'Aurore* which is awaited with bated breath by both traditionalists and Liberals—the latter waiting with trepidation to discover what new aspect of the "Conciliar Church" he will expose as tyranny, heresy or hypocrisy. He has come to be looked upon as the voice of the ordinary French Catholic, and because he refused to silence that voice he has been subjected to severe pressure from his superiors in the Dominican Order. No comment needs to be made regarding the parallel between the persecution he suffered for his resistance to the Nazi tyranny and that which he now suffers for his resistance to the tyranny of the "Conciliar Church."

In his column in *L'Aurore* dated 8 July 1976 he gave vent to an impassioned *cri du coeur* in protest at the coldness and hostility shown by the French Bishops to the newly ordained priests from Ecône. Had they been Muslims, Communists, Protestant ministers, or Buddhist monks they would have been received with open arms; churches would have been placed at their disposal. But they were traditionalist Catholic priests—so the doors of the "Conciliar Church" were slammed in their faces. Father Bruckberger's article follows.

The Order of Melchisedech

"Once again we return to the subject of Ecône and to the priests ordained there by Mgr. Lefebvre. One knows that they were ordained illicitly, that is to say without the permission and against the wishes of the Pope, but nobody denies that they are true, validly ordained priests; nobody casts doubts on their fervor or on their priestly zeal.

Immediately after ordination, these young men return to their home parishes. In former days, I well remember, such a newly ordained priest was the pride of the entire parish. Everyone flocked to his first Mass, which was celebrated in an atmosphere of joyous devotion and reverence; of gratitude for the precious gift which God had bestowed upon the entire Christian people. Bells pealed, and the sweet smell of incense filled the church. When the Mass was ended, even the old men knelt to receive the blessing of this young, newly ordained priest.

This was the reception the new priests from Ecône were given by their relatives and friends; not so by the official clergy, whose behavior was crude in the extreme. By "official clergy" I mean those now in charge of our churches and cathedrals. We know that discord exists among bishops; was it really necessary to extend the burden of discord to those young men, at the very moment when they had so joyfully given their entire youth to God?

Closed Doors

It was Cardinal Marty who initiated this contemptible ostracism; at last he has shown himself in his true colors. While all types of liturgical abuses are tolerated in our churches; while one church in Paris is used for Moslem services, it is these young priests alone who find the doors of their parish churches closed in their faces; young priests of Jesus Christ, the anointing oils of the ordination still fresh upon their hands; young priests who bring no threat, but solely their new powers of Consecration. Ousted from their parish churches, they are forced to celebrate Mass in secret as during the Reign of Terror. One blushes with shame at the very thought.

However severe the Church may have been during my childhood, showing at times the austere face of Jansenism, never did She show the implacable, cold cruelty which in France today She shows to those of Her sons whose sole aim is to preserve the purity of their Faith and of their vocation. Is this what is called a "Pastoral Church"? Is this the Church of the Good Shepherd, carrying the lamb upon His shoulders? Is it even, as Cardinal Marty claims, "A church which wishes to obey its Lord in the service of contemporary man"? He Who has the words of eternal life for our salvation, is He not also a "present day" man?

Your Eminence, I am going to tell you what horrifies me in you. Christianity has taught us that in the depths of man there exists something impenetrable, something which could well be called his spiritual "heart." This "heart" does not beat to the rhythm of time: it beats secretly to the rhythm of eternal life. When confined within the limits of time, it ceases to beat, as it always does. It is when this "heart-beat" is on the point of stopping that the priest of Jesus Christ brings the spiritual oxygen cylinder. Your Eminence, you are condemning these young priests in the name of "your time" of which, in any case, you know little. Fear, yes, fear the sentence which will be pronounced, not by them, not by me, but by Another Who is above us all in eternity.

But, Your Eminence, the surprising part of your declaration, your trump card, so to speak, was: "Allow me to tell you once again, that in our present difficulties it is not merely a matter of Latin or of the cassock. Far more is at stake: the unity of the Church is threatened, the Eucharistic Mystery in its fullness of truth is threatened." Your Eminence, your words are indeed true, they are indeed frank; they are terribly frank; they are terribly true. They re-affirm what I have been constantly repeating in this chronicle. They are the very words used by Mgr. Lefebvre. So, for once, we are in agreement and the door is now open for discussion.

The Return of the Pharisees

Nothing could be more legitimate, nothing more traditional than to base the unity of the Church on the truth of the Eucharist. The Eucharist is the sacrement of that unity, for the Body of Christ is the common heritage of the Church. It is around this Body that the members of the Church gather. The Mystical Body of Christ is sanctified by participating in the Eucharistic Body of Christ, either by receiving Holy Communion or by making a Spiritual Communion. One calls to mind the words found in St. Matthew: "Wheresoever the body shall be, there shall the eagles also be gathered together." The Eucharist is not a meal for the unlettered; still less is it a banquet for the intellectual; it is, as it were, the prey of the eagle, a bird which is not given to relinquishing its prey for its shadow. That is the heart of the matter. Who best safeguards the unity of the Church: those who keep the reality of the Eucharistic Body of Christ, or those who lightly relinquish the substance for the shadow?

Catholicism is the religion of the Incarnation. God lifts us up to Himself through the Humanity of Jesus Christ, made present throughout the centuries and throughout the world by outward signs known as sacraments. To betray those rites is to betray Jesus Christ in His reality; it is to endanger the salvation of man for whom these rites were instituted by Jesus Christ Himself, rites which have been carefully fostered by the Church since Her foundation. Herein lies the cause of the turmoil within the Church; the crisis of Ecône is but a symptom of the turmoil.

Your Eminence, when, as you say, the unity of the Church and the mystery of the Eucharist in the fullness of its truth are at stake, we find it extremely worrying, not to say distasteful, to find you reducing the affair of Ecône to a mere disciplinary matter, to find you donning the cap of a Doctor in Canon Law, when, in fact, the very Church is at stake.

In former days the Pharisees posed as groping defenders of

the Law against One Who was both the Consummation and Supreme Justification of the Law."

THE CATHOLIC MASS

In the *Supplément-Voltigeur* to *Itinéraires* (No. 40 of July 1976), Jean Madiran made it quite clear why these young priests had been treated in the manner described by Father Bruckberger.

"During the days preceding the ordinations to the priesthood at Ecône on 29 June, messages and envoys from the Vatican thronged about Mgr. Lefebvre, promising him that all would be well if he accepted the new missal, imposed it on his priests, and himself concelebrated the New Mass publicly with a representative of Paul VI. The promise was no doubt false, but it was significant—it showed that the assurance given to Mgr. Lefebvre all through 1975 by the official inquisitors, that in the proceedings against him liturgy was not in question, was a trick: the truth was that it was liturgy alone, or liturgy above all, that was in question—it was a question of the Mass of Article 7 which was to take the place of the traditional Mass.

A similar trickery had pretended in 1970 to correct Article 7 promulgated in 1969. The same trick, in the Council, had put forward the *nota praevia explicativa* on collegiality. In all these similar cases the sequel showed and the facts proved that it was an imposture designed to lull Catholic resistance with illusory, merely verbal, guarantees, destined to remain dead letters. The trick was used often enough for it to be exposed.

It is indeed the Mass of Article 7 that the holders of ecclesiastical power wish to impose on the Church; and it is indeed

the Catholic Mass which they intend shall disappear progressively and which in fact is progressively disappearing.

As it becomes more serious, the situation becomes daily
clearer. Mgr. Lefebvre has perceived that in reality whatever
is undertaken against him on a variety of pretexts has one
principal purpose: *to stop priests being ordained to say the
Catholic Mass.*   The present holders—real holders, but unworthy—of the apostolic succession will not tolerate the Mass
unless in one form or another it is the Mass of Article 7. The
real battle is there.

The young priests ordained at Ecône on 29 June are beginning in their priestly life opposed, scorned, insulted; calumniated and abused in the press; subjected to administrative persecution. They are thus already in the likeness of Our
Lord.

These young priests have been validly ordained to say the
Catholic Mass. By them, for our salvation, the Catholic Mass
will continue. We kneel before them, we kiss their consecrated hands, and we thank God.''

12 July 1976
Preliminary Note by Mgr. Lefebvre

On 12 July 1976, Mgr. Lefebvre makes public, by communicating it to the *Agence France-Presse,* his third letter to
Paul VI, that of 22 June 1976. He precedes this communication with a preliminary note:

**The letter which follows (Letter to Paul VI of 22 June 1976) is the
third of the same kind addressed to the Holy Father within the last
year. It was forwarded to him by the mediation of the Berne Nunciature to which it had been sent on 22 June in answer to the letter of
H.E. Mgr. Benelli which the Nuncio in Berne communicated to me on**

17 June (and which was dated 12 June). This letter of 17 June forbade me to proceed with the ordinations on 29 June.

On Sunday 27 June, a special envoy of the Secretariat of State came to join me at Flavigny-sur-Ozerain in France, when I was preaching the retreat to the ordinands. The letter he brought me from H.E. Mgr. Benelli (of 25 June) made out that it was an answer to the annexed letter.

It confirms the prohibition of the ordinations and the threat of sanctions, but it makes no allusion to the possibility of a dialogue even with a mediator.

It thus appears impossible to approach the basic problem, which is the agreement of the *Conciliar Church*, as H. E. Mgr. Benelli himself calls it in his last letter, and the *Catholic Church*.

Let there be no mistake. It is not a question of a difference between Mgr. Lefebvre and Pope Paul VI. It is a question of the radical incompatibility between the *Catholic Church* and the *Conciliar Church*, the Mass of Paul VI being the symbol and the program of the Conciliar Church.

† Marcel Lefebvre

The letter of 22 June 1976 has been included under this date.

17 July 1976
Letter of Mgr. Lefebvre to Pope Paul VI

This is the fourth letter of Mgr. Lefebvre to Pope Paul VI. It is the first in which Mgr. Lefebvre "approaches the basic problem," the three preceding letters doing no more, essentially, than asking to be heard.

This letter is extremely compact in substance: it says, in summary, all that Mgr. Lefebvre would have said to Pope Paul VI if this pope had not, for years, systematically refused to see him and to hear him.

Most Holy Father,

All access permitting me to reach Your Holiness being forbidden me, may God grant that this letter reaches you to express to you my feelings of profound veneration, and at the same time to state to you, with an urgent prayer, the object of our most ardent desires, which seem, alas!, to be a subject of dispute between the Holy See and numerous faithful Catholics.

Most Holy Father, deign to manifest your will to see the Kingdom of Our Lord Jesus Christ extended in this world,

> by restoring the Public Law of the Church,
>
> by giving the liturgy all its dogmatic value and its hierarchical expression according to the Latin Roman rite consecrated by so many centuries of use,
>
> by restoring the Vulgate to honor,
>
> by giving back to catechisms their true model, that of the Council of Trent.

By taking these steps Your Holiness will restore the Catholic priesthood and the Reign of Our Lord Jesus Christ over persons, families, and civil societies.

You will give back their correct concept to falsified ideas which have become the idols of modern man: liberty, equality, fraternity and democracy—like your Predecessors.

Let Your Holiness abandon that ill-omened undertaking of compromise with the ideas of modern man, an undertaking which originates in a secret understanding between high dignitaries in the Church and those of Masonic lodges, since before the Council.

To persevere in that direction is to pursue the destruction of the Church. Your Holiness will easily understand that we cannot collaborate in so calamitous a purpose, which we should do were we to close our seminaries.

May the Holy Ghost deign to give Your Holiness the grace of the gift of fortitude, so that you may show in unequivocal acts that you are truly and authentically the Successor of Peter, proclaiming that there is no salvation except in Jesus Christ and in His Mystical Spouse, the Holy Church, Catholic and Roman.

And may God . . .

† Marcel Lefebvre

22 July 1976
Notification of Suspension *a Divinis*

Letter from the Secretariat of the Congregation for Bishops, with the reference 514/76.

Monseigneur,

On 6 July 1976 (Prot. N. 514/76) Cardinal Sebastiano Baggio sent you a formal monition, according to the terms of which you were made aware of the canonical penalties which would be inflicted on you if proof of resipiscence did not reach the Congregation of Bishops within ten days of the receipt of the monition.

Seeing that:

—on the one hand, Mgr. the Apostolic Nuncio in Switzerland attests that you received, on 11 July, the formal monition from the Cardinal Prefect of this Congregation, and that you signed a certificate of reception as evidence of the fact;

—and that, on the other hand, the interval of ten days has passed without the hoped-for proof of resipiscence reaching the offices of this same Congregation;

—in execution of the instructions left by Cardinal Baggio, at present absent from Rome, I have referred to His Holiness.

The Holy Father has informed me that he has received from you a letter dated 17 July. In his eyes, it could not unhappily be considered satisfactory—on the contrary. I may even tell you that he is very distressed by the attitude to him shown in that document.

In consequence the Sovereign Pontiff Paul VI, on 22 July 1976, in conformity with canon 2227, in virtue of which the penalties that can be applied to a bishop are expressly reserved to him, has inflicted on you suspension *a divinis* provided for in canon 2279, 2, 2⁰, and has ordered that it take immediate effect.

The undersigned Secretary of the Congregation for Bishops has been commissioned to inform you of this in the present letter.

But, as you may well think, it is with great sorrow that the Holy Father resolved to take this disciplinary measure, because of the scandal caused to the Christian people by your obstinacy, after so many fraternal attempts to turn you from the blind alley in which you are proceeding. His Holiness cherishes the hope that you will again reflect on this, and he begs Our Lord to inspire you with the resolve to re-establish as soon as possible your communion with him.

Given at Rome, in the offices of the Congregation of Bishops, 22 July 1976.

Signed: (illegible)

Interview Given to the *Nouvelliste* of Sion, Valais, Switzerland, at Ecône on 3 August 1976 and Printed on 4 August 1976

Journalist: Aren't you heading towards schism?

Mgr. Lefebvre: When someone says to me, "You are going to cause a schism," I answer that it is not I who am causing a schism; I am remaining in a completely traditional line. So I remain united to the Church of two thousand years, and I am doing nothing other than what has been done for two thousand years, than what I was congratulated for doing, for the same thing, I am condemned! It is as if I am expelled, I am almost excommunicated; finally I am suspended, whereas I am doing exactly the same thing as I did for thirty years of my life, during which time I was given every possible and imaginable honor.

No one will take from me my conviction that something

has happened in the Church. A new direction was taken at the Council, under the direction of Liberal Cardinals who had contacts with Freemasonry, and who desired that openness to the world that is so pleasing to the Freemasons; an openness to the world that resulted in the Declaration on Religious Liberty which is practically, in fact, the equality of all religions. So no more Catholic State, no more affirmation that the Church alone possesses the truth, and so many other things that obviously oppose us to the Council. The whole problem is there, the whole "drama of Ecône," if it can be called that, is there. Personally, therefore, I think that it is not I who am causing a schism. Let me be shown in what I am causing a schism, let me be tried. I asked to be tried before the Congregation of the Faith, if I am truly opposed to the Catholic faith, if I am truly against the discipline of the Church.

I claim that now, since the Council, the authority in the Church—I do not say the Pope, for I do not know what the influence of the Pope is on the orders that are given. But those who hold power, at least the Roman Congregations, are in the process of leading the Church into schism.

What is schism? It is a break, a break with the Church. But a break with the Church can also be a break with the Church of the past. If someone breaks with the Church of two thousand years, he is in schism. There has already been a council which was declared schismatic. Well, it is possible that one day, in twenty years, in thirty, in fifty years—I don't know—the Second Vatican Council could be declared schismatic, because it professed things which are opposed to the Tradition of the Church, and which have caused a break with the Church.

8 August 1976
The Petition of the Eight

Eight of the most distinguished Catholics in France sent
the following communication to the Press:

"A certain number of personages of the literary and artis-
tic world communicate this letter which they are sending to
the Pope on the subject of Mgr. Lefebvre.

8 August 1976

Most Holy Father,

The sanctions that have just been taken against Mgr. Lefebvre and his Seminary at Ecône have aroused great emotion
in France. Quite apart from traditionalists strictly so-called,
it is the majority of French Catholics who feel themselves
affected. For years they have been disturbed about the evolution of religion. They say nothing because they are not
qualified to speak. They simply withdraw. It is Cardinal
Marty himself who recently revealed to us that, between
1962 and 1975, Sunday Mass-going has fallen in the Paris
parishes by 54 per cent. Why? Because the faithful no longer
recognize their religion in the new liturgy and methods of
evangelization.

Nor do they recognize it in the catechism that is now
taught to their children, in the contempt for basic morality,
in the heresies professed by accepted theologians, in the political character given to the Gospel.

They welcomed the Council with joy, because they saw in
it the announcement of a rejuvenation, a certain suppleness
brought to structures and rules which time had little by little
hardened, a more fraternal welcome to those seeking truth
and justice without yet having the benefit of the great heritage of the Church. But what has happened did not meet
their expectation. They have the impression now of being
present at the sack of Rome. Was it not yourself, Holy Father, who spoke of the self-destruction of the Church? The

fact is that in France that self-destruction is at its height—and we are witnessing it.

About Monseigneur Lefebvre and the Seminary at Ecône these rank and file Catholics know very little. But what they have been learning about them little by little from newspapers, radio, and television rather evokes their sympathy. Monseigneur Lefebvre spent the best years of his life in missionary activity. He was Apostolic Delegate in Africa. Your predecessor, Pope John XXIII, who esteemed him greatly and loved him, nominated him to the Central Commission for the preparation of the Council.* He formed generations of seminarians. Of the priests from his seminaries, four became bishops, and it was yourself who made one of them, Monseigneur Thiandoum, a Cardinal. How could such a bishop who, all his life, has served the Church in a signal manner, suddenly become a stranger? Is he not rather the bishop whose portrait Vatican II seems to have painted: a bishop strong in faith, turned towards the mission, open to the world to be evangelized? Grieved at the ruin of the French seminaries, and convinced that vocations were not lacking amongst the young, he opened a seminary which, strictly faithful to the norms of Vatican II itself and of the Congregation for Catholic Education, offered to those who wished to enter there a life of prayer, study, and discipline. At once candidates flocked in, and the seminary was filled. The great majority of "rank and file Catholics" of whom we speak know all that now.

The unity of the Church is the argument which we see put forward everywhere to justify the severe measures taken against Ecône. But, Holy Father, if the little nucleus of Ecône is crushed, division will be made much worse! For the division is not between Monseigneur Lefebvre and the other French bishops. It is in the very heart of the hierarchical

*Pius XII, even more than John XXIII, loved and esteemed Mgr. Lefebvre.

Church, which lets so many rites, practices and opinions
develop with impunity that there is a risk that we shall soon
have as many of them as there are priests and communities.
It is the swarming of these little inner schisms, it is this pro-
liferation of individual religions, which is the mark of the
Church in France—for we are speaking only for France. And
there is an explosion of disobedience to Rome, to the Pope,
to the Council, in all that concerns the liturgy, the priesthood, the formation of seminarians, and the faith itself.
Strange Masses—sometimes ecumenical—and which have
nothing to do with the Mass of Paul VI are celebrated with
the greatest impunity. Is every "Eucharistic celebration"
permitted except the traditional Mass? Can every church be
open to Moslems, Israelites, Buddhists, but closed only to
priests in soutanes? Is every dialogue to be welcomed with
Freemasons, communists, atheists, but condemned with traditionalists? Is the hierarchy in France more prone to imposing a certain new spirit than to announcing and defending
the truths of the faith?

There, Holy Father, you have what the basic stratum of
the Christian people, whom we are here evoking, end by asking themselves. Every day brings us the echoes—ever stronger,
ever more numerous—of their stupefaction and their anguish
and that is why we turn to you, for to whom should a Catholic turn if not the Pope, Successor of Peter, Vicar of Jesus
Christ? We lay our petition at your feet. What petition? That
for love and pardon. It is, rather, a lamentation, a groan, that
we hope will rise to you. We are not versed in Canon Law,
and we do not doubt that Roman condemnations have juridical foundation.   But it is precisely excessive juridicism,
legalism, and formalism which seemed to us to have been
banished by Vatican II. Could not this serious legal action
taken against Monseigneur Lefebvre and his seminary be re-
considered? Could not the love you feel for the Christian
people of France prevail over a rigor which, striking the most

famous of our defenders of Tradition, will finish in inflicting an incurable wound on that people? Could not charity inspire the restoration of unity in the unique Truth? It seems to us that the traditional Mass and the priesthood of all time could be capable of finding their place in the consolidation and extension of a Church that has never ceased to keep Her essential dogmas and forms, through Her successive adaptations to the vicissitudes of history. What would become of a Church without priests and without Mass?

It is by this act of confidence, Holy Father, that we wish to bear witness to our loyalty to the Roman Pontiff, sure, as we are, of being heard by the Father of all Catholics, holder of the powers given to him from the beginning by the Founder to lead the Church to the end of the world.

Michel Ciry
Michel Droit
Jean Dutourd
Rémy*
Michel de Saint Pierre
Louis Salleron
Henri Sauguet
Gustave Thibon"

15 August 1976
Letter of Pope Paul VI to Mgr. Lefebvre

To Our venerated Brother Marcel Lefebvre.

On this Feast of the Assumption of the Most Holy Virgin Mary, We desire to assure you of Our remembrance, accompanied with a special prayer for a positive and speedy solution of the question which concerns your person and your actions with regard to Holy Church.

Our remembrance is expressed in this fraternal and paternal wish:

*Colonel Rémy is possibly the most distinguished living hero of the French Resistance.

The words "fraternal" and "paternal" do not make us forget the reality. Pope Paul VI refused to hear Mgr. Lefebvre before condemning him. And, in his discourse to the consistory on 24 May 1976, he publicly denounced Mgr. Lefebvre and those who follow him as being without feeling, without sincerity, and without good faith.

. . . that you would carefully consider, before the Lord and before the Church, in the silence and the responsibility of your conscience as a bishop, the insupportable irregularity of your present position.

There was an additional irregularity, the cause of all the subsequent irregularities: the irregularity of the procedure by which Mgr. Lefebvre was clandestinely judged and unjustly condemned.

It is not in conformity with truth and with justice. It arrogates to itself the right to declare that Our apostolic ministry deviates from the rule of faith, and to judge as unacceptable the teaching of an Ecumenical Council held with a perfect observance of the ecclesiastical norms: those are extremely serious accusations.

So Paul VI rejects the accusations as *serious* and not as *false*. In accord with the constant attitude of the Holy See in this affair, he does not deny the Liberal and Modernist tendencies of his pontificate, he denies that there is a right to challenge them; he does not claim that the Council was faultless, he affirms that the ecclesiastical norms were observed. It is the argument from authority, hypertrophied to the point of becoming the sole criterion of the just and the true. Once again, it is unconditional obedience to the Pope and the Council—what is demanded is servile submission.

Your position is not in accordance with the Gospel and in accordance with the faith.

Mgr. Lefebvre's position would not, in fact, be "in accordance with the Gospel and in accordance with the faith" if he were opposed to the principle of pontifical and conciliar authority. But that is not so. He is opposed to the manner, accidental (and faulty), with which that authority has been exercised for some fifteen years. Faced with that, Paul VI does again what he had already done in his consistorial discourse of 24 May: he confuses the challenging (in principle) of an authority with the challenging (in fact) of its exercise; in other words, he answers as though Mgr. Lefebvre were demanding a Church without Pope and without Council, which would, in fact, be out of conformity with Gospel and faith. The question raised by Mgr. Lefebvre, in this regard, is whether the authority itself is exercised "in conformity with Gospel and faith" in the way it conducts conciliar evolution. By reason of the circumstances, this question is neither gratuitous, nor trivial, nor temerarious. It cannot be put aside indefinitely without examination.

To persist in this course would do great harm to your consecrated person and to those who follow you, in disobedience to Canon Law. Instead of providing a remedy for the abuses which it is desired to correct, that would add another, of incalculable gravity.

Have the humility, Brother, and the courage, to break the illogical bond which makes you a stranger, hostile to the Church, the Church to which you have been of such service and which you desire still to love and edify. How many souls are expecting from you this example of heroic and simple faithfulness!

It is not stated what bond and what illogicality are meant.

Invoking the Holy Spirit, and trusting to the Most Holy Virgin Mary this hour which is, for you and for Us, decisive and bitter, We pray and We hope.

Paul, PP VI.

27 August 1976
An Appeal by Twenty-eight French Priests
to Pope Paul VI

During a spiritual conference on 27 August 1976, a group of twenty-eight French priests, mostly parish clergy, in no way involved in the traditionalist movement, addressed a plea to His Holiness Pope Paul VI to take the appropriate measures to calm the emotion created in France by the affair of the Seminary at Ecône. Protesting their total loyalty to the Holy See, these priests point out at length to the Holy Father the disorders which the exercise of their ministry has brought to their notice in France, particularly in catechetics, in the liturgy, and in the workings of the episcopal commissions for collegiality.*

27 August 1976

Most Holy Father,
    In the midst of the drama which has caused such disquiet among French Catholics for nearly two months, it is towards Your Holiness that we turn with filial respect to present this plea on behalf of His Grace Monseigneur Lefebvre and the young men who have gone to him to ask him to form them and lead them to the priesthood. Many voices have already been raised to make known the consternation experienced by the faithful when they heard of the severe sanctions imposed upon the founder of Ecône and the priests ordained by him. Many of these expressed themselves with a dignity and a concern for the Church which must be recognized. But these were the voices of lay people. All honor to them. It is as priests and fully cognizant of the responsibilities of our priestly ministry that we wish to address Your Holiness,

*The text of this appeal was published in the *Courrier de Rome*, No. 161, September 1976.

protesting loudly our fidelity and our submission to the Holy See.

An inquiry conducted by a reputable public opinion poll has made clear the extent of the popular feeling: 28 per cent of French Catholics gave their spontaneous support to Mgr. Lefebvre. Such a number calls for reflection, but in our pastoral experience, as priests in direct contact with the Christian people, it is neither exaggerated nor surprising. It is because of the extent and the depth of the distress that has been revealed that we beg Your Holiness to relent.

Although these lay people, admitting perhaps their understandable ignorance of Canon Law, may have revealed their anguish to Your Holiness with a freedom and frankness which did not diminish by an iota the respect with which they venerate the successor of St. Peter, quite the contrary, we as priests cannot ignore the law of the Church in the matter of ecclesiastical incardination. Although we cannot fail to recognize the very real and very serious questions which the decisions and actions of His Grace Monseigneur Lefebvre pose from the canonical standpoint, neither can we hide from ourselves the fact that this legal standpoint is only one aspect of the problem. What is most essential, and also relative to the very purpose of Canon Law, is the defense of the Faith and its promotion for the growth of the Church and the extension of the Kingdom of God.

This fundamental truth, far from favoring a typically subversive opposition between law and life, between the letter of the law and justice which the law must serve, recalls on the contrary the existence of higher principles and the ultimate purposes in the light of which positive law, which is necessarily limited and relative, must be used in the interests of justice and the vitality of the Church in order to avoid juridicism, that rightly denounced evil. *Summum jus, maxima injuria,* as the ancients used to say. Justice should always (in the Church) be at the service of Christ's charity and the salvation of souls: *Salus animarum, lex suprema.*

It is thus appealing to these higher principles, which we know are held most dear to the heart of Your Holiness, that we submit our plea that Your Holiness may find, as you alone have the power, a solution which will save Catholics and the Church from the terrible damage which must inevitably follow the present division if a remedy is not swiftly found.

1. Since it is primarily the law which is in question, what reply can one make to those who voice their deep anxiety at the fact that in the events leading up to the actual drama there is no indication of normal legal procedures having been observed, procedures demanded by the gravity of the affair in question and that of the measures finally taken? To stress a single point among many which have cropped up, one can only be very surprised to learn that the report of the canonical visitation of the Seminary at Ecône in November 1974 was never sent to its superior; and this at a time when the Seminary's canonical status had been termed "vague," that is uncanonical, even by voices in authority. And why, one must also ask, was this visitation and its report not taken into consideration when the decision to suppress the Priestly Fraternity of St. Pius X was taken in May 1975?

We beg Your Holiness to forgive us for returning to these sad events. We believe that it is our duty to recall them, as these events, and others like them, explain the perplexity of the faithful, and the hardening of attitudes, in a manner which would normally be incomprehensible, even among genuine servants of God and of the Church.

2. What other reaction can the faithful and the clergy themselves manifest when, while these events are taking place, they witness the freedom and impunity enjoyed by almost all the "assassins of the faith," as His Eminence Cardinal Daniélou designated them? The brutal force of such an expression may shock, but it only reflects the truth of the situ-

ation. It is hardly necessary to recall the facts that lie at the basis of this situation. Cardinal Seper and Cardinal Wright have for years been in possession of many dossiers concerning the new catechism which the offical commissions of episcopal collegiality impose on the dioceses of France. These obligatory courses contain neither the "truths" nor the "means" necessary for salvation and yet years have passed without any action being taken against the authors or the propagators of this catechesis. They thus pursue their work of destroying the faith under cover of the Bishops' authority which they have usurped.

The situation concerning the liturgy is similar. With the uncertainty of the law, the innovators are no longer few in number but many. A religious was able to list more than one hundred and fifty "Eucharistic Prayers" put officially at the disposal of priests, not to mention the directions given by official bodies for the free composition of the eucharistic liturgy. All these directions have but one point in common, the rejection of Catholic truth—particularly where it concerns the sacramental function of the priest, the Real Presence of Christ, and the fact that the Mass is the true Sacrifice of the Cross. In this area also, most Holy Father, the Vatican Congregations were informed according to the prescribed forms, but the sanctions demanded by these blasphemous violations of divine law have never been taken. The result is that the innovators continue their work with an ever greater audacity. One bishop even tolerates those concelebrations, if such a word can be used, which for months have been taking place involving a priest of his diocese and a Protestant pastor, causing as much scandal to sincere Protestants as to faithful Catholics. Other prelates preside over meetings where the agenda of the JOC (Young Catholic Workers) is a cover-up for action which is more trade-unionist and political than apostolic, and where the official "eucharistic celebration" is an open denial of the Gospel. And what

can be said about the establishment of General Absolution as
the norm, an innovation which tends in practice to suppress
the Sacrament of Penance, and which in many places has already supplanted it?

*These facts, Most Holy Father, are no longer exceptional.
They are daily occurrences.* And it is this which explains why
millions of French people, Catholics and even unbelievers,
have made manifest their sympathy for the person and the
actions of Mgr. Lefebvre. Catholics and large sections of the
general public have recognized that he was reacting against
the "self-destruction of the Church" which Your Holiness
has denounced personally. It is to this reaction that they have
said "Yes." It would be tragic to ignore the appeal contained
in this massive popular manifestation.

3. As to the very serious basic questions concerning the conciliar and post-conciliar situation taken as a whole and in its
reality: a certain manner of referring to the "Conciliar
Church" cannot effectively be accepted; nor is it possible to
deny the destruction of the Faith, or its large-scale abandonment by the faithful which, in spite of happily large exceptions, is obvious to any attentive observer. We recall the insistence with which, on two occasions in 1974, Your Holiness
personally declared the need to "re-examine" what has been
done for "the last ten years": firstly in the Bull announcing
the Holy Year on 23 May, and secondly a month later in
your discourse to the Cardinals on 22 June.

The task is immense, certainly, but if twenty-eight per cent
of Catholics reacted immediately by approving Mgr. Lefebvre
whom they recognize quite simply as a pastor who is openly
fighting the ills which afflict them all: if forty-eight per cent
of these feel that the Church has gone "too far," if fifty-two
per cent of practicing Catholics declare they are anxious and
troubled by the current evolution of the Church, and if — and
it is the Archbishop of Paris himself who has told us this —
from 1962 to 1975, fifty-four per cent of Catholics in Paris

have ceased attending Mass, it shows that there is something seriously wrong, and that appropriate measures should be taken as a matter of urgency.

It is these measures which the Christian people are asking for today, and we believe that it is our duty as priests to confirm this in our small way to Your Holiness. We can bear witness that these statistics, revealed in the daily press, do in fact reflect exactly what our daily parish experience teaches us. Certainly, there are still generous souls whose devotion is often admirable, and their spirit of prayer and sacrifice sometimes attains to heroism. It is nevertheless a fact that these are only a very few, while the numbers abandoning the Church are growing; thousands leave the Church and the seminaries continue to empty, although vocations exist. Where can we send them, these young men who ask where they can go to receive a priestly formation? There is not a single seminary in France (and voices more authoritative than ours can confirm this) where the norms of Catholic priestly formation, such as they have recently been formulated once again by the competent authority, are truly observed.

There again, Most Holy Father, it seems that the cause of the *malaise* is not to be found among persons—you are aware of the difficulties of our Bishops—under the burden of the structures and orientations which have followed the Council. Is not Collegiality, as it is exercised in practice by the commissions in which its authority is invested, one of the prime causes of the present situation in the seminaries of France, as it is in catechetics and the liturgy? Stemming from this, among a very great number of priests, among the young aspiring to the priesthood, and among the faithful, there is a temptation to discouragement and to disgust and to revolt. There is a grave risk of this feeling growing and aggravating the harm already done unless these grievances are dealt with; and to achieve this words will not suffice, adequate measures must be taken at once.

4. What measures? It is not for us to point them out to Your Holiness. It is, however, permitted for us to indicate to your paternal heart *two areas* where your personal intervention seems to us most urgent.

(a) The first is that of the Ecône affair: *a revision of the procedure* which has resulted in the present drama appears necessary. We think particularly of the young priests, of their debt of gratitude to the Seminary at Ecône and to its founder and to the faithful who have supported them. If a certain hardening of attitudes has already become apparent this is a matter not only of immediate gravity but has even more serious implications for the future. The factors which have contributed to this situation must not be forgotten, and we have already cited the principal ones. The Church in France is already short of priests. The salvation of souls demands that a solution conforming to justice and charity be found.

(b) The second area is that of the *Liturgy*. Numerous questions arise, as much from the point of view of the law as that of practice. Contrary to the view of Father Congar, we do not believe that the books he cites (in *La Croix* of 20 August 1976) reply to these questions. In fact, they only cite and analyze parts of the dossier. The situation is, in fact, one of almost unrestricted pluralism, as long as the "fruits of creativity" go in the direction of evolution. The absolute rights of creativity and research are proclaimed as the supreme law. This claim has been made and it would be hard to deny that it describes the current situation accurately. In such a situation it must be recognized that there is a permanent provocation even for those who, without denying the validity of the *Ordo Missae* instituted in 1969, see that in practice no one is concerned but those priests and faithful who, in opposition to the aberrations to which this evolution leads, attached themselves from the introduction of the *Novus Ordo* to an *Ordo* with a tradition of more than one thousand years.

In the name of what do they forbid this *Ordo* which the law promulgated by Your Holiness has not abrogated? We are in the midst of total pluralism and it is precisely because the faithful see that everything is, in fact, tolerated (even what is manifestly unlawful), that they are deeply shocked to find that the only victims of intolerance are those who in the present drama appeal to tradition in liturgical matters.

Now that the unity of Catholic liturgy has been shattered (we are speaking of France where we are the witnesses of unbelievable division), it is not by proscribing the only rite with a thousand years of tradition in the Roman Church that we shall find the means of achieving unity. On the contrary, it is clear that the recognition of the established position of the old Roman rite within the Catholic Church would be an act of conciliation capable of contributing in no small way to calming troubled spirits and healing wounds, not to mention all the other benefits which could be expected to accrue.

It is with full confidence that we send this request to Your Holiness. We well remember the words of your Profession of Faith (*Credo of the People of God*) of 30 June 1968: "Within the body of this Church the rich variety of liturgical rites and legitimate diversity in theological and spiritual heritage and particular custom, far from detracting from this unity demonstrates it yet more vividly." On 14 December last did not Your Holiness recall again, when addressing the Patriarch Dimitrios, all the benefits which can and do derive from "the respect of a legitimate liturgical diversity, at once spiritual, disciplinary, and theological"? Such words are a great encouragement to us, particularly as they seem to echo the Council which declared that: "Holy Mother Church holds all lawfully recognized rites to be of equal right and dignity: that She wishes to preserve them in the future and foster them in every way" (Liturgy Constitution, No. 4). Certainly the Council goes on to say that there is need for "revisions," but when these end up by creating a new rite, are we not conforming to the sovereign law of the Church in this matter by suggesting that the wish manifested by the Council to preserve and favor all manner of rites legitimately recognized, especially the oldest and most venerable, applies in a very particular way to the rite of the Roman Church, the most venerable of them all?

Most Holy Father, as respectful and submissive sons, we place this supplication in your hands, but it is also as priests and pastors conscious of their positions of responsibility which the Church has conferred upon them in the care of souls. Love of Christ's unique Church, so sadly torn apart from within, is the motive which has inspired us. It is the love of Christ and the love of our brothers which Our Saviour Himself has confided to you His Vicar here below. It is the love of Our Lady so gloriously proclaimed by you "Mother of the Church."

Be pleased, Your Holiness, to accept together with our supplication the homage of our most profound and filial respect, and to grant us the grace of your Apostolic Benediction.*

*The letter was signed by twenty-eight diocesan priests, parish priests, and chaplains.

XIII

29 August 1976
The Mass at Lille

THE MASS AT LILLE was an event of considerable importance. Firstly, it constituted in the most dramatic manner possible the response of the Archbishop to his suspenion, the terms of which forbade him to celebrate Mass. Secondly, it enabled him to put his case to an audience of millions around the world. Thirdly, it was clearly as a result of the impact made by this Mass that the Pope felt obliged to receive the Archbishop despite repeated Vatican claims that this would never be done until he made an act of submission to the "Conciliar Church." Fourthly, the reporting of this Mass and its background provides one of the clearest instances of the extent to which the Catholic and secular press is prepared to go to misrepresent the Archbishop. Fortunately, I was present at the Mass with some friends and can thus provide a first-hand account of what took place. I also have the complete text of the Archbishop's controversial sermon and have had access to a professionally made recording which includes every word.

Among the allegations made concerning the Mass at Lille
is that it was intended by the Archbishop as an act of public
defiance, a huge public demonstration against the authority
of the Holy See. Nothing could be further from the truth.
Lille is, of course, in the Archbishop's own native region of
France. He had been asked by some of his friends and relations to offer Mass there on 29 August and had agreed.
It was to be a semi-private occasion for two or three hundred
people at the most. But the media got to learn of the proposed Mass and began building it up into an act of contes-
tation, a trial of strength between the Archbishop and the
Pope. Then, as a result of this publicity, traditionalists from
further afield got to know about the Mass and began to make
inquiries about its venue as they wished to attend. This posed
the organizers and the Archbishop himself with a problem
as they had not made arrangements to cope with a congregation of more than a few hundred. The Archbishop's decision was unequivocal—the arrangements that had been
made were to stand and those from further afield were to be
discouraged from coming. That this was indeed the case is
also something to which I can add my personal testimony.
After learning of the proposed Mass I had thought it might
be appropriate to arrange for a few hundred British Catholics
to go to Lille as a gesture of solidarity with Mgr. Lefebvre
in the face of the Vatican sanctions. But I did not want to
do this without being certain that there would be a public
Mass with sufficient space for everyone wishing to attend.
I arranged for a phone call directly to the Archbishop at
Ecône and his personal reply was quite definite: the Mass
was to be private, he did not want anyone from outside Lille
to come, and anyone planning to do so should be discouraged. This was only one week before the Mass was scheduled
to take place.

During the week before the Mass it became clear to the organizers that several thousand of the faithful were going to

arrive whether the Archbishop wanted them to or not and so, at the last minute, they decided to hire the vast auditorium of the International Fair in Lille. This, they reckoned, would be more than sufficient to cope with any number that might arrive. This was reported in the British secular press on Saturday, 28 August, and so I made a last-minute decision to attend and, just before midnight, I left London's Victoria Station on the boat train with just one friend.

We met a few more traditionalists on the boat and arrived at Lille early on Sunday morning. On our way to the International Fair we were most impressed by the zeal and organization of the Lille Catholics. Stewards with arm-bands were strategically posted along the route to indicate the way and coaches had been laid on for those who felt unable to walk. There were very few police in evidence—a dozen or so traffic police at the most. When we reached the perimeter of the large grounds in which the Fair is situated a steady stream of cars had already begun to arrive. However, when I entered the huge auditorium I feared that an error of judgment had been made. A local paper which I had bought at the station gave the seating capacity as 10,000 and there was clearly room for several thousand people to stand. Under the circircumstances a congregation of 4,000 would have been a remarkable gesture of support for the Archbishop—but such a number would have appeared lost in this vast hall. I could already envisage the line the press—the Catholic press in particular—would take. The headlines would read: HALL ONLY HALF FULL FOR LEFEBVRE MASS. However, as the time for the Mass drew nearer the line of cars and procession of pedestrians grew more and more dense and, having waited outside for a friend coming by car, I found that at about 10:45 all the seats had been taken, the standing space was packed and it appeared that I would not be able to get into the auditorium. I managed to insert myself into a jam-packed mass of people which was literally inching its way along a corridor towards the auditorium. A number of young stewards did their best to persuade those inside to cram themselves up even more closely to allow a few more in. At least one report claimed that the stewards were Gestapo types wearing jackboots! I can testify that all those I saw were extremely inoffensive looking young men wearing leisure suits and that I did not notice a single jackboot anywhere in the congregation! A Soviet paper reported the presence of thousands of Italian fascists although, newspaper reporters apart, there did not appear to be a single Italian present.

The Archbishop's enemies have also spared no effort to publicize the fact that the journals of extreme right-wing political groups were being sold outside the auditorium, including *Aspects de la France*—the journal of *Action française*. What the papers did not point out is that on at least three occasions before the Mass an announcement was made that the Archbishop did not want any literature sold outside the auditorium and that if this was done it would be in opposition to his wishes. When this matter was raised during a press conference given by the Archbishop on 15 September 1976 (the full text of which was published in *Itinéraires* of December 1976) he made the following points: he was displeased at the fact that *Aspects de la France* had been sold outside the auditorium at Lille; he did not read this journal; he did not know those who produced it; he had never met Charles Maurras;* he had not even read his works; and he was thus ignorant of his political philosophy.

It needs to be appreciated that political attitudes in France cannot be assessed on the basis of attitudes in English-speaking countries. In France political feeling tends to be more polarized, more extreme, and far more deeply felt than in England. It can only be understood in the light of the French Revolution and subsequent history—particularly the inter-

---

*Founder of *Action française*.

war period and the German occupation. At the risk of a serious over-simplification, it is reasonable to state that up to the Second World War Catholicism in France tended to be identified with right-wing politics and anti-Catholicism with the left. Since the war, and especially since Vatican II, the official French Church has veered sharply to the left and has adopted all the postures identified with the Liberal consensus which is accepted throughout the West, e. g. on the virtues of the Viet Cong and the evils of capitalism. Thus, a large proportion of right-wing Catholics was predisposed to support any religious movement opposed to the policies of the French hierarchy. The political views of some of the French Catholics who support the Archbishop would certainly be odious to many English-speaking traditionalists— although such views are more understandable (if not acceptable) within the French context. However, if they wish to support the Archbishop (and not necessarily for the right reasons) there is nothing he can do about it. His own alleged right-wing political philosophy is nothing more than straightforward Catholic social teaching as expounded by the Popes for a century or more. Those familiar with this teaching need only read his book *A Bishop Speaks* to see at once that his so-called "political" utterances are no more than paraphrases of teaching contained in papal encyclicals. The French hierarchy has replaced this social teaching with diluted Marxism to such an extent that anyone adopting the Catholic position is now automatically accused of fascism. Whenever the Archbishop is accused of intermingling the traditional faith and right-wing politics a demand should be made that chapter and verse be provided to substantiate the allegation. The almost invariable Liberal response will be to ignore such a demand but, if a reply is given, it will be found that what is being objected to is the consistent teaching of the Popes.

What should be quite obvious is that Mgr. Lefebvre cannot prevent anyone who wishes to support him from doing so.

It is quite certain that there is no formal link whatsoever between Mgr. Lefebvre and any political party in any country. He has a right to his own political views, so have his priests, so have those who support him. But support for the Archbishop does not involve adherence to any political standpoint, only to the traditional faith, the traditional liturgy, and the social teaching of the Popes.

The congregation at Lille certainly represented a balanced cross-section of French society. In its 31 August issue, *Le Monde,* which has never attempted to disguise its hostility towards the Archbishop, commented on the make-up of the congregation in terms which coincided exactly with my own impression. Contrary to reports that the atmosphere of the Mass was political rather than religious, the report affirmed that for the vast majority of those present it was "an act of piety, a gesture of solidarity with a bishop who was the object of sanctions, a gesture of fidelity to the traditional Church . . . Men were in a definite majority, there were large numbers of young people, and entire families with their children . . . the general impression was of a normal parish congregation with a far from negligible proportion of workers." The same report adds that everyone from Lille seemed to know what was going on. The duty clerk in the ticket office at the station told *Le Monde's* reporter: "I'm broken-hearted at not being free to go to the Mass. I'm 100 per cent behind Mgr. Lefebvre. I haven't put a foot inside my parish church for ages because of the clowning that goes on there; they don't get so much as a *sou* (cent) out of me any more." On the way to the Mass his taxi driver also declared himself to be a strong supporter of Mgr. Lefebvre.

The extent of the Archbishop's support in France was made clear in an opinion poll published earlier in the month by the newspaper *Progrès de Lyon* and reported in *The Times* on 14 August. It revealed that while 28 per cent of Catholics approved of the Archbishop's stand only 24 per cent opposed it, the rest being indifferent or unwilling to express an opinion. In typical fashion, the London *Universe* (England's largest-circulation Catholic weekly) withheld the figures from its readers and informed them that the poll had revealed that the great majority of French Catholics "are more concerned about matters other than Mgr. Lefebvre." Similarly, among the glaring inaccuracies in its report on the Mass at Lille it claimed that there were 200 riot police on duty at the Mass—there was not a riot policeman in sight—and that the sermon carried hints of anti-semitism when, in fact, there was not a single phrase in the whole sermon referring to the Jews, even indirectly.

The Mass at Lille was celebrated with immense fervor and great dignity. A report in *Le Monde* remarked on Mgr. Lefebvre's serenity and tranquil dignity despite the strain he must have been undergoing since his suspension. The volume and quality of the congregational participation in the sung parts of the Mass—with more than twelve thousand Catholics from at least six countries singing *una voce,* with one voice, and broadcast to millions on TV and radio, provided the most effective possible rebuttal to the nonsensical claim that the traditional Mass provides an obstacle to congregational participation.

The complete text of the sermon will not be given here. Most of it is simply a restatement of points made in other sermons contained in this book and it is extremely long— about 8,500 words. Under the circumstances, particularly the overcrowding in the hall, a much shorter sermon might have been far more effective. But the Archbishop, clearly affected by the emotional nature of the occasion and the frequent applause from the congregation, probably went on for a much longer time than he had intended. He makes no secret of the fact that his sermons are not written beforehand. He begins with a few ideas of what he would like to say and carries on from there, with the result that he sometimes makes remarks which had not been planned and which, perhaps, he might rather not have made. However, lest it be alleged that this sermon has been omitted to cover up some of the controversial passages in it, these passages will be quoted in full, together with some other important passages.

The Archbishop began his sermon as follows:

My Dear Brethren,

Before addressing a few words of exhortation to you, I should like first to dispel some misunderstandings. And to begin with, about this very gathering.

You can see from the simplicity of this ceremony that we made no preparations for a ceremony which would have gathered a crowd like the one in this hall. I thought I should be saying Holy Mass on the 29 August as it had been arranged, before a few hundreds of the faithful of the Lille region, as I have done often in France, Europe, and even America, with no fuss.

Yet all of a sudden this date, 29 August, through press, radio and television, has become a kind of demonstration, resembling, so they say, a challenge. Not at all: this demonstration is not a challenge. This demonstration is what you wanted, dear Catholic brethren, who have come from long distances. Why? To manifest your Catholic faith; to manifest your belief; to manifest your desire to pray and to sanctify yourselves as did your fathers in faith, as did generations and generations before you. That is the real object of this ceremony, during which we desire to pray, pray with all our heart, adore Our Lord Jesus Christ Who in a few moments will come down on this altar and will renew the sacrifice of the Cross which we so much need.

I should like also to dispel another misunderstanding. Here I beg your pardon, but I have to say it: it was not I who called myself head of the traditionalists. You know who did that not long ago in solemn and memorable circumstances in Rome. Mgr. Lefebvre was said to be the head of the traditionalists. I do not want to be head of the traditionalists, nor am I. Why? Because I also am a simple Catholic. A priest and a bishop, certainly; but in the very conditions in which you find yourselves, reacting in the same way to the destruction of the Church, to the destruction of our faith, to the ruins piling up before our eyes.

Having the same reaction, I thought it my duty to form priests, the true priests that the Church needs. I formed those priests in a "Saint Pius X Society," which was recognized by the Church. All I was doing was what all bishops have done for centuries and centuries. That is all I did—something I have been doing for thirty years of my priestly life. It was on that account that I was made a bishop, an Apostolic Delegate in Africa, a member of the central pre-conciliar commission, an assistant at the papal throne. What better proof could I have wanted that Rome considered my work profitable for the Church and for the good of souls? And now when I am doing the same thing, a work exactly like what I have been doing for thirty years, all of a sudden I am suspended *a divinis,* and perhaps I shall soon be excommunicated, separated from the Church, a renegade, or what have you! How can that be? Is what I have been doing for thirty years liable also to suspension *a divinis?*

I think, on the contrary, that if then I had been forming seminarians as they are being formed now in the new seminaries I should have been excommunicated. If then I had taught the catechism which is being taught in the schools I should have been called a heretic. And if I had said Mass as it is now said I should have been called suspect of heresy and out of the Church. It is beyond my understanding. It means something has changed in the Church; and it is about that that I wish to speak.

The next passage to be cited evoked a great deal of unfavorable comment, principally because of the use of the word "bastard," particularly with reference to priests emerging from the reformed seminaries. Liberals were quick to seize upon this passage to imply that the Archbishop had intended to be personally offensive to these young priests. Nothing could be further from the truth. A careful reading of the controversial passage will show that the Archbishop was making a valid analogy and using the word with great precision. Unfortunately the word "bastard" sounds far more offensive in English than in French and for this reason I could wish that the Archbishop had found some other term for making his point.

As the text will make clear, he first takes up an image met with frequently in the Old Testament, and often phrased in terms far more blunt than those of the Archbishop, that the infidelities of the Jewish people constituted adultery. Israel was the spouse of Yahweh; when the Jews strayed to the "high places" to participate in pagan cults this constituted an adulterous liaison. The great temptation facing Catholics since the French Revolution has been to enter into an adulterous liaison with Liberalism, the pervading spirit of our times. Since Vatican II, large sections of the Church have succumbed to this temptation, none more evidently than the French hierarchy. Similarly, an attempt has been made to unite (in a clearly adulterous manner) Catholic and Protestant worship and doctrine. Thus many of the young priests emerging from our seminaries today (and I have personal experience of this) are a confused mixture of Liberalism and Protestantism, with possibly some vestigial Catholicism. Such is their confusion that they could not name their spiritual ancestry if asked, and to term them doctrinal bastards is blunt but accurate. Anyone who has attended a typical celebration of the New Mass will hardly need to be told that to call it a bastard rite is, if anything, an understatement. The controversial passage reads as follows:

The union desired by these Liberal Catholics, a union between the Church and the Revolution and subversion is, for the Church, an adulterous union, adulterous. And that adulterous union can produce only bastards. And who are those bastards? They are our rites: the rite of Mass is a bastard rite, the sacraments are bastard sacraments—we no longer know if they are sacraments which give grace or which do not give grace. We no longer know if this Mass gives the Body and Blood of Our Lord Jesus Christ or if it does not give them. The priests coming out of the seminaries do not themselves know what they are. In Rome it was the Archbishop of Cincinnati who said: "Why are there no more vocations? Because the Church no longer knows what a priest is." How then can She still form priests if She does not know what a priest is? The priests coming out of the seminaries are bastard priests. They do not know what they are. They do not know that they were made to go up to the altar to offer the sacrifice of Our Lord Jesus Christ, to give Jesus Christ to souls, and to call souls to Jesus Christ. That is what a priest is. Our young men here know that very well. Their whole life is going to be consecrated to that, to love, adore, and serve Our Lord Jesus Christ in the Holy Eucharist.

The adulterous union of the Church with the Revolution is consolidated with dialogue. When the Church entered into dialogue it was to convert. Our Lord said: "Go, teach all nations, convert them." But He did not say to hold dialogue with them so as not to convert them, so as to try to put us on the same footing with them.

Error and truth are not compatible. We must see if we have charity towards others, as the Gospel says: he who has charity is one who serves others. But those who have charity should give Our Lord, they should give the riches they possess to others and not just converse with them and enter into dialogue on an equal footing. Truth and error are not on the same footing. That would be putting God and the Devil on the same footing, for the Devil is the father of lies, the father of error.

We must therefore be missionaries.

We must preach the Gospel, convert souls to Jesus Christ and not engage in dialogue with them in an effort to adopt their principles. That is what this bastard Mass and these bastard rites are doing to us, for we wanted dialogue with the Protestants and the Protestants said to us: "We will not have your Mass; we will not have it because it contains things incompatible with our Protestant faith. So change the Mass and we shall be able to pray with you. We can have intercommunion. We can receive your sacraments. You can come to our churches and we can come to yours; then it will be all finished and we shall have unity." We shall have unity in confusion, in bastardy. That we do not want. The Church has never wanted it. We love the Protestants; we want to convert them. But it is not loving them to let them think they have the same religion as the Catholic religion.

The next passage to be quoted was the most controversial in the whole sermon. It contains a reference to Argentina, about 150 words long out of a sermon of about 8,500 words, and it is the passage which was seized upon by Liberals, secular and Catholic, to categorize the entire speech as political and even to go as far as to compare Mgr. Lefebvre with Hitler! This is what the Archbishop said:

There will be no peace on this earth except in the reign of Our Lord Jesus Christ. The nations are at war—every day we have page after page of the newspapers about it, we have it on radio and television. Now because of a change of Prime Minister they are asking what can be done to improve the economic situation, what will strengthen the currency, what will bring prosperity to industry, and so on. All the papers in the world are full of it. But even from an economic point of view Our Lord Jesus Christ must reign, because the reign of Our Lord Jesus Christ is the reign of the principles of love, indeed of the commandments of God which give society its balance, which make justice and peace reign in society. It is only when society has order, justice, and peace that the economy can prevail and revive. That is easily seen. Take the Argentine Republic as an example. What state was it in just two or three months ago? Complete anarchy, brigands killing right and left, industries totally ruined, factory owners seized and held to ransom, and so on. An incredible revolution, and that in a country so beautiful, so balanced, and so congenial as the Argentine Republic, a Republic which could be extraordinarily prosperous and enormously wealthy. Now there is a government of principle, with authority, which brings back order into life and stops the brigands murdering; and lo and behold! the economy is reviving, workers have employment, and they can return to their homes knowing that no one is going to knock them on the head because they will not strike when they do not wish to strike. That is the reign of Our Lord Jesus Christ that we want; and we profess our faith, saying that Our Lord Jesus Christ is God.

Before making any comment on this passage I will quote an explanation which the Archbishop gave himself when questioned upon it during a press conference on 15 September 1976.* Let it be noted once again that the passage in question is one of about 150 words in a sermon of about 8,500 words. The following question was posed to the Archbishop:

"You have recently been reproached with your sympathy for régimes like that in Argentina. Is this true or false?"
The Archbishop's answer reads as follows:

I have just been talking to you about principles, I might say political principles, which one may have, the political principles of the Church. She has principles, political principles, principles for society, for She considers that society is created by God, like the family. The family has its laws: there are father, mother, and child; and each has a law and a position in the family. Similarly in civil society. The Church considers that it is a creature of God, and that this creature of God also has its laws so that it can develop normally and give all its members the fullest possibility for their own development. Of course we want governments to observe these laws. I took that example, but I might have taken another, for, as you know, I do not write my speeches—a pity, perhaps —but I do not think about them well in advance. So, trying to give an example of Christian order, of the notion people have of Christian order which brings things back to peace and justice, with the hierarchy which is necessary in a society, I quoted this example because it is recent and known to everybody, and also because the situation was really frightful, the Argentine being in a state of anarchy, with assassinations and abductions—a situation on the brink of the abyss, on the verge of

*Itinéraires, No. 208, December 1976, p. 127.

total anarchy. A government then took over, but I think that, given the ideas of some of these men (I know some of the Argentinian bishops and I was there myself not long ago), I think that these men who took over the government did so in a Christian spirit. That they are not governing perfectly, that they exaggerate, that not everything is perfect, I do not doubt for a moment (I do not think that any government in the world has ever been perfect); but they did, I think, return to principles of justice, and that is why I gave that example. I said: you see that when Christian principles are restored a society is rediscovered which can live, which is livable, in which people can live, where they need not always be asking themselves if they are going to be assassinated at the street corner, or be robbed, or have a bomb in their garden, and so on. All I wanted to do was give an example: but that does not mean I am a supporter of the government of the Argentine or of the government of Chile. I might have used Chile as an example. I could perhaps have quoted governments which were in total anarchy and which then re-established order. Such an order might be tyrannical, and then it is a different matter: we are not talking of introducing slavery. I must say that I did not use that example so as to support the government in the Argentine or to play politics. I do not play politics.

I would not wish to make any detailed comments on the régimes in Argentina and Chile as I have made no detailed personal study of them. What is perfectly clear is that in both cases the military only took over the government because life had been made literally impossible by the previous régimes. Let British or American readers spend a few moments calculating the precise meaning of an 800 per cent inflation rate, let them calculate the cost of the basic necessities of life multiplied eightfold and decide just how tolerable they would have found régimes which had brought about such a state of affairs. It must also be remembered that in both countries Marxist terrorists consider themselves bound by no ethical norms in achieving their aims. During my own military service I had personal experience of two terrorist campaigns, in Malaya and Cyprus, and, leaving aside the question as to whether right is on the side of the military or the terrorists, it is hard for the security forces to conform to the rule book when dealing with men who violate civilized standards of behavior. To take Northern Ireland as an example, there can be no doubt that the situation there has been caused by an unjust partition of Ireland and unjust treatment of the Catholic population. The Catholics have a legitimate grievance which they have been unable to rectify through the accepted political channels. Nonetheless, when a soldier or policeman has seen his comrades blown to pieces by a terrorist bomb, or seen the carnage in a bomb-blasted shop, with women and children lying dead or bleeding from lost limbs, he is not likely to think much about the historical background when he gets his hands on a gunman. He should—but he doesn't. It is wrong but understandable. It is thus quite unjust for Liberals, Catholic or otherwise, to sit in judgment on the régimes in Chile and Argentine when they have no first- and probably even little second- or even third-hand knowledge of the background to the current situation in these countries. It is also a fact that the governments of Chile and Argentina have been subjected to a campaign of systematic defamation in the secular and Catholic press. To take just one example, those who rely for their information on the British Catholic press would imagine that the prisons of Chile are bursting with political prisoners when, in fact, there is not a single political prisoner in the entire country.*

*The last political prisoner in Chile (the Communist ex-Senator Jorge Montes) was released on 17 June 1977 and allowed to travel to East Germany in exchange for eleven East German political prisoners, *Chile Today*, No. 33 (12 Devonshire Street, London, W1). For a factual background account of the Chilean situation read *The Church of Silence in Chile*, 450 pp., $7 postpaid from Lumen Mariae Publications, P. O. Box 99455, Erieview Station, Cleveland, Ohio 44199. Available in Britain from Augustine Publishing Co. Essential background reading on this topic is contained in two valuable *Approaches* supplements, "Dossier on Chile," and "Hatred and Lies Against Latin America," which prove, *inter alia*, that Amnesty International has published false information, e.g. alleging that people are missing who are not missing at all.

As regards Argentina, the far from right-wing French journal *L'Express* admitted in its issue of 30 August, the day after the sermon at Lille, that:

> General Videla, brought to power by a *coup d'état*, has managed at the last moment to save the economic situation of the country. With an 800 per cent inflation during the last twelve months of Isabel Peron's presidency, with no means of paying off its debts abroad, the Argentine was on the verge of bankruptcy. By freezing prices and freezing salaries, inflation has been brought down by at least 3 per cent a month . . . . The Argentine can resume its development on a solid foundation.

As for the *"coup d'état"* of the Argentinian armed forces, on their side there was neither ambition nor despotism. They would have preferred (like the Brazilian armed forces in 1964) not to have to intervene. But there was nobody else. The *Courrier de Paul Dehème* makes that clear in its No. 7,967 of 16 September 1976:

> The Argentinian armed forces refused for a long time to act, and on 24 March 1976, when they made their decision, the chaos had reached such a pitch that they could no longer delay. I remind you, moreover, of what I wrote to you on 17 March, a week before their seizure of power: "The armed forces are going to have to make draconian decisions whether they like it or not."

The major part of the Archbishop's sermon was concerned with an impassioned defense of the traditional faith and a scathing indictment of the "Conciliar Church"—a Church in which consecrated churches are put at the disposal of Muslims but withheld from faithful Catholics wishing to offer the traditional Mass. The Archbishop laid stress on the need for traditionalists to put their case in a restrained and unaggressive manner:

> We are against no one. We are not commandos. We wish nobody harm.

All we want is to be allowed to profess our faith in Our Lord Jesus Christ.

So, for that reason, we are driven from our churches. The poor priests are driven out for saying the Old Mass by which all our saints were sanctified: Saint Jeanne d'Arc, the holy Curé of Ars, the little Thérèse of the Child Jesus were sanctified by this Mass; and now priests are driven brutally, cruelly, from their parishes because they say the Mass which has sanctified saints for centuries. It is crazy. I would almost say it is a story of madmen. I ask myself if I am dreaming. How can this Mass have become some kind of horror for our bishops and for those who should preserve our faith? But we will keep the Mass of Saint Pius V because the Mass of Saint Pius V is the Mass of twenty centuries. It is the Mass of all time, not just the Mass of Saint Pius V; and it represents our faith, it is a bulwark of our faith, and we need that bulwark.

We shall be told that we are making it a question of Latin and soutanes. Obviously it is easy that way to discredit those you disagree with. But Latin has its importance; and when I was in Africa it was marvelous to see those crowds of Africans of different languages - we sometimes had five or six different tribes who did not understand one another — who could assist at Mass in our churches and sing the Latin chants with extraordinary fervor. Go and see them now: they quarrel in the churches because Mass is being said in a language other than theirs, so they are displeased and they want a Mass in their own language. The confusion is total, where before there was perfect unity. That is just one example. You have just heard the epistle and gospel read in French—I see no difficulty in that; and if more prayers in French were added, to be said all together, I still see no difficulty. But it still seems to me that the body of the Mass, which runs from the offertory to the priest's Communion, should remain in a unique language so that all men of all nations can assist together at Mass and can feel united in that unity of faith, in that unity of prayer. So we ask, indeed we address an appeal to the bishops and to Rome: will they, please, take into consideration our desire to pray as our ancestors did, our desire to keep the Catholic faith, our desire to adore Our Lord Jesus Christ and to want His reign. That is what I said in my last letter

to the Holy Father—and I thought it really was the last, because I did not think the Holy Father would have written to me again.

The Archbishop also laid stress on the fact that while Communists and Freemasons were welcome in the Vatican, Catholic traditionalists were not. An audience of millions throughout the world was able to see at first hand the mask being torn from the face of the "Conciliar Church"—a Church characterized by harshness, hypocrisy, intolerance, and calculated cruelty to its most faithful children: a Church prepared to sacrifice its doctrinal and liturgical patrimony in the interests of an illusory ecumenical goal. There can be little doubt that it was the embarrassment resulting from this public exposure that resulted in the subsequent papal audience for the Archbishop.

It is also obvious that this massive demonstration of support for the Archbishop came as a great shock to the Vatican. Technically, after his suspension, not a single Catholic should have been present at the Mass, and the local bishops had reminded the faithful of this and warned that they should not be present even out of curiosity. It is also worth restating the fact that this Mass was in no way intended as a major public demonstration of support for the Archbishop and the traditional faith—it was made public only at the last minute. Had the Archbishop wished to arrange a demonstration of the massive support he enjoys and asked for this to be organized through the month of August it is doubtful whether there would have been a building in France large enough to accommodate the congregation.

The message which came from Lille was clear. The régime in the Vatican had insisted that the first, the only duty of Catholics was to accept all its directives without question. It wanted absolute and blind obedience. If it forbade today what it commanded yesterday it was not for the faithful to reason why but to obey. But the Catholics present at Lille showed, by their presence, that with Mgr. Lefebvre their commitment is to the traditional faith. In so far as the Vatican upholds that faith it will enjoy their support; where it fails to build up the Body of Christ but introduces measures which effectively undermine it then they will say "No," even to the Pope himself.

XIV

The Audience with Pope Paul VI

11 September 1976
Communiqué from the Vatican Press Office

His Excellency Mgr. Marcel Lefebvre came yesterday to Castelgandolfo to ask the Holy Father for an audience.

He was received this morning at 10:30.

His Holiness, after pointing out that the problems raised had been and were always followed by the Pope with the keenest and most constant attention, invited him, in words especially and intensely paternal, to reflect on the situation he had created, a situation gravely damaging to the Church, as well as on his personal responsibility with regard to the group of the faithful who follow him and to the whole ecclesial community, and before God.

11 September 1976
Archbishop Lefebvre is Received in Audience
by His Holiness Pope Paul VI

The following account of Mgr. Lefebvre's audience with Pope Paul VI is entirely in the Archbishop's own words. The first part is taken from a press conference given at Ecône on

15 September, the full text of which was published in *Itiné-raires* No. 208, pp. 100-116. The second part is taken from a conference given to the seminarians at Ecône on 18 September. The full text is included in *Itinéraires* No. 208, pp. 136-154. In neither case was the Archbishop speaking from a prepared text, which explains a somewhat disjointed style in places.

PART I

I tell you quite sincerely that this meeting with the Pope was for me altogether unexpected. Certainly I had been wanting it for several years. I had asked to meet the Holy Father, to talk to him about my seminary, my work—I might say to give him joy because I was still able, in spite of the circumstances, to manage to form some priests, to help the Church in the formation of priests. But I never succeeded. I was always told that the Pope had not time to receive me. Then, little by little, when the seminary was penalized, the difficulties were obviously greater, with the result that I was never able to get through the bronze door. But after those events (the suppression of the seminary and the suppression of the Fraternity) the condition set for my seeing the Holy Father was that I submit to the Council, the post-conciliar reforms, and the post-conciliar orientations desired by the Holy Father—that is, practically, the closure of my seminary. That I did not accept. I could not accept the closure of my seminary or the cessation of ordinations in the seminary, because I consider that I am doing constructive work, I am building the Church, not pulling it down, though the demolition is going on all around me. I consider that I cannot in conscience collaborate in the destruction of the Church. That brought us to a complete deadlock: on the one side the Holy See was imposing conditions which meant the closure of the seminary, and on the other side I would not have the seminary closed. It seemed, therefore, that dialogue was impossible. Then, as you know, that penalty of suspension *a divinis* was imposed, which is very serious in the Church, especially for a bishop: it means that I am forbidden to perform acts corresponding to my episcopal ordination—no Mass, no sacraments, no administering of sacraments. Very serious. That shocked public opinion, and it so happened that a current of opinion was formed in my favor. It was not I who sought it: it was the Holy See itself which gave tremendous publicity to the suspension and to the seminary. You represent all the means for the diffusion of news, and it was your job to give people what they wanted by speaking of this event. That set moving a wave of opinion which, to say the least, was unexpected by the Vatican.

So the Vatican found itself in a rather delicate and tiresome situation in face of public opinion, and that, I think or at least imagine, is why the Pope wanted to see me after all, but not officially through the usual channels: I did not see Mgr. Martin, who usually arranges audiences, nor did I meet Cardinal Villot—I met no one. It so happened that I was at Besançon preparing for Mass when I was told: "There is a priest come from Rome who would like to see you after Mass. It is very urgent and very important." I said: "I'll see him after Mass."

So after Mass we retired to a corner of the room where we happened to be, and this priest, Don Domenico La Bellarte I think—I did not know him, having never in my life set eyes on him—said to me: "The Archbishop of Chieti, my superior, saw the Holy Father recently, and the Holy Father expressed a desire to see you." I said to him: "Look, I've been wanting to see the Holy Father for five years. They always impose conditions, and they will impose the same conditions again. I do not see why I should go to Rome now." He insisted, saying: "There has been a change. Something has changed at Rome in the situation with regard to you." "Very well. If

you can assure me that the Archbishop of Chieti will accom-
pany me to the Holy Father, I have never refused to see the
Holy Father and I am willing to go."

I then promised him that I would go to Rome as soon as
possible. I had the ceremony at Fanjeaux, so I went to Fanjeaux and afterwards went direct by car to Rome. I tried to
get in touch with that priest, and I met him in Rome, where
he said to me: "You had better, all the same, write a bit of a
letter to the Holy Father which I can give to Mgr. Macchi, his
secretary, and then you will be able to see the Holy Father."
I said: "But what sort of letter? There is no question of
my asking pardon or saying that I accept beforehand whatever will be imposed on me. I will not accept that." Then
he said to me: "Write anything. Put something on paper
and I'll take it at once to Castelgandolfo." I wrote expressing
my deep respect for the person of the Holy Father and saying that if there were, in the expressions I had used in
speeches and writings, anything displeasing to the Holy Father, I regretted them; that I was always ready to be received,
and hope to be received, by the Holy Father. I signed the
letter, and that was that.* The priest did not even read the
little note I had written but put it in an envelope. I addressed
the envelope to the Holy Father and we set off for Castelgandolfo. He went in to the palace. We remained a while outside. He went to see Mgr. Macchi, who said to him: "I cannot

---

*Regarding the precise text of the letter, the following note was printed in
Itinéraires, No. 207, November 1976, p. 188: "Mgr. Lefebvre's Request to Pope
Paul VI for an Audience." The text of this letter has not been published. We
asked Mgr. Lefebvre about the matter, and this is his answer:
   That request for an audience was composed very quickly; I have no copy of it,
but, as far as I remember, this is an exact reproduction of its substance:
   "Most Holy Father,
      Will Your Holiness be pleased to accept the assurance of my respectful vene-
ration? If in my words or my writings certain expressions have displeased Your
Holiness, I am exceedingly sorry. I am still hoping that Your Holiness will kindly
grant me an audience, and I assure you of my respectful and filial feelings.
                                                           + Marcel Lefebvre
                                                      Rome, 10 September 1976."

give you an answer at once. I will let you know about seven this evening." That was last Thursday evening. And in fact at seven I got a telephone call in my house at Albano. I was told: "You will have an audience with the Holy Father tomorrow at ten-thirty."

PART II

So, the next day, Saturday, at quarter past ten, I went to Castelgandolfo, and there I really believe the Holy Angels had driven out the Vatican employees because I had come back there: there were two Swiss Guards at the entrance, and after that I encountered only Mgr. X (not Mgr. Y: their names are very alike). Mgr. X, the Canadian, conducted me to the lift. Only the lift man was there, that is all, and I went up. The three of us went up to the first floor, and there, accompanied by Mgr. X, I went through all the rooms: there are at least seven or eight before you come to the Holy Father's office. Not a living soul! Usually—I have often been to private audience in the days of Pope Pius XI, Pope Pius XII, Pope John XXIII, and even Pope Paul VI—there is always at least one Swiss Guard, always a gendarme, always several people: a private chamberlain, a monseigneur who is present if only to keep an eye on things and prevent incidents. But the rooms were empty—nothing, absolutely nothing. So I went to the Holy Father's office, where I found the Holy Father with Mgr. Benelli at his side. I greeted the Holy Father and I greeted Mgr. Benelli. We seated ourselves at once, and the audience began.

The Holy Father was lively enough at the beginning—one could almost call it somewhat violent in a way: one could feel that he was deeply wounded and rather provoked by what we are doing. He said to me:

"You condemn me, you condemn me. I am a Modernist.

I am a Protestant. It cannot be allowed, you are doing an evil work, you ought not to continue, you are causing scandal in the Church, etc. . . " with nervous irritability.

I kept quiet, you may be sure.

After that he said to me:

"Well, speak now, speak. What have you to say?"

I said to him:

"Holy Father, I come here, but not as the head of the traditionalists. You have said I am head of the traditionalists. I deny flatly that I am head of the traditionalists. I am only a Catholic, a priest, a bishop, among millions of Catholics, thousands of priests and other bishops who are torn and pulled apart in conscience, in mind, in heart. On the one side we desire to submit to you entirely, to follow you in everything, to have no reserves about your person, and on the other side we are aware that the lines taken by the Holy See since the Council, and the whole new orientation, turn us away from your predecessors. What then are we to do? We find ourselves obliged either to attach ourselves to your predecessors or to attach ourselves to your person and separate ourselves from your predecessors. For Catholics to be torn like that is unheard of, unbelievable. And it is not I who have provoked that, it is not a movement made by me, it is a feeling that comes from the hearts of the faithful, millions of the faithful whom I do not know. I have no idea how many there are. They are all over the world, everywhere. Everybody is uneasy about this upset that has happened in the Church in the last ten years, about the ruins accumulating in the Church. Here are examples: there is a basic attitude in people, an interior attitude which makes them now unchangeable. They will not change because they have chosen: they have made their choice for Tradition and for those who maintain Tradition. There are examples like that of the religious Sisters I saw two days ago, good religious who wish to keep their religious life, who teach children as their parents want them to be taught—many parents bring their children to them because they will receive a Catholic education from these religious. So, here are religious keeping their religious habit; and just because they wish to preserve the old prayer and to keep the old catechism they are excommunicated. The Superior General has been dismissed. The bishop has been five times, requiring them to abandon their religious habit because they have been reduced to the lay state. People who see that do not understand. And, side by side with that, nuns who discard their habit, return to all the worldly vanities, no longer have a religious rule, no longer pray—they are officially approved by bishops, and no one says a word against them! The man in the street, the poor Christian, seeing these things cannot accept them. That is impossible. Then it is the same for priests. Good priests who say their Mass well, who pray, who are to be found in the confessional, who preach true doctrine, who visit the sick, who wear their soutane, who are true priests loved by their people because they keep the Old Mass, the Mass of their ordination, who keep the old catechism, are thrown on the street as worthless creatures, all but excommunicated. And then priests go into factories, never dress as priests so that there is no knowing what they are, preach revolution—and they are officially accepted, and nobody says anything to them. As for me, I am in the same case. I try to make priests, good priests as they were made formerly; there are many vocations, the young men are admired by the people who see them in trains, on the underground; they are greeted, admired, congratulated on their dress and bearing; and I am suspended *a divinis*! And the bishops who have no more seminarians, no young priests, nothing, and whose seminaries no longer make good priests—nothing is said to them! You understand, the poor average Christian sees it clearly. He has chosen and he will not budge. He has reached his limit. It is impossible.''

"That is not true. You do not train good priests," he said to me, "because you make them take an oath against the Pope."

"What!" I answered. "An oath against the Pope? I who, on the contrary, try to give them respect for the Pope, respect for the successor of Peter! On the contrary, we pray for the Holy Father, and you will never be able to show me this oath which they take against the Pope. Can you give me a copy of it?"

And now, officially, the Vatican spokesmen have published in today's paper, where you can read it, the Vatican denial, saying that it is not true, that the Holy Father did not say that to me: the Holy Father did not say to me that I made my seminarians and young priests take an oath against the Pope. But how could I have invented that? How invent anything of the kind? It is unthinkable. But now they deny it: the Holy Father did not say it. It is incredible. And obviously I have no tape recording. I did not write out the whole conversation, so I cannot prove the contrary materially. But my very reaction! I cannot forget how I reacted to that assertion by the Holy Father. I can still see myself gesturing and saying: "But how, Holy Father, can you possibly say such a thing! Can you show me a copy of the oath?" And now they are saying it is not true. It is extraordinary!

Then the Holy Father said to me, further:

"It is true, is it not, that you condemn me?"

I had the strong impression that it all came back rather to his person, that he was personally hurt:

"You condemn me, so what ought I to do? Must I hand in my resignation and let you take my place?"

"Oh!" I put my head in my hands.

"Holy Father, do not say such things. No, no, no, no!"

I then said:

"Holy Father, let me continue. You have the solution of the problem in your hands. You need say only one word to the bishops: receive fraternally, with understanding and charity, all those groups of traditionalists, all those who wish to keep the prayer of former days, the sacraments as before, the catechism as before. Receive them, give them places of worship, settle with them so that they can pray and remain in relation with you, in intimate relation with their bishops. You need say only one word to the bishops and everything will return to order and at that moment we shall have no more problems. Things will return to order. As for the seminary, I myself shall have no difficulty in going to the bishops and asking them to implant my priests in their dioceses: things will be done normally. I myself am very willing to renew relations with a commission you could name from the Congregation of Religious to come to the seminary. But clearly we shall keep and wish to continue the practice of Tradition. We should be allowed to maintain that practice. But I want to return to normal and official relations with the Holy See and with the Congregations. Beyond that I want nothing."

He then said to me:

"I must reflect, I must pray, I must consult the Consistory, I must consult the Curia. I cannot give you an answer. We shall see."

After that he said to me: "We will pray together."

I said: "Most willingly, Holy Father."

We then said the *Pater Noster, Veni Creator,* and an *Ave Maria,* and he then led me back very pleasantly, but with difficulty—his walk was painful, and he dragged his legs a little. In the room to the side he waited until Don Domenico came for me; and he had a small medal given to Don Domenico. We then left. Mgr. Benelli did not open his mouth; he did nothing but write all the time, like a secretary. He did not bother me at all. It was as though Mgr. Benelli were not present. I think it did not trouble the Holy Father, just as it did not trouble me, because he did not open his mouth, and gave no sign.

I then said twice again that he had the solution of the problem in his hands. He then showed his satisfaction at having had this interview, this dialogue. I said I was always at his disposal. We then left.

Since then, they are now relating what they like in the newspapers, the most fantastic inventions—that I accepted everything, that I made a complete submission; then they said it was all to the contrary—that I had accepted nothing and conceded nothing. Now they are telling me, in effect, that I lied, that I am inventing things in the conversation I had with the Holy Father. My impression is that they are so furious that this audience took place unforeseen, without going through the usual channels, that they are trying in every way to discredit it, and to discredit me as well. Clearly they are afraid that this audience puts me back in favor with many people, who are saying: Now, if Monseigneur has seen the Holy Father, there are no more problems: he is back again with the Holy Father. In fact, we have never been against the Holy Father and have always wanted to be with the Holy Father.

Moreover, I have just written to him again because Cardinal Thiandoum was so insistent on that* so that he could have a short note from me to take to the Holy Father. I said to him: "Good. I am ready to write a short letter to the Holy Father (though I am beginning to think that this correspondence is endless), I want to thank the Holy Father for granting me this audience." I did that, and thanked the Holy Father.

The Holy Father had said in the course of the conversation: "Well, at least we have a point in common: we both want to stop all these abuses that exist at present in the Church, so as to give back to the Church Her true counte-

---

*The Cardinal had been spending some days with Mgr. Lefebvre.

nance, etc . . ."

I answered: "Yes, absolutely."

So I put in my letter that I was ready to collaborate with him, he having said in the course of the audience that at least we had a point in common, to give the Church back Her true countenance and to suppress all the abuses in the Church. In that, I was quite ready to collaborate, and indeed under his authority. I said nothing, I think, which would promise too much, as giving back Her true countenance to the Church is what we are doing.

When I also said to him that I was, in fact, basing myself on "pluralism," I said:

"But, after all, with the present pluralism how would it be to let those also who want to keep Tradition be on the same footing as the others? It is the least that could be granted us." I said: "I do not know, Holy Father, if you know that there are twenty-three official eucharistic prayers in France."

He raised his arms to heaven and said: "Many more, Monseigneur, many more!"

So then I said to him:

"But, if there are many more, if, even so, you add another, I do not see how that can harm the Church. Is it a mortal sin to keep up Tradition and do what the Church has always done?"

You see, the Pope seems well-informed.

So now I think we must pray and hold firm. There may be some among you who were shocked at the suspension *a divinis*, and, I should say, by my rejection of the suspension *a divinis*. Of course. I understand. But that rejection is part, and I say it should be seen as part, of our refusal to accept the judgment that came to us from Rome. All that is the same thing. It is part of the same context; it is all linked together. Is that not so? So I do not see why I should accept this suspension since I did not accept the prohibition of ordaining, nor accept the closing of the seminary and the closing and destruction of the Fraternity. That would mean that I should have accepted from the moment of the first sentence, of the first condemnation: I should have said Yes, we are condemned, we close the seminary and end the Fraternity. Why did I not accept that? Because it was done illegally, because it is based on no proof and no judgment. I do not know if you have had occasion to read what Cardinal Garrone himself said in an interview: our meeting with Mgr. Lefebvre in Rome with the three Cardinals was not a tribunal. He said that openly. It is what I have always said myself. It was a conversation. *I have never found myself before a tribunal.* The Visitation was not a tribunal; it was an enquiry, not a judgment. So there was no tribunal, no judgment, nothing: I have been condemned like that without being able to defend myself, with no monition, nothing in writing, nothing. No! It is not possible. All the same, justice exists. So I rejected that condemnation, because it was illegal and because I was not able to make my appeal. The way that happened is absolutely inadmissible. We have been given no valid reasons for our condemnation. Once that sentence has been rejected, there is no valid reason for not rejecting the others, for the others always rest on that one. Why have I been forbidden to ordain? Because the Fraternity was "suppressed" and the seminary should have been closed. So I have no right to ordain. I reject that because it is based on a judgment that is false. Why am I suspended *a divinis*? Because I ordained when I had been forbidden to do so. But I do not accept that sentence about ordinations precisely because I do not accept the judgment that was pronounced. It is a chain. I do not accept the chain because I do not accept the first link on which the entire condemnation was built. I cannot accept it.

Moreover, the Holy Father himself did not speak to me of the suspension, he did not speak to me of the seminary, of anything. On that subject, nothing, nothing at all.

That is the situation as it is at present. I think that for you, clearly—and I understand—it is a drama, as it is for me; and I think we desire from our heart that normal relations will be resumed with the Holy See. But who was it who broke off normal relations? They were broken at the Council. It was at the Council that normal relations with the Church were broken, it was at the Council that the Church, separating Herself from Tradition, departing from Tradition, took up an abnormal attitude to Tradition. It is that which we cannot accept; we cannot accept a separation from Tradition.

As I said to the Holy Father: "In so far as you deviate from your predecessors, we can no longer follow you." That is plain. It is not we who deviate from his predecessors.

When I said to him: "But look again at the texts on religious liberty, two texts which formally contradict one another, word for word (important dogmatic texts, that of Gregory XVI and that of Pius IX, *Quanta Cura,* and then that on religious liberty, they contradict one another, word for word); which are we to choose?"

He answered: "Oh, leave those things. Let us not start discussions."*

Yes, but the whole problem is there. In so far as the new Church separates itself from the old Church we cannot follow it. That is the position, and that is why we maintain Tradition, we keep firmly to Tradition; and I am sure we are being of immense service to the Church. I should say that the Ecône seminary is basic to the battle we are waging. It is the Church's battle, and it is with that idea that we should position ourselves.

Unhappily, I must say that this conversation with the Holy Father has left me with a painful impression. I had precisely the impression that what he was defending was himself personally:

---

*See Appendix IV.

"You are against me!"

"I am not against you, I am against what separates us from Tradition; I am against what draws us towards Protestantism, towards Modernism."

I had the impression that he was considering the whole problem as personal. It is not the person, it is not Mgr. Montini: we regard him as the successor of Peter, and as successor of Peter he should pass on to us the faith of his predecessors. In so far as he does not pass on the faith of his predecessors he is no longer the successor of Peter. He becomes a person separated from his duty, denying his duty, not doing his duty. There is nothing I can do: I am not to blame. When Fesquet of *Le Monde*—he was there in the second row two or three days ago—said: "But in fact you are alone. Alone against all the bishops. What on earth can you do? What sense is there in combat of that sort?"

I answered: "What do you mean? I am not alone, I have the whole of Tradition with me. Besides, even here I am not alone. I know that many bishops privately think as we do. We have many priests with us, and there are the seminary and the seminarians and all those who come our way."

And Truth is not made by numbers: numbers do not make Truth. Even if I am alone, and even if all my seminarians leave me, even if I am abandoned by the whole of public opinion, it is all the same to me. I am attached to my catechism, attached to my Credo, attached to the Tradition which sanctified all the saints in heaven. I am not concerned about others: they do as they wish; but I want to save my soul. Public opinion I know too well: it was public opinion which condemned Our Lord after acclaiming Him a few days before. First, Palm Sunday: then, Good Friday. We know that. Public opinion is not to be trusted at all. Today it is for me, tomorrow it is against me. What matters is fidelity to our faith. We should have that conviction and stay calm.

When the Holy Father said to me:

"But, after all, do you not feel within you something which reproaches you for what you are doing? You are making a huge scandal in the Church. Is there not something which reproaches you?"

I replied: "No, Holy Father, not at all!"

He answered: "Oh! Then you are irresponsible."

"Perhaps," I said. I could not say otherwise. If I had anything to reproach myself with I should stop at once.

Pray well during your retreat, because I think things are going to happen—they have been happening for a long time, but the further we go the more often we come to critical points. All the same, the fact that God has allowed me to meet the Holy Father, to tell him what we think, and to leave the whole responsibility for the situation, now, in his hands—that is something willed by God. It remains for us to pray, begging the Holy Ghost to enlighten him and to give him courage to act in a manner which could clearly be very hard for him. I see no other solution. God has all the solutions. I could die tomorrow. We should pray also for the faithful who maintain Tradition that they may always preserve a strong, firm attitude, but not an attitude of contempt for persons, insult to persons, insult to bishops. We have the advantage of possessing the Truth—we are not at fault—just as the Church has the superiority over error of having the Truth: that superiority is Hers.

Because we have the conviction that we are upholding the Truth, Truth must plot our course, Truth must convince. It is not our person, it is not outbursts of anger, or insults to people, which will give added weight to Truth. On the contrary, that could cast doubt upon our possession of the Truth. Becoming angry and insulting shows that we do not completely trust in the weight of Truth, which is the weight of God Himself. It is in God that we trust, in Truth which is God, which is Our Lord Jesus Christ. What can be surer than that? Nothing. And little by little that Truth

makes, and will make, its way. It must. So let us resolve
that in our expressions and attitudes we shall not despise
and insult people, but be firm against error. Absolute firmness, without compromise, without relaxation, because we
are with Our Lord—it is a question of Our Lord Jesus Christ.
The honor of Our Lord Jesus Christ, the glory of the Blessed
Trinity is at stake—not the infinite glory in heaven, but the
glory here below on earth. It is Truth; and we defend it at
any cost, whatever happens.

I thank you all for praying for these intentions, as I believe you did during the vacation, and I thank all those who
had the kindness to write me a few words during the vacation
to say and show their sympathy and affection during these
times, which are always something of a trial. God certainly
helps us in this fight: that is absolutely certain. But, all the
same, it is trying. It would be such happiness to work with
all those who have responsibility in the Church and who
ought to work with us for the kingdom of Our Lord.

We remain united. Make a good retreat so that you will be
able to undertake a profitable year of studies.

14 September 1976
Declarations by the Director of the Press Office

Fr. Panciroli, Director of the Vatican Press Office, read the
following declarations on 14 September. They were repro-
duced in Italian in *L'Osservatore Romano* of 15 September.
This translation is from the French version published in *La
Documentation Catholique* and reproduced in *Itinéraires*,
No. 207, pp. 190-191.

**To the question put to me by a journalist I am authorized to answer:
It is not true that Mgr. Lefebvre signed a document of submission**

before being received by the Holy Father. Before being received, he himself brought to Castelgandolfo a short letter in which he asked the Holy Father for an audience, in courteous terms which gave room for hope of a possible and always desirable submission on his part.

To another journalist who asked if the Abbé La Bellarte or other persons had been instrumental, in agreement with the Holy See, in preparing this audience, I am authorized to answer:

Neither the Abbé La Bellarte nor anyone else was given such a mission. There was no previous understanding, either direct or indirect. Mgr. Lefebvre presented himself unexpectedly at the papal residence in Castelgandolfo and asked for an audience by the letter mentioned above. The Holy Father decided to receive him, above all because, though he was suspended *a divinis,* he was still a bishop who had come in person to the house of the common Father, in very special circumstances, and also because, as we have already said, his request for an audience was so formulated as to allow the Holy Father hope of a repentance.

I take this opportunity to put you on your guard against news-stories which, in different countries, are unjustifiable embellishments of this sad episode.*

16 September 1976
Letter of Mgr. Lefebvre to Pope Paul VI

The occasion and the reason for this courtesy letter are explained by Mgr. Lefebvre in his conference to his seminarians. Cardinal Thiandoum had been spending a few days at Ecône with Mgr. Lefebvre: "Cardinal Thiandoum was so insistent on having a bit of writing from me to bring to the Holy Father" etc.

The text was published in *Itinéraires,* No. 208, p. 131.

---

*The episode which Fr. Panciroli calls "sad" cannot be other than the reception of Mgr. Lefebvre by Pope Paul VI. Fr. Panciroli was perhaps "authorized" to express such a judgment—but by whom, exactly?

Most Holy Father:

Taking advantage of His Eminence Cardinal Thiandoum's meeting with Your Holiness, I am anxious to thank you for your kindness in granting me an interview at Castelgandolfo.

As Your Holiness said: we are united by a point in common—the ardent desire to see the end of all the abuses which are disfiguring the Church.

How I long to collaborate in that salutary work with Your Holiness and under your authority, so that the Church may recover her true countenance.

Hoping that the interview Your Holiness granted me will bear fruit pleasing to God and salutary for souls, I beg you to accept my respectful and filial wishes in Christ and Mary.

† Marcel Lefebvre

17 September 1976
Letter from Mgr. Lefebvre to Dr. Eric de Saventhem

In its issue number 217 of November 1977, *Itinéraires* published the *Saventhem Dossier*. This consisted of fourteen documents taking up 52 pages of the issue. The documents consist of a correspondence (concerning the illegal prohibition of the traditional Mass) conducted by Dr. de Saventhem with Cardinal Knox, Prefect of the Congregation for Divine Worship and the Sacraments; Cardinal Villot, the Secretary of State; and Archbishop Benelli, then Substitute (deputy) to the Secretary of State. This correspondence is of considerable historical importance and it is to be hoped that it will be made available in English.* Firstly, the fact that the prohibition of the traditional rite is an abuse of power is proved in the clearest possible terms by one of Europe's foremost laymen who is also a lawyer. He makes his case, in his capacity

*Substantial extracts were translated in *Approaches*, No. 60, March 1978.

as President of the international federation *Una Voce,* in the politest and most respectful terms possible; he is answered sometimes curtly, sometimes rudely, but most often with a stony silence. It is the almost invariable experience of anyone who has corresponded with members of the hierarchy in the "Conciliar Church" that the correspondence will be brought to an abrupt conclusion the moment that the person writing produces evidence to prove his point. This has been particularly true with parents, priests, and teachers who have worked to restore orthodoxy in catechetics.

In the March 1978 issue of *Approaches,* Hamish Fraser comments on the *Saventhem Dossier* in the light of the Vatican II Constitution on the Church (*Lumen Gentium*) which states (No. 37), after quoting Canon 682, that the laity have the right: "to disclose (to their pastors) their needs and desires with that liberty and confidence which befits children of God and brothers of Christ." It goes on:

"By reason of the knowledge, competence, or pre-eminence which they have, the laity are sometimes empowered—indeed sometimes obliged—to manifest their opinion on those things which pertain to the good of the Church. If the occasion should arise this should be done through the institutions established by the Church for that purpose and always with truth, courage, and prudence; and with reverence and charity towards those who, by reason of their office, represent the person of Christ."

Thus the theory—but the *Saventhem Dossier* shows the reality. Hamish Fraser comments:

"It cannot be denied that Dr. de Saventhem is one of the most distinguished, erudite, and responsible laymen in the whole of Catholic Europe. Yet when, after going through the prescribed channels, he most respectfully requests no more than satisfactory answers or explanations concerning certain questions which have for years been causing intense anguish to loyal Catholics throughout the Universal Church, in the person of Cardinals Villot and Knox he meets with stony silence, and is denounced as disobedient for even daring to ask such questions."

Archbishop Lefebvre has a good number of critics who, far from being Liberal, are every bit as orthodox as he is but insist that he should work within the establishment and make respectful representations through the proper channels. Such people failed to understand (or did not want to understand) the manner in which the Church was administered during the pontificate of Pope Paul VI. The *Saventhem Dossier* exposes what became a standard procedure, a procedure which had already long been evident to anyone who *really* wanted to know.* It is quite obvious that some of the Archbishop's orthodox critics did not *really* want to accept the truth. They made their private representations, which were ignored, and then sat back claiming they had done their duty. The fact that Mgr. Lefebvre was actually taking practical steps to salvage something of the Catholic faith from the wreckage of the Latin Church made them feel uneasy and caused resentment rather than admiration.

In his letter to Cardinal Villot dated 15 August 1976, Dr. de Saventhem had concluded with three requests, which are referred to in the letter from Mgr. Lefebvre which follows. These requests were:

1. That Rome should revise its recent liturgical legislation in

---

*One of the most dramatic pieces of evidence to show the futility of attempting to work through the established channels in the "Conciliar Church" was provided when Canon George Telford resigned as Vice-Chairman and Secretary to the Department for Catechetics of the Education Commission of the National Conference of Bishops of England and Wales. Together with his letter of resignation he sent a statement of the reasons for his decision, namely that he had come to see the futility of fighting for orthodox catechetics without any effective episcopal support. The entire catechetical establishment of England and Wales is in the hands of Liberals who are using their position to destroy the faith. Some bishops regret this privately—none are prepared to take effective steps to prevent it. Canon Telford's statement was published in *Christian Order* in April 1977. It was not even mentioned in the "official" Catholic press.

the near future and accord the pre-conciliar rites the right of peaceful co-existence alongside the revised rites.

2. That as a provisional measure with effect from Advent of that year any priest should be free to celebrate the Mass of St. Pius V for groups who desired it providing they were submissive to the Magisterium of Pope Paul VI.

3. From the same date the restriction should be lifted which only allowed aged or infirm priests to utilize the traditional rite if there were no people present (*sine populo*).

Having received a copy of this letter, Mgr. Lefebvre wrote to Dr. de Saventhem on 17 September 1976.

Monsieur le Président,

I have read with great interest the extract from your last letter to His Eminence the Cardinal Secretary of State, with the three requests you submitted to him. I congratulate you on this initiative, and I wish with all my heart that it will be received in Rome with understanding.

The fact is, it was necessary for me to denounce the new rites as "bastard" rites and to say that the new rite of Mass is "the symbol of a new faith, a Modernist faith"; and one of the chief reasons for that was the rigor of the attempt to proscribe the old rites. That rigor can be explained only on the hypothesis that the purpose was to drive out of the Church, along with those venerable rites, the doctrines of which they are the expression.

If the proscription of our old rites were lifted, that could be taken as a sign that Rome does not wish to impose on us, by means of a completely altered *lex orandi*, a new law of faith. And if, thenceforward, those venerable rites recovered, in the lived liturgy of the Church, the rights and honors due to them, that would be striking evidence that the Church called "Conciliar" allows us to profess the same faith, and to draw from the same sacramental sources, as the Church of all time.

True, the renewed rites present problems even if they are proposed to the Church as merely experimental. Yet, however serious these problems, we should be able to discuss them calmly with the competent authorities, without finding ourselves accused at every turn of failing in authentic loyalty to the Church.

As to the work of priestly formation which I undertake in my seminaries, it is centered wholly, as you know, on the inexhaustible mystery of the Holy Mass. That is why, for the celebration of Mass, we keep the old Missal which seems to me to enable both the celebrant and the congregation to have a more intense participation in that mystery. The same would be true for the other sacramental rites: I am sure that in their old form they give expression, better than in the new forms, to the riches of their dogmatic content, and that they therefore have a greater evangelical and pastoral effectiveness.

For the universal Church I hope, as you do, for the peaceful coexistence of the pre- and post-conciliar rites. Priests and people could then choose to which "rite-family" they would belong. Time would then let us know God's judgment on their comparative values for truth and for their salutary effect on the Catholic Church and on the whole of Christendom.

With my respectful and cordially devoted wishes in Christ and Mary.

† Marcel Lefebvre

17 September 1976
Statement by the Vatican Press Office

In its issue of 18 September 1976, L'Osservatore Romano published the following statement made on 17 September by Father Panciroli, Director of the Vatican Press Office. It concerns the revelation made by the Archbishop that the Pope had accused him of making his seminarians take an oath against the Pope. Mgr. Lefebvre answered Father Panciroli on 18 September, and his reply will be included under that date. Father Panciroli also alleged that the Pope had offered to receive Mgr. Lefebvre on five occasions which are listed in his statement. Readers have only to refer to the instances quoted by Father Panciroli which are recorded in this book under the appropriate dates to note that it was made clear to the Archbishop that he must make a total surrender to the "Conciliar Church" before the Holy Father would receive him. To quote an instance not cited by Father Panciroli, in the handwritten letter to Cardinal Villot included under the date 21 February 1976, Pope Paul states: "We consider that before being received in audience Mgr. Lefebvre must renounce his inadmissible position concerning the Second Ecumenical Vatican Council and measures which We have promulgated or approved in matters liturgical and disciplinary."

Mgr. Lefebvre most certainly did not renounce his position and it was quite clearly as a result of the unfavorable light in which the Mass and the sermon at Lille had placed the Vatican that it was decided to back down on this frequently reiterated pre-condition for an audience.

Father Panciroli's statement reads as follows:

Mgr. Lefebvre has said that during his audience with the Holy Father he learned that he was being falsely accused of demanding from his seminarians an oath against the Pope. Yesterday evening, speaking on "Antenne 2" of French Television, he said the same thing in even greater detail, asserting that the Holy Father said to him: "You require from your seminarians an oath against the Pope." According to the ex-Archbishop of Tulle this would prove that the Pope is ill-informed, and even roused against him by calumnies, "no doubt to stop him receiving him." Mgr. Lefebvre, according to the story, challenged the Pope to show him the text of the oath.

Well, I can assure you that during the course of the audience with the Pope there was never any question of an oath against the Pope which Mgr. Lefebvre was alleged to demand from his seminarians. This is news to the Holy See, which has heard of it only from the mouth of Mgr. Lefebvre in the interview in question and in the press conference the next day. It had never been heard of before, even as a theory.

The Pope has never said anything of the kind. Mgr. Lefebvre has never asked the Pope to let him have the text of the oath.

As for the insinuation that this "calumny" of the "oath" was invented to prevent the Pope receiving Mgr. Lefebvre, it seems to me that we have sufficient proof to the contrary in the fact that the Holy Father has five times let Mgr. Lefebvre know he would be happy to receive him, requiring nothing from him beforehand but a sign of repentance or at least of good will.

1. In the autograph letter of 29 June 1975 we read: "He (the Pope) awaits with impatience the day when he will have the happiness of opening his arms to you, to manifest a re-found communion, when you have responded to the demands he has just formulated. Now he trusts this intention to the Lord, who rejects no prayer."

2. At his meeting with Mgr. Lefebvre on 19 March 1976, Monseigneur the Substitute (Archbishop Benelli) spoke to him in the same sense.

3. In the consistorial discourse on 24 May 1976 the Holy Father said: "We await them (Mgr. Lefebvre and his collaborators) with open heart, our arms ready to embrace them."

4. In the letter addressed on 9 June 1976 by Monseigneur the Substitute to the Nuncio in Switzerland, which he brought to the knowledge of Mgr. Lefebvre, it says: "He (the Pope) has said, and he says again today, that he is ready to welcome him (Mgr. Lefebvre) as soon as he has given public testimony of obedience to the present successor of Saint Peter and of his acceptance of Vatican Council II."

5. P. Dhanis repeated the same thing to Mgr. Lefebvre when he met him on 27 June 1976. And in a Press Office answer to a question, published in *L'Osservatore Romano* of 28 August, 1976, it was said: "The arms of the Pope are open."

18 September 1976
Communiqué from Mgr. Lefebvre

The Director of the Vatican Press Office alleges that in the audience

I had with the Holy Father on Saturday, 11 September, the Pope did not accuse me of making my seminarians take an oath against the Pope. I am ready to swear on the Crucifix that that accusation was made by the Pope.

Staggered by that accusation I asked him if he could get me the text of the oath.

How otherwise could I have thought of putting that statement in the mouth of the Holy Father? For the oath never existed, either in fact or in my mind.

It is incredible that the Director should tell such outright lies.

Ecône, 18 September 1976.

This statement was published in *Itinéraires*, No. 208, p. 135.

7 October 1976
Letter to Friends and Benefactors
(No. 11)

Dear Friends and Benefactors:

Since the appearance of my last letter, at Eastertime, so many more events have marked out the history of our work which has since become a center of universal interest: yet another proof, if such was needed, that the people of our time can still be stirred by religious problems and that these problems have a much more important impact on our society than is generally believed.

At the beginning of these events a great many among you have shared their sorrow, their sympathy, and sometimes their worries with us. All have assured us of their fervent prayers. We have received thousands of letters and telegrams and it has been impossible for us to reply to each individually. You will find, therefore, in these lines the expression of our profound gratitude. May they also be a source of encouragement and hope for you.

To help you make those persons who know little about us understand the reasons for our attitude, we insist on two things which seem to us to be very important: the disciplinary aspect and the theological aspect, or the aspect of Faith.

One does not condemn without judgment and one cannot judge if the cause cannot be given a hearing in the forms which assure its perfect and free defense before a tribunal. But we have been condemned without judgment, without being able to plead our cause, and without appearing before any tribunal. From this arbitrary and tyrannical condemnation of the Society of Saint Pius X and its Seminary follow the interdiction of Ordinations and the suspension which concerns us personally. Considering the evident nullity of the first sentence, we do not see how the sentences which are its follow-up can be valid. That is why we are not taking any account of the decisions of an authority which abuses its power.

If it was only a question of a juridical problem and if the unjust sentences only concerned us personally, we would submit in a penitential spirit. However, to this juridical aspect is attached a much more serious motive, that of the safeguard of our Faith.

In fact, these decisions constrain us to submit ourselves to a new orientation in the Church, an orientation which is the result of an "historic compromise" between Truth and Error.

This "historic compromise" was brought about in the Church by the acceptance of Liberal ideas which were put into operation after the Council by the men of the Liberal Church who succeeded in taking the reins of power in the Church.

It is put into concrete form by the dialogue with the Protestants which has led to the liturgical reform and to the decrees concerning inter-communion and mixed marriages. Dialogue with Communists has resulted in the giving over of entire nations to Socialism or to Marxism, such as Cuba, Viet Nam, and Portugal. Soon it will be Spain, if not Italy. Dialogue with Freemasons has concluded in liberty of worship, liberty of conscience, and freedom of thought which means the suffocation of Truth and morality by error and immorality.

It is in this betrayal of the Church that they would like us to collaborate by bringing us into line with this orientation which has so often been condemned by the Successors of Peter, and by preceding Councils.

We refuse this compromise in order to be faithful to our Faith, our Baptism, and our unique King, Our Lord Jesus Christ.

This is why we will continue to ordain those whom Providence leads to our Seminary, after having given them a formation which is completely in conformity with the doctrine of the Church, and faithful to the Magisterium of the Successors of Peter.

This year we should have fourteen new priests and we are accepting thirty-five new seminarians, of whom four will be postulants to the brotherhood. We have the great pleasure of welcoming several Italians and Belgians. All of these candidates are on the retreat which starts the academic year.

During this time our priories are being slowly fitted out. Three of these will become active during 1977. We are being asked for everywhere. The groups of faithful Catholics are growing considerably and the priests are not yet numerous enough.

We are greatly counting on your spiritual and material support to permit us to continue the most necessary work for the renovation of souls, the formation of true priests, not to mention that of brothers and nuns.

On 26 September last, two brothers made their profession and two received the habit, while on 29 September we had the pleasure of receiving the profession of Sister Mary

Michael, who is of Australian origin and is the first nun of the Society, as well as the blessing of the habit of three American postulants. Eight new women presented themselves to the postulancy on 20 September last.

Fortunately, we are not alone in maintaining the holy Tradition of the Church in this domain. The novitiates of men and women multiply in spite of the trials which they are suffering from those who should rather bless them.

With the help of Jesus, Mary, and Joseph we hope that the end of this persecution that we are unjustly suffering is forthcoming. God will not abandon His Church even if he allows Her to suffer the Passion of Her Divine Founder.

That in every domain we may make Our Lord Jesus Christ to reign!

This is our aim.

May God bless you by the mediation of Our Lady of the Rosary.

† Marcel Lefebvre
7 October 1976

XV

The October Condemnation

11 October 1976
Letter of Pope Paul VI to Archbishop Lefebvre

This letter was not published by the Vatican until December and the translation given here was published by the Catholic Information Office of England and Wales on 11 December 1976 in its official journal, *Infoform*. In a prefatory note to the Pope's letter, the CIO claims that:

> Until now the Holy See refused to publish this firm but fraternal letter, in order to give Archbishop Lefebvre all the time he needed for reflection. But the Archbishop has failed to give the reply that the Pope was waiting for. Instead, he has allowed a distorted interpretation of the Pope's intervention to be spread, and has continued his own activities . . . . In these circumstances, His Holiness has to think, as a pastor, not only of bringing one of his brethren back to full ecclesial communion but also of preventing advantage being taken of the good faith

of a part of the Christian people through accusations that sin seriously
against truth and the unity of the Church.

The full text of Pope Paul's letter follows and it is not
necessary to be an expert in the techniques of public relations to realize at once that it is a straightforward propa-
ganda exercise designed for public consumption.

The "distorted interpretation" referred to concerns a
complaint made by the Archbishop that one of the conditions laid down as a prerequisite for a reconciliation between himself and the Holy See was that he should hand over
all the assets of the Society of St. Pius X to the Vatican.
This complaint is described by the CIO as "a sin against
truth." As the text of the letter makes clear, the demand
was made and therefore in making his protest the Arch-
bishcp was doing no more than stating the truth.

There is no little irony in the English Catholic Information Office, of all institutions, accusing anyone of attempting to take advantage of the good faith of the Christian
people by sinning against the truth. As one priest commented
to me, regarding the manner in which the CIO had distorted
the facts in another instance, it ought really to be entitled
"the Catholic Misinformation Office." Unfortunately, the
secular media in England tend to confine their reporting of
Catholic events to an uncritical reproduction of CIO hand-
outs. The BBC is particularly notable in this respect. As far
as its reporting of Catholic affairs is concerned it might be
a branch of the CIO.

On 11 September 1976, the CIO issued a disgraceful
attack upon Archbishop Lefebvre in which advantage was
certainly "taken of the good faith of a part of the Christian
people through accusations that sin seriously against truth."
The substance of this attack was later reproduced in a
pamphlet issued by the Catholic Truth Society under the
name of Monsignor George Leonard, Chief Information Offi-

cer of the CIO. Despite repeated letters which I wrote to him, he refused either to substantiate or withdraw these accusations, which I subsequently exposed as totally false in an article which was published in *Christian Order* of January 1977, and subsequently in a pamphlet entitled *Archbishop Lefebvre—The Truth,* which had to be reprinted three times within six months.*

The Text of the Pope's Letter

To Our Brother in the Episcopate
Marcel Lefebvre, Former Archbishop-Bishop of Tulle

When We received you in audience on 11 September last at Castelgandolfo, We let you freely express your position and your desires, even though the various aspects of your case were already well known to Us personally. The memory that We still have of your zeal for the faith and the apostolate, as well as of the good you have accomplished in the past at the service of the Church, made Us and still makes Us hope that you will once again become an edifying subject in full ecclesial communion. After the particularly serious actions that you have performed, We have once more asked you to reflect before God concerning your duty.

We have waited a month. The attitude to which your words and acts publicly testify does not seem to have changed. It is true that We have before Us your letter of 16 September in which you affirm: "A common point unites us: the ardent desire to see the cessation of all the abuses that disfigure the Church. How I wish to collaborate in this salutary work, with Your Holiness and under your authority, so that the Church may recover Her true countenance." How must these few words to which your response is limited—and which in themselves are positive—be interpreted? You speak as if you have forgotten your scandalous words and gestures against ecclesial communion—words and gestures that you have never retracted.

*Available from Augustine Publishing Co. and the Angelus Press.

As these "scandalous words and gestures" are not specified it is hard to decide to what the Holy Father can be referring. Is it scandalous to reiterate the traditional teaching of
the Church; to protest against abuses; to demand that Catholic children should be taught their faith; to celebrate Mass in
the manner utilized by so many popes and holy priests for
five centuries—and in all essentials for 1,000 years? No, if we
are to look for scandal we should look to those bishops who
cooperate in the devastation of the Lord's vineyard or, if
they do not actively cooperate, make not the least effort to
intervene in the interests of orthodoxy. Dietrich von Hildebrand writes:

"One of the most horrifying and widespread diseases of
the Church today is the lethargy of the guardians of the Faith
of the Church. I am not thinking here of those bishops who
are members of the 'fifth column,' who wish to destroy the
Church from within, or to transform it into something completely different. I am thinking of the far more numerous
bishops who have no such intentions, but who make no use
whatever of their authority when it comes to intervening
against heretical theologians or priests, or against blasphemous performances of public worship. They either close their
eyes and try, ostrich-style, to ignore the grievous abuses as
well as appeals to their duty to intervene, or they fear to be
attacked by the press or the mass media and defamed as re-
actionary, narrow-minded, or medieval. They fear men more
than God. The words of St. John Bosco apply to them: 'The
power of evil men lives on the cowardice of the good.' One
is forced to think of the hireling who abandons his flocks to
the wolves when one reflects on the lethargy of so many
bishops and superiors who, though still orthodox themselves,
do not have the courage to intervene against the most flagrant heresies and abuses in their dioceses or in their orders.

But it is most especially infuriating when certain bishops,
who themselves show this lethargy towards heretics, assume a

rigorously authoritarian attitude toward those believers who are fighting for orthodoxy, and who are thus doing what the bishops ought to be doing themselves! .... The drivel of heretics, both priests and laymen, is tolerated; the bishops tacitly acquiesce in the poisoning of the faithful. But they want to silence the faithful believers who take up the cause of orthodoxy, the very people who should by rights be the joy of the bishops' hearts, their consolation, a source of strength for overcoming their own lethargy. Instead, these people are regarded as disturbers of the peace . . . The failure to use holy authority to protect the holy Faith leads necessarily to the disintegration of the Church."*

If we are looking for scandal we need only look as far as the campaign to destroy the Society of St. Pius X. It is in perfect conformity with the spirit of the "Conciliar Church" that legitimate resistance to an abuse of power should be termed scandalous, and not the abuse of power itself.

You do not manifest repentance, even for the cause of your suspension *a divinis*.

It is precisely the Archbishop's refusal to submit to an abuse of power that caused his suspension. It is those guilty of the abuse of power who should repent.

You do not explicitly express your acceptance of the authority of the Second Vatican Council and of the Holy See—and this constitutes the basis of your problem—and you continue in those personal works of yours which the legitimate Authority has expressly ordered you to suspend.

The Acts of the Second Vatican Council are only Acts of

The Devastated Vineyard (Franciscan Herald Press, 1973), pp. 3-6. (Now out of print.)

the Ordinary Magisterium. The Council Fathers deliberately chose not to invest even one conciliar document with that infallible status which demands immediate and total acceptance. Mgr. Lefebvre's attitude is the correct attitude of a Catholic towards documents of the Ordinary Magisterium— to receive them with respect and to accept them where they conform with Tradition but to exercise a prudent reserve where they do not—for in such cases the possibility of error does exist.* What Pope Paul demanded was that the Archbishop must accept the *fallible* Acts of Vatican II as if they were *infallible*. Not only was the Archbishop required to accept all the Acts of the Council itself—as has been shown in this book on several occasions, he was required to accept the post-conciliar orientations. Where the Acts of the Council themselves are concerned, there is no bishop in the world who comes closer to implementing them than Mgr. Lefebvre. The only documents he refused to sign were those on *The Church in the Modern World* and *Religious Liberty*. His reasons for doing so are set out in Appendix IV.

Ambiguity results from the duplicity of your language.

Yes, it is quite true. Pope Paul VI is accusing Mgr. Lefebvre of ambiguity and duplicity after approving *in forma specifica* all the devious actions taken against the Archbishop —and this must include an invitation to a discussion which turned out to be a trial (see p. 45).

On Our part, as We promised you, We are herewith sending you the conclusions of Our reflections.

1. In practice you put youself forward as the defender and spokesman of the faithful and of priests "torn apart by what is happening in

---

*See *The Ordinary Magisterium of the Church Theologically Considered* by Dom Paul Nau, O.S.B., p. 26. Available from *Approaches*, 1 Waverley Place, Saltcoats, Ayrshire, Scotland, KA21 5AX.

the Church," thus giving the sad impression that the Catholic Faith and the essential values of Tradition are not sufficiently respected and lived in a portion of the People of God, at least in certain countries.

As Mgr. Lefebvre made clear during his sermon at Lille, he has never put himself forward as the leader of the traditionalists (see Chapter XIII). The Vatican thus invests him with a title to which he has never laid claim, and then attacks him for laying claim to it! Another example of the "Conciliar Church" in action!

If Mgr. Lefebvre has given the impression that the essential values of Tradition are not respected in certain countries, he is doing no more than state a fact which has been so obvious for so long that it is something which truly faithful Catholics now take for granted. The fact that there is not a single hierarchy in the West prepared to uphold and teach the truths and traditions of our faith is now accepted as quite normal rather than a cause of scandal. Organizations such as Pro Fide in Great Britain or Catholics United for the Faith in the U.S.A., which have never been connected with Mgr. Lefebvre, have produced thousands of pages of documented evidence detailing liturgical, doctrinal, and catechetical abuses which almost invariably remain uncorrected. This is a charge which I would not have the least difficulty in proving where Great Britain is concerned. When they are presented with irrefutable proof that their catechetical directors are preventing Catholic children from learning their faith, the reaction of British bishops is to ignore the interests of the children and leap to the defense of their "experts." I repeat, this is something I can prove if challenged.

In a message to the People of God issued on 11 October 1977, the Synod of Bishops included the following:

" . . . the vitality and strength of the entire catechetical activity of the Church is clearly felt almost everywhere. This has produced excellent results for the renewal of the entire community of the Church .... Despite some areas which cause concern, the number of present initiatives in this field, visible almost everywhere, is striking. Over the past ten years, in all parts of the world, catechesis has become a primary source of vitality leading to a fruitful renewal of the entire community of the Church."

There is only one possible comment regarding this statement—it is quite untrue. As a result of the initiatives taken over the past ten years the results are indeed striking—the accelerating decomposition of the Church throughout the West. To paraphrase once more a statement by Tacitus with which I concluded my book *Pope John's Council*: "When they create a wilderness they call it a renewal."

But in your interpretation of the facts and in the particular role that you assign yourself, as well as in the way in which you accomplish this role, there is something which misleads the People of God and deceives souls of good will who are justly desirous of fidelity and of spiritual and apostolic progress.

When the Synod of Bishops met to vote upon the document just cited it was approved almost unanimously. If the Pope had wished to accuse bishops of misleading the People of God and of deceiving souls of good will, there was clearly no lack of suitable candidates for such a reproach—the fact that he reserved it for one of the very few bishops to whom it is not applicable is another example of the Conciliar Church in action.

Deviations in the faith or in sacramental practice are certainly very grave, wherever they occur. For a long period of time they have been the object of Our full doctrinal and pastoral attention.

What exactly did Pope Paul mean by his "full doctrinal and pastoral attention"? The manner in which he exercised

his authority was well described by Hamish Fraser in the
July 1977 issue of *Approaches*. He comments:

"Having promulgated the New Mass, which was intended
by its authors to initiate a permanent liturgical revolution,
Pope Paul undoubtedly bears a terrifying responsibility for
the consequent liturgical (as well as doctrinal) chaos. Similarly, he bears grave responsibility for the subversion of Catholic education. On the one hand, although details concerning
catechetical subversion have been reported to the Holy See
time and again, nothing has been done to discipline the bishops guilty of imposing heretical catechisms on the schools
under their control. On the other hand, by sanctioning the
continued use of the New (Dutch) Catechism (subject only to
its carrying an Appendix adverting to its most egregious
errors, which Appendix is simply ignored by those who use
this compendium of Neo-Modernist heresies), he gave great
comfort to the New Catechists responsible for catechetical
subversion . . . . Pope Paul must bear responsibility for the
breakdown of Law within the Church and the consequent
abuse of power at all levels. His pontificate, probably the
most disastrous in history, has been characterized less by 'a
suspense of the functions of the *ecclesia docens*' (teaching
Church—Cardinal Newman's description of the state of affairs in the fourth century), than by a suspense of the *ecclesia sanctificans* (the sanctifying Church) and of the *ecclesia
gubernans* (the governing Church) . . . . It is undoubtedly
true that, but for this partial suspense of the functions of the
ecclesia docens, and the near total chaos concerning the
functions of the *ecclesia sanctificans* and the *ecclesia gubernans,* there would have been no need for Mgr. Lefebvre to
found the Ecône seminary and there would certainly have
been no danger whatsoever of his coming into conflict with
the Holy See."

Mr. Fraser's allegations concerning the total inactivity of
the Holy See in the face of liturgical, doctrinal, and catechet-

ical abuses are fully corroborated by the letter sent to Pope
Paul by twenty-eight French priests on 27 August 1976 and
included in this book under that date.

**Certainly one must not forget the positive signs of spiritual renewal
or of increased responsibility in a good number of Catholics . . .**

With all due respect to the late Holy Father, there is not
one indication of renewal anywhere in the Church which can
be ascribed to Vatican II. There are, it is true, fruitful and in-
spiring apostolates such as that of Mother Teresa of Calcutta;
however, this was not inspired by Vatican II but pre-dated it.
An indication of the true nature of the fruits of Vatican II is
provided in Appendix VIII to my book *Pope John's Council.*

**. . . or the complexity of the cause of the crisis: the immense change
in today's world affects believers at the depth of their being, and
renders ever more necessary apostolic concern for those "who are
far away." But it remains true that some priests and members of the
faithful mask with the name "conciliar" those personal interpretations
and erroneous practices that are injurious, even scandalous, and at times
sacrilegious.**

Take careful note: sacrilege is being committed; the
Council is used to justify sacrilege; and it is the Pope him-
self who testifies to this fact. It is quite clear that any fault
Mgr. Lefebvre might be guilty of would pale into insignifi-
cance beside a single act of sacrilege—but it was against Mgr.
Lefebvre alone that the Pope took positive action.

**But these abuses cannot be attributed either to the Council itself or
to the reforms that have legitimately issued therefrom, but rather to
a lack of authentic fidelity in their regard. You want to convince the
faithful that the proximate cause of the crisis is more than a wrong interpretation of the Council, and that it flows from the Council itself.**

Pope Paul was correct in stating that Archbishop Lefebvre claims that the Council is the cause of the crisis but the Pope contradicted all the available evidence in claiming that neither the Council nor the official reforms could, in fact, be blamed for the erroneous, scandalous, and indeed, sacrilegious practices which exist. It must be clearly understood that in making such a statement the Pope was expressing his opinion on a question of fact—i.e.: Have or have not the official reforms helped to create the atmosphere which engendered the abuses? Pope Paul said "No"; Mgr. Lefebvre said "Yes." In a dispute concerning a matter of fact we must base our decision upon the available evidence and not upon the status of the parties concerned. In his diary giving the background to the encyclical *Apostolicae Curae,* Cardinal Gasquet relates how, in January 1895, Pope Leo XIII explained to Cardinal Vaughan that a small concession on the part of the Holy See would bring the majority of Englishmen into communion with Rome. He asked for the Cardinal's help in achieving this objective. The Cardinal felt bound to tell the Pope bluntly that his opinion had no "foundation in fact." Subsequent events proved the Cardinal to be right and the Pope to have been completely mistaken—he had put too much faith in the opinions of ecumenically-minded French priests who were totally ignorant of the situation in England. No one in authority likes to admit making an error of judgment and there is a natural tendency among subordinates never to suggest that their superiors have erred. A prelate of lesser character than Cardinal Vaughan would not have spoken so bluntly; the same can be said of St. Paul, Bishop Grosseteste, and St. Catherine of Siena—to name but three of those who have rightly rebuked the Pope of their day for pursuing policies which harmed the Church (See Appendix II). Pope Paul's personal prestige had become inextricably linked with the Council and the post-conciliar reforms and orientations to which he was committed. It is an incontestable fact that never in the history of the Church had there been so sudden and so widespread a decomposition of Catholicism. Historians will certainly record that the Pontificate of Pope Paul VI proved to be the most disastrous during the history of the Church. There is, however, considerable scope for a difference of opinion on the reason for this collapse.

One version, and it is a version which deserves consideration, is that a series of sincere but misguided pontiffs failed to keep pace with an unprecedented advance in human progress, that they failed to adapt the Gospel to the profound developments manifest in every other branch of society and contented themselves with repeating archaic and stereotyped formulae that were meaningless to a mankind which had "come of age." The capital fault of these pontiffs had been to fail to "read the signs of the times." These particular signs were, through the intervention of the Holy Ghost, made manifest to the Fathers of the Second Vatican Council, who at last undertook the urgently needed task of adaptation. It is argued that due to the short-sighted policies of pontiffs prior to Pope John XXIII, the Church was totally unprepared for this process of adaptation and that, to a large extent, it had come too late. Thus, this school of thought argues, the decomposition of the Church would have come anyway; Pope Paul and his policies are in no way to blame (except where he tried to uphold the traditional positions as in the case of *Humanae Vitae*); and if it had not been for the post-conciliar orientations the disaster would have been even greater.

Archbishop Lefebvre's view is that it is precisely the post-conciliar reforms and orientations to which Pope Paul himself was committed, and the virtual *carte blanche* which this Pope had given to Modernists to undermine the faith in any way that suited them (rarely opposing them with anything more than pious exhortations), to which the present crisis is due. Humanly speaking, it would have been almost impossible for Pope Paul VI to admit this—even to himself. He would have thus admitted not simply that his pontificate had been the most disastrous in the history of the Church but that his policies had been responsible for the disaster. When someone in authority initiates a policy which does not succeed, the almost invariable reaction is to find some explanation other than that the policy itself was wrong. When an education official introduces a new system of teaching reading which results in illiterate children, he will blame the teachers, their methods, lack of parental cooperation—anything and anyone but his own judgment. The history of the papacy makes it clear that the popes themselves are only too human. We should not be surprised that Pope Paul attempted to justify the orientations to which he was committed—it would have been a miracle of grace if he had not. If we read the history of the papacy we shall find many occasions when we could wish miracles of grace had occurred but didn't!

This has been a long comment on a short passage in the Pope's letter—but it involves what is perhaps the most crucial issue for faithful Catholics in the whole controversy between the Archbishop and Pope Paul VI. The faithful Catholic tends to presume that anyone who disagrees with the Pope on any topic whatsoever must certainly be wrong—and he cannot be condemned for this attitude as it has been one that has been inculcated for centuries, particularly in Protestant countries. "Keep the faith" has been equated with "Give uncritical support to every papal act and opinion." Now that it has come to the point that there can be a contradiction between keeping the faith and supporting the Pope, few orthodox Catholics are able to make the necessary distinction. I am not arguing here that the Pope's interpretation of the reasons for the crisis is incorrect and that of Archbishop Lefebvre correct, simply that the Pope could be mistaken. I will leave readers to examine the evidence presented in my book *Pope John's Council* and decide for themselves whether or not it establishes that the Council and the official reforms and orientations are responsible for the present crisis.

I will content myself here with citing just one specific example. I am sure that every orthodox Catholic, whatever his views about Mgr. Lefebvre, would agree that there has been a great decline in reverence towards the Blessed Sacrament, particularly among children. Pope Paul VI insisted that this has nothing to do with the official reform, Mgr. Lefebvre insists that it does. Before the reform children knelt to receive Holy Communion on the tongue from the consecrated hands of a priest. Now it is quite common for them to receive it standing, in the hand, from one of their teachers or even from a fellow pupil. How can it be argued that these revolutionary changes have not contributed to the decline in reverence? Yet these revolutionary changes were official orientations to which the Pope himself was committed.

> **Moreover, you act as if you had a particular role in this regard. But the mission of discerning and remedying the abuses is first of all Ours; it is the mission of all the bishops who work together with Us. Indeed, We do not cease to raise Our voice against these excesses: Our discourse to the Consistory of 24 May last repeated this in clear terms. More than anyone else We hear the suffering of distressed Christians, and We respond to the cry of the faithful longing for faith and the spiritual life. This is not the place to remind you, Brother, of all the acts of Our Pontificate that testify to Our constant concern to insure for the Church fidelity to the true Tradition, and to enable Her with God's grace to face the present and the future.**

Pope Paul was quite correct in stating that the Pope and the Bishops have a mission to discern and remedy abuses—but having a mission is not the same as discharging it faithfully.

The "acts" to which the Pope referred consisted in the main only of words, and even here he made only generalized condemnations. The legion of Modernists which proliferated throughout the Church, often in official positions, could rest assured that its members would remain exempt from specific papal condemnation; this was reserved for Mgr. Lefebvre. Cardinal Heenan remarked as early as 1968 that the Pope: ". . . constantly returns to the theme of the erroneous teaching of theology. Unfortunately, his condemnations are made in general terms. Since nobody knows which theologians are being condemned it is impossible for bishops to take any action."* As for the response of the bishops to "the suffering of distressed Christians"—as many distressed Christians can confirm, appeals to bishops frequently remain unanswered, a convenient way of avoiding responsibility. And when an answer is received, that given to the People of God by the Synod of Bishops regarding catechetics is only too typical— a great renewal, we are told, is taking place in every country!

Finally, your behavior is contradictory. You want, so you say, to remedy the abuses that disfigure the Church; you regret that authority in the Church is not sufficiently respected; you wish to safeguard authentic faith, esteem for the ministerial priesthood and fervor for the Eucharist in its sacrificial and sacramental fullness. Such zeal would, in itself, merit Our encouragement, since it is a question of exigencies which, together with evangelization and the unity of Christians, remain at the heart of Our preoccupations and of Our mission. But how can you at the same time, in order to fulfil this role claim that you are obliged to act contrary to the recent Council, in opposition to your brethren in the Episcopate, to distrust the Holy See itself—which you call the "Rome of the Neo-Modernist and Neo-Protestant tendency"—and to set yourself up in open disobedience to Us? If you truly want to work "under Our authority," as you affirm in your last private letter,

*The Tablet, 18 May 1968, p. 488.

it is immediately necessary to put an end to these ambiguities and contradictions.

Mgr. Lefebvre's behavior is not in the least contradictory. Respect for authority does not involve an obligation to submit to an abuse of power. True respect for authority means that where it is abused it must be resisted—witness the case of Bishop Grosseteste (see Appendix II).

2. Let us come now to the more precise requests which you formulated during the audience of 11 September. You would like to see recognized the right to celebrate Mass in various places of worship according to the Tridentine rite. You wish also to continue to train candidates for the priesthood according to your criteria, "as before the Council," in seminaries apart, as at Ecône. But behind these questions and other similar ones, which we shall examine later on in detail, it is truly necessary to see the intricacy of the problem: and the problem is *theological*. For these questions have become concrete ways of expressing an ecclesiology that is warped in essential points.

All that Mgr. Lefebvre wishes to do is to uphold the teachings and traditions which he upheld as a bishop during the pontificates of Popes Pius XII and John XXIII. Pope Paul's response can only mean that he considered the ecclesiology of the pre-conciliar Church to be warped. Well, it's a point of view!

What is indeed at issue is the question—which must truly be called fundamental—of your clearly proclaimed refusal to recognize, in its whole, the authority of the Second Vatican Council and that of the Pope. This refusal is accompanied by an action that is orientated towards propagating and organizing what must indeed, unfortunately, be called a rebellion. This is the essential issue, and it is untenable.

To repeat a point which has been made already, the Archbishop does not refuse to recognize the authority of the Second Vatican Council—he refuses to accord its documents with the status of infallible Acts of the Extraordinary Magisterium when, as Pope Paul himself admitted, they are only Acts of the Ordinary Magisterium which, although infallible on occasions, can be fallible and even contain error. And the action described by the Pope as a "rebellion" is no more than a refusal to submit to an abuse of power. It is not the position of Mgr. Lefebvre which is untenable.

> Is it necessary to remind you that you are Our brother in the Episcopate and moreover—a fact that obliges you to remain even more closely united to the See of Peter—that you have been named an assistant to the Papal Throne? Christ has given the supreme authority in His Church to Peter and to the Apostolic College, that is, to the Pope and to the College of Bishops *una cum Capite*. In regard to the Pope, every Catholic admits that the words of Jesus to Peter determine also the charge of Peter's legitimate successors: " . . . whatever you bind on earth will be bound in heaven" (Mt 16:19); " . . . feed my sheep" (Jn 21:17); "confirm your brethren" (Lk 22:32).

There is no little irony in the fact that whereas Archbishop Lefebvre would accept what the Pope has written here in its totality, it is stated in the Agreement on Authority, produced by the Anglican-Roman Catholic International Commission in 1976, that:

"Claims on behalf of the Roman Sec as commonly presented in the past have put a greater weight on the Petrine texts (Matt. 16. 18, 19; Luke 22. 31, 32; John 21. 15-17) than they are generally thought to be able to bear. However, many Roman Catholic scholars do not now feel it necessary to stand by the former exegesis of these texts in every respect (para. 23a)."

Thus the interpretation which the Pope has placed upon these texts is challenged by Catholic bishops appointed to this Commission by the Vatican in an Agreement published with the approval of the Vatican. It is true that the three Agreed Statements have not been approved by the Vatican, only approval to publish them has been given; and that they only represent the personal opinions of the signatories. But up to this point not one of these three betrayals of the faith has been denounced by the Vatican, nor has any action been taken to discipline the bishops concerned. Unlike Mgr. Lefebvre, they could count on an effusive welcome from Pope Paul whenever they cared to visit the Vatican. This is something which Bishop C. Butler, one of the Catholic signatories, pointed out with considerable relish in a broadcast on BBC Radio on 9 October 1977, when he stated:

"The Roman Catholic members of this Commission didn't choose themselves, they were chosen by the authorities at Rome, the authorities at Rome didn't presumably intend to choose either inefficient people or people whose loyalty to the Church and her traditions was in doubt, that these members have been able unanimously to sign each of these statements as they came along, that the statements were communicated to Rome and, of course, on the Anglican side to the Archbishop of Canterbury, before they were published, that the first of these statements has now been before the world for six years, and if we have seriously compromised the Catholic faith or shown intentional or unintentional disloyalty to it, all I can say is that it is about time the Church authorities stepped in and either sacked us or showed that they disapproved."

Bishop Butler is, of course, speaking with his tongue in his cheek here. He knows very well that in the "Conciliar Church" no one will be disciplined for betraying the faith, only for upholding it.

And the First Vatican Council specified in these terms the assent due to the Sovereign Pontiff: "The pastors of every rank and of every rite and the faithful, each separately and all together, are bound by the duty of hierarchical subordination and of true obedience, not only in questions of faith and morals, but also in those that touch upon discipline and the government of the Church throughout the entire world. Thus, by preserving the unity of communion and profession of faith with the Roman Pontiff, the Church is a single flock under one Pastor. Such is the doctrine of Catholic truth, from which no one can separate himself without danger for his faith and his salvation" (Dogmatic Constitution, *Pastor Aeternus,* ch. 3, DZ 3060). Concerning bishops united with the Sovereign Pontiff, their power with regard to the universal Church is solemnly exercised in the Ecumenical Councils, according to the words of Jesus to the body of the Apostles: " . . . whatever you bind on earth shall be bound in heaven" (Mt. 16:19). And now in your conduct you refuse to recognize, as must be done, these two ways in which supreme authority is exercised.

An important distinction must be made here between a refusal to recognize the existence of an authority and a refusal to submit to it in a particular instance. Those who refuse to accept the existence of the papal prerogatives *as such* are guilty of schism and heresy. Those who refuse to submit to the exercise of papal authority in a particular instance are only guilty of disobedience; if the instance in question involves an abuse of power this disobedience involves not guilt but merit. This distinction between schism and disobedience is explained in the *Dictionnaire de Théologie Catholique* by no less an authority than Father Yves Congar, a virulent opponent of Mgr. Lefebvre.

Pope Paul continues:

Each bishop is indeed an authentic teacher for preaching to the people entrusted to him that faith which must guide their thoughts and conduct and dispel the errors that menace the flock. But, by their nature, "the charge of teaching and governing . . . cannot be exercised except in hierarchical communion with the head of the College and

with its members " (Constitution *Lumen Gentium*, 21; cf. also 25).
A fortiori, a single bishop without a canonical mission does not have,
in actu expedito ad agendum, the faculty of deciding in general what
the rule of faith is or of determining what Tradition is. In practice you
are claiming that you alone are the judge of what Tradition embraces.

Needless to say, Mgr. Lefebvre has never made any such
claim. All that he is doing is what every Catholic—bishop,
priest, or layman—has not simply the right but the duty to
do, and that is to speak up in defense of the faith when it is
endangered no matter by whom. Thus when Pope John XXII
claimed in 1331 that the souls of the just do not enjoy the
Beatific Vision immediately after death, but must await the
final judgment of God on the Last Day, he was rightly denounced by some Franciscan theologians who demanded
that he be brought before a council for trial and condemnation. The Pope appointed a commission of theologians to
examine the question; the commission convicted him of
error; he made a public retraction on 3 December 1334 and
died the next day.

Similarly, the General Instruction (*Institutio Generalis*)
to the New Order of the Mass was approved by Pope Paul VI.
Certain articles, notably Article 7, provoked such outrage
among the faithful that the Pope felt himself bound to order
their correction. Had the faithful waited for those with a
canonical mandate to denounce these articles they would
still be waiting!

You say that you are subject to the Church and faithful to Tradition, by the sole fact that you obey certain norms of the past that
were decreed by the predecessor of Him to Whom God has today
conferred the powers given to Peter. That is to say, on this point also,
the concept of "Tradition" that you invoke is distorted. Tradition is
not a rigid and dead notion, a fact of certain static sort which at a
given moment of history blocks the life of this active organism which

is the Church, that is, the Mystical Body of Christ.

On the contrary, particularly where the liturgy is concerned, it is Mgr. Lefebvre who is the defender of that salutary development expounded by Cardinal Newman. It is the proponents of the New Mass who wish to fly in the face of history and impose a rigid, dead, static notion of liturgical development by reverting to more primitive liturgical forms on the grounds that what is earlier must be better. This is an attitude that was condemned most forcefully by Pope Pius XII in his encyclical *Mediator Dei* (paras. 64-69).

It is up to the Pope and to Councils to exercise judgment in order to discern in the traditions of the Church that which cannot be renounced without infidelity to the Lord and to the Holy Spirit—the deposit of faith—and that which, on the contrary, can and must be adapted to facilitate the prayer and the mission of the Church throughout a variety of times and places, in order better to communicate it, without an unwarranted surrender of principles. Hence Tradition is inseparable from the living Magisterium of the Church, just as it is inseparable from Sacred Scripture. "Sacred Tradition, Sacred Scripture, and the Magisterium of the Church . . . are so linked and joined together that one of these realities cannot exist without the others, and that all of them together, each in its own way, effectively contribute under the action of the Holy Spirit to the salvation of souls" (Constitution *Dei Verbum,* 10).

This is all true, but it does not follow that every decision of ecclesiastical authority is automatically infallible and could not constitute an abuse of power.

With the special assistance of the Holy Spirit, the Popes and the Ecumenical Councils have acted in this common way. And it is precisely this that the Second Vatican Council did.

Quite the contrary. Vatican II, in contrast with preceding Councils, took the unprecedented step of declaring that it had not availed itself of the special assistance of the Holy Ghost given to Ecumenical Councils when it stated specifically that none of its teaching was to be considered infallible. In an address delivered on 12 January 1966, Pope Paul himself stated explicitly:

"Some ask what authority—what theological qualification —the Council has attached to its teachings, knowing that it has avoided solemn dogmatic definitions backed by the Church's infallible teaching authority. The answer is familiar to those who remember the conciliar declaration of 6 March 1964, repeated on 16 November 1964. In view of the pastoral character of the Council, it has avoided pronouncing in an extraordinary way dogmas carrying the note of infallibility. Nevertheless its teachings carry the weight of the supreme ordinary teaching authority."

Pope Paul thus contradicted himself in claiming that Vatican II acted precisely as previous councils had done. This is precisely what it did not do!

Nothing that was decreed in this Council, or in the reforms that We enacted in order to put the Council into effect, is opposed to what the two-thousand-year-old Tradition of the Church considers as fundamental and immutable. We are the guarantor of this, not in virtue of Our personal qualities but in virtue of the charge which the Lord has conferred upon Us as legitimate Successor of Peter, and in virtue of the special assistance that He has promised to Us as well as to Peter: "I have prayed for you that your faith may not fail" (Lk 22:32). The universal episcopate is guarantor with Us of this.

As Appendix IV will show, some teaching in the Declaration on Religious Liberty is opposed to what a series of popes has taught consistently with the authority of the Supreme Ordinary Magisterium, possibly even in an extraordinary and infallible manner in the encyclical *Quanta Cura*. It has also been the consistent teaching of the Magisterium that Catholics should not take part in the services of heretical or schismatic bodies, yet this is now encouraged. This prohibition derives from the very nature of the Church founded by Christ. Those who organize religious services outside and in opposition to the one, true Church are in opposition to Christ Himself, Whose Mystical Body the Church is. To permit Catholics to take part in services organized by, say, Protestants must be, and is, taken to imply that these bodies are legitimate branches of the Church.

Now if it is conceded that previous teaching on Religious Liberty and common worship was erroneous, or at least not immutable, why should we have any confidence that the teaching of Vatican II is correct? We are reduced to the situation that it is only teaching which has been solemnly declared as infallible to which we can give our wholehearted acceptance! The great French bishop Bossuet recognized the importance of the continuity of teaching in a pastoral letter to the new Catholics of his diocese:

"We never disparage the faith of our fathers but hand it on exactly as we have received it. God willed that the truth should come down to us without any evident novelties. It is in this way that we recognize what has always been believed and, accordingly, what must always be believed. It is, so to speak, from this word *always* that the truth and the promise derive their authority, an authority which would vanish completely the moment an interruption was discovered anywhere."

The example concerning common worship illustrates this point perfectly. Unless the Vatican expects the faithful to behave like robots, programmed to change direction at the whim of their controller, what reaction does it expect of us when in 1963 (in accord with a 2,000-year tradition) we are taught that it is wrong to worship with heretics and then

in 1964 (Decree on Ecumenism) we are taught that it is not
wrong?

**Again, you cannot appeal to the distinction between what is dog-
matic and what is pastoral, to accept certain texts of this Council and
to refuse others. Indeed, not everything in the Council requires an
assent of the same nature: only what is affirmed by definitive acts as an
object of faith or as a truth related to faith requires an assent of faith.**

And there is not a single document of the entire Council
which demands the assent of faith.

**But the rest also forms part of the solemn Magisterium of the
Church, to which each member of the faithful owes a confident acceptance and a sincere application.**

This is quite true, but in the accepted sense of the assent
to be given to the teaching of the Ordinary Magisterium, particularly with regard to novelties. Once again, Dom Nau's
study which was referred to on page 178 should clarify the
nature of this assent for those in any doubt concerning the
difference between the Ordinary and Extraordinary Magisterium. It should be added that this study is intended to re-
inforce the authority of the Ordinary Magisterium and not
to diminish it in any way.

It must also be noted with respect to this passage from
the Pope's letter that he most certainly does *not* require each
and every member of the faithful to accept and apply the
teaching of the Council. The Council *ordered* (Liturgy Constitution, para. 116) that Gregorian Chant be given pride of
place in liturgical services. Apart from those institutes controlled by Mgr. Lefebvre, this instruction is almost universally
ignored—and ignored with impunity.

You say moreover that you do not always see how to reconcile cer-

tain texts of the Council, or certain dispositions which We have enacted in order to put the Council into practice, with the wholesome Tradition of the Church and in particular with the Council of Trent or the affirmations of Our predecessors. These are for example: the responsibility of the College of Bishops united with the Sovereign Pontiff, the new *Ordo Missae*, ecumenism, religious freedom, the attitude of dialogue, evangelization in the modern world . . . . It is not the place, in this letter, to deal with each of these problems. The precise tenor of the documents, with the totality of its nuances and its context, the authorized explanations, the detailed and objective commentaries which have been made, are of such a nature to enable you to overcome these personal difficulties. Absolutely secure counsellors, theologians, and spiritual directors would be able to help you even more with God's enlightenment, and We are ready to facilitate this fraternal assistance for you.

On 18 June 1977 the Secretariat of State received an offer from the Archbishop to "accept *all* the texts of Vatican II either in their obvious meaning or in an official interpretation which ensures their full concordance with the authentic teaching of the Church." His offer, together with other proposals aimed at healing the breach with the Vatican, was rejected as unacceptable by Pope Paul in a letter dated 20 June 1977. These documents will be dealt with under their respective dates.

But how can an interior personal difficulty—a spiritual drama which We respect—permit you to set yourself up publicly as a judge of what has been legitimately adopted, practically with unanimity, and knowingly to lead a portion of the faithful into your refusal?

This is a far from subtle attempt to insinuate that the Archbishop is the instigator of resistance to the reforms of the "Conciliar Church." On the contrary, this resistance long predated the emergence of the Archbishop and his seminary as focal points of inspiration and encouragement to Catholics wishing to remain true to the traditional faith. For example, the Latin Mass Society of England and Wales sent every priest in the country a copy of the *Critical Study* of the New Mass sent to the Pope by Cardinals Ottaviani and Bacci in 1969. The name of the Archbishop was hardly known in Britain at that time. I support the Archbishop because he upholds the beliefs and traditions which I *already* upheld when I first came to know of him.

If justifications are useful in order to facilitate intellectual acceptance —and We hope that the troubled or reticent faithful will have the wisdom, honesty, and humility to accept those justifications that are widely placed at their disposal—they are not in themselves necessary for the assent of obedience that is due to the Ecumenical Council and to the decisions of the Pope. It is the ecclesial sense that is at issue.

The type of justification given to the faithful has already been indicated in the response of the 1977 Synod of Bishops to documented complaints concerning the "New Catechetics" —that we are in the presence of an almost universal and fruitful catechetical renewal!

In effect you and those who are following you are endeavoring to come to a standstill at a given moment in the life of the Church. By the same token you refuse to accept the living Church, which is the Church that always has been: you break with the Church's legitimate pastors and scorn the legitimate exercise of their charge.

The term "the living Church" is yet another novelty. The Pope says that it is the Church that always has been, but the use of the term "living" only makes sense in opposition to "dead"—just as the term "Conciliar Church" only makes sense in opposition to the "Preconciliar Church." As has already been stated, where the liturgy is concerned it is the "living Church" which wishes to reverse a process of development lasting almost 2,000 years under the guidance of the Holy Ghost by reverting to what it terms more "primitive forms"—precisely the argument used by the Protestant Reformers when they made similar changes to destroy the sacrificial nature of the Mass. The term "living Church" is also a useful example of the manner in which the language used in the "Conciliar Church" is approximating more and more closely to the Newspeak of *Nineteen Eighty-Four*. In Newspeak words frequently imply the opposite of their apparent meaning, and we now have the term "living Church" used to describe a Church which has not been closer to dying since the Arian crisis—when a weak Pope confirmed the excommunication of the great champion of orthodoxy, St. Athanasius. There are no signs of new vitality anywhere in the Church today—whatever is vital and fruitful is a survival from the "Preconciliar (dead?) Church." The frenetic hysteria of the Pentecostal movement—so often cited as a sign of renewal—is one of the clearest indications of approaching death, the final paroxysms of the dying body. But the Body of Christ cannot die—the Church has been written off on many occasions but has always survived—just as She will survive the present crisis—if only as a remnant. It is far from fanciful to see Ecône as a source of the antibodies which are already emerging to fight the contagion and restore the Mystical Body to health.

And so you claim not even to be affected by the orders of the Pope, or by the suspension *a divinis*, as you lament "subversion" in the Church.

Is it not clear proof of the extent of the subversion in the Church during the Pontificate of Pope Paul VI that Her most courageous and orthodox bishop was suspended *a divinis* for the crime of forming orthodox priests? As has already been made clear in this book on several occasions, the refusal

of the Archbishop to accept any of the sanctions following
his refusal to close his seminary is not more than the logical
corollary of his contention that the order to do this was
unjust.

Is it not in this state of mind that you have ordained priests without dimissorial letters and against Our explicit command, thus creating
a group of priests who are in an irregular situation in the Church and
who are under grave ecclesiastical penalties? Moreover, you hold that
the suspension you have incurred applies only to the celebration of
the sacraments according to the new rite, as if they were something
improperly introduced into the Church, which you go so far as to call
schismatic, and you think that you evade this sanction when you ad-
minister the formulas of the past and against the established forms
(cf. 1 Cor 14:40).

Mgr. Lefebvre has indeed referred to the "Conciliar
Church" being in schism, but in a light-hearted manner. He
has a highly-developed sense of humor and can be provocative at times. When charged with being in schism he has replied that in so far as it has broken with the Traditional
Church it is the "Conciliar Church" which is in schism. However, he has always made it clear that he recognizes the authority of the Pope, a fact proved by all his letters to Pope
Paul. They are not the letters of a bishop who is seriously
maintaining that the Pope is in schism!

From the same erroneous conception springs your abuse of celebrating the Mass called that of St. Pius V.

So it is now an abuse to celebrate a form of Mass dating
back in all essentials over 1,000 years and which, during that
time, has been a source of sanctification for countless millions of the faithful. Well, it's a point of view!

You know full well that this rite had itself been the result of successive changes, and that the Roman Canon remains the first of the Eucharistic Prayers authorized today.

Yes, but the Roman Mass had developed by a gradual and natural process for over 1,000 years until it was finally codified by St. Pius V. I have provided its history in some detail in my pamphlet *The Tridentine Mass.** Surely the Holy Father, or whoever wrote this letter for him, cannot expect any Catholic with a rudimentary knowledge of Church history to take seriously a comparison between the evolution of the traditional Mass and the concoction of a *new* Mass (something the Council did not order) within the space of a few years and with the cooperation of heretics. Leaving aside the fact that the New Mass has been constructed in such a fashion that it can be celebrated in a form containing hardly a reference to the sacrificial nature of the Mass, in which form it is entirely acceptable to some Protestants. The New Mass has also proved to be a disaster pastorally and aesthetically. No layman was better qualified to comment on the liturgy than Dietrich von Hildebrand. He wrote:

"The new liturgy was simply not formed by saints, *homines religiosi,* and artistically gifted men, but has been worked out by so-called experts, who are not at all aware that in our time there is a lack of talent for such things. Today is a time of incredible talent for technology and medical research, but not for the organic shaping of the expression of the religious world. We live in a world without poetry, and this means that one should approach the treasures handed on from more fortunate times with twice as much reverence, and not with the illusion that we can do it better ourselves."**

*Available from Augustine Publishing Company and the Angelus Press.

***The Devastated Vineyard* (Franciscan Herald Press, 1973), p. 70. For full documentation concerning the participation of Protestant observers in the compilation of the New Mass see my pamphlet *The Roman Rite Destroyed.*

The present reform derived its *raison d'être* and its guidelines from the Council and from the historical sources of the Liturgy.

In my pamphlet *The Roman Rite Destroyed* I have quoted from such irreproachable authorities as Cardinal Heenan, Archbishop R. J. Dwyer, and Father Louis Bouyer to the effect that the liturgical reform is far more radical than that envisaged by the Council Fathers (who were given the opportunity of discussing only general principles). It is actually a contradiction of both what the Fathers intended and the entire papally-approved liturgical movement of the present century.

It enables the laity to draw greater nourishment from the word of God.

In this case it seems permissible to wonder why millions of Catholics who attended the Old Mass have ceased attending since the imposition of the New.

Their more effective participation leaves intact the unique role of the priest acting in the person of Christ.

This statement is quite true in that only the priest can consecrate, but in practice many of the changes have served to obscure the nature of the unique priestly role. This minimization has occurred by allowing the laity to perform functions which had been reserved to the celebrant in the Tridentine Mass. Sacred vessels which only he could touch are now handled by all and sundry; laymen and women can now read the lessons or preach the sermons; only his consecrated hands had been allowed to touch the host—now it can be distributed by teen-aged girls into the hands of standing communicants. No distinction is made in the new Eucharistic Prayers between the role of the celebrant and that of the congregation. With Eucharistic Prayer II in particular, the priest can appear to be no more than the spokesman for a con-celebrating congregation.

We have sanctioned this reform by Our authority, requiring that it be adopted by all Catholics.

The original General Instruction (*Institutio Generalis*) to the New Mass and the new rite of Baptism were also sanctioned by the Pope's authority—but they subsequently required modifications in the interests of orthodoxy. It is not correct to state that the Pope has required *all* Catholics to adopt it—the Instruction applies only to Catholics of the Roman Rite and does not affect the Eastern Churches. Nor has it ever been made clear whether such variants of the Roman Rite as the Dominican Rite are affected. Nor is it certain that the Pope has imposed the New Mass with the required legal forms necessary to make it mandatory even for the Roman Rite. But this is a very complex question which will be examined in detail in my book *Pope Paul's New Mass*.

If, in general, We have not judged it good to permit any further delays or exceptions to this adoption, it is with a view to the spiritual good and the unity of the entire ecclesial community, because for Catholics of the Roman Rite, the *Ordo Missae* is a privileged sign of their unity.

With all due respect to the late Holy Father, such a claim constitutes a mockery of the faithful. Where in the Roman Rite is that unity which was once its most precious characteristic? There are now so many permutations officially permitted that it is possible for every priest in any diocese to celebrate the Mass in a different manner—not to mention the countless unofficial and even sacrilegious variations which are perpetrated throughout the West with total impunity. In their book *Les Fumées de Satan,* André Mignot and Michel de Saint Pierre have presented nearly 300 pages of documented instances of catechetical and liturgical abuses—selected from 4,000 cases which they had investigated. All the examples they give can be substantiated with names, dates, and places. Every Catholic who reads French should obtain a copy. It will have a place in history as perhaps the most terrifying indictment of the "Living Church" yet assembled. And what was the reaction of the French bishops? Without making the least attempt to deny the factual nature of the documentation in the book they issued the most vicious public denunciation of the authors. No less a person than Father Henri Bruckberger sprang to their defense. Father Bruckberger is a hero of the French Resistance and the most distinguished man of letters among the French clergy today. As for the French bishops, he wrote:

"They knew Michel de Saint Pierre and André Mignot only too well; they knew that the authors had such respect for the sacred character of the episcopacy that, in formulating so outrageous a communiqué the bishops knew that they risked neither a beating nor a summons before the courts, which they fully deserved. Thus our bishops are transformed into men without fear for the simple reason that they are not putting themselves at risk . . . . They have the sudden temerity of men overcome with terror who try to cover up facts which accuse them personally. This episcopal communiqué constitutes the most terrible admission. Our bishops have acknowledged publicly not only that they are aware of the abuses brought to light in *Les Fumées de Satan,* but that they are the knowing and willing accomplices. Here and now the object of the book has been achieved. It is the hour when Tartuffe's mask has been torn away completely."*

The type of abuse cited in *Les Fumées de Satan* is com-

---

* *Toute L 'Eglise en Clameurs* (Paris, 1977), p. 195. Tartuffe is a religious hypocrite, the principal character in a play by Moliere with the same title.

mon to all the countries of the West—as is the complicity of all the Western hierarchies whose members, if they don't actually approve of the abuses, tolerate them. The only form of Mass which they will not tolerate is the one they were ordained to offer. So much for the New Mass as "a privileged sign" of the unity of the Catholics of the Roman Rite.

It is also because, in your case, the old rite is in fact the expression of a warped ecclesiology, . . .

It is quite true that the Tridentine Mass is the most fitting expression of the traditional Faith, the Faith expressed with such clarity by the Council of Trent. The Tridentine Mass expresses clearly the concept of a Church with Her eyes fixed firmly on heaven; a solemn sacrifice offered to a transcendent, omnipotent God; the exalted role of the priest at the altar as mediator between God and man. A warped ecclesiology? Well, it's a point of view!

. . . and a ground for dispute with the Council and its reforms, under the pretext that in the old rite alone are preserved, without their meaning being obscured, the true sacrifice of the Mass and the ministerial priesthood. We cannot accept this erroneous judgment, this unjustified accusation, nor can We tolerate that the Lord's Eucharist, the sacrament of unity, should be the object of such division (cf. 1 Cor 11:18), and that it should even be an instrument and sign of rebellion.

The issue here is whether the Archbishop's judgment is correct or erroneous. I have already provided ample evidence in my pamphlet *The Roman Rite Destroyed* to prove that the doctrines of "the true sacrifice of the Mass and the ministerial priesthood" are, at the very least, expressed far less clearly in the new rite than the old, particularly where Eucharistic Prayer II is used. The most conclusive proof of this is the fact that a number of Protestants are cited in the pamphlet as stating that they are happy with the new prayers and recognize a Protestant theology in them. This is the most striking corroboration there could be of Mgr. Lefebvre's allegation—which is, of course, that put forward in the *Critical Study* sent to Pope Paul by Cardinals Ottaviani and Bacci. It is also only necessary for anyone conversant with Protestant eucharistic theology to examine the traditional Mass carefully and make a note of any prayers he considers incompatible with Protestant belief. He will find at once that almost all such prayers have been eliminated from the new rite.

Of course there is room in the Church for a certain pluralism, but in licit matters and in obedience. This is not understood by those who refuse the sum total of the liturgical reform; nor indeed on the other hand by those who imperil the holiness of the real presence of the Lord and of His Sacrifice.

What we are witnessing in the Church today is not pluralism but anarchy—anarchy in which anything is tolerated but the traditional Mass. Those guilty of irreverence and sacrilege are (occasionally) rebuked in general terms—but their excesses are tolerated.

In the same way there can be no question of a priestly formation which ignores the Council.

As was shown on pages 69-70, there can be no doubt that Ecône comes closer to the norms laid down by the Council and subsequent instructions than almost any other seminary in the West.

We cannot therefore take your requests into consideration because it is a question of acts which have already been committed in rebellion against the one true Church of God. Be assured that this severity is not dictated by a refusal to make a concession on such and such a point of

discipline or liturgy, but, given the meaning and the extent of your acts in the present context, to act thus would be on Our part to accept the introduction of a seriously erroneous concept of the Church and of Tradition. This is why, with the full consciousness of Our duties, We say to you, Brother, that you are in error. And with the full ardour of Our fraternal love, as also with all the weight of Our authority as the Successor of Peter, We invite you to retract, to correct yourself and to cease from inflicting wounds upon the Church of Christ.

3. Specifically, what do We ask of you?

(a) First and foremost a Declaration that will rectify matters, for Ourself and also for the People of God who have a right to clarity and who can no longer bear without damage such equivocations.

This Declaration will therefore have to affirm that you sincerely adhere to the Second Vatican Council and all its documents—*sensu obvio*—which were adopted by the Council Fathers and approved and promulgated by Our authority. For such an adherence has always been the rule, in the Church, since the beginning in the matter of Ecumenical Councils.

It is not a question of the Archbishop's accepting all the documents, there are only two that he didn't sign. And, as has been pointed out already, when he offered to accept these in June 1977, on the understanding that they would be interpreted in the light of the traditional teaching, his offer was rejected. And once again, the Pope is referring to Vatican II as if it did not differ from preceding Ecumenical Councils. He is asking the Archbishop to give the assent due to the Extraordinary Magisterium to documents of the Ordinary Magisterium.

It must be clear that you equally accept the decisions that We have made since the Council in order to put it into effect, with the help of the Departments of the Holy See; among other things, you must explicitly recognize the legitimacy of the reformed liturgy, notably of the *Ordo Missae*, and Our right to require its adoption by the entirety of the Christian people.

In his letter delivered to the Vatican on 18 June 1977, the Archbishop asked for co-existence of the old and new rites, which makes it quite clear that he accepts the legitimacy of the new. In the Archbishop's letter to Dr. Eric M. de Saventhem dated 17 September 1976 he had already made this point, stating that he would be prepared to accept the peaceful co-existence of the two rites with the faithful being given the choice of which "family" of rites they preferred to adhere to. The text of this letter is included under the date given.

You must also accept the binding character of the rules of Canon Law now in force which, for the greater part, still correspond with the content of the Code of Canon Law of Benedict XV, without excepting the part which deals with canonical penalties.

As far as concerns Our person, you will make a point of desisting from and retracting the grave accusations or insinuations which you have publicly levelled against Us, against the orthodoxy of Our faith and Our fidelity to Our charge as the Successor of Peter, and against Our immediate collaborators.

It is significant that the Pope gives no details of these alleged accusations. Those who have read this far will have noted the profound respect of the Archbishop towards the person of the Pope, either when writing to him or speaking of him. This respect is also manifest throughout Mgr. Lefebvre's book, *A Bishop Speaks*. The Archbishop explained his own attitude to the person of Pope Paul VI and to other bishops in an address delivered in Montreal on 31 May 1978.

"Pray for the Pope; pray that God will guide him to abandon the path along which he has allowed himself to be led, a path which is not the way of the good God. Ecumenism is not God's way. Pray for the Bishops, do not insult them. I do not think that a single expression of disrespect towards the Holy Father can be found anywhere in my writings. I do not insult the Bishops. I consider them to be my brothers and I pray for them that they will return to the way of the Tradition of the Church. I am sure that this will happen one day. We must have confidence. We are passing through a tornado; the only anchor to which we can attach ourselves is the tradition of the Church because it cannot err; our Catholic faith has been, is, and will always be the same."*

With regard to the Bishops, you must recognize their authority in their respective dioceses, by abstaining from preaching in those dioceses and administering the sacraments there: the Eucharist, Confirmation, Holy Orders, etc., when these Bishops expressly object to your doing so.

Finally, you must undertake to abstain from all activities (such as Conferences, publications, etc.) contrary to this Declaration, and formally to reprove all those initiatives which make use of your name in the face of this Declaration.

It is a question here of the minimum to which every Catholic Bishop must subscribe: this adherence can tolerate no compromise. As soon as you show Us that you accept its principle, We will propose the practical manner of presenting this Declaration. This is the first condition in order that the suspension *a divinis* be lifted.

(b) It will then remain to solve the problem of your activity, of your works, and notably of your seminaries. You will appreciate, Brother, that in view of the past and present irregularities affecting these works, We cannot go back on the juridical suppression of the Priestly Fraternity of St. Pius X.

What cruel irony! Has there ever been an instance in the history of the Church involving more irregularities, more disregard for the most elementary demands of justice than in

Le Doctrinaire, July/August 1978, p. 8.

the suppression of the Society of St. Pius X?

> This has inculcated a spirit of opposition to the Council and to its implementation such as the Vicar of Christ was endeavoring to promote. Your Declaration of 21 November 1974 bears witness to this spirit; and upon such a foundation, as Our Commission of Cardinals rightly judged, on 6 May 1975, one cannot build an institution or a priestly formation in conformity with the requirements of the Church of Christ.

So once more the Declaration is the only evidence that can be cited against the Archbishop and the "spirit" of his Fraternity. Remember the origin of this Declaration, remember the manner in which the Cardinals conducted their inquiry, and then the case against the Archbishop can be evaluated at its true worth. As for the spirit that permeates certain "approved" seminaries, a young friend of mine, who is totally orthodox and a student at an English seminary, told me that when the Vatican issued its recent Declaration on Sexual Ethics it was not simply rejected but ridiculed by staff and students alike. He added that such is the unanimity among staff and students in their rejection of papal teaching that he sometimes has to fight off serious doubts as to whether they could be right and he could be wrong for accepting it.

> This in no way invalidates the good element in your seminaries, but one must also take into consideration the ecclesiological deficiencies of which We have spoken and the capacity of exercising a pastoral ministry in the Church of today.

The ecclesiological difficulties cited consist of the Archbishop's Declaration! And now we have yet another neologism—the "Church of today." One fact to which any seminarian from Ecône could testify is that wherever they go it is made abundantly clear to them that they are precisely what "the Church of today" wants—the Church, of course, being the faithful. The seminarians are approached wherever they go, on public transport, in the streets, by ordinary Catholics, who say to them, "How wonderful to see a real priest again!"

If by his reference to the "Church of today" the Holy Father is implying that the so-called "modern man" needs a new type of priest, then he has been effectively answered by Dietrich von Hildebrand, who has made it clear that this so-called "modern man" does not exist—he is a myth.

"As long as one only refers to the immense change in the external conditions of life brought about by the enormous technological development which has taken place, then one is referring to an indubitable fact. But this outward change has had no fundamental influence on man—on his essential nature, on the sources of his happiness, on the meaning of his life, on the metaphysical nature of man. And yet only some such fundamental change in man would have any bearing at all on his ability to understand the language in which the Church has been announcing the Gospel of Christ to mankind for thousands of years.

A knowledge of modern history and an unprejudiced view of it could not fail to convince anyone that the 'modern man' who is radically different from the men of all other periods is a pure invention, or rather, a typical myth."*

Faced with these unfortunate mixed realities, We shall take care not to destroy but to correct and save as far as possible. This is why, as supreme guarantor of the faith and of the formation of the clergy, We require of you first of all to hand over to Us the responsibility of your work, and particularly for your seminaries. This is undoubtedly a heavy sacrifice for you, but it is also a test of your trust, of your obedience, and it is a necessary condition in order that these semi-

*The Devastated Vineyard, p. 9.

naries, which have no canonical existence in the Church, may in the future take their place therein.

The Archbishop is thus asked to hand over the responsibility for his work as a test of his trust. Cardinal Mindszenty had also been asked to put his trust in Pope Paul VI. We learn from his memoirs that he was given a solemn promise by the Pope's personal envoy that his "titles of archbishop and primate" would not be affected if he agreed to leave Hungary (p. 223). After he had arrived in Rome he was told by the Pope: "You are and remain Archbishop of Esztergom and primate of Hungary. Continue working, and if you have difficulties, always turn trustfully to Us" (p. 239). And then, "exactly on the twenty-fifth anniversary of my arrest, I was pained to receive a letter from the Holy Father dated 18 December 1973, in which His Holiness informed me with expressions of great appreciation and gratitude that he was declaring the archiepiscopal See of Esztergom vacant" (p. 246). The Cardinal begged Pope Paul to rescind this decision not because he desired to cling to office but to avoid sowing confusion in the minds of the Hungarian faithful. Despite this plea, on the twenty-fifth anniversary of the Cardinal's show trial the news of his removal from his see was published as if he had resigned voluntarily. He issued the following statement:

"A number of news agencies have transmitted the Vatican decision in such a way as to imply that Jozef Cardinal Mindszenty has voluntarily retired . . . . In the interests of truth Cardinal Mindszenty has authorized his office to issue the following statement:

Cardinal Mindszenty has not abdicated his office as Archbishop nor his dignity as Primate of Hungary. The decision was taken by the Holy See alone" (p. 246).

It is only after you have accepted the principle, that We shall be able to provide in the best possible way for the good of all the persons involved, with the concern for promoting authentic priestly vocations and with respect for the doctrinal, disciplinary and pastoral requirements of the Church. At that stage We shall be in a position to listen with benevolence to your requests and your wishes, and, together with Our Departments, to take in conscience the right and opportune measures.

As for the illicitly ordained seminarians, the sanctions which they have incurred in conformity with Canons 985, 7 and 2374 can be lifted, if they give proof of a return to a better frame of mind, notably by accepting to subscribe to the Declaration which We have asked of you. We count upon your sense of the Church in order to make this easy for them.

This makes it clear that the formation given at Ecône must be regarded as satisfactory if the only condition required to regularize the position of those ordained there is subscription to a declaration.

As regards the foundations, houses of formation, "priories," and various other institutions set up on your initiative or with your encouragement, We likewise ask you to hand them over to the Holy See, which will study their position, in its various aspects with the local episcopate. Their survival, organization, and apostolate will be subordinated, as is normal throughout the Catholic Church, to an agreement which will have to be reached, in each case, with the local bishop—*nihil sine Episcopo*—and in a spirit which respects the Declaration mentioned above.

This constitutes a straightforward demand that the assets of the Society of St. Pius X be handed over to the Vatican—and simply for protesting against this demand the Archbishop is accused of spreading "a distorted interpretation of the Pope's intervention." The buildings belonging to the Society, and which constitute its assets, have been purchased with the contributions of tens of thousands of Catholics specifically because they wished their money to be used to preserve the traditional Church and not to finance the "Conciliar Church," the "Living Church," the "Church of today." It would be an offense against justice to put buildings purchased with these donations at the service of the "Conciliar Church."

All these points which figure in this letter, and to which We have given mature consideration, in consultation with the Heads of Departments concerned, have been adopted by Us only out of regard for the greater good of the Church. You said to Us during our conversation of 11 September: "I am ready for anything, for the good of the Church." The response now lies in your hands.

If you refused—*quod Deus avertat*—to make the Declaration which is asked of you, you would remain suspended *a divinis.* On the other hand, Our pardon and the lifting of the suspension will be assured you to the extent to which you sincerely and without ambiguity undertake to fulfil the conditions of this letter and to repair the scandal caused. The obedience and the trust of which you will give proof will also make it possible for Us to study serenely with you your personal problems.

May the Holy Spirit enlighten you and guide you towards the only solution that would enable you on the one hand to rediscover the peace of your momentarily misguided conscience but also to insure the good of souls, to contribute to the unity of the Church which the Lord has entrusted to Our charge, and to avoid the danger of a schism. In the psychological state in which you find yourself, We realize that it is difficult for you to see clearly and very hard for you humbly to change your line of conduct: is it not therefore urgent, as in all such cases, for you to arrange a time and place of recollection which will enable you to consider the matter with the necessary objectivity? Fraternally, We put you on your guard against the pressures to which you could be exposed from those who wish to keep you in an untenable position, while We Ourself, all your Brothers in the Episcopate, and the vast majority of the faithful await finally from you that ecclesial attitude which would be to your honor.

In order to root out the abuses which we all deplore and to guarantee a true spiritual renewal, as well as the courageous evangelization to which the Holy Spirit bids Us, there is needed more than ever the help and commitment of the entire ecclesial community around the Pope and the Bishops. Now the revolt of one side finally reaches and risks accentuating the insubordination of what you have called the "subversion" of the other side: while, without your own insubordination, you would have been able, Brother, as you expressed the wish in your last letter, to help Us, in fidelity and under Our authority, to work for the advancement of the Church.

Therefore, dear Brother, do not delay any longer in considering before God, with the keenest religious attention, this solemn adjuration of the humble but legitimate Successor of Peter. May you measure the gravity of the hour and take the only decision that befits a son of the Church. This is Our hope, this is Our prayer.

From the Vatican, 11 October 1976.

Paulus PP. VI.

XVI

The End of a Momentous Year

November 1976
Manifesto of the Catholic Academics

The undersigned Catholic members of university faculties wish to give public expression to their personal convictions, and to affirm the communion of thought which unites them with Mgr. Lefebvre. Like him they hold not to "one" tradition amongst others but to Catholic Tradition, to the truth of which so many martyrs have borne and are still today bearing witness. They deeply regret that many priests and most of the bishops no longer teach Christians what they must believe to be saved. They deplore the decadence of ecclesiastical studies, and the ignorance of Christian philosophy, the history of the Church, and the ways of spiritual perfection in which future priests are left. They are angered by the contempt shown by so many clerics for Greco-Latin culture; for that culture is not simply a garment:

the Church is embodied in it. They hope for a renaissance of
the Church, in which justice will be done to intelligence and
to holiness, in which the worship of the Blessed Sacrament
of the Altar will be restored, the reign of Jesus Christ over
the Nations will be proclaimed. Devoted to the unity of the
Church, strong in their faith, animated with that hope, they
salute the brave bishop who has dared to stand up, to break
the conspiracy of silence, and to appeal to the Pope for full
justice for the faithful people. *

The names of the first signatories to the appeal, thirty university teachers, were appended.

16 November 1976
Extracts from an Interview with Michael Davies

Mgr. Lefebvre granted an interview to Michael Davies at
the Great Western Hotel, Paddington, London, on 16 November 1976. This interview was published in *The Remnant*
on 17 February 1977. Before publication it was sent to the
Archbishop with a request that he should study it carefully
and confirm that it was an accurate account of what he had
said and represented his thinking on the points raised. It was
returned with a handwritten note from the Archbishop
stating: "Oui, ces réponses correspondent bien à mes pens-
ées."

Michael Davies: Monseigneur, it is alleged that the stand you
are taking is based on political rather than doctrinal considerations.
Mgr. Lefebvre: This is completely untrue.

*The text of this manifesto appeared in *Itinéraires*, No. 209, January 1977.

Michael Davies: The Catholic Information Office (of England and Wales) has initiated a publicity campaign intended to link you with *Action française.* Have you ever been associated with this movement?

Mgr. Lefebvre: Never.

Michael Davies: It is frequently alleged that you "refuse" Vatican II, that you claim any sincere Catholic must "reject" the Council. These allegations are very vague. I presume that you accept that Vatican II was an Ecumenical Council properly convoked by the reigning Pontiff according to the accepted norms.

Mgr. Lefebvre: That is correct.

Michael Davies: I presume that you accept that its official documents were voted for by a majority of the Council Fathers and validly promulgated by the reigning Pontiff.

Mgr. Lefebvre: Certainly.

Michael Davies: In a letter published in *The Times* on 18 August this year (1976) I stated that your position vis-à-vis the Council was as follows. Would you please read this passage carefully and tell me whether it does state your position accurately?

The reforms claiming to implement the Council were intended to initiate an unprecedented renewal but, since the Council, the history of the Church throughout the West has been one of stagnation and decline; the seeds of this decline can be traced back to the Council itself as those holding Neo-Modernist and Neo-Protestant views were able to influence the formation of some of the official documents by the inclusion of ambiguous terminology which has been used to justify the abuses which are now apparent to all. Thus, while accepting the Council documents as official statements of the Magisterium, we have the right and duty to treat them with prudence and to interpret them in the light of Tradition.

Mgr. Lefebvre: That is precisely my position.

Michael Davies: It is frequently alleged that you believe the

New Mass *per se* to be invalid or heretical. Is this true?

Mgr. Lefebvre: Not at all. But I believe an increasing number of celebrations of the New Mass to be invalid due to the defective intention of the celebrant.*

Michael Davies: It is alleged that you intend to consecrate one or more bishops to continue your work. Is this true?

Mgr. Lefebvre: It is totally untrue.

Michael Davies: It has been alleged both in Britain and the U.S.A. that in an interview with *Der Spiegel* you announced plans for establishing "a Church independent of Rome." Did you, in fact, make such a statement and have you any such plans?

Mgr. Lefebvre: I most certainly did not make such a statement and I most definitely do not intend to set up a Church independent of Rome.

Footnote to this Interview

As regards *Action française,* in a lengthy press conference given at Ecône on 15 September 1976, Mgr. Lefebvre stated that he had not known the late Charles Maurras (founder of the movement); he had not even read his books; he is not linked with *Action française* in any way; he does not read its journal *Aspects de la France*; he does not know those who edit it; he regretted the fact that it was being sold outside the hall in which his Mass at Lille was celebrated.

As regards the Documents of Vatican II, Mgr. Lefebvre signed fourteen of the sixteen documents and only refused to sign the ones on The Church in the Modern World and on Religious Liberty. On 18 June 1977, in an attempt to achieve a conciliation with the Vatican, a memorandum from Mgr. Lefebvre was delivered to the Secretariat of State offering, *inter alia,* to "accept all the texts of Vatican II, either in their

---

*The Archbishop confirmed that this is still his opinion in a handwritten letter to me dated 17 October 1978.

obvious meaning or in an official interpretation which insures their full concordance with the authentic tradition of the Church." The Archbishop's proposals for a reconciliation were rejected by the Pope as unacceptable. A detailed account of these proposals was printed in *The Remnant* of 31 July 1977, pp. 9-10.

As regards the validity of the New Mass, in his book, *A Bishop Speaks*, Mgr. Lefebvre writes (p. 159): "I shall never say that the new *Ordo Missae* is heretical, I shall never say that it cannot be a sacrifice. I believe that many priests—above all those priests who have known the old *Ordo*—certainly have very good intentions in saying their Mass. Far be it from me to say everything is wrong with the new *Ordo*. I do say, however, that this new *Ordo* opens the door to very many choices and divisions."

29 November 1976
Letter of Pope Paul VI to Mgr. Lefebvre

To Our brother in the episcopate Marcel Lefebvre,
formerly Archbishop-Bishop of Tulle.

Once more We address Ourselves directly to you, dear brother, after having prayed for a long time and asked Our Lord to inspire Us with words able to touch you. We do not understand your attitude. Can you have decided to attach no importance to the word of the Pope? Before rejecting the appeal of the Church, your Mother, have you at least taken time to reflect and pray?

As for Us, it seems that silence would have been becoming the day after your visit in September and after Our letter of 11 October. But We continue to hear of new initiatives which lead to a deepening of the ditch you are digging: the ordination on 31 October, your book,* your

---

*The book referred to here is entitled *I Accuse the Council*. It contains Mgr. Lefebvre's conciliar interventions and other relevant source material and is indispensable for every serious student of Vatican II and the present crisis. It is available in French only at present but an English translation will be produced in Spring 1980 by the Angelus Press.

declarations, your many journeys on which you take no account of local bishops.

This very day, therefore, We resolve, with regret, to authorize publication of Our last letter. God grant that knowledge of the exact text of that admonition may put an end to the calumnious interpretations of it that have been spread and may help the Christian people to see clearly and to strengthen its unity.

The "calumnious interpretations" refer to the claim that the Pope had required Mgr. Lefebvre to hand over to the Holy See all the assets of the Society of St. Pius X. As this is exactly what he did demand (see p. 341), interpretations which are perfectly exact cannot possibly be calumnious.

Conscious of the gravity of the moment We adjure you at the same time, with very special solemnity and insistence, to change the attitude which sets you in opposition to the Church, to return to the true Tradition and to full communion with Us.

From the Vatican, 29 November 1976.

Paulus PP. VI.

3 December 1976
Letter of Mgr. Lefebvre to Pope Paul VI

Holy Father,

His Excellency, Monseigneur the Nuncio in Berne, has just delivered to me Your Holiness's last letter. Dare I say that every one of these letters is like a sword going through me, for I am so desirous of being in full accord with and full submission to the Vicar of Christ and the Successor of Peter, as I think I have been, the whole of my life.

But that submission can be made only in the unity of the faith and in the "true Tradition," as Your Holiness says in your letter.

Tradition, being, according to the teaching of the Church, Christian doctrine defined for ever by the solemn Magisterium of the Church, it carries a character of immutability which obliges, to the assent of faith, not only the present generation but future generations as well. The sovereign pontiffs, the Councils, can make the deposit explicit, but they must transmit it faithfully and exactly, without changing it.

But how can the statements in the Declaration on Religious Liberty be reconciled with the teaching of Tradition? How can the liturgical reform be reconciled with the teaching of the Council of Trent and with Tradition? How reconcile the working out of ecumenism with the Magisterium of the Church and Canon Law concerning the relations of the Church with heretics, schismatics, atheists, unbelievers, public sinners?

The new departures of the Church in these domains imply principles contrary to the solemn and continuous teaching of the Church, contrary to that "true Tradition" to which Your Holiness alludes, Tradition which is unchangeable because defined solemnly by the authority of your predecessors and preserved intact by all the successors of Peter.

To apply the notion of life to the Magisterium, to the Church, and also to Tradition, does not allow of a minimizing of the concept of the immutability of defined faith, because faith in that case borrows its character of immutability from God Himself, *immotus in se permanens* while being the source of life, as are the Church and Tradition.

Saint Pius X in his encyclical *Pascendi Dominici Gregis* has clearly shown the danger of false interpretations of the terms "living faith," "living tradition."

It is this sad proof of the incompatibility of the principles of the new orientations with Tradition or the Magisterium that we come up against.

Could it, please, be explained to us how man can have a

natural right to error? How can there be a natural right to cause scandal? How can the Protestants who took part in the liturgical reform state that the reform allows them from now on to celebrate the Eucharist according to the new Rite? How, then, is that reform compatible with the affirmations and the canons of the Council of Trent? And, finally, what are we to think of reception of the Eucharist by persons not of our faith, the lifting of excommunication from those belonging to sects and organizations which openly profess contempt for Our Lord Jesus Christ and our holy religion, that being contrary to the truth of the Church and to all Her Tradition?

Is there, since Vatican Council II, a new conception of the Church, of Her truth, of Her Sacrifice, of Her priesthood? It is on those points that we seek enlightenment. The faithful are beginning to be disturbed and to understand that it is no longer a question of details but of what constitutes their faith and therefore of the foundations of Christian civilization.

There, in brief, is our deep concern, compared with which the whole operation of the canonical or administrative system is nothing. As it is a question of our faith, it is a question of eternal life.

That said, I accept everything that, in the Council and the reforms, is in full conformity with Tradition; and the Society I have founded is ample proof of that. Our seminary is perfectly in accordance with the wishes expressed in the Council and in the *Ratio fundamentalis* of the Sacred Congregation for Catholic Education.

Our apostolate corresponds fully with the desire for a better distribution of the clergy and with the concern expressed by the Council on the subject of the sanctification of clerics and their life in community.

The success of our seminaries with the young is clear proof that we are not incurably immobilized but are perfectly adapted to the needs of the apostolate of our times. That is why we beg Your Holiness to consider above all the great spiritual benefit that souls can draw from our priestly and missionary apostolate which, in collaboration with diocesan bishops, can bring about a true spiritual renewal.

To seek to force our Society into accepting a new orientation which is having disastrous effects on the whole Church is to compel it to disappear, like so many other seminaries.

Hoping that Your Holiness will understand, on reading these lines, that we have but one purpose, to serve Our Lord Jesus Christ, His glory and His Vicar, and to bring about the salvation of souls, we beg you to accept our respectful and filial wishes in Christ and Mary.

† Marcel Lefebvre
Former Archbishop-Bishop of Tulle
on the Feast of St. Francis Xavier
3 December 1976.

Chronological Index

1905-1968. . . . . **1-10**
        An outline of Mgr. Lefebvre's life
        up to his retirement in 1968.

7 October 1970. 12
        Opening of the Seminary at Ecône.

1 November 1970 12
        The Society of St. Pius X canonically established.

26 March 1974 35
        Meeting convened in Rome
        to discuss the Society of St. Pius X.

30 April 1974 36
        Meeting between Mgr. Mamie and Mgr. Lefebvre.

23 June 1974 37
        The Commission of Cardinals decides upon
        an Apostolic Visitation of the Seminary.

11-13 November 1974. 37
        The Apostolic Visitation takes place.

21 November 1974 . . . . **37-40**
        The "Declaration" of Mgr. Lefebvre.

21 January 1975 41
        The Commission of Cardinals meets to discuss
        the report of the Apostolic Visitors.

24 January 1975 43
        Mgr. Mamie informs the Commission of Cardinals that
        he wishes to withdraw canonical approval from
        the Society of Saint Pius X.

25 January 1975 44-45
Mgr. Lefebvre invited for a "discussion"
with the Commission of Cardinals.

13 February 1975 & 3 March 1975 45-49
Mgr. Lefebvre meets the Commission of Cardinals.
His account of the meetings.

19 March 1975 49-51
Mgr. Lefebvre writes to the Abbé de Nantes
affirming that he will never break with Rome.

25 April 1975 51
Cardinal Tabera authorizes Mgr. Mamie to withdraw
canonical approval from the Society of St. Pius X.

6 May 1975 51
Mgr. Mamie notifies Mgr. Lefebvre of this decision.

6 May 1975 57-63
The Commission of Cardinals condemns Mgr. Lefebvre.
Text of the condemnation and commentary.

8 May 1975 63-67
L'Osservatore Romano attacks Mgr. Lefebvre.

9 May 1975 67
Mgr. Mamie makes his decision public.

21 May 1975 73-74
Letter from Mgr. Lefebvre to Cardinal Staffa
appealing against the decision.

25 May 1975 75-81
Mgr. Lefebvre leads the *Credo* Holy Year
Pilgrimage to Rome.

25 May 1975 81-86
Mgr. Lefebvre's sermon, *The One True Religion,*
the complete text.

27-29 May 1975 87-101
Events at Ecône.

31 May 1975 103-104
First letter of Mgr. Lefebvre to Pope Paul VI.

2 June 1975 104
Mgr. Mamie publishes the text of the condemnation
of Mgr. Lefebvre by the Commission of Cardinals.

5 June 1975 104
Mgr. Lefebvre's lawyer lodges the Archbishop's appeal
with the Court of the Apostolic Signature in Rome.

6 June 1975 105-106
Statement of Dr. Eric de Saventhem.

10 June 1975 106
Mgr. Lefebvre's appeal is rejected.

14 June 1975 108
The Archbishop's second appeal.

15 June 1975 111
Fr. Pierre Épiney, the Parish Priest of Riddes,
dismissed for his support of the Archbishop.

29 June 1975 112-122
First letter of Pope Paul VI to Mgr. Lefebvre.
Text and commentary.

29 June 1975 129
Ordinations at Ecône.

15 July 1975 130-131
Letter from Mgr. Lefebvre to Hamish Fraser
claiming that Cardinal Villot is determined to
destroy the Society of St. Pius X.

21 July 1975 131
Cardinal Garrone urges French-speaking seminarians
to transfer to Pontifical French Seminary in Rome.

8 September 1975 134-135
Second letter of Pope Paul VI to Mgr. Lefebvre.

24 September 1975 135
Second letter of Mgr. Lefebvre to Pope Paul VI.

27 October 1975 136-142
Letter from Cardinal Villot to the Presidents of
Episcopal Conferences. Text and commentary.

12 December 1975 142-157
Mgr. Mamie publishes a commentary on Mgr. Lefebvre's
Letter to Friends and Benefactors (No. 9).
Text of this letter and Mgr. Mamie's commentary.

13 February 1976 157-163
Louis Salleron's interview with Mgr. Lefebvre published
in *La France Catholique-Ecclesia.*

21 February 1976 163-166
Letter from Pope Paul VI to Cardinal Villot
commenting on the Salleron interview.
Text and commentary.

21 April 1976 168-171
Letter from Mgr. Benelli to Mgr. Lefebvre.

24 May 1976 173-191
The Allocution of Pope Paul VI to the Consistory
of Cardinals. Text and commentary.

12 June 1976 193-196
Letter from Mgr. Benelli to the Apostolic Nuncio in
Berne instructing him to inform Mgr. Lefebvre that he
must refrain from conferring orders. Text and commentary.

22 June 1976 196-197
Third letter of Mgr. Lefebvre to Pope Paul VI.

25 June 1976 197-200
Letter from Mgr. Benelli to Mgr. Lefebvre repeating this

instruction and stating that the seminarians must submit to the "Conciliar Church." Text and commentary.

29 June 1976 201-214
The ordinations at Ecône including the complete
text of Mgr. Lefebvre's sermon.

1 July 1976. 215-216
The suspension of Mgr. Lefebvre,
declaration of the Vatican Press Bureau.

4 July 1976. 216-225
The Mass in Geneva, sermon of Mgr. Lefebvre
at the First Solemn Mass of Fr. Denis Roch.

6 July 1976. 225-226
Letter from Cardinal Baggio to Mgr. Lefebvre
explaining the terms of his suspension.

8 July 1976. 227-231
An article by Fr. Henri Bruckberger, O. P.,
condemning the hostility shown to the newly ordained
priests from Ecône by the French Hierarchy.

12 July 1976. 232-233
Mgr. Lefebvre makes public his letter to the Pope
of 22 June. Text of the explanatory note.

17 July 1976. 233-235
Fourth letter of Mgr. Lefebvre to Pope Paul VI.

22 July 1976. 235-236
Notification of the Suspension *a divinis*. Letter from the
Secretariat of the Congregation for Bishops to Mgr. Lefebvre.

3 August 1976. 236-237
Interview given to the *Nouvelliste* of Sion
by Mgr. Lefebvre.

8 August 1976. 238-241
The Petition of the Eight.

15 August 1976. 241-243
Third letter of Pope Paul VI to Mgr. Lefebvre.
Text and commentary.

27 August 1976. 244-252
An appeal by twenty-eight French priests
to Pope Paul VI.

29 August 1976. 253-271
The Mass at Lille.

11 September 1976 273
Communiqué from the Vatican Press Office concerning
the audience of Mgr. Lefebvre with Pope Paul VI.

11 September 1976 273-288
Mgr. Lefebvre's account of his audience with Pope Paul VI.

14 September 1976. 288-289
Declaration by the Director of the Vatican Press Office.

16 September 1976. 289-290
Fifth letter of Mgr. Lefebvre to Pope Paul VI.

17 September 1976. 290-294
Letter from Mgr. Lefebvre to Dr. Eric de Saventhem.

17 September 1976. 294-296
Statement by the Vatican Press Office accusing Mgr.
Lefebvre of lying about his interview with the Holy Father.

18 September 1976. 296-297
Communiqué from Mgr. Lefebvre refuting this allegation.

7 October 1976 297-300
Letter to Friends & Benefactors (No. 11).

11 October 1976. 301-343
Fourth letter of Pope Paul VI to Mgr. Lefebvre.
Text and commentary.

November 1976. 345-346
            Manifesto of the Catholic Academics.

16 November 1976 346-349
            Interview with Michael Davies.

29 November 1976 349-350
            Fifth letter of Pope Paul VI to Mgr. Lefebvre.

3 December 1976 350-353
            Sixth letter of Mgr. Lefebvre to Pope Paul VI.

APPENDIX I

SAINT ATHANASIUS
THE TRUE UPHOLDER OF TRADITION

What happened over 1600 years ago is repeating itself today, but
with two or three differences: Alexandria is today the whole Universal
Church, the stability of which is being shaken, and what was undertaken at that time by means of physical force and cruelty is now being
transferred to a different level. Exile is replaced by banishment into the
silence of being ignored; killing, by assassination of character.

> Mgr. Rudolf Graber, Bishop of Regensburg,
> *Athanasius and the Church of Our Time*, p. 23.

The object of this appendix is not to explain the nature
of the Arian heresy but to prove that a bishop who is faithful
to tradition could be repudiated, calumniated, persecuted,
and even excommunicated by almost the entire episcopate,
the Pope included. Obviously, this would be an abnormal
situation. A Catholic can normally presume that the majority
of bishops in union with the Pope will teach sound doctrine;
he would be imprudent not to conform his belief and behavior to their teaching. But this is not always the case as
the present situation of the Church demonstrates. There is
hardly a diocese in the English-speaking world where the
bishop insures that Catholic children are taught sound doctrine, where Catholic moral and doctrinal teaching are not
contradicted with impunity from the pulpit, where liturgical abuses which sometimes amount to sacrilege remain
unrebuked. Writing of the time of St. Athanasius, St. Jerome
made his celebrated remark:*"Ingemuit totus orbis et arianum
se esse miratus est"*—"The whole world groaned and was
amazed to find itself Arian." The Catholic world in the West
today finds itself in a state of accelerating disintegration but
for the most part does not groan and certainly does not seem
amazed. Indeed, most of the bishops repeat *ad nauseam* that
things have never been better, that we are living in the most

APOLOGIA PRO MARCEL LEFEBVRE

flourishing period of the Church's history. A bishop like the late Mgr. R. J. Dwyer, of Portland, Oregon, who had the courage to speak out and describe the situation in the Church as it really is was looked upon as an eccentric, as a crank, as a trouble-maker. The International Commission for English in the Liturgy (ICEL) received fulsome praise from the bishops of the U.S.A. for the liturgical translations now inflicted upon English-speaking Catholics. Archbishop Dwyer spoke of:

> . . . the inept, puerile, semi-literate English translation which has been foisted upon us by the ICEL—the International Commission for English in the Liturgy—a body of men possessed of all the worst characteristics of a self-perpetuating bureaucracy, which has done an immeasurable disservice to the entire English-speaking world. The work has been marked by an almost complete lack of literary sense, a crass insensitivity to the poetry of language, and even worse by *a most unscholarly freedom in the rendering of the texts, amounting at times, to actual misrepresentation.*[1] (My emphasis.)

These are strong words. Archbishop Dwyer stood almost alone in denouncing ICEL — but did this make him wrong? It is the truth that matters. Are his criticisms correct or not? If they are then it would not have mattered if every other English-speaking bishop had denounced him. As Appendix II will show, Robert Grosseteste, a thirteenth-century Bishop of Lincoln, was as solitary as Archbishop Dwyer when he made his protest at the iniquitous practice of Pope Innocent IV appointing relations to benefices which they would not so much as visit, simply to provide them with a source of income. The other bishops tolerated the practice, just as most bishops today tolerate unorthodox catechetics and ICEL—but this did not make Bishop Grosseteste wrong.

The Arian Heresy

In his celebrated *Essay on the Development of Christian Doctrine,* Cardinal Newman wrote:

Arianism had admitted that Our Lord was both the God of the Evangelical Covenant, and the actual Creator of the Universe; but even this was not enough, because it did not confess Him to be the One, Everlasting, Infinite, Supreme Being, but as one who was made by the Supreme. It was not enough in accordance with that heresy to proclaim Him as having an ineffable origin before all worlds; not enough to place Him high above all creatures as the type of all the works of God's Hands; not enough to make Him the King of all Saints, the Intercessor for man with God, the Object of worship, the Image of the Father; not enough because it was not all, and between all and anything short of all, there was an infinite interval. The highest of creatures is levelled with the lowest in comparison to the One Creator Himself.[1]

The Council of Nicea (325) defined that the Son is consubstantial (*homoousion*) with the Father. This meant that, while distinct as a person, the Son shared the same divine and eternal nature with the Father. If the Father was eternal by nature, then the Son must also be eternal. If the Father was eternal and the Son was not then clearly the Son was not equal with the Father. The term *homoousion* thus became the touchstone of orthodoxy. In her standard history of heresies, M. L. Cozens writes:

No other word could be found to express the essential union between the Father and the Son, for every other word the Arians accepted, but in an equivocal sense. They would deny that the Son was a creature as other creatures—or in the number of creatures—or made in time, for they considered him a special creation made before time. They would call Him "Only-begotten," meaning "Only directly created" Son of God.* They would call Him "Lord Creator," "First-born of all creation"; they even accepted "God of God" meaning thereby "made God by God." This word (*homoousion*) alone they could not say without renouncing their heresy.[3]

The Council of Nicea had been convoked by the Emperor Constantine, who insisted upon acceptance of its definitions. Arius was excommunicated. But a good number of bishops signed the Creed only as an act of submission to the Emperor, including Eusebius of Caesarea, and Eusebius of Nicomedia. They were, according to Cozens:

> Men of worldly character, they disliked dogmatic precision and wished for some comprehensive formula which men of all opinions could sign while understanding it in widely diverging senses. To these men the precise and exact faith of an Athanasius and the obstinate heresy of Arius and his plain-spoken followers were equally distasteful.
>
> "Respectable, tolerant, broadminded" would be their ideal of religion. They therefore brought forward, instead of the too definite, ineradicable *homoousion*—of *one* substance—the vaguer term *homoiousion*, i. e., of *like* substance. They sent letters far and wide couched in seemingly orthodox and fervent language, proclaiming their belief in Our Lord's divinity, ascribing to Him every divine prerogative, anathematizing all who said He was created in time:** in short, saying all the most orthodox could ask, *except* that they substituted their own *homoiousion* for the *homoousion* of Nicea.[4]

It is possible to interpret the term "of like substance" in an orthodox sense, i. e. exactly like, identical. But it can also be interpreted as meaning *like in some respects but not in others,* i. e., as *not* identical. A candle is like a star in that it generates heat and light, but it most certainly is not a star.

---

*Arius taught that Christ was the only being *directly* created by God and that having been created, He then created the rest of the universe on behalf of the Father. The rest of creation is, therefore, created directly by the Son and only indirectly by the Father.

**Arius taught that Christ was created before time began.

But a comparison between a candle and a star could be taken as an example of almost perfect precision of language when set beside a comparison between a being that is created (even before time began) and a being that is uncreated. A mood soon grew up among many of the bishops and the faithful that too much fuss was being made about the distinction between *homoousion* and *homoiousion.* They considered that more harm than good was done by tearing apart the unity of the Church over a single letter, over an *iota* (the Greek letter "i"). They condemned those who did this, to quote Cozens again, as:

. . . over-rigid precisians, more anxious about terminology than about fraternal charity.

Meanwhile these latter, foremost among them Athanasius, at first deacon and disciple of Alexander, Bishop of Alexandria, and afterwards his successor, refused to modify in any way their attitude. Steadfastly they refused to accept any statement not containing the *homoousion* or to communicate with those who rejected it.[5]

Athanasius and his supporters were right. That one letter, that *iota,* spelled the difference between Christianity as *the* faith founded and guided by God incarnate, and *a* faith founded by just another creature. Indeed, if Christ is not God, it would be blasphemous to call ourselves Christians.

St. Athanasius: Defender of the Nicene Faith

The Catholic Encyclopedia is far from exaggerating when it describes the life of St. Athanasius as a "bewildering maze of events." It would not be practical here to outline even the principal incidents of his truly amazing career, the various councils which declared for and against him, his excommunications, his expulsions from and restorations to his see, his relations with a formidable list of emperors, with his brother-bishops, with the Roman Pontiffs. It can also be added that in some cases the dates affixed to events in his life are only approximate. Those given here may not correspond with those found in other studies.

Athanasius was born around the year 296 and died in 373. He became Bishop of Alexandria within five months of the Council of Nicea, at the age of about thirty. Hardly had the Council Fathers dispersed when intrigues to restore the fortunes of Arius began. Eusebius, Bishop of Nicomedia, was able to gain favor with the Emperor chiefly through the influence which he exerted upon Constantia, sister of Constantine. He eventually prevailed upon the Emperor to recall Arius from exile. Constantine was induced to write to Athanasius ordering him to admit Arius to communion in his own see of Alexandria. He wrote:

> On being informed of my pleasure, give free admission to all who are desirous of entering into communion with the Church. For if I learn of your standing in the way of any who were seeking it, or interdicting them, I will send at once those who shall depose you instead, by my authority, and banish you from your see.[6]

After various intrigues, Athanasius was eventually banished to Gaul, and Arius returned to Alexandria but fled in the face of the wrath of the populace. He eventually arrived in Constantinople where he was struck dead in so dramatic a manner that no one doubted that, as Athanasius remarked, "there was displayed somewhat more than human judgment."[7]

The Emperor Constantine died in 337 and the Empire was shared among his three sons. The fortunes of Athanasius are more bewildering than ever during this period. The See of Peter was occupied by Pope St. Julius I from 337 to 352. Pope Julius consistently and courageously upheld the cause of Athanasius and the faith of Nicea. In 350 the entire Empire was united under Constantius following the murder of his brother Constans (another brother having vanished from the scene soon after the death of Constantine). Constantius was an Arian.

The Fall of Pope Liberius

On 17 May 352, Liberius was consecrated as Pope. He immediately found himself involved in the Arian dispute.

He appealed to Constantius to do justice to Athanasius. The imperial reply was to summon the bishops of Gaul to a council at Arles in 353-354, where, under threat of exile, they agreed to a condemnation of Athanasius. Even Liberius' legate yielded. When the Pope continued to press for a council more widely representative, it was assembled by Constantius at Milan in 355. It was threatened by a violent mob and the Emperor's personal intimidation: "My will," he exclaimed, "is canon law." He prevailed with all save three of the bishops. Athanasius was once more condemned and Arians admitted to communion. Once more papal legates surrendered and Liberius himself was ordered to sign. When he refused to do so, or even to accept the Emperor's offerings, he was seized and carried off to the imperial presence; when he stood firm for Athanasius' rehabilitation, he was exiled to Thrace (355) where he remained for two years. Meanwhile, a Roman deacon, Felix, was intruded into his see. The people refused to recognize the imperial anti-pope. Athanasius himself was driven into hiding and his flock abandoned to the persecution of an Arianizing intruder. When he visited Rome in 357, Constantius was besieged by clamorous demands for Liberius' restoration. Subservient bishops around the court at Sirmium subscribed in turn to doctrinal formulas more or less ambiguous or unorthodox. In 358, a formula drawn up by Basil of Ancyra, declaring that the Son was of *like* substance with the Father, *homoiousion*, was officially imposed.[8]

The opposition to the anti-pope Felix made it imperative for Constantius to restore Liberius to his see. But it was equally imperative that the Pope should condemn Athanasius. The Emperor used a combination of threats and flattery to attain his objective. Then followed the tragic fall of Liberius. It is described in the sternest of terms in Butler's *Lives of the Saints:*

About this time Liberius began to sink under the hardships of his exile, and his resolution was shaken by the continual solicitations of Demophilus, the Arian Bishop of Beroea, and of Fortunatian, the temporizing Bishop of Aquileia. He was so far softened, by listening to flatteries and suggestions to which he ought to have stopped his ears with horror, that he yielded to the snare laid for him, to the great scandal of the Church. He subscribed to the condemnation of St. Athanasius and a confession or creed which had been framed by the Arians at Sirmium, though their heresy was not expressed in it; and he wrote to the Arian bishops of the East that he had received the true Catholic faith which many bishops had approved at Sirmium. The fall of so great a prelate and so illustrious a confessor is a terrifying example of human weakness, which no one can call to mind without trembling for himself. St. Peter fell by a presumptuous confidence in his own strength and resolution, that we may learn that everyone stands only by humility.[9]

According to *A Catholic Dictionary of Theology* (1971), "This unjust excommunicaton [of St. Athanasius]   was a moral and not a doctrinal fault."[10]   Signing one of the "creeds" of Sirmium was far more serious (there is some dispute as to which one Liberius signed, probably the first). The *New Catholic Encyclopedia* (1967), describes it as "a document reprehensible from the point of view of the faith."[11] Some Catholic apologists have attempted to prove that Liberius neither confirmed the excommunication of Athanasius nor subscribed to one of the formulae of Sirmium. But Cardinal Newman has no doubt that the fall of Liberius is an historical fact. [12]   This is also the case with the two modern works of reference just cited and the celebrated *Catholic Dictionary*, edited by Addis and Arnold. The last named points out that there is "a fourfold cord of evidence not easily broken," i. e., the testimonies of St. Athanasius, St. Hilary, Sozomen, and St. Jerome. It also notes that "all the accounts are at once independent of and consistent with each other."[13]

The New Catholic Encyclopedia concludes that:

Everything points to the fact that he [Liberius] accepted the first formula of Sirmium of 351 . . . it failed gravely in deliberately avoiding the use of the most characteristic expression of the Nicene faith and in particular the *homoousion.* Thus while it cannot be said that Liberius taught false doctrine, it seems necessary to admit that, through weakness and fear, he did not do justice to the full truth. [14]

It is quite nonsensical for Protestant polemicists to cite the case of Liberius as an argument against papal infallibility. The excommunication of Athanasius (or of anyone else) is not an act involving infallibility, and the formula he signed contained nothing directly heretical. Nor was it an *ex cathedra* pronouncement intended to bind the whole Church, and, if it had been, the fact that Liberius acted under duress would have rendered it null and void.

However, despite the pressure to which he was submitted, Liberius' fall reveals a weakness of character when compared with those such as Athanasius, who did remain firm. Cardinal Newman comments:

His fall, which followed, scandalous as it is in itself, may yet be taken to illustrate the silent firmness of those others of his fellow-sufferers, of whom we hear less, because they bore themselves more consistently. [15]

This is a judgment with which the *New Catholic Encyclopedia* concurs:

Liberius did not have the strength of character of his predecessor Julius I, or of his successor Damasus I. The troubles that erupted upon the latter's election indicate that the Roman Church had been weakened from within as well as from without during the pontificate of Liberius. His name was not inscribed in the Roman Martyrology.[16]

Tradition Upheld by the Laity

The fall of Pope Liberius needs to be considered within the context of a failure by the vast majority of the episcopate to be faithful to its commission; only then can the full extent of the heroism of St. Athanasius be appreciated (together with a few other heroic bishops such as St. Hilary, who supported him faithfully). Cardinal Newman cites numerous Patristic testimonies to the abysmal state of the Church at that time. In Appendix V to the third edition of his *Arians of the Fourth Century*, we read:

A. D. 360. St. Gregory Nazianzen says, about this date: "Surely the pastors have done foolishly; for, excepting a very few, who either on account of their insignificance were passed over, or who by reason of their virtue resisted, and who were to be left as a seed and root for the springing up again and revival of Israel by the influence of the Spirit, all temporized, only differing from each other in this, that some succumbed earlier, and others later; some were foremost champions and leaders in the impiety, and others joined the second rank of the battle, being overcome by fear, or by interest, or by flattery, or, what was the most excusable, by their own ignorance." (*Orat.* xxi. 24).

Cappadocia. St. Basil says, about the year 372: "Religious people keep silence, but every blaspheming tongue is let loose. Sacred things are profaned; those of the laity who are sound in faith avoid the places of worship as schools of impiety, and raise their hands in solitude, with groans and tears to the Lord in heaven." *Ep.* 92. Four years after he writes: "Matters have come to this pass: the people have left their houses of prayer, and assemble in deserts,—a pitiable sight; women and children, old men, and men otherwise infirm, wretchedly faring in the open air, amid most profuse rains and snow-storms and winds and frosts of winter; and again in summer under a scorching sun. To this they submit, because they will have no part in the wicked Arian leaven." *Ep.* 242. Again: "Only one offense is now vigorously punished,—an accurate observance of our fathers' traditions. For this cause the pious are driven from their countries, and transported into deserts." *Ep.* 243.

In this same appendix, the Cardinal also included an extract from an article he had written for the *Rambler* magazine in July 1859.[17] The article dealt with the manner in which, during the Arian crisis, divine tradition had been upheld by the faithful more than by the episcopate. Three phrases in this article had been misinterpreted when first published, and Newman now took the opportunity of clarifying them in the appendix. The gist of these clarifications will be provided in footnotes. Here is Newman's assessment of the manner in which the laity, the Taught Church (*Ecclesia docta*), upheld the traditional faith rather than what is known today as the Magisterium or the Teaching Church (*Ecclesia docens*)—that is, the bishops united to the Roman Pontiff:

It is not a little remarkable, that, though historically speaking, the fourth century is the age of doctors, illustrated, as it is, by the Saints Athanasius, Hilary, the two Gregories, Basil, Chrysostom, Ambrose, Jerome, and Augustine (and all those saints [were] bishops also, except one), nevertheless in that very day the Divine tradition committed to the infallible Church was proclaimed and maintained far more by the faithful than by the episcopate.

Here, of course, I must explain:—in saying this then, undoubtedly I am not denying that the great body of the Bishops were in their internal belief orthodox; nor that there were numbers of clergy who stood by the laity and acted as their centres and guides; nor that the laity actually received the faith in the first instance from the Bishops and clergy; nor that some portions of the laity were ignorant and other portions were at length corrupted by the Arian teachers, who got possession of the sees, and ordained an heretical clergy:—but I mean still, that in that time of immense confusion the divine dogma of Our Lord's divinity was proclaimed, enforced, maintained, and (humanly speaking) preserved, far more by the *Ecclesia docta* than by the *Ecclesia docens*; that the body of the Episcopate [*] was unfaithful to its commission, while the body of the laity was faithful to its baptism; that at one time the Pope, at other times a patriarchal, metropolitan, or

*Where Newman uses the term "body" he means "the great preponderance," the majority.

374 APOLOGIA PRO MARCEL LEFEBVRE

other great sees, at other times general councils [*] said what they should not have said, or did what obscured and compromised revealed truth; while, on the other hand, it was the Christian people, who, under Providence, were the ecclesiastical strength of Athanasius, Eusebius of Vercellae, and other great solitary confessors, who would have failed without them . . . .

On the one hand, then, I say, that there was a temporary suspense of the functions of the *Ecclesia docens*. [**] The body of bishops failed in their confession of the faith.

The True Voice of Tradition

What, then, are the lessons we can learn from the fall of Liberius, the triumph of Arianism, the witness of Athanasius, and the fortitude of the body of the faithful? Newman provides us with the answers, recognizing that what has happened once can happen again. In his July 1859 *Rambler* article, he wrote:

I see, then, in the Arian history, a palmary example of a state of the Church, during which, in order to know the tradition of the Apostles, we must have recourse to the faithful; for I fairly own, that if I go to writers, since I must adjust the letter of Justin, Clement, and Hippolytus with the Nicene Doctors, I get confused: and what revives me and reinstates me, as far as history goes, is the faith of the people. For I argue that, unless they had been catechized, as St. Hilary says, in the orthodox faith from the time of their baptism, they never could have had that horror, which they show, of the heterodox Arian doctrine. Their voice, then, is the voice of tradition . . . .

*Newman is not referring to any of the recognized Ecumenical ("from the whole world") Councils of the Church, of which there were none in the period he is describing. He is referring to gatherings of bishops large enough to come under the classification of the Latin word *generalia*.

**Newman explains that by "a temporary suspense of the functions of the *Ecclesia docens*" he means "that there was no authoritative utterance of the Church's infallible voice in matters of fact between the Nicene Council, A. D. 325, and the Council of Constantinople, A. D. 381."

It is also historically and doctrinally true, as Newman stressed in Appendix V to *The Arians of the Fourth Century*, "that a Pope, as a private doctor, and much more Bishops, when not teaching formally, may err, as we find they did err in the fourth century. Pope Liberius might sign a Eusebian formula at Sirmium, and the mass of Bishops at Ariminum or elsewhere, and yet they might in spite of this error, be infallible in their *ex cathedra* decisions."

Finally, what the history of this period proves is that, during a time of general apostasy, Christians who remain faithful to their traditional faith may have to worship outside the official churches, the churches of priests in communion with their lawfully appointed diocesan bishop, in order not to compromise that traditional faith; and that such Christians may have to look for truly Catholic teaching, leadership, and inspiration not to the bishops of their country as a body, not to the bishops of the world, not even to the Roman Pontiff, but to one heroic confessor whom the other bishops and the Roman Pontiff might have repudiated or even excommunicated. And how would they recognize that this solitary confessor was right and the Roman Pontiff and the body of the episcopate (not teaching infallibly) were wrong? The answer is that they would recognize in the teaching of this confessor what the faithful of the fourth century recognized in the teaching of Athanasius: the one true faith into which they had been baptized, in which they had been catechized, and which their confirmation gave them the obligation of upholding. In no sense whatsoever can such fidelity to tradition be compared with the Protestant practice of private judgment. The fourth-century Catholic traditionalists upheld Athanasius in his defense of the faith that had been handed down; the Protestant uses his private judgment to justify a breach with the traditional faith.

The truth of doctrinal teaching must be judged by its conformity to Tradition and not by the number or authority of those propagating it. Falsehood cannot become truth, no matter how many accept it. Writing in 371, St. Basil lamented the fact that:

The heresy long ago disseminated by that enemy of truth, Arius, grew to a shameless height and like a bitter root it is bearing its pernicious fruit and already gaining the upper hand since the standard-bearers of the true doctrine have been driven from the churches by defamation and insult and the authority they were vested with has been handed over to such as captivate the hearts of the simple in mind. [21]

But there will never be a time when the faithful who wholeheartedly wish to remain true to the Faith of their Fathers need have any doubt as to what that faith is. In the year 340 St. Athanasius wrote a letter to his brother bishops throughout the world, exhorting them to rise up and defend the faith against those he did not hesitate to stigmatize as "the evil-doers." What he wrote to them will apply until the end of time when God the Son comes again in glory to judge the living and the dead:

The Church has not just recently been given order and statutes. They were faithfully and soundly bestowed on it by the Fathers. Nor has the faith only just been established, but it has come to us from the Lord through His disciples. May what has been preserved in the Churches from the beginning to the present day not be abandoned in our time; may what has been entrusted into our keeping not be embezzled by us. Brethren, as custodians of God's mysteries, let yourselves be roused into action on seeing all this despoiled by others. [22]

NOTES

This appendix is available in an expanded version as a separate pamphlet published by *The Remnant*. It is available from The Angelus Press. Some of the works referred to in the notes have been abbreviated as follows:

AFC J. H. Newman, *Arians of the Fourth Century* (London, 1876).
CD   W. Addis and T. Arnold, *A Catholic Dictionary* (London, 1925).
CDT J. H. Crehan, ed., *A Catholic Dictionary of Theology* (London, 1971).
CE   *The Catholic Encyclopedia* (New York, 1913).
HH   M. L. Cozens, *A Handbook of Heresies* (London, 1960), available from The Angelus Press.
NCE *New Catholic Encyclopedia* (New York, 1967).
PG   Migne, *Patrologia Graeca.*

1. *National Catholic Register,* 2 March 1975.
2. *The Development of Christian Doctrine* (London, 1878), p. 143.
3. HH, p. 34.
4. HH, pp. 35-36.
5. HH, p. 36.
6. AFC, p. 267.
7. AFC, p. 270.
8. E. John, ed., *The Popes* (London, 1964), p. 70.
9. A. Butler, *The Lives of the Saints* (London, 1934), II, p. 10.
10. CDT, III, 110, col. 2.
11. NCE, VIII, 715, col. 1.
12. AFC, p. 464.
13. CD, p. 522, col. 2.
14. NCE, VIII, 715, col. 2.
15. AFC, pp. 319-320.
16. NCE, VIII, 716, col. 2.
17. *The Rambler,* Vol. I, new series, Part II, July 1859, pp. 198-230. This article had been written to refute criticisms of an unsigned article he had contributed to the May 1859 issue of *The Rambler,* of which he was editor.
18. "Des heiligen Kirchenlehrers Basilius des Grossen ausgewählte Schriften," in *Bibliothek der Kirchenväter* (Kösel-Pustet, Munich, 1924), I, 121.
19. PG XXVII, col. 219.

THE RIGHT TO RESIST AN ABUSE OF POWER

Part One
Robert Grosseteste : Pillar of the Papacy

The Redemptorist *Christian Encounter* is one of the most widely read Sunday bulletins circulating in Britain. Its issue of 11 May 1975 contained a short account of the life of Robert Grosseteste, Bishop of Lincoln, who was born in 1175, or thereabouts, and died in 1253. The fact that 1975 may mark the eighth centenary of his birth could account for the article.

It is a matter for regret that the few brief details given in the bulletin will be all that most of its readers will ever learn of Bishop Grosseteste; most Catholics will not know this much and the majority would not even recognize his name. This is a pity as Robert Grosseteste is quite possibly the greatest Catholic the English Church has yet produced, not excluding St. John Fisher, St. Thomas More, or Cardinal Newman. He is also one of England's truly outstanding scholars, famous throughout the world for his learning and intellect.

Among the details given in *Christian Encounter* is the fact that as well as being a great scholar and a great reformer, Robert Grosseteste "might have been canonized if he hadn't opposed the papacy in matter of Church practice." This, then, is the explanation of his neglect among English Catholics—he did not simply oppose the Pope but refused to obey a papal command. "I disobey, I contradict, I rebel," was his answer to an order from the Pope which had been phrased carefully to exclude any legal loophole which might provide an excuse not to comply. As every theologian is aware, it is possible for a pope to fall into error and it is a matter of free debate among theologians as to what, if any, action could be taken in such a case. What is interesting in the case of Robert Grosseteste is that heresy was not involved. He was not claiming to defend Catholic doctrine, but refusing to implement a practical directive from the Pope which he considered harmful to the Church. The first and natural reaction of the Catholic reader will be to say: "Then he must have been wrong." When the facts have been presented it would be surprising to find even one who would not say without any hesitation: "He was certainly right."

Robert Grosseteste was born in very humble circumstances in the village of Stow in Suffolk. He has been described as "a man of universal genius" by one of England's outstanding modern historians, Sir Maurice Powicke, formerly Regius Professor of Modern History in the University of Oxford.[1] As a student he was considered a prodigy of remarkable efficiency in the liberal arts and of wide learning and dexterity in legal and medical matters. He was one of the first chancellors of Oxford University and, according to Professor Powicke, perhaps "the greatest of her sons"—a truly staggering tribute when the list of those sons is considered. Had he not been a churchman he would still have a world reputation as a natural scientist, a man with a truly scientific mind at whose clear-headedness and insight contemporary historians of science are bound to marvel. He knew Greek and Hebrew, was an outstanding student of the Greek Fathers, and was responsible for many translations and commentaries including the first complete Latin version of Aristotle's *Ethics.* Notes in his handwriting demonstrate his familiarity with such authors as Boethius, Cicero, Horace, Seneca, Ptolemy, and the Christian poets.[2]

Bishop Grosseteste was also a great biblical scholar, "an unwearied student of the Scriptures," in the words of a contemporary who disagreed with him profoundly on some issues.[3] He had a most exalted view of the Bible and considered it to be the basis, the primary source for the spiritual formation of the clergy and their preaching and teaching. "All pastors after reciting the offices in Church," he ordered, "are to give themselves diligently to prayer and reading of Holy Scripture, that by understanding of the Scriptures they may give satisfaction to any who demand a reason concerning hope and faith. They should be so versed in the

teaching of Scripture that by reading of it their prayer may
be nourished, as it were, by daily food."[4]

He became Bishop of Lincoln in 1235 at the age of six-
ty. As bishop he was distinguished by the "conviction that
the cure of souls directed by a responsible and singleminded
episcopate must be the aim of ecclesiastical policy . . . . "[5]
This has always been the aim of the great Catholic reformers
such as Pope Gregory the Great, but even this saint could not
have been more determined or more consistent than Robert
Grosseteste in making the salvation of souls the guiding principle of all his policies and actions. He regarded this duty as a
truly fearful responsilibity which he hardly dared accept: "I,
as soon as I became bishop, considered myself to be the over-
seer and pastor of souls, and lest the blood of the sheep be
required at my hand at the strict Judgement, to visit the
sheep committed to my charge."[6] He not only set himself
the highest possible standards of pastoral solicitude but demanded the same high standards from all those subordinate to him and from his superiors in the Church, including
the Pope himself. Needless to say, such an attitude was not
calculated to win popularity. His principal aim was to achieve
"the reformation of society by a reformed clergy."[7] He
was famous throughout England for the severity of his visi-
tations. Strict continency was required from the clergy; they
must reside in their benefices; they must reach a required
standard in learning; they must not take fees for enjoining
penances or any other sacred ministration; directions are giv-
en regarding reverence in celebrating Mass and carrying the
Blessed Sacrament to the sick; care must be taken that the
Canon of the Mass is correctly transcribed; since the observance of the ten commandments is vital to the salvation of
souls, they must be expounded to the people frequently;
the divine office is to be recited in its entirety with devout
attention to the meaning of the words so that there is a living
offering and not a dead one; parish priests must be ready to
visit the sick day or night lest anyone should die without the
Sacraments; special attention must be given to the religious
education of children; and, as was mentioned above, great

stress was laid upon the importance of Holy Scripture. His objective was to "raise the standard of the clergy alike in their preaching and teaching as well as in their moral conduct."[8]   Bishop Grosseteste's concept of the pastoral ideal was set out in his famous "sermon" which he delivered in person at the Council of Lyons in 1250 at the age of seventy-five:

> The pastoral charge does not consist merely in administering the sacraments, saying the canonical hours, celebrating Masses, but in the truthful teaching of the living truth, in the awe-inspiring condemnation of vice and severe punishment of it when necessary. It consists also in feeding the hungry, giving drink to the thirsty, covering the naked, receiving guests, visiting the sick and those in prison, especially those who belong to the parish, who have a claim upon the endowments of their church. By the doing of these things is the people to be taught the holy duties of the active life.[9]

Another notable characteristic of Bishop Grosseteste was "his mystical veneration for the plenitude of papal power."[10] This veneration for the pope's plenitude of power, *plenitudo potestatis,* is of paramount importance in considering his subsequent refusal to obey Pope Innocent IV. Attempts have been made to portray him as some sort of proto-Anglican, which may account for the fact that he is held in greater esteem in the Church of England than among English Catholics. The truth is that: "The most striking feature about Grosseteste's theory of the constitution and function of the ecclesiastical hierarchy is his exaltation of the papacy. He was probably the most fervent and thoroughgoing papalist among medieval English writers."[11]   In 1239, in a discourse on the ecclesiastical hierarchy addressed to the Dean and Chapter of Lincoln, he wrote:

> For this reason after the pattern of the ordinance made in the Old Testament, the lord Pope has the fullness of power over the nations and over kingdoms, to root up and to pull down, and to waste and destroy, and to build and to plant . . . . Samuel was like the sun of the people,

among the people of Israel, just as the lord Pope is in the universal Church and every bishop in his diocese.[12]

For Robert Grosseteste:

The Vicar of Christ was the lynch pin upon which the whole fabric of the Church depended; but he was the Vicar of Christ and woe betide if he fell short of his awful responsibilities. Orthodox minds were more outspoken than they were in post-Tridentine days in their criticism of papal behavior.[13]

In a letter to a papal legate written in about 1237 he warns:

But God forbid, God forbid that this most Holy See and those who preside in it, who are commonly to be obeyed in all their commands, by commanding anything contrary to Christ's precepts and will, should be the cause of a falling away. God forbid that to any who are truly united to Christ, not willing to go in any way against His will, this See and those who preside in it should be a cause of falling away or apparent schism, by commanding such men to do what is opposed to Christ's will. [14]

Bishop Grosseteste regarded with horror even the idea of disobeying the legitimate use of any lawful authority in the Church or State. He considered us bound by God's Commandments to honor and obey our spiritual parents even more than our earthly parents. He was fond of quoting the text that the sin of disobedience is the sin of witchcraft (1 Samuel 15:23).[15] Obedience is the *only* response to legitimate authority exercising itself within its competence. But authority only exists within its limits, set by commission or delegation, and always by the law of God. There is no authority outside those limits—*ultra vires*—and the answer to an invocation of authority beyond them can be a refusal which is not disobedience but an affirmation that the person giving the command is abusing his power. To give an obvious example, Catholics are bound to obey the civil authority but

when, under Elizabeth I, the government made assisting at
Mass illegal, those Catholics who continued doing so were not
disobedient. The government had exceeded its authority and
was guilty of an abuse of power; a refusal to submit to an
abuse of power is *not* disobedience. Medieval political theory
included the right of resistance to tyranny which was "im-
ported into the domain of ecclesiastical polity."[16]   It is the
common teaching of some of the greatest Catholic theologians that, in the words of Suarez, it is licit to resist the Pope
"if he tried to do something manifestly opposed to justice
and the common good."

Robert Grosseteste certainly believed that the Pope possessed the plenitude of power which he had the right to exercise freely; but he accepted the medieval view that this was
not arbitrary power given to the Pope to use as *he* liked, but
was an office entrusted to him and "instituted for the service
of the whole Body."[17] The Pope's power had been given
to him for the cure of souls, to build up the Body of Christ
and not to destroy it. He was the Vicar of Christ, *not* Christ
Himself, and must exercise his power in accordance with the
will of Christ and never in manifest opposition to it. God
forbid, as he had said, that the Holy See should be the
cause of an apparent schism by commanding faithful Catholics to do what was contrary to Christ's will.

The issue which provoked Bishop Grosseteste's refusal to
comply with what he considered to be an abuse of papal
power was that of the papal provision of benefices. He was a
man who would allow no compromise on a matter of principle and this was a question which could not have been more
directly concerned with the cure of souls. Where he was concerned, there were two considerations which must come before all else when appointing a priest who was to be a true
pastor of his people—the pastor must be spiritually worthy
of his awe-inspiring office and must live among his flock. This
will seem so obvious to a contemporary Catholic that it hardly needs stating, but at that time there were many who did
not consider that the cure of souls was the only or even the
prime function of a benefice. A system existed in which cer-

tain benefices came under the "patronage" of important figures in Church and State who were entitled to appoint their nominees when a vacancy occurred, subject to certain conditions. These patrons often used the livings they controlled to provide a source of income for men who would never even visit their flocks, let alone offer them any form of pastoral care. "It would be wrong to regard this system simply as an abuse; it must have seemed to contemporaries the only way of supporting the necessary bureaucracy in Church and State." [18]   It must be remembered that almost all the offices in what would now be considered as the state bureaucracy (a term which is not intended to be pejorative) were filled by clerics who had to get an income from somewhere. It is obvious that in both Church and State the Pope and King alike would find it more convenient if the incomes of these bureaucrats could be paid from a source other than their own pockets. But to Robert Grosseteste this was a perversion in the precise meaning of the term, "it reduced the pastoral care to a thing of secondary importance, whereas in his view only the best brains and energy available were good enough for the work of saving souls."[19]

The Bishop had:

. . . .no hesitation in rejecting presentations to benefices, if those who were presented lacked the qualifications which he considered necessary for the cure of souls, whoever were the patrons, whether laymen, friends of his own, monastic bodies, or even in the last resort, as time went on, the Pope himself. [20]

A papal provision took the form of a request from the Pope to an ecclesiastic to appoint a papal nominee to a canonry, a prebend, or a benefice. The process began as a trickle, became a stream, and the stream a flood. Executors were appointed to insure that papal mandates were obeyed and this led to a great deal of subsidiary corruption; for example, they would use their authority to obtain benefices for their own friends or in return for a bribe. The papal nominees rarely resided in their benefices, could not speak the language

of the country if they did, and spent most of their revenues
in Italy. It was Robert Grosseteste's elevated concept of both
the pastoral and papal office which led him to oppose such
practices. He accepted that, in virtue of his plenitude of power, the Pope had the right to make nominations to benefices
and where this right was properly exercised he was prepared
to accept it.[21] But both papal power and the provision to
a benefice had one end—*the salvation of souls.* The Pope had
been given the power to nominate men to pastoral offices
only to build up the Body of Christ through the effective
cure of souls; and how could the cure of souls be advanced
by alien pastors, who never even saw their flocks and were
interested only in the gold they could obtain from them?
"Where Grosseteste showed his originality and clear-sightedness was in seeing this system of exploitation as one of the
root causes of spiritual inefficiency." [22] He was a man of
genius and vision who thought not simply of the contemporary situation but of the future, and of the corrupting effect
such a system must have upon the life of the Church, an insight which time proved to be only too accurate.

    He resisted these papal provisions by every legitimate
means at his disposal, particularly by the skillful use of
Canon Law to defer the need to comply. In 1250, at the
age of eighty, he made a journey to the papal court at Lyon
and confronted the Pope in person.

**He stood up alone, attended by nobody but his official Robert
Marsh . . . Pope Innocent IV sat there with his cardinals and the members of his household to hear the most thorough and vehement attack
that any great Pope can ever have heard at the height of his power.** [23]

    The gist of his accusation was that the Church was suf-
fering because of the decline in pastoral care.

**The pastoral office is straitened. And the source of the evil is to
be found in the papal Curia, not merely in its indifference but in its
dispensations and provisions of the pastoral care. It provides bad shepherds for the flock. What is the pastoral office? Its duties are numerous,**

and in particular include the duty of visitation .... [24]

How an absentee pastor could visit his flock was something beyond even the Pope's power to explain! It is worth noting that, as in all things, Bishop Grosseteste taught by example as well as by precept and, in an unprecedented act, had resigned all his own prebends, but for the one in his own Cathedral Church of Lincoln, a step which evoked ridicule rather than respect from his more worldly contemporaries. "If I am more despicable in the eyes of the world," he wrote, "I am more acceptable to the citizens of heaven." [25]

Unfortunately his heroic visit to Lyon was of no avail, and it was heroic not simply for the manner in which he pointed out the failings of the Pope and his court to their faces, but for the very fact that a man of his age even undertook such an arduous journey under thirteenth-century conditions. The priorities of the Pope differed from those of the Bishop. Innocent IV had become dependent upon the system of papal provisions to maintain his Curia and to bribe allies to fight in his interminable wars with the Emperor Frederick II. His political ambitions took precedence over the cure of souls.

In 1253, the Pope nominated his own nephew, Frederick of Lavagna, to a vacant canonry in Lincoln Cathedral. The mandate ordering Bishop Grosseteste to appoint him was something of a legal masterpiece in which the careful use of *non obstante* clauses ruled out every legal ground for refusal or delay. This, then, was the Bishop's dilemma. He was faced with a perfectly legal command from the Sovereign Pontiff, which apparently must be obeyed, and yet the demand, though legal, was obviously immoral, a clear abuse of power. The Pope was using his office as Vicar of Christ in a sense quite contrary to the purpose for which it had been entrusted to him. The Bishop saw clearly that there is an important distinction between what a pope has a legal right to do and what he has a moral right to do. His response was a direct refusal to obey an order which constituted an abuse of authority. The Pope was acting *ultra vires*, beyond the limits of his authority, and hence his subjects were not bound to obey him.

It is of great importance to note that Robert Grosseteste made this stand not because he failed to appreciate or to respect the papal office but as a result of his exalted appreciation of and respect for papal authority.

In his attitude to the papacy Grosseteste was at once loyal and critical. It was just because he believed so passionately in the papal power that he hated to see it misused . . . . If there had been more loyal and disinterested critics like Grosseteste, it would have been better for all concerned. [26]

Lesser men could and did acquiesce in what was wrong, using a facile concept of obedience as their justification. True loyalty does not consist in sycophancy, in telling a superior what he probably wants to hear, in using obedience as an excuse for a quiet life. Had there been more "loyal and disinterested critics" like Bishop Grosseteste, prepared to stand up to the Pope and tell him where his own policies or those of his advisors were wrong, then the Reformation might never have taken place. But men of courage and principle will always be the exception, even in the episcopate, as was made clear in England when the Reformation did come and only St. John Fisher made a stand for the Holy See.

Bishop Grosseteste refused to appoint Frederick of Lavagna to the canonry in Lincoln Cathedral. The letter in which he expressed most strongly his resistance to what he considered to be the unrighteous demands of the Pope was addressed to "Master Innocent," a papal secretary then resident in England. (Some historians have mistakenly concluded that the letter was addressed to Pope Innocent IV himself.) This is his answer to the papal mandate:

No faithful subject of the Holy See, no man who is not cut away by schism from the Body of Christ and the same Holy See, can submit to mandates, precepts, or any other demonstrations of this kind, no, not even if the authors were the most high body of angels. He must needs repudiate them and rebel against them with all his strength. Because of the obedience by which I am bound, and of my love of my union with the Holy See in the Body of Christ, as an obedient son I disobey, I contradict, I rebel. You cannot take action against me, for my every word and act is not rebellion but the filial honor due by God's command to father and mother. As I have said, the Apostolic See in its holiness cannot destroy, it can only build. This is what the plentitude of power means; it can do all things to edification. But these so-called provisions do not build up, they destroy. They cannot be the works of the blessed Apostolic See, for "flesh and blood," which do not possess the Kingdom of God "hath revealed them," not "our Father which is in heaven." [27]

Commenting on this letter in his study, *Grosseteste's Relations With The Papacy and The Crown,* W. A. Pantin writes:

> There seem to be two lines of argument here. The first is that since the *plenitudo potestatis* exists for the purpose of edification and not destruction, any act which tends to the destruction or the ruin of souls cannot be a genuine exercise of the *plenitudo potestatis* . . . . The second line of argument is that if the Pope, or anyone else, should command anything contrary to Divine Law, then it will be wrong to obey, and in the last resort, while protesting one's loyalty, one must refuse to obey. The fundamental problem was that while the Church's teaching is supernaturally guaranteed against error, the Church's ministers, from the Pope downwards, are not impeccable, and are capable of making wrong judgements or giving wrong commands. [28]

"You cannot take action against me," Bishop Grosseteste had warned—and events proved him to be correct. Innocent IV was beside himself with fury when he received the Bishop's letter. His first impulse was to order his "vassal the king" to imprison the old prelate—but his cardinals persuaded him to take no action.

> You must do nothing. It is true. We cannot condemn him. He is a Catholic and a holy man, a better man that we are. He has not got his

equal among the prelates. All the French and English clergy know this
and our contradiction would be of no avail. The truth of this letter
which is probably known to many, might move many against us. He is
esteemed as a great philosopher, learned in Greek and Latin literature,
zealous for justice, a reader in the schools of theology, a preacher to the
people, an active enemy of abuses.[29]

This account was written by a man who had no love for the
bishop—Matthew Paris, executor of the mandate which
Grosseteste had refused to implement. But Matthew recognized the greatness and sincerity of Robert Grosseteste and
was stirred by it.

Innocent IV decided that the most prudent course would
be to take no action and in that same year the aged Bishop of
Lincoln died. Robert Grosseteste was a great scholar, a great
Englishman, a universal genius, perhaps the greatest son of
Oxford, and above all one of the greatest of all Catholic bishops, a true *bonus pastor* who would willingly have laid down
his life for his flock.

He knew everybody and feared nobody. At King Henry's request
he instructed him on the nature of an anointed king, and in so doing
courteously reminded him of his responsibility for the maintenance of
his subjects in peace and justice and of his duty to refrain from any interference with the cure of souls. He would allow no compromise on
matters of principle. The common law of the land should be applied
in the light of equity, the dictate of conscience, and the teaching of
the natural law, as revealed in the Scriptures, implicit in the working of
a Divine Providence, and conformable to the teaching and guidance of
Christ in the Church Militant on earth. [30]

There were many reports of miracles at his tomb in
Lincoln, which soon became a center of veneration and pilgrimage. Repeated attempts were made to secure his canonization; but these were met with little sympathy by the Holy
See. [31] His only rival as the greatest of all English bishops
is St. John Fisher, whose loyalty and love for the Holy
See certainly did not exceed that of Bishop Grosseteste. It

is quite certain that had this thirteenth-century bishop occupied his see under Henry VIII he would have joined St. John Fisher on the scaffold and died for the Pope. It seems equally certain that had the Bishop of Rochester lived during the pontificate of Innocent IV he would have joined Robert Grosseteste in opposing a flagrant abuse of papal power. Who knows, the saintly Bishop of Lincoln may yet be canonized.

NOTES

The following works are referred to in the notes as indicated:

RG   D. A. Callus, ed., *Robert Grosseteste* (Oxford, 1955).
KHLE   F. M. Powicke, *King Henry III and the Lord Edward* (Oxford, 1950).
RGBL   M. Powicke, *Robert Grosseteste, Bishop of Lincoln*, Bulletin of the John Rylands Library, Manchester, Vol. 35, No. 2, March 1953.

1. RGBL, p. 482.
2. D. A. Callus, "Robert Grosseteste as Scholar," RG, pp. 1-69.
   A. C. Crobie, "Grosseteste's Position in the History of Science," RG, pp. 98-120.
   B. Smalley, "The Biblical Scholar," RG, pp. 70-97.
3. Matthew Paris, executor of the papal mandate which Robert Grosseteste refused to implement, RG, p. 170.
4. RG, pp. 168-169.
5. KHLE, p. 287.
6. RG, p. 150.
7. RG, p. 85.
8. RG, p. 146ff.
9. RG, p. 170.
10. KHLE, p. 287.
11. RG, p. 183.
12. RG, p. 185.
13. RGBL, p. 503.
14. RG, p. 189.
15. RG, p. 188.
16. O. Gierke, *Political Theory of the Middle Ages* (Cambridge, 1968), p. 36.
17. Ibid.
18. RG, p. 181.
19. RG, p. 182.
20. RG, p. 158.
21. RG, pp. 158-159.

22. RG, p. 182.
23. RGBL, p. 504.
24. KHLE, p. 284.
25. RG, xix.
26. RG, p. 197.
27. KHLE, p. 286.
28. RG, pp. 190-191.
29. KHLE, p. 287.
30. RG, xxi.
31. E. W. Kemp, "The Attempted Canonization of Robert Grosseteste," RG, pp. 241-246.

Part Two
The Abuse of Ecclesiastical Power

According to Catholic theologians and canon lawyers, a prelate can abuse his position in a number of ways, which include the imposition of unjust laws or failure to guard and transmit the deposit of Faith, either by remaining silent in the face of heresy or even by teaching heresy himself. A Catholic has the right to refuse obedience in the first case and a duty to oppose the prelate in the second. Their consensus regarding law in general is that the legislator should not simply refrain from demanding something that his subjects would find impossible to carry out, but that laws should not be too difficult or distressing for those subjected to them. St. Thomas explains that, for a law to be just, it must conform to the demands of reason and have an effect which is both good and for the benefit of those for whom it is intended. A law can cease to bind without revocation on the part of the legislator when it is clearly harmful, impossible, or irrational.[1] This is particularly true if a prelate commands anything contrary to divine precept. (*Praelato non est obediendum contra praeceptum divinum.*) In support of this teaching St. Thomas cites Acts 5:29: "We ought to obey God rather than men." He teaches that not only would the prelate err in giving such an order but that anyone obeying him would sin just as certainly as if he disobeyed a divine command. (". . . *ipse peccaret praecipiens, et ei obediens, quasi contra praeceptum Domini agens . . .").*[2]

Dealing with the question as to whether subjects are bound to obey their superiors in all things he explains that: "Now sometimes the things commanded by a superior are against God. Therefore superiors are not to be obeyed in all things."[3]

Where a matter of faith is involved, resistance is not a right but a duty for the faithful Catholic. The only correct course of action is that taken by Eusebius and so highly praised by Dom Guéranger in his *Liturgical Year:*

On Christmas Day, 428, Nestorius (Patriarch of Constantinople), profiting from the immense crowd assembled to celebrate the birth of the Divine Child to Our Lady uttered this blasphemy from his episcopal throne: "Mary did not give birth to God; her son was only a man, the instrument of God."

At these words a tremor of horror passed through the multitude. The general indignation was voiced by Eusebius, a layman, who stood up in the crowd and protested. Soon a more detailed protest was drafted in the name of the members of the abandoned Church, and numerous copies spread far and wide, declaring anathema on whoever should dare to say that He Who was born of the Virgin Mary was other than the only begotten Son of God. This attitude not only safeguarded the Faith of the Eastern Church, but was praised alike by Popes and Councils. When the shepherd turns into a wolf the first duty of the flock is to defend itself. As a general rule, doctrine comes from the bishops to the faithful, and it is not for the faithful, who are subjects in the order of Faith, to pass judgment on their superiors. But every Christian, by virtue of his title to the name Christian, has not only the necessary knowledge of the essentials of the treasure of Revelation, but also the duty of safeguarding them. The principle is the same, whether it is a matter of belief or conduct, that is of dogma or morals. Treachery such as that of Nestorius is rare in the Church; but it can happen that, for one reason or another, pastors remain silent on essential matters of faith.

Dom Guéranger then insists that, when the Faith is compromised by someone in authority in the Church, the true Christian is the one who makes a stand for the truth rather than the one who does nothing under the specious pretext of submission to lawful authority.

To sum up what has been demonstrated so far, normally subjects must be obedient to lawful authority in Church and State but they have the right to resist harsh and harmful laws which do not contribute to the common good. They must never compromise the Faith under the pretext of obedience. "When the shepherd becomes the wolf the flock must defend itself."

Few Catholics concerned to uphold orthodoxy within the

Church during these troubled times would dispute this. Catholics in English-speaking countries do not normally have to contend with shepherds who have actually become wolves but with shepherds who permit wolves to ravage their flocks, shepherds who condemn any of the sheep who have the temerity to complain. Such bishops are not the exception, they have become the norm. Dietrich von Hildebrand denounces them with the burning indignation of an Old Testatment prophet:

> They either close their eyes and try, ostrich-style, to ignore the grievous abuses as well as appeals to their duty to intervene, or they fear to be attacked by the press or the mass-media and defamed as reactionary, narrow-minded, or medieval. They fear men more than God. The words of St. John Bosco apply to them: "The power of evil men lives on in the cowardice of the good." . . . One is forced to think of the hireling who abandons his flocks to the wolves when one reflects on the lethargy of so many bishops and superiors who, though still orthodox themselves, do not have the courage to intervene against the most flagrant heresies and abuses of all kinds in their dioceses or in their orders.[4]

Dr. von Hildebrand is in perfect conformity with the authorities who have already been cited when he denies that the faithful have the duty of automatic obedience to their bishops in the present state of the Church. He shows with admirable clarity that the mark of a truly faithful Catholic can be a refusal to submit to heretical or compromising bishops.

> Should the faithful at the time of the Arian heresy, for instance, in which the majority of the bishops were Arians, have limited themselves to being nice and obedient to the ordinances of these bishops, instead of battling heresy? Is not fidelity to the true teaching of the Church to be given priority over submission to the bishop? Is it not precisely by virtue of their obedience to the revealed truths which they received from the Magisterium of the Church, that the faithful offer resistance? . . . .

The drivel of the heretics, both priests and laymen, is tolerated; the bishops tacitly acquiesce to the poisoning of the faithful. But they want to silence the faithful believers who take up the cause of orthodoxy, the very people who should by all rights be the joy of the bishops' hearts, their consolation, a source of strength for overcoming their own lethargy. Instead, these people are regarded as disturbers of the peace. [5]

"Is not fidelity to the true teaching of the Church to be given priority over submission to the bishop?" asks Dr. von Hildebrand. "Yes, it is," replies St. Thomas Aquinas together with every reputable theologian who has examined the subject. There can be very few faithful Catholics who would refuse to align themselves with St. Thomas and Dietrich von Hildebrand on this point—with one reservation. Many, if not most, would add the proviso: "Unless the bishop in question is the Bishop of Rome." Some are quite unwilling to admit, even to themselves, that an occasion could ever arise when a Catholic should justifiably refuse obedience to the Sovereign Pontiff. However sincere such people may be, they display a lamentable ignorance of Church history and Catholic theology.

Professor Marcel de Corte of the University of Liège can be ranked with Dr. von Hildebrand as one of the outstanding Catholic philosophers of our time. He has noted that the attitude of these Catholics towards the Pope is tantamount to the claim that he is inerrant, that his every decision, his every word, is divinely inspired, that he is, in fact, a divine oracle. Writing in the March 1977 issue of the *Courrier de Rome* he remarked:

For them it is as if the *person* of the Pope were, *as such*, infallible, and as if all his words, all his directives, all his judgments in all matters, even those foreign to religion, could never be subject to error, though the whole history of the Church protests against that conviction which is close to idolatry.

There have been Popes whose doctrine was near-heresy, Honorius and Liberius for example. There were others whose faith, hope and

charity could hardly be perceived behind the disorders of their conduct. And there were some whose faults, stupidity, blunders, extravagances, and weaknesses in the government and administration of the
Church were such that the divine organism entrusted to their care was
more than once shaken. It is enough to read the twenty or so volumes
of Ludwig von Pastor's *History of the Popes* to be convinced of that.

Few readers will possess this huge work but some will
own the very scholarly one-volume work on the same subject,
The Popes, edited by Eric John and published by Burns and
Oates in 1964. It is only necessary to glance through the brief
lives of the Popes in this book to find literally hundreds of
examples of "faults, stupidity, blunders, extravagances, and
weaknesses" among the Popes. A few of these examples will
suffice to make the point:*
    The pontificate of Pope Zosimus lasted for one year
only, from 417-418.

His knowledge and prudence were insufficient for his task of governing the Church, and he was a weak man who blustered and yielded.
Within a few days of consecration he conferred on Patroclus, Bishop
of Arles, a usurper of the see, unscrupulous in his methods, what
amounted to legatine authority over all the bishops of southern Gaul,
and reprimanded them harshly when they defended their rights . . . .
Zosimus ordered the rehabilitation of an African priest, Apiarius, de-
graded by his bishop for his immoral life.

Pope Boniface II (530-532) attempted to nominate his
successor, "an ambitious and unscrupulous deacon named
Vigilius. His action, however, met with such general disap-
probation that he rescinded the decree." Here is an example
of a pope who was clearly in the wrong, who met with legitimate resistance, and eventually abandoned his misguided
policy. Pope Zosimus had refused to budge when opposed on
equally just grounds.

---

*References are not provided for these quotations as they can all be found in the
accounts of the lives of the Popes to whom they refer.

This did not prevent Vigilius from eventually obtaining the papacy. Pope St. Silverius was unjustly deposed in 537 and Vigilius elected in his place. St. Silverius was handed over "to Vigilius and his slaves. He was taken to the island of Palmaria where on 11 November his resignation was extorted. On 2 December 537 he died, a victim of ill use and starvation. The guilt of his death rests primarily on Vigilius. The Church honors him as a martyr."

After becoming Pope "letters frankly Monophysite* addressed to the Monophysite bishops are attributed to Vigilius and reputable Catholic scholars believe in his authorship. In view of his shifty and unscrupulous character . . . we may be disposed to agree." The Emperor Justinian was anxious to reconcile his Monophysite subjects and hoped to achieve a compromise with them by condemning three authors of whom they did not approve. "These writings proposed for anathema were known as the 'Three Chapters.' Though the condemnation would not reject [the Council of] Chalcedon,** it must derogate from its authority, and would therefore be a sop to the Monophysites." The Emperor wished Vigilius to condemn the Three Chapters. "A pitiful history of vacillation and evasion followed." One of the writings was a letter by a Bishop Ibas which had been read at Chalcedon and pronounced orthodox. A Council of Oriental bishops falsely claimed that the letter of Bishop Ibas was not the document read at Chalcedon. The Council excommunicated Pope Vigilius, who then surrendered. He "condemned the Chapters and even endorsed the Council's lie about Ibas' letter on pain of heresy for disputing it. It was perhaps the greatest humiliation in the history of the papacy."

---

*Monophysitism : The doctrine that in the Person of the Incarnate Christ there was but a single Divine Nature, as against the orthodox teaching of a double Nature, Divine and Human, after the Incarnation.
**The Council of Chalcedon (451) condemned those who deny the title *Theotokos* ('God-bearer') to Our Lady. A denial of this title implied that the Humanity of Christ is separable from His Divine Person. It also condemned those who denied any distinction between Our Lord's Divine and Human natures. Catholic teaching is that the Second Person of the Blessed Trinity is one Divine Person with *two* natures, Divine and Human.

Pope Honorius I (625-628), though orthodox in his personal belief, wrote letters which could be interpreted in a heretical sense. "The progress of the heresy [Monothelitism], the clear revelation of its character after Honorius' death, and the use made by the heretics of his approving letters, compelled the General Council of 680 to condemn Honorius along with the Patriarch Sergius. This condemnation was sustained by Pope Leo II and repeated by subsequent popes."

The case of Pope Honorius poses a particular problem for those who claim that the Pope is inerrant. If Honorius did not really favor heresy then Leo II erred in condemning him, but if Leo II did not err in his condemnation then Honorius was guilty of favoring heresy.

Pope Sergius III (904-911):

. . . certainly took the papacy by force, but he is customarily regarded as a legitimate pope. Legitimate he may have been but suitable he certainly was not . . . . This unscrupulous man who ruled the Church so arrogantly held a Roman Council which overturned the acts of the Council of 898 . . . . the execration of some undoubted popes by this terrible man, were enough to cause scandal. Many of the better men of the day resisted and a bitter conflict arose.

Here is another example of good Catholics justly resisting a bad pope.

Pope John XII was "a scandal to the whole Church . . . John conducted himself in the manner of a layman, preferring hunting to church ceremonies, and largely indifferent to Church matters . . . It was said that he was struck with a paralysis while visiting his mistress. He died on 14 May 964, without confession or receiving the Sacraments."

Pope Alexander II (1061-1073) made a sincere effort to introduce much needed reforms into the Church. "Both in northern Italy, and to a lesser extent in England, reform had served as a cloak for dirty politics without the Pope realizing he was being used by men less scrupulous than himself."

St. Gregory VII (1073-1085) was able to humiliate the Emperor Henry IV "but it proved to be a political mistake."

Pope Gregory IX (1227-1241) "commissioned a convert from heresy, the Dominican Robert le Bougre, a sadistic monster who was later burned himself, as his inquisitor in France."

A French pope, Martin IV (1281-1285) had served the King of France before Pope Urban IV called him to the Curia. "An ardent patriot, Martin IV was the devoted servant of Charles, and all else was now sacrificed to French interests. Charles was made a senator of Rome for life. Seven new cardinals were created, four of them Frenchmen. Those appointed to offices in the Papal States by the previous pope were now displaced in favor of Frenchmen."

Pope Boniface IX (1389-1404):

. . . increased the taxation of the Church and sold provisions and expectatives for ready cash. Indulgences were multiplied, to be gained by an offering of money with little regard paid to the essential spiritual conditions. In the year 1400 the Pope proclaimed a Holy Year and allowed would-be pilgrims to the shrines of Rome to forgo the arduous journey for a sum roughly equivalent to what they would otherwise have spent. The bankers of Europe were called in to collect the offerings which they divided equally with the Pope. There can be little doubt that Boniface IX, who treated the whole business simply as a political problem, was guilty of simony on a massive scale.

Pope Sixtus IV (1471-1484) had one dominating idea, "the desire to advance his family and obtain for it a leading position in Italy. Other popes had engaged in nepotism, some out of family loyalty and others from political considerations: but under him it became the chief influence in papal policy."

Pope Innocent VIII (1484-1492) was:

. . . a kindly and genial man [but] he lacked the personality and intellectual capacity for the office of pope. His morals were equally unsuitable, and he openly avowed his illegitimate children . . . To the open scandals caused by the pope's morals and policies — the advancement of his bastard Franceschetto, and his collaboration with the heathen — were added the results of corruption in the Curia. Administrative incompetence and the expenses of foreign policy in the early years of his pontificate led both to an increase in the sale of offices and to the creation of new posts in order that they might be sold. The number of papal secretaries was increased to twenty-six and the new posts sold for 62,400 ducats, while fifty-two *Plumbatores* were appointed to seal bulls, each of whom paid 2,500 ducats for his appointment.

Despite the fact that all these citations appear in an approved and highly praised work of Catholic scholarship, many Catholics will be shocked to read them. They reveal that men totally unsuited for the highest office to which a human being can rise have been elected to the office of Sovereign Pontiff. They reveal that popes have appointed unworthy officials; that popes have been deceived by unscrupulous men; that policies they initiated have done harm to the Church; that they have subordinated the good of the Church to political policies, to the interests of a particular country or their family. If true, these statements reveal that to be elected pope guarantees neither impeccability nor inerrancy. But as the Church has never taught that the pope is impeccable or inerrant, no Catholic should shirk facing up to the truth. Mention was made earlier of Baron von Pastor's *History of the Popes.* A most interesting article on this work appeared in the 19 July 1940 issue of *The Commonweal,* at that time one of the most reputable and orthodox publications in the English-speaking Catholic world. The first volume of Baron von Pastor's great work was published in 1886—the last in 1933. The article in *The Commonweal* comments:

> The circumstances of the time were favorable to Pastor. The nineteenth century had seen an unprecedented development of the historical sciences, and nowhere was this development more remarkable than in Germany, where Pastor was trained. Immense stores of authentic materials were made available to historians, and the publication of manuscripts and documents, of the fruits of individual and collective research, of historical monographs of every kind and of reviews which gave expression to the findings and opinions of every school of thought

increased on all sides. Leo XIII gave further impetus to this movement when in 1883 he opened to historians the incomparable riches of the Vatican archives.

Pope Leo performed an even greater service by his letter on the study of history, in which he declared that the Church has nothing to fear from the truth and desires only that the truth be known. He reaffirmed the norms by which all sound historical scholarship must be guided; the first law of history is, "Never tell a lie," and the second, "Do not fear to tell the truth." It is understandable, though deplorable, that many who observe the first cannot bring themselves to fulfill the second. From this selective obedience arises the grave abuse by which history, maimed and distorted, is made the unprofitable servant of unsound apologetics. Cardinal Newman remarked that the endemic fidget about giving scandal is itself the greatest of scandals, and we may paraphrase his famous comment on literature by saying that we may expect a sinless history only from a sinless people.

Pastor's freedom from the criminal trait of accommodating his matter is an imperishable glory for Catholic historical readership and is surely not the least of the reasons for the esteem in which his work is held by Catholic and non-Catholic scholars alike.

Conservative Catholics who ignore the truth and insist that every decision of Pope Paul VI was divinely inspired cannot hope to be vindicated by history. For many centuries there was an unfortunate tendency for Catholic apologists to adapt the facts to suit the case. Thus Liberius neither signed one of the creeds of Sirmium nor confirmed the excommunication of St. Athanasius (see Appendix I); Honorius did not write the letter for which he was condemned—it was a forgery; Bishop Grosseteste did not write the letter denouncing Pope Innocent IV—it was also a forgery.

An ability to face up to the truth is a sign of a strong and informed faith. Had the Church taught that every pope is impeccably virtuous this could not be reconciled with the life of Pope Alexander VI—but as the Church has never taught that the popes are impeccable, Alexander VI may be a source of scandal but he is not an impediment to faith. It should never be forgotten that the first pope actually denied Our Lord—perhaps this was intended as a lesson and a warning to us. Certainly, not even the most dissolute of St. Peter's successors ever descended to the extent of denying Christ.

Professor de Corte comments:

> One must have a very weak faith to be upset by this human side of the Church. One can, indeed, suffer in one's feelings; but the solidity, the *Amen*, of our response to the action of God in the One, Holy, Catholic and Apostolic Church should never be damaged by it: God writes straight with crooked lines, says the Portugese proverb, He always draws good from evil; and we know from Scripture that the time of universal apostasy will be followed by the glory of eternity.
>
> The epidemic of the kind of deification of the Pope which is raging, in different degrees, in Catholic souls, and which inclines them, again in different degrees, to an absolute obedience to his injunctions in any domain whatsoever, is relatively recent. The Middle Ages, for example, knew nothing of it. It certainly cannot be said that that period, the most brilliant in the history of Christianity, ever cast doubt on the spiritual primacy of the papacy in the order of faith. The struggles between the Empire and Rome, however violent they were, respected the fundamental principle of the Catholic faith. When Dante, with a sort of ferocity, put Boniface VIII, the Pope gloriously reigning at the time he wrote, into the abysses of Hell, in company with some of his predecessors, he did not, like Luther, condemn to a shameful execution the Papacy itself as the principal organ of the Church.

Professor de Corte has touched here upon what is perhaps the most important distinction to be made in this discussion —the distinction between schism and disobedience. This distinction is discussed in *Le Dictionnaire de Théologie Catholique* by no less a person than Fr. Yves Congar, O. P., an implacable critic of Mgr. Lefebvre and the traditionalist movement.[6] Father Congar writes that schism involves a refusal to accept the existence of legitimate authority in the Church, e. g. Luther's rejection of the papacy to which Professor de Corte referred. Father Congar explains that the refusal to accept a decision of legitimate authority in a particular instance does not constitute schism but disobedience. A Catholic who misses Mass on Sunday without good cause is disobedient but not schismatic—and his disobedience constitutes a sin. But disobedience to an unlawful command, a refusal to submit to an abuse of power, can be meritorious. It was not Bishop Grosseteste who sinned in refusing to appoint the Pope's nephew as a canon of Lincoln Cathedral but the Pope who sinned by using offices intended for the cure of souls as a means of obtaining revenue for his relatives. But how can such a viewpoint be reconciled with the teaching of *Pastor Aeternus*, the dogmatic constitution of the First Vatican Council on the Church and particularly papal authority?

> We teach and declare that, in the disposition of God, the Roman Church holds the pre-eminence of ordinary power over all the other churches; and that this power of jurisdiction of the Roman Pontiff, which is truly episcopal, is immediate. Regarding this jurisdiction, the shepherds of whatever rite and dignity and the faithful, individually and collectively, are bound by a duty of hierarchical subjection and of sincere obedience; and this not only in matters that pertain to faith and morals, but also in matters that pertain to the discipline and government of the Church throughout the whole world. When, therefore, this bond of unity with the Roman Pontiff is guarded both in government and in the profession of the same faith, then the Church of Christ is one flock under one supreme shepherd. This is the doctrine of Catholic truth; and no one can deviate from this without losing his faith and his salvation. [7]

In their zeal to uphold papal authority some Catholics interpret these words as if they invested the Sovereign Pontiff with an authority which he has never possessed and could never possess. Probably without realizing it, they are claiming, implicitly if not explicitly, that the Pope possesses absolute or arbitrary power, i.e. that the Church has been placed at his disposal to be governed at his whim. But the authority of the Pope is neither absolute nor arbitrary—the idea that *Pastor Aeternus* might be interpreted in this manner was considered ridiculous during the debates of the First Vatican Council and attempts to include clauses intended to exclude such an interpretation were treated as absurd. One American Father, Bishop Verot of Savannah, proposed a canon stating: "If anyone says that the authority of the Pope in the Church is so full that he may dispose of everything by his mere whim, let him be anathema." He was told that the Fathers had not come to Rome "to hear buffooneries." [8]

Bishop Freppel of Angers (France) had been professor of theology at the Sorbonne and was one of the theologians who were called to Rome to prepare for the Council. During the debate on the Pope's power of jurisdiction he commented:

> Absolutism is the principle of Ulpian in the Roman law, that the mere will of the prince is law. But who has ever said that the Roman Pontiff should govern the Church according to his sweet will, by his nod, by arbitrary power, by fancy, that is without the laws and canons? We all exclude mere arbitrary power; but we all assert full and perfect power. Is power arbitrary because it is supreme? Are civil governments arbitrary because they are supreme? Or a General Council confirmed by the Pope? Let all this confusion of ideas go! Let the genuine doctrine of the schema* be accepted in its true, proper, genuine sense, without preposterous interpretations. [9]

Bishop Zinelli was Relator (Spokesman) for the Deputation of the Faith, the body charged with explaining the meaning of the schemas to the Fathers. In answer to the Melchite Patriarch of Antioch he explained that papal power was not absolutely monarchical because the form of Church government had been instituted by Christ and could not be abolished even by an ecumenical council. "And no one who is sane can say that either the Pope or the Ecumenical Council can destroy the episcopate or other things determined by divine law in the Church." [10]

If the power of the Pope is neither absolute nor arbitrary it must obviously be limited. The most obvious and

---

*Preparatory document which the Fathers could discuss and amend.

most important limitation upon the plenitude of papal power (*plenitudo potestatis*), mentioned on a number of occasions during the debates of the First Vatican Council, is no less than that upon which Bishop Grosseteste based his refusal to obey Pope Innocent IV:

> As I have said, the Apostolic See in its holiness cannot destroy, it can only build. This is what the plenitude of power means; it can do all things to edification. But these so-called provisions do not build up, they destroy (see p. 389).

This is precisely the point made by Bishop d'Avanzo of Calvi, another spokesman for the Deputation of the Faith, during the Vatican I debate on papal authority:

> Therefore Peter has as much power as the Lord has given to him, not for the destruction, but for the building up of the Body of Christ that is the Church. [11]

Sylvester Prierias was a prominent Dominican opponent of Martin Luther and defended papal authority in his *Dialogus de Potestate Papae* (1517). He accepted that the Pope could abuse his position and used the terminology of Bishop Grosseteste—that the Pope possessed his power only to build, not to destroy:

> Thus, were he to wish to distribute the Church's wealth, or Peter's Patrimony among his own relatives; were he to wish to destroy the Church or to commit an act of similar magnitude, there would be a duty to prevent him, and likewise an obligation to oppose him and resist him. The reason being that he does not possess power in order to destroy, and thus it follows that if he is doing so it is lawful to oppose him.

Sufficient evidence has already been presented to make it clear that *Pastor Aeternus* does not oblige Catholics to accept that the Pope has absolute or arbitrary power, or that all legislation which he promulgates in accordance with prescribed legal norms must necessarily be above criticism. Doctrinal teaching promulgated with the Pope's infallible teaching authority comes into a special category and every Catholic is bound to give it full internal and external consent. Commenting on the possibility of a conflict between conscience and papal authority, Cardinal Newman explains:

> Next, I observe that, conscience being a practical dictate, a collision is possible between it and the Pope's authority only when the Pope legislates, or gives particular orders, and the like. But a pope is not infallible in his laws, nor in his commands, nor in his acts of State, nor in his administration, nor in his public policy. [12]

Opposition to any papal command is not something to be contemplated lightly. Indeed, it would be better to err in the direction of unthinking and unqualified obedience than to adopt the Modernist attitude of submitting every papal decision to our personal judgment. Cardinal Newman warns:

> If in a particular case it (conscience) is to be taken as a sacred and sovereign monitor, its dictate, in order to prevail against the voice of the Pope, must follow upon serious thought, prayer, and all available means of arriving at a right judgment on the matter in question. And further, obedience to the Pope is what is called "in possession"; that is, the *onus probandi* of establishing a case against him lies, as in all cases of exception, on the side of conscience. Unless a man is able to say to himself, as in the Presence of God, that he must not, and dare not, act upon the Papal injunction, he is bound to obey it, and would commit a great sin in disobeying it. *Prima facie* it is his bounden duty, even from a sentiment of loyalty, to believe the Pope right and to act accordingly. [13]

This is an admonition which traditionalists should always keep in the forefront of their minds. There can be no source of action which a Catholic should undertake with more fear and trembling than that of disobeying a papal command. Such an act can only be prompted by the certainty that to obey the Pope would be to disobey God ("We ought to obey

God rather than men" [Acts 5:29]).

Cardinal Newman stresses that if a man is sincerely convinced that "what his superior commands is displeasing to
God, he is bound not to obey." [14]　He adds that:

> The word "Superior" certainly includes the Pope; Cardinal Jacob-
> atius brings out this point clearly in his authoritative work on Coun-
> cils, which is contained in Labbe's collection, introducing the Pope
> by name: "If it were doubtful," he says, "whether a precept (of the
> Pope) be a sin or not, we must determine thus: that, if he to whom
> the precept is addressed has a conscientious sense that it is a sin and
> injustice, first it is his duty to put off that sense; but, if he cannot, nor
> conform himself to the judgment of the Pope, in that case it is his
> duty to follow his own private conscience, and patiently to bear it if
> the Pope punishes him."—lib. iv. p. 241. [15]

It was in this context that Newman remarked:

> Certainly, if I am obliged to bring religion into after-dinner toasts
> (which indeed does not seem quite the thing) I shall drink—to the
> Pope, if you please,—still, to Conscience first, and to the Pope after-
> wards. [16]

A Distinction: Legal and Moral Norms

The above sub-title appears on page 394 of Karl Rahner's
book *Studies in Modern Theology* which was published in
English in 1965. Father Rahner makes an important distinction between what is *legally valid* and what is *morally valid.*
He cites an example of a papal act which would be legally
valid but morally illicit which has some similarity to the case
of Bishop Grosseteste and Innocent IV.

> Take the case of a pope's deposing a competent and pious bishop
> without any objective reason, merely in order to promote one of his
> relatives to the post. It could hardly be proved that such a deposition
> is legally invalid. There is no court of appeal before which the Pope

and his measure could be cited. The Pope alone has the competence of competence, that is, he alone judges in the last juridical instance on earth whether in a given act he has observed those norms by which in his own view that act is to be judged. But for all the unassailable legal validity of such a measure, such a deposition would be immoral and an actual offense against the divine right of the episcopate, though not an offense extending to the proper sphere of doctrine.

One hundred years ago, in May 1879, Joseph Hergenröther was created Cardinal together with John Henry Newman. The Cardinal, one of the greatest theologians of his time, was called to Rome to assist in the preparatory work for the First Vatican Council. He was acknowledged as one of the most effective apologists for and interpreters of the Council. Pope Pius IX was one of his most fervent admirers. Cardinal Hergenröther made it quite clear that by no stretch of the imagination could the powers of jurisdiction ascribed to the Pope by the Council be considered as arbitrary or unrestricted.

The Pope is circumscribed by the consciousness of the necessity of making a righteous and beneficent use of the duties attached to his privileges . . . . He is also circumscribed by the respect due to General Councils and to ancient statutes and customs, by the rights of bishops, by his relation with civil powers, by the traditional mild tone of government indicated by the aim of the institution of the papacy—to "feed"— and finally by the respect indispensable in a spiritual power towards the spirit and mind of nations. [17]

Cardinal Hergenröther's reference to ancient customs is very pertinent to the refusal of Mgr. Lefebvre and traditionalists in general to accept the New Mass. Cardinal Jean de Torquemada* was the most influential champion of the papal primacy in the fifteenth century. His *Summa de Ecclesia* (1489) is a systematic treatise on the Church, defending the infallibility and plenitude of papal power. This work

*Uncle of Tomas de Torquemada, the Grand Inquisitor.

forms the basis of the arguments of the most notable defenders of the primacy up to the First Vatican Council—such theologians as Domenico Jacobazzi and Cajetan, Melchior Cano, Suarez, Gregory of Valencia, and Bellarmine. Cardinal Torquemada taught that the Pope could become a schismatic by breaking with tradition, particularly with respect to worship:

> The Pope can separate himself without reason purely by his wilfulness from the body of the Church and from the college of priests by not observing what the universal Church by apostolic tradition observes . . . or by non-observance of what was ordered universally by the universal councils or by the Apostolic See, especially in respect to the divine cult if he does not want to observe what concerns the universal rite of the Church's worship.[18]

Similarly, the wholesale reversal of traditional customs and ceremonies could, in the opinion of Francisco de Suarez (1548-1617), result in the Pope actually becoming a schismatic. Suarez is usually considered the greatest Jesuit theologian and was called by Pope Paul V *"Doctor eximius et pius."* For Suarez, schism, in the specifically theological sense, is a cleavage in the one Church. This need not involve formal heresy but can include one who retains the faith but in his actions and conduct is unwilling to maintain the unity of the Church. Suarez writes:

> The Pope can be a schismatic if he does not want to have union and bond with the whole body of the Church, as he should, if he attempts to excommunicate the whole Church, or if he wants to abolish all ecclesiastical ceremonies, which are confirmed by apostolic tradition as Cajetan remarks.[19]

It is an indisputable fact that never in the history of the Church has any Pope presided over so wholesale an abolition of traditional customs and ceremonies as Pope Paul VI. The only comparable revolution was that of the Protestant Reformation—but this was done by men who were openly acting outside the unity of the Church.

Father Rahner also uses a similar example to illustrate a morally illicit papal act:

> Imagine that the Pope, as supreme pastor of the Church, issued a decree today requiring all the uniate churches of the Near East to give up their Oriental liturgy and adopt the Latin rite . . . The Pope would not exceed the competence of his jurisdictional primacy by such a decree, and the decree would be legally valid.
>
> But we can also pose an entirely different question. Would it be morally licit for the Pope to issue such a decree? Any reasonable man and any true Christian would have to anwer "no." Any confessor of the Pope would have to tell him that in the concrete situation of the Church today such a decree, despite its legal validity, would be subjectively and objectively an extremely grave moral offense against charity, against the unity of the Church rightly understood (which does not demand uniformity), against possible reunion of the Orthodox with the Roman Catholic Church, etc., a mortal sin from which the Pope could be absolved only if he revoked the decree.
>
> From this example one can readily gather the heart of the matter. It can, of course, be worked out more fundamentally and abstractly in a theological demonstration:
>
> 1. The exercise of papal jurisdictional primacy remains even when it is legal, subject to moral norms, which are not necessarily satisfied merely because a given act of jurisdiction is legal. Even an act of jurisdiction which legally binds its subjects can offend against moral principles.
> 2. To point out and protest against the possible infringement against moral norms of an act which must respect these norms is not to deny or question the legal competence of the man possessing the jurisdiction.* [20]

Father Rahner asserts that "there can be a right and even a duty to protest" against a morally illicit act "even where the legality of an act of ecclesiastical authority cannot be

---

*Father Rahner is here making the same point to be found in Father Congar's article on schism in *Le Dictionnaire de Théologie Catholique*, i. e. that to question the use made of authority in a particular instance without denying or rejecting that authority does not constitute schism.

questioned."[21] He refrains from discussing the nature such a protest might take but censures in the most scathing terms those who insist that any act of an ecclesiastical superior, the Pope included, cannot be contested if legally valid. (Note that this was written before 1965.) His indictment can be applied directly to those conservative Catholics who attack traditionalists simply because they oppose legally valid papal legislation. It would be a different matter if they contested the grounds upon which traditionalists protest, e. g. it is a matter for debate as to whether the New Mass constitutes a break with tradition, has compromised true Eucharistic doctrine, and leads to liturgical abuse, etc. But when they deny that a Catholic ever has the right to contest *any* legally valid papal act there is no room for debate. Such an assertion is nonsensical: there is nothing to discuss.

Has the example of papal interference with liturgical custom, chosen by Fathers Rahner and Suarez, ever been applied in practice? The answer is "yes," and on at least two occasions. During the pontificate of St. Victor (189-198) a dispute arose due to the fact that some Asiatic Christians did not conform their system for reckoning the date of Easter to that of Rome, with the result that Easter was celebrated on different days in different parts of the Church.

Victor bade the Asiatic Churches conform to the custom of the rest of the Church, but was met with determined resistance by Polycrates of Ephesus, who claimed that their custom derived from St. John himself. Victor replied with excommunication. St. Irenaeus, however, intervened, exhorting Victor not to cut off whole Churches on account of a point which was not a matter of faith. He assumes that the Pope can exercise the power but urges him not to do so. Similarly the resistance of the Asiatic bishops involved no denial of the supremacy of Rome. It indicates solely that the bishops believed St. Victor to be abusing his power in bidding them renounce a custom for which they had apostolic authority . . . Saint Victor, seeing that more harm than good would come from insistence, withdrew the imposed penalty. [22]

Similarly, a number of Popes including Nicholas II, St. Gregory VII, and Eugenius IV attempted to impose the Roman rite upon the people of Milan. The Milanese even went to the extent of taking up arms in defense of their traditional liturgy (the Ambrosian rite) and they eventually prevailed. As a rite with a prescription of two centuries it was not affected by the promulgation of *Quo Primum* in 1570.* [23]

Pope John XXII actually taught heresy in his capacity as a private doctor. (Many papal utterances express no more than the personal opinion of the Pope and do not involve the teaching authority of the Church.) Pope John XXII taught that there was no particular judgment; that the souls of the just do not enjoy the beatific vision immediately; that the wicked are not at once eternally damned; and that all await the judgment of God on the Last Day. The Pope was denounced as a heretic by some Franciscans and then appointed a commission of theologians to examine the question. The commission found that the Pope was in error and he made a public recantation. [24]

One of the most serious cases of papal error was that of Pope Sixtus V. This well-meaning pontiff considered himself to be a biblical scholar and Latinist of no small ability and decided to intervene personally in the revision of the Vulgate which had been ordered by the Council of Trent.

Sixtus V, though unskilled in this branch of criticism, had introduced alterations of his own, all for the worse. He had even gone so far as to have an impression of this vitiated edition printed and partially distributed, together with the proposed Bull enforcing its use. He died, however, before the actual promulgation and his immediate successors at once proceeded to remove the blunders and call in the defective impression. [25]

---

*Sadly, it was "reformed" on the lines of the Roman Rite after Vatican II but whether or not its traditional character has been destroyed I am unable to say.

The Rebuke at Antioch

St. Paul's rebuke to St. Peter at Antioch (Gal. 2) provides a classic example of an occasion when the Pope himself needs to be corrected. Peter's behavior in not eating with the Gentile converts was not in conformity with his own convictions or the truth of the Gospel. He was also endangering both the liberty of the Gentiles and the Jews from the Mosaic Law and, although not guilty of doctrinal error, he was, at the least, exerting moral pressure on behalf of the Judaizers.[26] St. Thomas comments:

> If the Faith be in imminent peril, prelates ought to be accused by their subjects, even in public. Thus, St. Paul, who was the subject of St. Peter, called him to task in public because of the impending danger of scandal concerning a point of Faith. As the Glossary to St. Augustine puts it: "St. Peter himself set an example for those who rule, to the effect that if they ever stray from the straight path they are not to feel that anyone is unworthy of correcting them, even if such a person be one of their subjects." [27]

To quote Suarez again:

> If [the Pope] lays down an order contrary to right customs one does not have to obey him; if he tries to do something manifestly opposed to justice and to the common good, it would be licit to resist him; if he attacks by force, he could be repelled by force, with the moderation characteristic of a good defense.[28]

Vitoria, his Dominican counterpart, writes: "If the Pope by his orders and his acts destroys the Church, one can resist him and impede the execution of his commands."[29]
Saint Robert Bellarmine considers that:

> Just as it is licit to resist the Pontiff who attacks the body, so also is it licit to resist him who attacks souls or destroys the civil order, or above all tries to destroy the Church. I say that it is licit to resist him by not doing what he orders and by impeding the execution of his

will; it is not licit, however, to judge him, to punish him, or depose him, for these are acts proper to a superior. [30]

Sufficient should now have been written to indicate that the right to resist the Pope has a solid foundation in Catholic theology although the circumstances which could justify such resistance would have to be of the utmost gravity. To repeat a citation by Cardinal Newman: "Unless a man is able to say to himself, as in the Presence of God, that he must not, and dare not, act upon the papal injunction, he is bound to obey it." The object of this appendix is limited to proving that under extraordinary circumstances a Catholic can have not simply the right but the duty to disobey the Pope. A related topic is that of the deposition of a heretical pope. It will be dealt with only briefly here.

Writing in *The Tablet* in 1965, Abbot (now Bishop) B. C. Butler posed the question as to the source of authority in the Church "if the Pope has disenfranchised himself by public heresy? Where at such a time is hierarchical authority? Where is the authority that can, not indeed depose a pope (no human authority can depose a pope), but declare that the *soi-disant* pope has lost his powers whether by heresy, schism, or lunacy?" [31]

It will be noted that Bishop Butler phrased his question carefully. He does not suggest that any authority on earth could either judge or depose the Pope but asks whether there is any authority competent to declare that the Pope has lost his powers. The First Vatican Council taught that: "They err from the right path of truth who assert that it is lawful to appeal from the judgments of the Roman Pontiffs to an Ecumenical Council, as to an authority higher than that of the Roman Pontiff." [32] Canon Law states clearly: *Prima sedes a nemine iudicatur*—"The first see can be judged by no one." (Canon 1556) On the other hand Canon 2314 states that: "All apostates from the Christian faith, and all heretics and schismatics: (1) are *ipso facto* excommunicated; (2) if after due warning they fail to amend, they are to be deprived of any benefice, dignity, pension, office, or other position which they may have in the Church, they are to be declared infamous, and clerics after a repetition of the warning are to be deposed.''

Clearly, if the Pope came into one of these categories he would incur the appropriate penalty—as a cleric he would be deposed but who could depose him as he has no superior? Theologians have answered this question in two ways. One school of thought, represented by St. Robert Bellarmine, taught that a heretical pope would be judged by God and cease *per se* to be pope: "The manifestly heretical pope ceases *per se* to be pope and head as he ceases *per se* to be a Christian and member of the Church, and therefore he can be judged and punished by the Church. This is the teaching of all the early Fathers."[33] The man the Church would be judging and punishing would not be the Pope, he would not even be a Catholic.

This is also the view taken in the classic manual on Canon Law by F. X. Wernz, rector of the Gregorian University and Jesuit General from 1906 to 1914. His work was revised by P. Vidal and last republished in 1952.[34]

The fact that the Pope had been deposed by God for heresy would need to be made known to the Church. This could be done by the declaration of a General Council. Cardinal Torquemada makes it clear that the Pope would not actually be judged by the Council—a Council cannot judge a pope nor is there any appeal from a pope to a Council. It would be a "declaratory sentence," a declaration that the Pope has lost his office through heresy or schism. "Properly speaking, the Pope is not deposed by the Council because of heresy but rather he is declared not to be pope since he fell openly into heresy and remains obstinate and hardened in heresy."[35]

Wernz-Vidal explain the position in very similar terms, i. e. the Pope is not deposed in virtue of the sentence of the Council but "the General Council declares the fact of the crime by which the heretical pope has separated himself from the Church and deprived himself of his dignity."[36]

In other words, the sentence merely declares publicly that the Pope has already been deposed: it is not the sentence which deposes him.

An important group of theologians including Cajetan, Suarez, and two Spanish Dominicans who were prominent in the debates at the Council of Trent—Melchior Cano and Dominic Soto, held a contrary view which was that it was the sentence of the Council which deprived the Pope of his office. This view does not appear tenable subsequent to the teaching of Vatican I which has already been cited, i. e. that there is no appeal from the judgment of a pope to a General Council. However, even the view that the General Council does not depose the Pope, but merely declares him to be deposed, raises extremely difficult problems. Who would summon a General Council since this is the prerogative of the Pope? What if the Pope could be persuaded to summon it but then refused to accept its decision? Fortunately, Pope John XXII submitted to the commission of theologians which declared his views on the Judgment to be heretical. Sixtus V died before his erroneous version of the Vulgate could be promulgated. The hypothesis of a heretical pope who either refused to summon a Council or refused to submit to its judgment, and did not die in the opportune manner of Pope Sixtus V, is one which would give even the very best theologians a great deal of food for thought. No attempt will be made to solve it here as it is only a hypothesis. The purpose of raising the matter of a papal deposition is to demonstrate that not only is it quite legitimate to resist the Pope if he is using his power to destroy the Church but that the far more serious step of actually deposing the Pope has been a matter for free debate among theologians.

Conclusion

The only possible conclusion to be drawn from the evidence provided in this appendix is that a Catholic has the right and sometimes the duty to oppose papal teaching or legislation which is manifestly unjust, contrary to the faith, or harmful to the Church. Such resistance has occurred during the history of the Church. Such a refusal could only be justified in the most exceptional circumstances when the fact that the subject was right and the Pope was wrong was not just probable but manifest. The conditions which Cardinal Newman set out as necessary preparation for such resistance should be observed stringently.

History must decide whether Archbishop Lefebvre had sufficient grounds for his refusal to obey Pope Paul VI. In the case of Bishop Robert Grosseteste there can be no reasonable doubt but that he was right and Pope Innocent IV wrong. What has happened once can always happen again and we can say with the saintly English Bishop, and in perfect loyalty to the Holy See: "God forbid that to any who are truly united to Christ, not willing in any way to go against His will, this See and those who preside in it should be a cause of falling away or apparent schism, by commanding such men to do what is opposed to Christ's will."

NOTES

CE *The Catholic Encyclopedia* (New York, 1913).

1. A comprehensive selection of citations from all the principal authorities is provided in an article by Fr. Raymond Dulac in the *Courrier de Rome*, No. 15, to which full acknowledgment is given.
2. ST, II-II, Q. XXXIII, a. VII, ad.5.
3. ST, II-II, Q. CIV, art.V, ad. 3.
4. *The Devastated Vineyard* (Franciscan Herald Press, 1973), pp. 3-4.
5. Ibid., p. 5.
6. *Dictionnaire de Théologie Catholique*, XIV, 1303, col.2.
7. Denzinger, 1827.
8. C. Butler, *The Vatican Council* (London, 1930), II, 80.
9. Ibid., pp. 84-85.
10. J. D. Mansi, *Sacrorum conciliorum nova et amplissa collectio* (Paris, 1857-1927), LII, 715.
11. Ibid.
12. *Difficulties of Anglicans* (London, 1876), p. 256.
13. Ibid., pp. 257-258.
14. Ibid., pp. 260-261.
15. Ibid., p. 261.

16. Ibid.
17. CE, XII, 269-270.
18. *Summa de Ecclesia* (Venice, 1560), lib. iv, parg. ii, cap. 11.
19. *De charitate, Disputatio XII de schismate, sectio I* (Opera Omnia, Paris, 1858), 12, 733ff.
20. K. Rahner, *Studies in Modern Theology* (Herder, 1965), pp. 394-395.
21. Ibid., p. 397.
22. CE, XII, 263, col. 2.
23. CE, I, 395, col. 2.
24. E. John, *The Popes* (London, 1964), p. 253.
25. CE, II, 412, col. 1.
26. *A Catholic Commentary on Holy Scripture* (London, 1953), p. 1116.
27. ST, II-II, Q. XXXIII, art. 5.
28. *De Fide*, disp. X, sect. VI, n. 16.
29. *Obras de Francisco de Vitoria*, pp. 486-487.
30. *De Summo pontifice* (Paris, 1870), lib. II, cap. 29.
31. *The Tablet*, 11 September 1965, p. 996.
32. D. 1830.
33. Bellarmine, *De Summo pontifice*, n. 30, lib. II, cap. 30.
34. Wernz-Vidal, *Jus Canonicum* (Rome, 1952).
35. *Summa de Ecclesia*, n. 18, lib.II, cap. 102.
36. Wernz-Vidal, *Jus Canonicum* (Rome, 1943), II, 518.

VATICAN II MORE IMPORTANT THAN NICEA

(This appendix originally appeared as an editorial by Jean Madiran in *Itinéraires* for November 1975.)

The truth is out at last: "The Second Vatican Council has no less authority and in certain respects is even more important than that of Nicea."* So speaks the new religion. Indeed it was a logical necessity that one day it should openly avow its ambition and its arrogance. This avowal is of great significance. The Council of Nicea is the first General Council. It lasted from May to June 325, it condemned the heresy of Arius; that is to say, it affirmed dogmatically the divinity of Our Lord Jesus Christ. It also promulgated the Nicene Creed, the first part of the *Credo* of the Mass where the Son of God is proclaimed consubstantial with the Father.**

The Second Vatican Council promulgated no infallible and irreformable teaching. It was pastoral and not dogmatic. But we have seen clearly that in reality it has become the standard practice to impart to the pastoral novelties of Vatican II as much authority and more importance than the dogmatic definitions of previous councils. Here, then, we witness this practice of conferring prestige by sleight of hand and then announcing it in formal terms in a categorically affirmative text. No matter how exalted the man whose signature adorns this text it is still inadequate to transform falsehood into truth. But it provides incontrovertible proof that this idea truly represents the thinking of the party now holding power in the Church.

Those who cherish and propagate this arrogant idea are the promoters, authors, and actors of the Second Vatican Council. It is their own work that they place on a higher level than the work of Nicea. They consider themselves to have

*A claim made by Pope Paul VI.

**Since the Council of Nicea the word "consubstantial" has been a touchstone of orthodoxy. It has been removed from the translation of the Creed currently in use in English-speaking countries.

held a *more important* council! They are not simply smug in their illusion; they proclaim it with an absolute assurance. After all, we know how consistent their scheming has been. Before Vatican II they announced the modest intention of holding the most important council yet to take place. Evidently, if it is more important than Nicea it must be the most important council in history!

It was only possible to entertain the idea of organizing a council of greater importance than any yet held by totally eclipsing every vestige of filial piety towards the history of the Church. It is nothing less than an abuse of power, a public fault, a scandal, to persist in this delusion after the event, confident of having succeeded, and to seek to impose this idea on others under threat of excommunication.

The pastoral novelties of Vatican II having been declared more important than the dogmatic definitions of previous councils, it follows that henceforth it is more serious to dispute the most trivial of these reforms than to reject an irreformable dogma. The conciliar reforms are so transitory that they are constantly becoming obsolete, moving along with the current, with the course of evolution. But Mgr. Lefebvre is pronounced outside the communion of the Church if he so much as questions their value. At the same time those who deny the virginal conception of Our Lord Jesus Christ, and those who teach that the Mass is no more than a simple commemoration, are still very much part of that communion. It is a novelty to define communion with the Church on such a basis. This is no longer the Catholic communion and so it is inevitable that sooner or later true Catholics must be excluded from it.

Although you are free to "re-interpret" every revealed dogma you are now obliged to venerate as beyond criticism the human novelties introduced into the government of the Church by the conciliar spirit. Is this clear?

However, criticism of the Council and its spirit is not ruled out providing it is to the effect that Vatican II was not sufficiently revolutionary, too timid in its innovations, too conservative, too attached to the apostolic tradition. On the same principle, there has been no condemnation of the new "music-hall" Masses with erotic dancers and Marxist songs as a deviation from the Mass of Pope Paul VI. Mass can be celebrated in any way at all as long as it is not according to the Roman Missal. Similarly, it is permissible to deride the Council as long as this is done in the interests of innovation, with a progressive intention. For although the Second Vatican Council is more important than the Council of Nicea, on the other hand it is less important than the "conciliar-evolution" to which it has given birth.

We must not be duped by the apparent concession which permits Nicea to retain at least as much authority as Vatican II, if not as much importance. This concession of "as much authority," now accepted at its face value, is in itself an insulting comparison. A pastoral council does not have as much authority as a dogmatic council. To recognize it as having as much is arbitrarily to grant the same authority to a transitory reform as to an irreformable dogma. It is subversive.

But it hasn't stopped there. We have been able to see where they would like to lead us since the years 1962-1966. When the review *Itinéraires* declared that it accepted the decisions of the latest council "in the context and living continuity of other councils" and "in conformity with preceding councils and all the teaching of the Magisterium," it was condemned by the French hierarchy on the grounds that this constituted a "rejection" of the Council. The review *Itinéraires* was condemned because, not having appreciated that Vatican II wished itself to be "more important than Nicea," it presumed that Vatican II must be interpreted according to the traditional Catholic rule of conformity to previous councils. This is the opposite of what the party in power intends to impose upon us. Nothing is to be retained from previous councils and the teaching of the Magisterium beyond what can be reconciled with the process of "conciliar evolution," the offspring of Vatican II.

We cannot go along with this.

Jean Madiran

Archbishop Lefebvre and Religious Liberty

Mgr. Lefebvre's opponents have accused him of rejecting the documents of Vatican II. The truth is that he signed fourteen of the sixteen documents and declined to sign two. The first of these, the Pastoral Constitution on the Church in the Modern World (*Gaudium et Spes*), does not directly contradict Catholic teaching but is so uncatholic in its ethos that it is hard to understand how any self-respecting bishop could have put his signature to it. A few of the deficiencies of this document can be discovered by referring to the entry *Gaudium et Spes* in the index of *Pope John's Council*.

Mgr. Lefebvre also refused to sign the Declaration on Religious Liberty (*Dignitatis Humanae*). In this case his objections were doctrinal. The documents of Vatican II come within the category of the Church's Ordinary Magisterium which can contain error in the case of a novelty which conflicts with previous teaching.* The Declaration contains a number of statements which it is not easy to reconcile with traditional papal teaching and in Article 2 there are two words, "or publicly," which appear to be a direct contradiction of previous teaching.

Paul H. Hallett of the *National Catholic Register* is probably America's most respected and erudite Catholic lay-journalist. On 3 July 1977 he noted that:

> **The Declaration on Religious Liberty is not a statement of faith. Neither does it appeal to the traditional teaching of the Church on religious freedom. Hence it is not disloyalty to faith to seek a clarification of its ambiguities. Nothing is gained by pretending that they do not exist.**

Mr. Hallett then went on to examine some of the unsatisfactory passages in the Declaration and concluded that "it

---

*See the *Approaches* supplement, *The Ordinary Magisterium of the Church Theologically Considered* by Dom Paul Nau, O. S. B.

is necessary that some things be made clearer and more in accord with tradition than they have been in the Religious Liberty Declaration." Unfortunately, the majority of Mgr. Lefebvre's critics, including "conservative Catholics," have been so eager to denounce the Archbishop that they have made no attempt to examine his case. Had they followed Mr. Hallett's example they would have found that there is a good deal to be said in favor of the Archbishop's position, and not only on the religious liberty issue. However, strident denunciations cost far less effort than careful research.

Pope Leo XIII warned in his encyclical *Libertas Humana* that there are certain so-called liberties which modern society takes for granted that every man possesses as a right. This is due to the fact that Liberals have been so successful in promoting their doctrines that some of their basic tenets are now accepted as self-evident truths even by Catholics. The essence of Liberalism is that the individual human being has the right to decide for himself the norms by which he will regulate his life. He has the right to be his own arbiter as to what is right and what is wrong. He is under no obligation to subject himself to any external authority. In the Liberal sense, liberty of conscience is the *right* of an individual to think and believe whatever he wants, even in religion and morality; to express his views publicly and persuade others to adopt them by using word of mouth, the public press, or any other means. The only limitation to be placed upon him is that he should refrain from causing a breach of public order. This means that the state must grant equal rights to all religions.

Pope Leo XIII condemned this theory in *Libertas Humana* when he taught that reason itself forbids the state "to adopt a line of action which would end in godlessness—namely to treat the various religions (as they call them) alike, and to bestow upon them promiscuously equal rights and privileges." Thus, a state in which Catholicism was the religion of the overwhelming majority of the inhabitants should be a Catholic state. In such a state civil law should be based upon the law of God, religious ceremonies at state functions should be conducted in accordance with the Catholic liturgy, and the Catholic Church should be given a privileged status in such spheres as education. This is because all authority is derived from God. Pope Leo XIII wrote in *Immortale Dei:*

For God alone is the true and supreme Lord of the world. Everything, without exception, must be subject to Him, and must serve Him, so that whosoever holds the right to govern holds it from one sole and single source, namely God, the Sovereign Ruler of all.

This is the teaching that forms the basis of the papal condemnation of democracy in the sense that this word is used today. The Popes have condemned democracy if by that term it is meant that those who govern do so as delegates of the people, that authority derives from the people, and that the law of the state *must* reflect what the majority of the people desires. According to this view, if the majority of the people wishes to permit divorce, abortion, euthanasia, or the sale of pornography, then the laws of the state must be adjusted accordingly. The teaching of the Church, as has just been shown in the quotation from *Immortale Dei,* is that authority is derived from God and that those who govern do so as His delegates. The Church is not opposed to democracy in the sense that the people choose those who govern them by means of a vote based on national suffrage. The Church is not committed to any particular form of government. She will co-operate with an absolute monarch or a parliamentary democracy. What She insists upon is that those who govern, however they are chosen, exercise their authority in accordance with the law of God, which no individual and no state can possibly have a *right* to violate. Given that God is, as Pope Leo XIII taught, "the Sovereign Ruler of all," the idea that a breach of His law can be a *right* and not an *abuse* is nonsensical. All men are subject to the power of Jesus Christ. Commenting on this in his encyclical *Quas Primas,* Pope Pius XI explained:

Nor is there any difference in this matter between the individual

and the family or the state; for all men, whether individually or collectively, are under the dominion of Christ. In Him is the salvation of the individual, in Him is the salvation of Society.

Given the existence of a Catholic state, there arises the question of the correct attitude of the civil authorities to minority religions. Writing in the September 1950 issue of the *American Ecclesiastical Review,* Mgr. George W. Shea explained:

> **Before another word is said on this subject, let it be noted at once that no Catholic holds or may hold that the state would be called upon to impose the Catholic faith on dissident citizens. Reverence for the individual conscience forbids this, and the very nature of religion and of the act of faith. If these be not voluntary they are nought.**

It is a fundamental principle of Catholic theology that no one must ever be forced to act against his conscience either in public or private (unfortunately this principle has not always been respected in the history of the Church). It is equally true that no one must be prevented from acting in accordance with his conscience in private (providing that no breach of the natural law is involved). Thus, for the most part, a policy of toleration towards the Jews was followed in the papal states. Jews were allowed to meet together for private worship but were not allowed to hold ceremonies in public or to proselytize among Catholics.* This last point brings us to the crucial issue in this appendix, i. e. that it has been the consistent teaching of the Popes that a Catholic state has the right to restrict the public expression of heresy. Thus, in a Catholic state, members of a Protestant sect could not be compelled to assist at Mass but they could be prevented from holding outdoor services, putting up notices outside their places of worship designating them as such, or advertising their services. This was the case in Malta when I served there with the British Army. Protestant ministers were

---

*See the article, "Toleration" in *The Catholic Encyclopedia.*

not so much as allowed to wear a Roman collar in the street—
a ruling which even applied to military chaplains. Similarly,
in a Catholic state, a Protestant could not be compelled to
profess belief in transubstantiation but could be prevented
from attacking the doctrine in public, either by the written
or the spoken word. Thus Father Francis J. Connell, C.SS.R.,
explained in 1949:

> Hence, just as the state can prohibit people from preaching the
> doctrine of free love, so it can prohibt them from preaching, to the
> detriment of Catholic citizens, the doctrine that Christ is not present
> in the Holy Eucharist. [1]

Father Connell also pointed out that although Catholic
states had the right to repress heresy this was not a duty.
Where a large minority religion existed within a Catholic state
more harm than good might result from attempting to limit
the public expression of heresy. In such cases heresy would
be tolerated as the lesser of two evils, e. g. to avoid the type
of civil war which occurred in attempting to suppress Protestantism in France. However, the distinction between what is
tolerated and what is a *right* is both obvious and important.

To sum up, the consensus of papal teaching is that a
Catholic state has the right but not the obligation to restrict
the public expression of heresy. Where repression would
cause more harm than good, toleration is the better policy.
The criterion which Catholic rulers must use in deciding their
policy towards religious minorities is the common good. The
purpose of civil society is to promote the common temporal
good of its citizens—that is, the good of its citizens in the
present life. But in view of the elevation of man to the supernatural life the common good must take account of man's
supernatural destiny. Hence, a Catholic government must do
all in its power to assist its citizens to observe the supernatural law of Christ. This can include measures to protect them
from exposure to heresy or immorality. Liberals claim that
any citizen has the right to propagate his views by any outlet
of the media providing this does not result in a breach of

public order. Paul Hallett noted that this can have too re-
stricted a meaning. In his article of 3 July 1977 he noted:

> It could and should include protection against anything that seri-
> ously threatens the welfare of the people. Thus a truly Christian state
> would repress the televising of a play denying the divinity of Christ,
> even though no palpable disturbance resulted.
>
> In his encyclical of 1864, *Quanta Cura,* Pius IX reprimanded
> those who, "contrary to the teaching of Holy Scripture and the Fa-
> thers, deliberately affirm that the best form of government is that
> in which no obligation is recognized in the civil power to punish, with
> specific penalties, the violators of the Catholic religion, save insofar
> as the public peace demands."

There are few Catholic countries today in which any attempt to restrict the public expression of heresy would not
do more harm than good but this does not change the fact
that a Catholic government has the right to take such action
where the common good demands it. Father Connell writes:

> But it is fully within their [civil rulers] right to restrict and to pre-
> vent public functions and activities of false religions which are likely to
> be detrimental to the spiritual welfare of the Catholic citizens or in-
> sulting to the true religion of Christ. Nowadays, it is true, greater evils
> would often follow such a course of action than would ensue if com-
> plete tolerance were granted; *but the principle is immutable.*[2] (My
> emphasis.)

The Church has frequently been accused of observing
double standards by claiming the same rights as other religions in such countries as the U.S.A. where She is in a minority and demanding a privileged status in such countries as
Malta or Spain where She is in the majority. Even those who
do not accept Her claim to be the One True Church should
at least be able to see that, in virtue of this claim, Her attitude is consistent and is based upon the rights of truth. Pope
Pius XII taught in his discourse *Ecco che gia un anno,* of 6

October 1946, that:

> The Catholic Church, as we have already said, is a perfect society and has as its foundation the truth of Faith infallibly revealed by God. For this reason, that which is opposed to this truth is, necessarily, an error, and the same rights which are objectively recognized for truth cannot be afforded to error. In this manner, liberty of thought and liberty of conscience have their essential limits in the truthfulness of God in Revelation.

This principle that "error has no rights" has been attacked by Liberals, Father John Courtney Murray in particular, on the grounds that error is an abstraction and hence cannot have rights. It was claimed that as only persons or institutions could have rights the formula "error has no rights is meaningless." This argument is not simply specious, it is silly. Father Connell demolished it in an article in the *American Ecclesiastical Review* in 1964:

> Some have tried to argue that while error has no rights, persons inculpably holding erroneous doctrines have the right to hold them. But it must be borne in mind that error can be believed, spread, and activated only by persons and so it is difficult to see what it would mean to say "error has no right to be spread" if one held at the same time "persons can have a right to spread error"—that is if "right" be taken in the same sense in both statements . . . . How can one have a genuine right to believe, spread, or practice what is objectively false or morally wrong? For a genuine right is based on what is objectively true and good. [3]

Such authors as Mgr. Shea and Father Connell faithfully reflect the teaching of the Popes who have condemned in the most forceful terms the belief that the state has no right to repress public heresy and that truth and error should be accorded equal right. Pope Pius VII termed it "disastrous and ever-to-be deplored heresy" (letter to Mgr. de Boulogne); Pope Gregory XVI condemned it as "the insanity" (*Mirari*

Vos); Pope Pius IX termed it "a monstrous error" (*Qui Pluribus*), "most pernicious to the Catholic Church, and to the salvation of souls" (*Quanta Cura*), "the liberty of perdition" (*Quanta Cura*), something which will "corrupt the morals and minds of the people" (*Syllabus of Errors*), something which propagates "the pest of indifferentism" (*Syllabus*); Pope Leo XIII termed it "a public crime" (*Immortale Dei*), "atheism, however it may differ from its name" (*Immortale Dei*), "contrary to reason" (*Libertas*).

Obviously, the insistence of the Popes upon the rights of truth is anathema to contemporary Liberalism in which unrestricted Liberty, including the liberty to propagate error, is the supreme norm. This liberty had been proclaimed in the Masonically inspired Rights of Man of the French Revolution and was subjected to one restriction only, the demands of public order. Papal teaching on the right of a Catholic state to repress error was embarrassing to such Catholic Liberals as Father Murray who wished to make Catholicism acceptable to contemporary American society. He was, no doubt, sincere in his efforts and considered them to be for the good of the Church. His principal argument was that the teaching of the Popes which has just been cited was related to a particular period in the history of the Church and was not of permanent validity. He was answered by no less an authority than Cardinal Ottaviani in an important article which appeared in the May 1953 issue of the *American Ecclesiastical Review:*

> The first fault of these persons consists in their failure to accept fully the *arma veritatis* and the teaching which the Roman Pontiffs during the past century, and particularly the reigning Pontiff Pius XII, have given to Catholics on this subject in encyclical letters, allocutions, and instructions of various kinds.
>
> To justify themselves these people assert that in the body of teaching imparted within the Church there are to be distinguished two elements, the one permanent, and the other transient. The latter is supposed to be due to the reflection of particular contemporary conditions.
>
> Unfortunately, they carry this tactic so far as to apply it to the

principles taught in pontifical documents, *principles on which the teachings of the Popes have remained constant so as to make these principles a part of the patrimony of Catholic doctrine.* (My emphasis.)

DIGNITATIS HUMANAE
The Declaration on Religious Liberty
of the Second Vatican Council

This Declaration is one of the most important documents of the Council. The ecumenical euphoria which followed Vatican II would not have been possible without it. No substantial ecumenical progress could have been made while the Church still insisted upon the right of a Catholic state to repress the public expression of heresy.

Paul Blanshard was America's most virulent anti-Catholic polemicist in the years preceding the Council. His particular *bête noire* was the Church's teaching on religious liberty. The fact that he had much to say in praise of *Dignitatis Humanae* (which will be abbreviated DH from now on) is a damning indictment of the extent to which the traditional teaching has been compromised. Blanshard claimed that DH "marked a great advance in Catholic policy, perhaps the greatest single advance in principle during all four sessions of the Council."[4] He was sufficiently perceptive to note that Article Two of the Declaration contained "the best paragraphs."[5] This is also the view of Mgr. Pietro Pavan, one of the theologians who collaborated with Fr. Murray in drafting and defending the Declaration. Mgr. Pavan wrote the commentary on DH which appears in Father Vorgrimler's highly praised *Commentary on the Documents of Vatican II.* (This commentary is highly praised because it endorses all the standard Liberal assumptions on the merits of the Council.) Mgr. Pavan states in his commentary that: "Article 2 is undoubtedly the most important article of the Declaration."[6] It could certainly be considered the most important article in any document of the Council as, until it is corrected by the Magisterium, it represents not simply a contradiction of consistently re-iterated, and possibly infallible, papal teaching but an implicit repudiation of the Kingship of Christ. Article 2 reads:

> This Vatican Synod declares that the human person has a right to religious freedom. This freedom means that all men are to be immune from coercion on the part of individuals or of social groups and of any human power, in such wise that in matters religious no one is to be forced to act in a manner contrary to his own beliefs.

Up to this point everything can be reconciled with the traditional doctrine. Article 2 continues:

> Nor is anyone to be restrained from acting in accordance with his own beliefs, whether privately . . .

The traditional teaching has still not been violated—but now comes the break with tradition:

> . . . or publicly, whether alone or in association with others, within due limits.

The phrase "within due limits" could have maintained harmony with previous papal teaching had these "due limits" been specified as "the common good." However, in conformity with the Masonic *Declaration of the Rights of Man* the "due limits" are later specified as "public order."
The Declaration continues:

> The Synod further declares that the right to religious freedom has its foundation in the very dignity of the human person, as this dignity is known through the revealed word of God and by reason itself.

It is important to bear in mind that from the moment the words "or publicly" were used, the term "religious freedom" in this Declaration includes freedom from restraint in the external forum, subject only to the requirements of public order. The sentence just cited is, then, neither in harmony with the revealed word of God nor reason. If there is one doctrine which is taught clearly throughout the Old Testament, it is that no one has a right to express religious error in the public forum—the penalty, mandated by God, was death. Are we to believe that God commanded men to be put to death for exercising what He had established as a human right? Nor is there anything reasonable in claiming that men have a natural right to teach error in public as long as this does not result in a breach of public order. The civil laws of slander and libel make this clear.

Mgr. Pavan comments:

. . . the right to religious freedom must be regarded as *a fundamental right of the human person* or as *a natural right, that is one grounded in the very nature of man*, as the Declaration itself repeats several times.[7] (Emphasis in original.)

Contrast this with a statement by Father Connell:

Beyond doubt, the expression "freedom of worship" is ordinarily understood by our non-Catholic fellow-citizens, when they advocate the "four freedoms," in the sense that every one has a natural God-given right to accept and to practice whatever form of religion appeals to him individually. No Catholic can in conscience defend such an idea of freedom of religious worship. For, according to Catholic principles, the only religion that has a right to exist is the religion that God revealed and made obligatory on all men; hence, man has a natural and God-given freedom to embrace only the true religion. One who sincerely believes himself bound to practice some form of non-Catholic religion is in conscience obliged to do so; but this subjective obligation, based on an erroneous conscience, does not give him a genuine right. A real right is something objective based on truth. Accordingly, a Catholic may not defend freedom of religious worship to the extent of denying that a Catholic government has the right, absolutely speaking, to restrict the activities of non-Catholic denominations in order to protect the Catholic citizens from spiritual harm.[8]

The Vatican II Declaration continues:

This right of the human person to religious freedom is to be recognized in the constitutional law whereby society is governed. This is to become a civil right.

Contrast this with the proposition condemned by Pope Pius IX in *Quanta Cura*, censuring those who:

... fear not to uphold that erroneous opinion most pernicious to the Catholic Church, and to the salvation of souls, which was called by Our Predecessor, Gregory XVI (lately quoted), the insanity (*deliramentum*) (Encyclical 13 August 1832): namely, "that liberty of conscience and of worship is the peculiar (or inalienable) right of every man, which should be proclaimed by law . . . ."

What Fr. Connell had stated no Catholic may defend is precisely what the Declaration defends and proclaims as a right. Thus Mgr. Pavan states in his commentary that: "In the religious sphere no man may be compelled to act against his conscience; and *no one may be prevented from acting according to his conscience.*" (My emphasis.)

It is not simply traditionalists who fail to see how the teaching of *Quanta Cura* and *Dignitatis Humanae* can be reconciled, how the latter can be said to be a development of the former. It is also very significant, in view of the important place held by *Quanta Cura* and the *Syllabus* in papal teaching on the subject of religious liberty, that *neither is referred to* in any of the footnotes to *Dignitatis Humanae*. In the many references to the teaching of "recent popes," not one of the texts cited affirms the right to religious freedom in the external forum. The breach with the traditional teaching can be narrowed down to two words in the Latin text of *Dignitatis Humanae*, "*et publice*" ("and in public"). Among the many non-traditionalists who have admitted the difficulty of proving a legitimate development between the traditional teaching and that of Vatican II are four Council *periti* (experts) whose testimony is of the very highest importance—the first three being the experts most influential in drafting the text of the Declaration itself. These experts are Fr. John Courtney Murray, S. J., Mgr. Pietro Pavan, Fr. Yves Congar, O. P., and Fr. Hans Küng.

Father Murray admitted openly that no one had been able to supply an explanation of how the teaching of *Dignitatis Humanae* constituted a development. He simply asserted that it was a development:

> The course of the development between the *Syllabus of Errors* (1864) and *Dignitatis Humanae Personae* (1965) still remains to be explained by theologians.[9]

Mgr. Pavan concedes that no previous papal teaching *agrees* with *Dignitatis Humanae*. The best he can come up with is that the teaching of some recent Popes "tended towards" it, including in this list Popes Pius XI and XII who had specifically re-affirmed the traditional position.

Mgr. Pavan writes:

> . . . there had, of course, been a doctrinal development, but that its last phase tended towards what was said in the Council documents, if it did not actually agree with it.

Fr. Congar writes, apropos Article 2 of *Dignitatis Humanae:*

> It cannot be denied that a text like this does *materially* say something different from the *Syllabus* of 1864, and even almost the opposite of propositions 15 and 77-9 of the document.[10]

An interview with Hans Küng published in the *National Catholic Reporter* on 21 October 1977 contained the following passage:

> In recent books he has stated that while conservatives do not have the right answers, they are often asking the right questions. And Lefebvre is no exception.
> "I think he is wrong, but nevertheless what he's arguing are *theoretically unresolved questions.*"

Lefebvre has every right to question the Council's Declaration on Religious Freedom, Küng says, because *Vatican II completely reversed Vatican I's position without explanation.*

"The Council evaporated the problem," Küng insists, because it called into question the doctrine of infallibility . . . He reminisces over the late night conversations with Father John Courtney Murray (the American who guided Council thought on religious liberty):

"The Council bishops said, 'It's too complicated to explain *how you can go from a condemnation of religious liberty to an affirmation of it purely by the notion of progress.*' "

For Küng the issue is still unresolved and cannot be settled without looking at permanence, continuity and the infallibility of doctrine. And to do that the bishops may well have to say that *what they uttered infallibly in the 19th century or before simply does not hold in the twentieth.* (My emphasis.)

Perhaps the most damning indictment of *Dignitatis Humanae* is the praise it received from the virulently anti-Catholic Paul Blanshard, who described it as marking "a great advance in Catholic policy, perhaps the greatest single advance in principle during all four sessions of the Council."[11]

The Declaration is commended by Blanshard because:

Catholicism after centuries of delay has finally caught up at least in part to the United Nations, to Western Protestantism, to Western democracies, and to the social democratic parties of Europe in advocating what had been written into the American Constitution more than 175 years before . . . The final statement on religious liberty was an important achievement. It will make the struggle for religious liberty throughout the world easier. From now on every libertarian can cite an official Catholic pronouncement endorsing the principle of liberty. [12]

But Blanshard positively exults in the fact that what has taken place is not a development but a *change* in doctrine. Vatican II had adopted Blanshard's position, he is pleased, but he is justifiably insistent that it can only have done this by reversing previous Catholic teaching. Having dedicated himself to opposing that teaching no one was better placed to know precisely what that teaching was. Blanshard writes with contempt of attempts to cover up a change in doctrine under the pretext of development. Such attempts are specious at the best and dishonest at the worst. Blanshard writes:

> The star of the American delegation was John Courtney Murray, whose chief function was to give the pedestrian bishops *the right words with which to change some ancient doctrines without admitting that they were being changed.* He built verbal bridges to the modern world very effectively, and the American bishops crossed over them joyously, delighted that they could be good American democrats and Catholic scholars at the same time. Murray argued that certain teachings of past leaders of Catholicism were not applicable at the present time in their original sense, since they had been designed to meet certain historic situations, and those situations had changed. Doctrine, he alleged, could "develop," a polite way of saying that it could change without any necessary admission that it had changed.
>
> This adroit formula for a "changeless" Church was frequently used at Vatican II by theologians who were bound by their Church's veneration for tradition, but it was not always accepted as worthy of honest men even by Jesuit leaders whose institutional past is commonly associated with such linguistic manipulation. In another connection, Father John C. Ford, S. J., of the Catholic University of America, declared after the end of the Council: "I do not consider it theologically legitimate or even decent and honest; to contradict a doctrine and then disguise the contradiction under the rubric: growth and evolution." [13] (My emphasis.)

Blanshard remarked that:

> I am often asked: Have you changed your opinion about the Catholic Church? The answer is "Yes," but only to the extent that the Catholic Church has changed. [14]

Although my treatment of this important issue has necessarily been brief, sufficient evidence should have been presented to make it clear that Paul Hallett was perfectly correct to state in his *National Catholic Register* article that: "Hence it is not disloyal to faith to seek a clarification of its ambiguities. Nothing is to be gained by pretending they do not exist." It should also be clear that the many Catholics (not all of them Liberals) who sneer at Mgr. Lefebvre, and reject his criticisms of the Declaration without having the courtesy and fairness to examine them, are acting most unjustly. It requires little effort and little integrity to condemn the Archbishop unheard simply because he criticizes Vatican II. Nor does it take much courage to do so, particularly when those who attack him can be virtually certain that no opportunity will be provided in the official Catholic press for the Archbishop's side of the case to be presented. Ironically, the Declaration of Religious Liberty is being defended by denying the Archbishop the liberty to express his views in public. In order to assist those who are fair-minded enough to study both sides of the case I have written a book on the subject of *Dignitatis Humanae* which should be published in 1980.

This appendix can best be concluded by quoting the final paragraph from Paul Hallett's 3 July 1977 article.

The Religious Liberty Declaration contains many excellent statements of principle, which need to be asserted against the rampant atheism that threatens all religion. All this is to the good. But for the protection of religion and not exclusively the Catholic religion—it is necessary that some things be made clearer and more in accord with tradition than they have been in the Religious Liberty Declaration.

NOTES

The American Ecclesiastical Review has been abbreviated as AER.

1. "Discussion of Government Repression of Heresy," *Proceedings III* (March 1949), pp. 98-101.
2. AER, No. 119, October 1948, p. 250.
3. AER, No. 151, February 1964, p. 128.
4. *Paul Blanshard on Vatican II* (Beacon Press, Boston, 1966), p. 339.
5. Ibid., p. 89.
6. H. Vorgrimler, ed., *Commentary on the Documents of Vatican II,* IV, 64.
7. Ibid., p. 65.
8. AER, No. 109, October 1943, p. 255.
9. W. Abbott, *The Documents of Vatican II* (America Press, 1967), p. 673.
10. *Challenge to the Church* (London, 1977), p. 44.
11. Blanshard, p. 339.
12. Ibid., pp. 88-89.
13. Ibid., pp. 87-88.
14. Ibid., Preface.

The Legal Background to the Erection and Alleged Suppression of the Society of Saint Pius X

by the Reverend Dr. Boyd A. Cathey

The first handful of seminarians of what was to become the Society of St. Pius X did their studies in the University of Fribourg. These young men had sought out Archbishop Marcel Lefebvre, then in semi-retirement in Rome (1969), and with him as superior established a house of formation in Fribourg, with the encouragement of the bishop of the diocese, François Charrière (cf. Letter to Archbishop Lefebvre, 18 August 1970). Within a few months it became evident that like other Catholic universities in the years following Vatican II, Fribourg was succumbing to Modernism. The decision was taken to form a religious institute, with a proper house of studies, at Ecône, in the Canton of Valais. Permission granted by Bishop Nestor Adam of Sion, Switzerland, the seminary opened its doors in October, 1970.

On 1 November 1970 the Society of St. Pius X was erected canonically in the diocese of Lausanne, Geneva, and Fribourg by Bishop François Charrière, under the provisions of canons 673-674, and 488: º3, º4, for a period of six years *ad experimentum*. The Society's statutes specify that it is a priestly society "of common life without vows, in the tradition of the Foreign Missionaries of Paris" (cf. Statutes of the Society of St. Pius X, No. 1).

Bishop Charrière's decree of erection approving these statutes reads as follows:

Given the encouragements expressed by Vatican Council II, in the decree *Optatam totius,* concerning international seminaries and the distribution of the clergy;

Given the urgent necessity for the formation of zealous and generous priests conforming to the directives of the cited decree;

Confirming that the Statutes of the Priestly Society correspond to its goals:*

We, François Charrière, Bishop of Lausanne, Geneva, and Fribourg, the Holy Name of God invoked and all canonical prescriptions observed, decree what follows:

1. The "International Priestly Society of St. Pius X" is erected in our diocese as a *"Pia Unio"* (Pious Union).**

2. The seat of the Society is fixed as the Maison Saint Pie X (St. Pius X House), 50, rue de la Vignettaz, in our episcopal city of Fribourg.

3. We approve and confirm the Statutes, here joined, of the Society for a period of six years *ad experimentum,* which will be able to be renewed for a similar period by tacit approval; after which, the Society can be erected definitely in our diocese by the competent Roman Congregation.

We implore divine blessings on this Priestly Society, that it may attain its principal goal which is the formation of holy priests.

Done at Fribourg, in our palace.

1st November 1970, on the Feast of All Saints,

François Charrière

The activity of the new Society of St. Pius X increased rapidly during the first four years of its existence. Archbishop Lefebvre received encouragement not only from many fellow bishops throughout the world, but also from Cardinal Hildebrando Antoniutti, the Prefect of the Sacred Congregation for Religious, and from Cardinal John Wright, Prefect of the Sacred Congregation for the Clergy.

On 18 February 1971, hardly five months after Ecône

---

*In view of the fact that allegations have been made that Archbishop Lefebvre was never authorized to found a seminary note carefully that the Decree of Erection authorizes the establishment of a "Priestly Society" for "the formation of zealous and generous priests" in an "international seminary."

**The Bishop's use of the expression *"pia unio"* here is a little confusing. A *"pia unio,"* as canons 707-708 make clear, is not normally a moral person. It means a lay association. A religious "society of the common life," as the approved statutes of the Society of St. Pius X specify it is, described in canon 673, is really very much like a religious institute but without public vows. It is possible that Bishop Charriere intended here *"pia domus"* since it is quite normal to erect a *"pia domus"* as the first step towards a new religious institute.

opened its doors, Cardinal Wright wrote Archbishop Lefebvre (translated from the Latin):

> With great joy I received your letter, in which your Excellency informs me of your news and especially of the Statutes of the Priestly Society. As Your Excellency explains, this Association, which by your action, received on 1 November 1970, the approbation of His Excellency François Charrière, Bishop of Fribourg, has already exceeded the frontiers of Switzerland, and several Ordinaries in different parts of the world praise and approve it. All of this and especially the wisdom of the norms which direct and govern this Association give much reason to hope for its success.
>
> As for this Sacred Congregation, the Priestly Society will certainly be able to conform to the end proposed by the Council, for the distribution of the clergy in the world.
>
> I am respectfully, Your Excellency,
> Yours in the Lord.
>
> J. Card. Wright, Prefect.

With all matters canonically in order before the so-called "suppression" of the Society of St. Pius X on 6 May 1975, newly ordained priests were incardinated into the diocese of Sigüenza-Guadalajara, Spain (by Bishop Laureano Castans Lacoma), and St. Denis de la Réunion (by former Bishop Georges Guibert, C.S.Sp.).

When a man is tonsured, thereby becoming a cleric, he must either be incardinated in a diocese or *"adscriptus"* in a religious institute or a society of the common life (c. 111). The word "incardination" is used only of a diocese, and religious or those seculars who are members of a society of the common life enjoying this privilege are *"adscripti"* not *"incardinati."*

Since the suppression, priests are "adscripted" into the Society, under the provisions of canon 111. As early as 1971 Archbishop Lefebvre had been assured by Cardinal Wright that within a short time the Society of St. Pius X would enjoy the privilege of adscription into the Society.* Moreover, it should be noted that on three occasions before the suppression priests received permission from the Sacred Congregation for Religious for adscription directly into the Society. In the opinion of noted canonists such as Father Emmanuel des Graviers and Don Salvatore di Palma this is sufficient to render the privilege of adscripting into the Society existent.

The success of the Society of St. Pius X could not continue for long without an eventual Modernist counter-attack. Thus, the French Bishops in 1974 labelled the Seminary of the Society a "wildcat" seminary (*"séminaire sauvage"*), an "illegal seminary." In November 1974 Rome sent an Apostolic Visitation which, ironically, only served to confirm the legality of the seminary. Why would Rome send an official Apostolic Visitation, as is normal with new seminaries, if there were no permission for it? Would it not have acted to close the seminary immediately after its foundation in 1970 if there had been some irregularity?

Following the Apostolic Visitation (November 1974), a special Commission of Cardinals was named by Pope Paul VI to "interview" Archbishop Lefebvre. Two long sessions occurred, on 13 February and 3 March 1975. His Excellency was given no transcript nor was he advised he was on trial (cfr. canons 1585: º1, º2142).

The only legal document available to the Commission on which a possible suppression could be based was the favorable Apostolic Visitors' report. Yet it was decided to authorize the "suppression" of the Society of St. Pius X and its seminary based on the Archbishop's "Declaration" of 21 November 1974, which the Commission condemned as "unacceptable to us on all points" (p. 58). Bishop Pierre Mamie, who had recently succeeded Bishop Charrière as Bishop of Lausanne, Geneva, and Fribourg, was accordingly instructed.

On 6 May 1975, Bishop Mamie wrote Archbishop Le-

---

*Cf. letter to Archbishop Lefebvre, 15 May 1971.

febvre: "I retire the acts and concessions granted by my predecessor in that which concerns the Priestly Society of St. Pius X, particularly the Decree of Erection of 1 November 1970." This action was completely illegal. The Society of St. Pius X, according to its Statutes approved by Bishop Charrière, is a priestly society "of common life without vows," coming under the provisions of canons 673-674 and 488, 03,04. As such the Society of St. Pius X could only be suppressed by the Holy See, which alone has the power to suppress such an institute erected under diocesan law (c. 493).

An appeal, protesting Bishop Mamie's illegal action, questioning the strange procedure of the Commission of three Cardinals, and challenging their competence in this matter, was lodged with the Supreme Tribunal of the Apostolic Signatura on 5 June 1975 (Letter of Archbishop Lefebvre to Dino Cardinal Staffa, 21 May 1975; this was followed by the appeal itself on 5 June). It was returned on 10 June, when the Prefect of the Signatura, the late Dino Cardinal Staffa, declared himself "incompetent," under canon 1556, to judge a decision approved *in forma specifica* by the Sovereign Pontiff (*"Prima sedes a nemine judicatur"*).

A second appeal was filed by the Archbishop's advocate, Corrado Bernardini, on 14 June 1975. To prevent its reception, Jean Cardinal Villot, the Secretary of State, personally intervened to interdict any further consideration of the question! (*La Condamnation sauvage de Mgr. Lefebvre*, 6th Edition, August 1976, p. 55, note).

Before analyzing these events, it might be helpful to explain the meaning of a confirmation *in forma specifica.* Dr. Neri Capponi, Professor of Canon Law in the University of Florence, Italy, in a study on the juridical problems in postconciliar legislation, resumes the teaching of canonists in a most important study of the juridical aspects of the postconciliar liturgical reform:*

Some Juridical Considerations on the Reform of the Liturgy. This invaluable study is available from the Angelus Press but readers are warned that it is of a technical nature and would not make easy reading for those unacquainted with Canon Law. It proves conclusively that no legal prohibition exists to prevent any priest celebrating the traditional Mass at any time.

The two forms of pontifical confirmation of acts emanating from inferior organs of government are the *confirmatio in forma communi* and the *confirmatio in forma specifica* respectively.* In the case of a provision *in forma communi* the provision confirmed, as we have seen, does not change its nature. For this reason if the inferior body has presumed to legislate *ultra vires* contrary to a preceding papal or conciliar law, or has sought to introduce principles contrasting with such laws, such legislation remains invalid regarding such part of it as is not in conformity with the higher legislation. But if the confirmation is *in forma specifica* the provision is thereby assumed by the higher authority, who makes it his own, remedying any invalidity it might have. It is presumed, in fact, in such cases that the higher authority is fully cognizant of the *ultra vires* element in the provision and wishes, by making it his own, to confirm it, abrogating or derogating from what had previously been laid down (p. 16).

In the case at hand, this would have involved necessarily a specific confirmation, first of all, of the illegal delegation by the Cardinals to Bishop Mamie of a power he in no way enjoyed, and secondly, of the illegal exercise of that power by Bishop Mamie. Cardinal Staffa seems to have based his written refusal to consider the appeal on this assumption (no doubt, he had other, *unwritten* reasons not to get involved!); "the contested act," he wrote to Mgr. Lefebvre on 10 June, "is only the execution of decisions taken by the Special Commission of three Cardinal Fathers, and approved by the Sovereign Pontiff '*in forma speciali* ' " (Letter cited in Yves Montagne, *L'Evêque suspens*, p. 158.)

This argument, however, doesn't seem to hold up under examination. As the Archbishop's advocate made clear in his second appeal, of 14 June, "the terms of the [Cardinals'] letter of 6 May 1975, that is 'It is with the full approval of His Holiness that we notify you . . . ' do not seem to speak of a specific approbation [that would make the act or decree a true pontifical act] but rather the customary approval which is ordinarily given by His Holiness for all decisions,

*See p. 114 for an explantion of these terms.

whether of Congregations, of the Apostolic Signatura, or of a special Cardinals' Commission." (Note, cited in *L'Evêque suspens*, pp. 159-160). Professor Capponi notes that curial officials tend to presume that certain formulae indicate confirmation *in forma specifica* without it following that the Pope must limit himself to these and that, in a case of doubt, it is presumed that one is dealing with a confirmation *in forma communi* (pp. 16-17).

Moreover, it is evident here that canon 1556 is cited out of its proper context. If we question the legitimacy of the acts of an extraordinary Commission of Cardinals, we do not thereby judge the pope, even if he had approved the Commission's existence or its acts *in forma specifica*. Rather, we question if, in effect, the Commission executed its mandate illegitimately by violating certain canonical prescriptions. According to one standard text on canonical procedure, Lega-Bardocetti (*Commentarius in judicia ecclesiastica*, Rome, 1941, Vol. II, p. 981), in such an hypothesis if an appeal from a judgment bearing on the essence of a question is excluded, nevertheless appeal is admitted for questions concerning the procedure (*procedendi modus respicientes*) and the procedure is rendered suspect. It was precisely on the *illegality* of the procedure followed that Archbishop Lefebvre's first appeal was based, that is, on the violation of norms which are prescribed to prevent unjust measures.

This argument applies for a measure taken by any organ, either ordinary or extraordinary, of the Holy See and approved *in forma specifica* by the Pope (cfr. "Justice et injustices romaines en l'Année Sainte de la Réconciliation 1975," *Courrier de Rome*, 153, January 1976, pp. 1-4). It should be stated that this was *not* the case with the action taken by Bishop Mamie, despite the pontifical approbation given to the letter signed by the three Cardinals. His suppression and the Cardinal's letter are two *different* documents; even if we were to admit that the latter had the approval of Pope Paul VI, the former would still be an illegitimate usurpation of authority, in flagrant violation of canon 493, and lacking the necessary confirmation (none has ever been produced, either by Rome or by Bishop Mamie). Cardinal Staffa's reply glaringly omits *any* mention of the measure taken by Bishop Mamie to "suppress" the Society of St. Pius X, and yet in a strictly juridical sense, this was the only action that really mattered.

Archbishop Lefebvre also appealed, protesting that the Commission of Cardinals was not competent to judge his "Declaration" of 21 November 1974, that rather the Sacred Congregation for the Doctrine of the Faith (former Holy Office) was "alone competent in such matters." Equally, a judgment of his "Declaration" could not be construed as a judgment of the seminary, especially since the results of the Apostolic Visitation were favorable.

Finally, the personal intervention of Cardinal Villot to prevent further consideration of these questions was anything but canonical. What did the Secretary of State have to fear if justice was on his side? As it is, the multiple irregularities and the obvious failure to render justice to Archbishop Lefebvre can only lead to one conclusion: the Society of St. Pius X continues to enjoy canonical existence, the measures taken against it and its founder lack validity.*

---

* FOOTNOTE BY MICHAEL DAVIES. An alternative view to that of Father Cathey can be found in the extract from *The Cambridge Review* cited on p. 125. As Father Cathey explains in the citation from Professor Capponi, subsequent papal approval *in forma specifica* can remedy an existing invalidity. Pope Paul gave such approval in his letter of 29 June (p. 113) and *The Cambridge Review* concluded that this approval was valid in law although "illicit in its violation of natural justice." Thus, even if Fr. Cathey's conclusion is disputed and the Society has been legally suppressed the Archbishop's refusal to submit can be justified on the grounds that natural justice has been violated (see pp. 121-124 and Appendix II).

INDEX

A Bishop Speaks, 9, 23, 257, 336, 349
Absolution (general), 248
Abuse of ecclesiastical power, 122-9, 175, 203-4, 290, 298, 305, 316, 317, 319, 321, 393-418, 422; see also Pope (rebellion, resistance)
Abuses: see also *Fumées de Satan*
  catechetical, 150, 190, 247, 249, 261 292, 307, 309, 363; see also New Church
  doctrinal, 66, 115, 128, 162, 179, 189, 190, 238, 247, 307, 309, 363, 436, 439; see also Scripture
  liturgical, 53, 66, 69, 77, 97, 110, 115, 116, 128, 150, 162, 179, 181, 184-5, 190, 228, 247, 249, 283, 307, 309, 321, 330-31, 363, 412
  moral, 115, 162, 179, 238, 279, 363
Action francaise, L' 26, 256, 347, 348
Acts of the Apostolic See, 175
Adam, Bishop Nestor, 12, 15, 35, 43, 44, 52, 59, 111-12, 131, 139, 158, 443
Alexander II, Pope, 399
Alexander VI, Pope, 402
Alta Vendita, 168
Ambrose, St., 117, 373
Ambrosian Rite, 127, 413
American Ecclesiastical Review, 428, 431, 432
Amnesty International, 267
Anglican-Roman Catholic Agreement on Authority, 317-18
Anglican-Roman Catholic International Commission, 317-18
Anti-clericalism, 3, 97
Anti-Modernist Oath, 147, 212
Anti-Semitism, 259
Antoniutti, Hildebrando Cardinal, 444
Anzevui, Rev. Jean, 4
Apologia Pro Vita Sua, x
Apostasy (general), 11, 188, 375, 403
Apostolicae Curae, 311
Apostolic Signature, Court of the, 42, 104, 108, 125, 130-31, 142, 447, 449
Approaches, 38, 42, 130, 178, 267, 290, 291, 306, 309, 425

Archaeologism (liturgical), 321 326-7
Archbishop Lefebvre—The Truth, ix, 303
Arianism, Arius, 327, 363-376, 395, 421
Arians of the Fourth Century, The, 372-4, 375
Aristotle, 380
Article 7, see *Institutio Generalis*
Aspects de la France, 256, 348
Athanasius, St. 47, 81, 117, 118, 327, 363-376, 402
Athanasius and the Church of Our Time, 363
Auctorem fidei, 147
Augustine Phamplet Series, x
Augustine, St., 220, 373, 414
Aurore, L', 70, 131, 191, 227
Authority (of the Pope), see Pope
Avanzo, Bishop d', 406

Bacci, Antonio Cardinal, 326, 334
Baggio, Sebastiano Cardinal, 225-6, 235
Baptism (new rite), 176, 331
Barbier, Rev. Emmanuel, 168
Barrielle, Rev. L.M., 54
Basic Norms for Priestly Training, 70
Basil, Bishop of Ancyra, 369
Basil, St., 372, 373, 375-6
BBC, 302, 318
Bellarmine, St. Robert, S.J., 410, 414, 416
Benedict XV, Pope, 336
Benelli, Archbishop Giovanni, 168-171, 193-6, 197-200, 232-3, 277, 281, 290, 296
Bernardini, Corrado, 447
Bible, see Ecumenical, Gospel, Scripture, Vulgate
Bishops, see College, Collegiality, Congregations, Episcopate
Blanshard, Paul, 433, 438, 439
Boniface II, Pope, 397
Boniface VIII, Pope, 403
Boniface IX, Pope, 400

Borgeat, M., 33
Bosco, St. John, 304, 395
Bossuet , Bishop Jacques-Bénigne, 323
Boulogne, Bishop Etienne-Antoine de, 431
Bouyer, Rev. Louis, 157, 330
Bruckberger, Rev. Henri, O.P., 191, 227-231,332
Bugnini, Archbishop Annibale, 53, 54, 80
Butler, Rev. Alban, 369-70
Butler, Bishop Christopher, O.S.B., 318, 415

Cajetan, Thomas De Vio Cardinal, O.P., 410, 417
Cambridge Review, The, 123-129, 450
Cano, Rev. Melchior, O.P., 410, 417
Canon Law, 19, 73, 93, 103-4, 107, 115, 121-2, 124-8, 140, 149, 162, 194, 199, 200, 203, 215, 225, 230, 235-6, 240, 243, 245-6, 336, 341, 351, 386, 393, 415, 416, 443-50; *see also* Incardination, Irregularity
Canons of St. Bernard, 12, 13, 88, 96
Capponi, Dr. Neri, 447-8, 449, 450
Carbonari, 168
Carbone, Mgr. Vincenzo, 8
Cardonnel, Rev. Jean, O.P., 104
Catechetics, *see* Abuses, New Church
Catherine of Siena, St., 311
Cathey, Rev. Dr. Boyd A., 443-450
Catholic Dictionary, A., 370
Catholic Dictionary of Theology, A., 370
Catholic Education, *see* Congregations
Catholic Encyclopedia, The, 367, 428
Catholic Herald, 110, 131
Catholic Information Office of England and Wales, ix, 301-3, 347
Catholic press, ix, 7, 21, 31, 126, 253, 255, 267, 292, 440
Catholic principles, *see* Church and State, Political, State
Catholic Social Order, *see* Social
Catholic State, *see* State
Catholics United for the Faith, 183, 307
Catholic Truth Society of England and Wales, ix, 302
Catholiques et Socialistes, 63

Chalcedon, Council of, 398
Chardin, *see* Teilhard de Chardin, Rev. P.S.J.
Charismatics, *see* Pentecostalism
Charrière, Bishop Francois, 12, 137, 443-7
Chile Today, 267
Christian Encounter, 379
Christianisme, see *Le Christianisme*
Christian Order, 292, 303
Chrysostom, St. John, 373
Church and State, 427; *see also* Separation, State
Church "Conciliar", *see* "Conciliar Church"
Church decline, *see* Decline
Church, Dogmatic Constitution on the, 291, 320
Church in the Modern World, Pastoral Constitution on the, 149, 158, 306, 348, 425
Church of Silence in Chile, The, 267
Church, the New, *see* New Church
Church under Occupation, The, 168
Cicero, 183
CIO, *see* Catholic Information Office
Ciry, Michel, 241
Clergy, *see* Congregations, *Histoire,* New Church, *Optatam Totius,* Priesthood, Priests
Coache, Rev. Louis, 36, 61, 107-9
Codex Juris Canonici, 73; *see also* Canon Law
Coetus Internationalis Patrum, 9, 32
College of Bishops, 174, 179, 325, 372
Collegiality, 10, 161, 175, 231, 244, 247, 249
Commentarius in judicia ecclesiastica, 449
Commentary on the Documents of Vatican II, 433
Commonweal, The, 401
Communion in the hand, 53, 55, 69, 97, 116, 174, 176, 179, 184, 314, 330
Communism, Communists, 13, 31, 147, 151, 189, 227, 240, 256, 270, 298
"Conciliar Church", 60, 109, 144, 152, 154, 176, 186, 190, 199, 204, 226, 227, 233, 248, 253, 268, 270, 291-3, 295, 305, 307, 308, 318, 325-8, 342 *see also* Post conciliar reforms, New Church

Congar, Rev. Yves, O.P., 250, 319, 403, 411, 437
Congregations (Roman) for:
Bishops, 106, 225, 235
Clergy, 19, 35, 46, 59, 67, 109, 122, 139, 444
Doctrine, 42, 73, 104, 106, 113, 115, 123, 129, 200, 237,450
Education, 35, 44-7, 59, 67, 139, 239, 352
Religious, 22, 35, 43, 46, 58, 59, 67, 139, 281, 444, 446
Worship and Sacraments, 53, 54, 110, 126, 127, 290
Connell, Rev. Francis J., C.S.S.R., 429-431, 435-6
Conscience, 144-6, 299, 390, 407-8, 426, 428, 431, 435
Constans, Emperor, 368
Constantine, Emperor, 366, 368
Constantinople, Council of, 374
Constantius, Emperor, 368, 369
Constitutions, *see* Vatican Council II
Contre-Réforme Catholique, La, 49, 50
Corcao, Gustavo, 191
Corriere della Sera, 66
Cosmao, Rev. Vincente, O.P., 4-7
Councils of the Church, 189, 321, 322, 335, 351, 409, 410, 423
authority of, 53, 177, 221, 306, 319, 423
Chalcedon, 398
Constantinople, 374
Jerusalem, 50
Lyons, 382
Nicea, 117, 118, 165, 185, 195, 365-6 368, 374, 421-3
Trent, 66, 127, 146, 182, 234, 325, 333, 351, 352, 413
Vatican I, 214, 318, 404,406, 409, 410, 415, 417, 438
Vatican II, *see* Vatican Council II
Courrier de Paul Dehème, 268
Courrier de Pierre Debray, 7
Courrier de Rome, 5, 7, 40, 42, 62, 175, 244, 396, 449
Cozens, M.L., 365-367
Cranmer, Archbishop Thomas, 186
Cranmer's Godly Order, 186
Credo of the People of God, 70, 116, 196, 251
Credo Pilgrimage, 50, 75-86, 87

Critical Study (of the New Mass), 326 334
Croix, La, 41, 61, 155, 250
Curé d'Ars, *see* Vianney

Damasus I, Pope St., 371
Daniélou, Jean Cardinal, S.J., 246
Dante Alighieri, 403
Davies, Michael, 346-8
Declaration, *see* Rights of Man, Sexual Ethics, Vatican Council II (Declarations)
Decline of the Church, 20, 21, 31-3, 39, 48, 50, 63, 64, 75-7, 119-121, 157, 188-9, 223, 238, 248-9, 252, 261, 347, 363; see also *Devastated*
De Corte, Prof. Marcel, 396, 403
Decree on Ecumenism, 324
Dei Verbum, 321
Delamare, Edith, 70-71
Delumeau, Jean, 7
Democracy, 146, 208, 427
Demophilus, Bishop of Beroea, 370
Deposit of the faith, 115, 143, 147, 148, 189, 212-14, 221, 323, 350-51
Derouet, Mgr., 66
Descamps, Bishop Albert, 37, 45, 46, 58, 60, 139
Des Graviers, Rev. Emmanuel, 62, 446
Desmazières, Bishop Etienne, 109
Devastated Vineyard, The, 305, 329, 339
Development of Christian Doctrine, An Essay on the, 365
Dhanis, Rev. Édouard, S.J., 200, 296
Dialogue, *see* New Church
Dialogus de Potestate Papae, 406
Dictionnaire de Théologie Catholique, Le, 319, 403, 411
Dignitatis Humanae, xiv, 149, 158, 178, 237, 285, 306, 322, 348, 351, 425, 426, 433-440; *see also* Religious Liberty
Dillion, Mgr. George F., 168
Dimitrios, Patriarch, 251
Disobedience, 27, 58-9, 65, 120-21, 144, 151-2, 180, 203-4, 212, 216, 222, 226, 240, 315, 319, 403-4, 408, 414-15; *see also* Obedience
Divine Law, 247, 405, 426, 429
Divine Revelation, see *Dei Verbum*

Divine Worship, *see* Congregations
Divini Redemptoris, 147
Doctrinaire, Le, 13, 337
Doctrinal abuses, *see* Abuses
Doctrine of the Faith, *see* Congregations
Documentation Catholique, La, 35, 54, 215, 288
Dogmatic Constitutions, see *Dei Verbum, Lumen Gentium*
Dominican Rite, 331
Drame d'Econe, Le, 4
Droit, Michel, 241
Dulac, Rev. Raymond, 181
Dutch Catechism, 179, 188, 309
Dutch Episcopate, 117, 148, 188
Dutourd, Jean, 241
Dwyer, Archbishop Robert J., 330, 364

Eastern Orthodox Church, 127, 143, 149, 150
Eastern Uniate Churches, 331
Ecumenical Bible, 211
Ecumenism:
  in general, xiii, 82-85, 100, 149, 270, 311, 323, 325, 336, 351, 433;
  see also Inter-communion, Worship in common
  Vatican II Decree, 324
Ecumenism as Seen by a Freemason, 149
Education, *see* Congregations
Elizabeth I, Queen of England, 384
English and Welsh Episcopate, 174, 292, 307
Epiney, Rev. Pierre, 12-18, 96, 111-12
Episcopate, *see* Dutch, English, French, German, National, Swiss, United States
Ethics, *see* Aristotle, Sexual
Eugenius IV, Pope, 413
Eusebius, Bishop of Caesarea, 366
Eusebius, Bishop of Nicomedia, 366, 368
Eusebius, Bishop of Vercellae, 374
Eusebius (layman), 393-4
Évêque suspens, L', 448, 449
Evolutionism, 145-6
Existentialism, 145
Express, L', 268
Extraordinary Magisterium, *see* Magisterium

Faith, *see* Deposit, Doctrinal, Traditional
Fascism, 257
Felici, Pericle Cardinal, 151
Felix, anti-pope, 369
Fesquet, Henri, 149, 286
Fisher, St. John, 379, 388, 390, 391
Fogazzaro, Antonio, 168
Ford, Rev. John C., S.J., 439
Foreign Missionaries of Paris, 443
Forma (in)
  communi, 114, 448, 449
  specifica, 36, 106, 114, 121, 123, 139, 306, 447-450
Fortunatian, Bishop of Aquileia, 370
France, *see* French (Episcopate, etc.), *Histoire des crises*
France Catholique-Ecclesia, La, 157, 163
France-Presse (Agence), 232
Fraser, Hamish, 130, 291, 309
Frederick II, Emperor, 387
Frederick of Lavagna, 387, 388
Freemason, Freemasonry, 97, 149, 168, 234, 237, 240, 270, 299, 432, 434; see also *Grand Orient, Masonic Infiltrations*
French Episcopate, xiii, 8, 20, 22, 23, 30, 40-42, 46, 66, 92, 161-2, 188, 227, 239, 240, 257, 262, 332, 423, 446
French National Center for Vocations, 20
French Revolution, 5, 228, 256, 262, 263, 432
French Seminary in Rome, 3, 26, 33, 131
Freppel, Bishop Charles-Emile, 405
Fribourg, University of, 12, 131, 443
Fumées de Satan, Les, 332

Garrone, Gabriel-Marie Cardinal, 35, 36, 44, 47, 48, 59, 62, 67, 71, 129, 131, 137, 139, 160, 162, 284
Gasquet, Francis Aidan Cardinal, 311
Gaudium et Spes, 149, 158, 306, 348, 425
General Instruction on the New Mass, see *Institutio Generalis*
German Episcopate, 148
Gospel Politicization of, 162, 238
Graber, Bishop Rudolf, 363

Grand Orient Freemasonry Unmasked,
168; *see also* Freemason
Graviers, *see* Des Graviers
Gregorian chant, 69, 324
Gregory the Great, Pope St., 381
Gregory VII, Pope St., 399, 413
Gregory IX, Pope, 400
Gregory XVI, Pope, 147, 149, 285, 431,
436
Gregory Nazianzen, St., 372, 373
Gregory of Nyssa, St., 373
Gregory of Valencia, 410
Grosseteste, Bishop Robert, 122, 311,
316, 364, 379-391, 402, 404, 406,
408, 418
*Grosseteste's Relations with the Papacy
and Crown,* 389
Guéranger, Dom Prosper, O.S.B., 393,
394
Guibert, Bishop Georges, 445
Gut, Benno Cardinal, 53

Hallet, Paul H., 425, 426, 430, 440
Hanu, José, 10, 18, 23, 37, 49, 62, 107,
108
Heenan, John Cardinal, 315, 330
Henry III, King of England, 390
Henry IV, Emperor, 399
Henry VIII, King of England, 391
Heresy, toleration of, 65-6, 70, 117, 129,
188, 238, 317-18, 351, 429, 430, 431,
435
Hergenröther, Joseph Cardinal, 409
Hilary, St., 370, 372, 373, 374
Hildebrand, Dr. Dietrich von, 304, 329,
339, 395-6
Hippolytus, St., 374
*Histoire des crises du clergé francais,
contemporain,* 7
History of the Popes, 397, 401
Holy Ghost Fathers, 3, 8, 9-10, 31, 32,
155, 222
Holy Office, *see* Congregations-
Doctrine
Honorius, I, Pope, 396, 399, 402
Houghton, Rev. Bryan, 181
Hourdin, Georges, 63
Humanae Vitae, 70, 116, 179, 312;
see also Sexual ethics
Humani Generis, 147
Humanism, xi-xiii

I Accuse the Council, 9, 349
Ibas, Bishop, 398
ICEL (International Commission for
English in the Liturgy), 364
IDOC (International Centre for Infor-
mation and Documentation), 148
Ignatius, St., 100
Illuminism, 5
Immortale Dei, 147, 427, 432
Incardination, 140, 201-4, 245, 445
Indifferentism, 82, 84, 211, 221, 237
299, 432; *see also* Religious
Liberty
Infallibility (papal), 178, 321-3, 371,
407
Infoform, 301
Innocent IV, Pope, 364, 382, 386-391,
402, 406, 408, 418
Innocent VIII, Pope, 400
Innocent, Master, 388
Institutio Generalis, 331
Article7, 66, 120, 175, 195, 231-2,
320
Intégrisme, 155
Intention, the priest's during Mass,
348, 349
Inter-communion, 85, 263, 298, 352
International Group of Fathers, 9, 32
Iraeneus, St., 412
Irish Catholic, 20
Irregularity (canonical), 200, 213, 216,
242, 337
Itinéraires, x, 7, 35, 38, 45, 49, 57, 64,
73, 108, 109, 119, 164, 182, 188, 191,
231, 256, 265, 274, 276, 288, 289,
290, 297, 346, 421

J'Accuse le Concile, see *I Accuse the
Council*
Jacobatius, Dominicus Cardinal, O.P.,
408; *see also* Jacobazzi
Jacobazzi, Rev. Domenico, O.P., 410
Jansenism, 229
Jerome, St., 363, 370, 373
Jerusalem, Council of, 50
Joan of Arc, St., 120, 269
JOC (Young Catholic Workers), 247
John the Apostle, St., 412
John XII, Pope, 399
John XXII, Pope , 320, 413, 417

John XXIII, Pope, 7, 8, 30, 52-5, 148, 239, 277, 312, 316
John, Eric, 397
John Paul II, Pope, xii
Jubilate Deo, 55
Judaism, 428
Juridicism, 240, 245
Justin, St., 374
Justinian, Emperor, 398

Kingsley, Charles, x
Knox, James Cardinal, 290, 292
Küng, Hans, 104, 106, 126, 437, 438

Labbe, Rev. Philippe, S.J., 408
La Bellarte, Rev. Domenico, 275, 281, 289
Lacoma, Bishop Laureano Castans, 445
Laity, 372-6
Lamennais, Rev. Félicité de, 147, 149
Lamentabili, 147
La messe catholique est-elle encore permise?, 54
Latin, 54-5, 67, 69, 110, 126, 229, 269, see also *Veterum Sapientia*
Latin Mass Society, 326
Law: see Canon, Divine, Natural
Le christianisme va-t-il mourir?, 7
Lefebvre, Madame, 2, 26
Lefebvre, Monsieur, 1, 2, 26
Le Floch, Père, 26
Lega-Bardocetti, 449
Legalism, 240, 245
Leo II, Pope St., 399
Leo XIII, Pope, 147, 311, 402, 426, 427, 432
Leonard Mgr. George, ix, x, 302
Liberalism, xiii, 12, 32, 39, 51, 71, 77, 144-154, 211, 223, 242, 257, 262, 264, 298, 426, 432, 433; *see also* Liberals, *Libertas*
Liberals, 9, 10, 21, 44, 53, 79, 109, 111, 122, 138, 145, 184, 187, 204, 227, 237, 264, 267, 292, 426, 429, 431, 440; *see also* Liberalism
Liberius, Pope, 118, 369-372, 374, 375, 396, 402
Libertas (encyclical), 426, 432; *see also* Religious Liberty
Light on Archbishop Lefebvre, ix

Liturgical revolution, 146, 180-81, 186, 190, 228, 240, 247, 249, 262, 298, 304, 309, 314, 334, 351, 352, 423; *see also* Abuses (liturgical), *Cranmer's*, New Church
Liturgical Year, 393
Liturgy: see *Apostolicae Curae*, *Critical Study*, ICEL, *Jubilate Deo*, *Mediator Dei*, *Memoriale Domini*, *Missale Romanum Mysterium Fidei*, New Mass, *Order of Melchisedech*, *Pope Paul's New Mass*, *Quo Primum*, Roman Rite Destroyed, *Sacrosanctum Concilium*, *Some Jurdical*, Traditional Mass, *Tridentine Mass*, *Una Voce*, Validity, *Veterum Sapientia*, Worship
Liturgy, Constitution on the, see *Sacrosanctum Concilium*
Lives of the Saints, 369-70
Lumen Gentium, 291, 320
Luther, Martin, 403, 406
Lyons, Council of, 382

Macchi, Mgr. Pasquale, 276
Madiran, Jean, x, xi, 119, 164, 187, 191, 231-2, 421-3; *see also Itinéraires*
Magisterium, 39-40, 43, 44, 115, 118, 146-8, 167, 173, 177-8, 299, 321, 324, 351, 395, 423, 433
   Extraordinary, 118, 177, 317, 322-4, 335, 351, 407
   Ordinary, 118, 152, 178, 306, 317, 322, 324, 335, 347, 404, 425; *see also* Nau
Mamie, Bishop Pierre, 35-6, 43, 44, 46, 49, 51-5, 57-9, 67, 68, 70-73, 103, 104, 124, 131, 134, 136, 139, 142, 154-7, 158, 215, 216, 446-50
Man (nature), 339; *see also* Rights
Manifesto of the Catholic Academics, 345-6
Marchioni, Mgr. Ambrogio, 193
Marriages (mixed), 298
Marsaudon, Yves, 149
Marsh, Robert, 386
Martin IV, Pope, 400
Marty, François Cardinal, 131, 223, 228, 229, 238, 248
Marxism, Marxists, 257, 266, 299

Masonic Infiltrations in the Church,
 168; *see also* Freemason
Mass: *see* Liturgy, New Mass, *Pope
 Paul's New Mass*, Traditional Mass,
 Tridentine Mass
Maurras, Charles, 348
Mayer, Mgr. Augustine, 35
Mediator Dei, 321
Memoriale Domini, 55, 116, 179, 185
Messe catholique, see *La messe
 catholique*
Mignot, André, 332
Mikulich, Rev. Milan, O.F.M., 22
Mindszenty, Jozef Cardinal, 340
Mirari Vos, 147, 149, 431-2
Missale Romanum, 116, 181
Mitre and Crook, 181
Modernism, Neo-Modernism, 12, 26,
 32, 37, 38-40, 50-51, 63, 66, 100, 151,
 179, 207, 211, 242, 286, 309, 315,
 347, 407, 443, 446; *see also*
 Anti-Modernist
Modernists, xii, 71, 120, 129, 148, 312,
 315
Monde, Le, 155, 258, 259, 286
Monophysitism, 398
Monothelitism, 399
Montagne, Yves, 448
Montes, Jorge, 267
More, St. Thomas, 379
Murray, Rev. John Courtney, S.J., 431,
 432, 433, 437, 438, 439,
Mysterium Fidei, 70, 116

Nantes, Abbé Georges de, 49, 105, 159
National Catholic Register, 425, 440
National Catholic Reporter, 437
National Episcopal Conferences,
 173-175
Natural Law, 103-4, 115, 121, 162, 203,
 390, 428
Nau, Dom Paul O.S.B., 178, 306, 324,
 425
Nestorius, 394
New Catholic Encyclopedia, 370, 371
New Church (the), 7, 65, 105, 136, 138,
 153-4, 189-190, 285, 293, 307, 338-9,
 342; *see also* "Conciliar Church"
catechetics, 7, 39, 190, 211, 223,
 238, 244, 247, 249, 261, 309, 326;
 see also Abuses, Dutch Catechism

dialogue, 240, 263, 325
Mass, *see* New Mass
priests, 39, 211, 223, 262-3; *see also*
 Ordination
sacraments, 39, 83, 262-3
seminaries, 39, 43, 249, 261, 262
theology, 7, 190, 238
unity, 263-4, 331, 333, 342
Newman, John Henry Cardinal, x, 76,
 128, 309, 321, 365, 370-75, 379, 402,
 407-9, 415, 418
New Mass, ix, 7, 39, 41, 43, 53, 54, 66,
 68, 76, 80, 110, 124, 126, 128, 171,
 175, 180, 182, 205, 206-211, 223,
 231, 233, 244, 250, 261, 262-3, 293,
 309, 321, 325, 329-331, 333-5, 348,
 349, 352, 409, 412; see also *Critical
 Study, Pope Paul's*
English version, 364
legal status, 181, 331
validity, 128, 208, 250, 348, 349
New Mass, The, 183
Nicea, Council of, *see* Councils
Nicholas II, Pope, 413
Nineteen Eighty-Four, 90, 130, 327
Nominalism, 145
Non-Christian Religions (Vatican II
 Declaration), 158
*Non, Entretiens de José Hanu avec
 Mgr. Lefebvre*, see Hanu
Nouvelliste, Le (Swiss), 112, 133, 142,
 154, 204, 217, 236
Novus Ordo Missae, see New Mass

Obedience, 27, 34, 120-21, 144, 151-2,
 157, 175-6, 177, 184, 186, 197, 199,
 212, 214, 242, 270, 285, 319, 334,
 339, 342, 383-4, 387, 389, 393-6,
 403-4, 407-8; *see also* Disobedience
Onclin, Mgr. Guillaume, 37, 46, 139
Optatam Totius, 443
Order of Melchisedech, The, xii
Ordinary Magisterium, *see*
 Magisterium, Nau
Ordination (new rite), xii
Orthodoxy of Catholic Doctrine, 22
Orwell, George, 90, 130
Osservatore Romano, L', 61, 63-8, 78,
 79, 105, 141, 173, 174, 183, 288, 294,
 296

Ottaviani, Alfredo Cardinal, 326, 334, 432
"Outside of Which Church?", 187-191
Oxford University, 380, 390

Palazzini, Rev. P., 109
Palmadon Salvatore di, 446
Panciroli, Rev. Romeo, 215, 288-9, 294-5; see also Vatican Press
Pantin, W.A., 389
Papal power, see Abuse, Pope (plenitude, rebellion, resistance)
Paris, Rev. Matthew, O.S.B., 390
Participation (in the Mass), 330
Pascendi Dominici Gregis, 71, 167, 351
Pastor, Ludwig von, 397, 401-2
Pastor Aeternus, 147, 319, 404, 406
Patroclus, Bishop of Arles, 397
Paul the Apostle, St., xv, 50, 311, 414
Paul V, Pope, 410
Paul VI, Pope, passim;
  Consistorial address, 115, 170, 171, 173-191, 194, 243, 314
  Letters to Archbishop Lefebvre, 112-121, 133-5, 143, 155, 156, 241-3, 303-343, 349-350
Pavan, Mgr. Pietro, 433, 435-7
Pedroni, Alphonse, 13, 14, 33
Pensée catholique, La, 7
Pentecostalism, Pentecostals, 39, 76-7, 181, 327
Peron, Isabel, 268
Perroud, Mgr., 36
Peter the Apostle, St., xv, 50, 370, 402-3, 414
Pistoia, Council of, 147
Pius V, Pope St., 127, 128, 182, 207, 213
Pius VI, Pope, 147
Pius VII, Pope, 431
Pius IX, Pope, 147, 149-50, 152, 168, 214, 285, 409, 430, 432, 436
Pius X, Pope St., 16, 26, 40, 71, 95, 147, 167, 351
Pius XI, Pope, 147, 211, 277, 427, 437
Pius XII, Pope, 4, 5, 7, 28, 29, 53, 147, 190, 191, 194, 239, 277, 316, 321, 430, 432, 437
Ploncard d' Assac, Jacques, 168
Pluralism (of rites), 247, 250, 283, 331, 334

Political principles, 265; see also State
Polycrates, Bishop of Ephesus, 412
Pope: see Popes (names, writings)
  authority, 184, 221, 382-3, 387; see also Dialogus, Infallibility, Magisterium
  authority, degrees of, 170
  authority, nature and limits of, 180, 387, 404-7, 409, 411
  confirmation of curial acts, 114, 448-9
  duty, 147-8, 152, 234-5, 285, 286, 309
  heresy of a, 413, 415-7
  plenitude of power, 382, 384, 386, 389, 406, 409
  rebellion against, 70, 176, 179, 184, 203
  resistance to abuse of power, 27, 39-40, 121-4, 175, 203, 204, 271, 305, 316, 319, 379-418
  schism of a, 410
Pope John's Council, 9, 21, 49, 53, 54, 68, 116, 138, 177, 182, 308, 310, 314
Pope Paul's New Mass, 54, 116, 183, 331
Popes (names): see Alexander, Benedict, Boniface, Damasus, Eugenius, Gregory, Honorius, Innocent, John, John Paul, Julius, Leo, Liberius, Martin, Nicholas, Paul, Peter, Pius, Sergius, Silverius, Sixtus, Urban, Victor, Zosimus
Popes (writings): see Apostolicae Curae, Auctorem Fidei, Credo of the People of God, Divini Redemptoris, Humanae Vitae, Humani Generis, Immortale Dei, Jubilate Deo, Lamentabili, Libertas, Mediator Dei, Memoriale Domini, Mirari Vos, Missale Romanum, Mysterium Fidei, Pascendi, Pastor Aeternus, Quanta Cura, Quas Primas, Qui Pluribus, Quo Primum, Syllabus, Veterum, Sapientia
Popes, The, 397
Post-conciliar reforms and orientations, 9, 17, 39, 46, 48, 51, 52, 56, 69, 96, 113, 115, 138, 143, 144, 150, 161-2, 164, 165, 173-4, 176, 178, 180, 184, 186, 187, 190, 243, 244, 248, 249, 274, 278, 306, 311-12, 314, 333, 338, 347, 351, 353, 421-3; see also Some Juridical

Powicke, Sir Maurice, 380
Prierias, Rev. Sylvester, O.P., 406
Priesthood, 146, 148, 209-10, 219, 234, 241, 261-3, 333, 352
Priests: *see* New Church, Ordination
    decline in numbers, 20, 63, 162, 222
    formation of true, 12, 20, 33-4, 40, 69, 116, 117, 143-4, 221-2, 239, 261, 279, 294, 299, 316, 352
Private judgment, 375
Pro Fide, 307
Progrès de Lyon, 258
Protestantism, Neo-Protestantism, xii, 37, 38-9, 51, 100, 145, 146, 150, 208, 219, 262, 263, 286, 315, 334, 347, 375, 429, 438
Protestants, 100, 143, 148, 149, 150, 220, 223, 247, 263-4, 298, 323, 329, 333, 352, 371, 428

Quanta Cura, 147, 149, 285, 323, 430, 432, 436
Quas Primas, 211, 427
Qui Pluribus, 432
Quo Primum, 413

Rahner, Rev. Karl, S.J., 408, 411, 412
Rambler, The, 373, 374
Reformation, xii, 223, 327, 388, 410
Reforms, *see* Post-conciliar, *Some Juridical*
Reid, Stuart, 110-11
Religious (Congregation for), *see* Congregations
Religious liberty, xiv, 146, 149, 299, 323, 325, 425-440; see also *Dignitatis Humanae*, Indifferentism, *Libertas*
Remnant, The, 38, 75, 81, 182, 188, 346, 349, 377
Rémy, Colonel, 241
Revolution, *see* French, Liturgical
Rhine Flows into the Tiber, The, 8
Rights of man, 234, 432, 434-5
Roch, Rev. Denis, 16, 216-20
Roman Congregations, *see* Congregations
Roman Rite Destroyed, The, 183, 329, 330, 333

Sacraments, 39, 83, 146, 147, 207, 212, 221; *see also New Church*
Sacrosanctum Concilium (Vatican II on liturgy), 69, 251, 324
Saint Pierre, Michel de, 241, 332
Salleron, Prof. Louis, xi, 5, 6, 157-163, 241
Sarum rite, 127
Sauguet, Henri, 241
Saventhem, Dr. Eric M. de, 105, 290-93, 336
Schism, 48, 188, 191, 236-7, 240, 319, 328, 342, 403-4, 410, 411, 416, 418
Scripture, 115, 156, 174, 321, 380-82, 390, 403, 430; *see also* Vulgate
    falsification of, 66, 190; *see also* Ecumenical, Gospel
Secretariat of State (Vatican), 63, 66, 70, 71, 125, 169, 233, 325, 348
Seminaries, see *Basic Norms*, New Church (priests, seminaries), *Optatam Totius*, Priesthood, Priests
Separation of Church and State, 146
Seper, Franjo Cardinal, 247
Sergius, Patriarch, 399
Sergius III, Pope, 399
Sexual ethics, 338; see also *Humanae Vitae*
Shea, Mgr. George W., 428, 431
Sigaud, Bishop Geraldo de Proenca, 151
Sillion, the, 147
Silverius, Pope St., xv, 398
Sixtus IV, Pope, 400
Sixtus V, Pope, 413, 417
Snyder, Rev. Urban, 188
Social order (Catholic), 264-6, 346
Socialism, 63, 299
Some Juridical Considerations on the Reform of the Liturgy, 447
Soto, Rev. Dominic, O.P., 417
Sozomen (historian), 370
Spiegel, Der, 348
Staffa, Dino Cardinal, 73, 108, 140, 142, 447, 448, 450
State, the Catholic, 5-6, 237, 346, 426, 428-430, 435; *see also* Church and State, Political
Studies in Modern Theology, 408
Suarez, Rev. Francisco, S.J., 384, 410, 412, 414, 417
Suenens, Leo Jozef Cardinal, 76-7, 189
Suisse romande (television), 4, 155

Summa de Ecclesia, 409
Swiss Episcopate, 41, 42, 43, 44, 52, 90, 92, 96, 133, 155
Syllabus of Errors, 147, 432, 436, 437

Tabera, Arturo Cardinal, 43, 45, 47, 51, 58, 59, 62, 67, 71, 103, 129, 139, 160
Tablet, The, 20, 315, 415
Tacitus, 308
Tartuffe, 332
Teilhard de Chardin, Rev. Pierre, S.J., 6-7
Telford, Canon George, 292
Teresa, Mother (of Calcutta), 310
Thérèse of the Child Jesus, St., 269
Thiandoum, Hyacinthe Cardinal, 7, 16, 205, 239, 282, 289, 290
Thibon, Gustave, 241
Thomas Aquinas, O.P., St., 69, 393, 396, 414
Thomism, 20
Times, The, 258, 347
Toleration of heresy, *see* Heresy
Torquemada, Jean de Cardinal, 409, 410, 416
Torquemada, Rev. Tomas de, O.P., 409
Toute L'Eglise en Clameurs, 332
Tradition, 19, 26, 38-40, 62, 65, 71, 72, 115, 120, 127, 129, 144, 147, 151-2, 155, 156, 163, 165, 168, 174-6, 178, 180, 206, 237, 241, 251, 278, 281, 283, 285-7, 300, 306, 307, 314, 320-22, 325, 328, 335, 337, 345, 347, 349-352, 363-376, 410, 421-3, 439; *see also* Traditional
Traditional faith, xii, 38-40, 62, 81-6, 100, 116-19, 148, 151-2, 165, 186, 207, 212, 214, 221, 240, 258, 268, 271, 279, 285, 298-9, 304, 325, 326, 333, 337, 351
Traditional Mass: xii, 15, 17, 20, 36, 39, 41, 43, 44, 67-8, 73, 77-80, 82, 83, 91-2, 100, 112, 116, 127-8, 146-7, 148, 155, 162, 173, 180, 181, 182, 183, 185-6, 189, 198, 206-211, 212, 213, 219, 221, 228, 230-32, 234, 250-52, 258-9, 263, 268-9, 279, 283, 290, 293-4, 304, 316, 328-330, 333, 334, 384, 421, 447; see also *Tridentine*
canonization of, 213

legal status, 127-8, 181, 213
true nature, 247, 260, 327, 333
Trent, *see* Councils of the Church
Tribune de Genève, La, 217
Tridentine Mass, The, 183, 329
Truth, 37, 43, 46, 82, 85, 145, 147, 149, 224-5, 241, 263, 286-8, 298-9, 323, 375-6, 430-35

Ulpian, 405
Una Voce, 105, 291
Unitatis Redintegratio (Vatican II on Ecumenism), 324
United Nations, 438
United States Constitution, 438
United States Episcopate, 364
Universal regligion, 211
Universe, The, 46, 259
Urban IV, Pope, 400

Validity: *see also* New Mass
legal, 203, 213, 408-18
moral, 203, 204, 404-18
Vatican Council I, *see* Councils
Vatican Council II
Authority of, 118, 148, 152, 177-8, 306, 322
Documents of:
Constitutions
on the Church (dogmatic), see *Lumen Gentium*
on the Church (pastoral), see *Gaudium et Spes*
on the Liturgy, see *Sacrosanctum Concilium*
on Revelation, see *Dei Verbum*
Declarations
on Non-Christian Religious, see *Nostra Aetate*
on Religous Liberty, see *Dignitatis Humanae*
Decrees
on Ecumenism, see *Unitatis Redintegratio*
on Training for the Priesthood, see *Optatam Totius*
Schismatic? 237
Spirit, of, 120, 182, 422; see also *Commentary on the Documents*

Vatican Encounter, 10, 49; *see also*
  Hanu
Vatican Press Bureau, 215, 273, 288,
  294, 296; *see also* Panciroli
Vaughan, Herbert Cardinal, 311
Verot, Bishop Augustine, 405
Veterum Sapientia, 54; *see also* Latin
Vianney, Jean-Marie, St., 269
Victor, Pope, St., 412
Vidal, Rev. P. S.J., 416
Videla, General Jorge, 268
Vigilius, deacon, 397, 398
Vigneron, Paul, 7
Villot, Jean Cardinal, xiii, 22-3, 42, 54,
  61, 63, 114, 130, 133, 136-142, 156,
  158, 159, 162, 163-4, 169, 201-2, 275,
  290, 292, 295, 447, 450
Vitoria, Rev. Francisco de, O.P., 414
Vocations, *see* Priests
Vorgrimler, Rev. Herbert, S.J., 433
Vulgate, 234, 413, 417

Wanderer, The, 183
Watine, Gabrielle, *see* Lefebvre,
  Madame Gabrielle
Wernz, Rev. Francis Xavier, S.J., 416
World War I, 1, 2, 26
World War II, xi, 2, 26, 257
Worship in common, 323; *see also*
  Inter-communion
Wright, John Joseph Cardinal, 19, 22,
  35, 45, 47, 59, 67, 71, 122, 129, 137,
  139, 160, 247, 444, 445

Young Catholic Workers, 247

Zinelli, Bishop, 405
Zosimus, Pope St., 397